The Chosen Image

The Chosen Image

Television's Portrayal of Jewish Themes and Characters

by
JONATHAN PEARL
and
JUDITH PEARL

McFarland & Company, Inc., Publishers
Jefferson, North Carolina, and London

British Library Cataloguing-in-Publication data are available

Library of Congress Cataloguing-in-Publication Data

Pearl, Jonathan.
    The chosen image : television's portrayal of Jewish themes
and characters / by Jonathan Pearl and Judith Pearl.
       p.   cm.
    Includes bibliographical references and index.
    ISBN 0-7864-0522-8 (library binding : 50# alkaline paper) ∞
    1. Jews on television.   I. Pearl, Judith.   II. Title.
PN1992.8.J48P43   1999
791.43'65203924 — dc21   98-45792
                                            CIP

Manufactured in the United States of America

McFarland & Company, Inc., Publishers
  Box 611, Jefferson, North Carolina 28640

To our parents
and to our children

Acknowledgments

This book is the fruit of more than fifteen years of intense study, research, labor, effort, and writing. Bringing such a work to completion and publication could not have been accomplished without the help and support of many people.

Going back to the origins of our work, we thank Professor Nathan Winter, Jonathan's doctoral dissertation advisor at New York University, for the years of education, fellowships, and practical experience. Even more significant were Dr. Winter's insight, vision, and guidance, which provided us the opportunity to research and write about a previously uncharted scholarly field. Also on the dissertation committee were Professor Rosalie Kamelhar, who lent much time, effort, insight, encouragement, and moral support, and Professor Christine Nystrom of the Department of Media Ecology, who provided invaluable technical assistance in helping to shape the dissertation. Thanks also to dissertation readers Professor Milton Arfa, whose interest in modern technology provided helpful perspectives on serious Jewish research, and Professor Cyrus Gordon, a man of unparalleled erudition and *menschlichkite*, with whom it was Jonathan's honor and privilege to engage in intense graduate study and who lent his scholarship and warmth in this endeavor. We express gratitude also to Lawrence Taishoff and Edith and Henry Everett for the interest and support that they expressed for the dissertation research.

For their assistance with Judith's master's thesis at Brooklyn College, we thank professors Donald MacLennan and Allen Lichtenstein.

The enormous amount of research time required to carry out this study was made so very pleasant and fruitful by Fay Schreibman (former director of the National Jewish Archive of Broadcasting), Leslie Slocum (librarian at the Television Information Office), and Kathy Loughney (research assistant at the Motion Picture, Broadcasting and Recorded Sound Division of the Library of Congress), as well as a number of other key individuals at these and other institutions. Their cooperation, expert assistance, and flexibility in scheduling appointments were of great value and are most appreciated.

We wish to thank those who were helpful in a variety of ways, including

Rena Schwarz, Robin Salzberg, Greg Hagg, Francine Raubvogel, Larry Raubvogel, and Deborah Hayn.

We particularly express gratitude to our children's grandparents, who have each provided us with various kinds of much needed support and advice over the years, for which they all have our great love and appreciation: to Saba and Nana (Rabbi Aaron Pearl and Cantor Sheila Pearl) from New Jersey, and Savta and Granddaddy (Zahava Velder and Professor Eli Velder) from Baltimore, who traveled here as they could to provide invaluable help in watching the children during some of our intense writing periods. We also express gratitude to our Aunt Judy and Uncle Allan Schwarz, with whom the children spent some fun days that provided us with significant blocks of time to write.

And we especially thank Grandpa and Grandma (Professor Nathan and Dorothy Schmukler), who have throughout been of inestimable help and without whom the final thrust — the last weeks, days, hours, and minutes before deadline in which the book was completed — would not have been possible. They watched, picked up, fed, amused, and grandparented our children almost daily and at a moment's notice during those crucial last weeks. Their help went well above and beyond — and we are truly grateful.

It is to the subjects of all that baby-sitting attention — our precious miracle children, Ayelet and Eitan — that we express our deepest awe, affection, and love. We thank them for their preschoolers' forbearance, allowing us to sit at the computer when playing with them would have been to everyone's greater delight.

Contents

Preface

While Jews have been known for millennia as the People of the Book, they could also well have been called, for the past fifty years, a people of television.

Although the significant Jewish presence in the Hollywood entertainment industry is legendary and has been the subject of much attention and some study, what has been overlooked is the Jewish presence *on television*. Contrary to the commonly held but inaccurate belief that serious Jewish issues and truly Jewish characters rarely find their way onto popular TV shows, our intense research — over the course of fifteen years and many thousands of hours of viewing shows — has revealed that literally hundreds of television dramas and comedies have featured Jewish themes over the past half century.

The Chosen Image is a study of Jewish images on popular television from 1948 through the 1996-97 TV season. It is the first book to explore this body of programming, blazing a trail across a previously neglected but vitally important field. This book, we envision, will serve as an indispensable resource and a pathfinding opus.

By "Jewish themes," we mean the explicit portrayal of issues relating to Jewish life, Jewish culture and traditions, and post–Biblical Jewish history. Our focus is on popular shows that prominently feature these issues as their primary story line or one of their central story lines.

"Popular shows" refers to the most widely watched programs on television: the TV dramas, situation comedies, miniseries, and made-for-television movies (rather than documentaries and news shows) broadcast during prime time. The prime-time evening hours (8 to 11 from Monday through Saturday and 7 to 11 on Sunday) attract the largest and broadest TV audience, drawing an average of nearly 96 million viewers every night. As the "heart" of the TV schedule, prime-time programming receives the bulk of the networks' expenditures, creative efforts, and concern over ratings.

For the first four decades of television, the most popular shows aired on the three major networks, ABC, CBS, and NBC, which regularly drew more than 90 percent of the TV audience. For this reason, the bulk of the shows we examine hail from these sources. However, in recent years the growth of cable

1

TV and the proliferation of new television networks and independent and public television stations have opened fresh programming opportunities, and original dramatic programs with Jewish themes now appear regularly on these venues. As these shows have been attracting ever increasing numbers of viewers (as well as critical acclaim and attention), they too are included where deemed particularly relevant or interesting. We have chosen 1948 as a departure point, for in that year "regular network service began ... large scale programming emerged," and "television finally began its explosive growth."[1]

We have not focused in this book on shows with only passing Jewish references or mere Jewish allusions (the isolated use, for example, of words like *kosher* or *oy vay*); an endless number of shows contain these. Nor do we dwell on programs that include "Jewish type" characters or characters with Jewish names who are not explicitly identified as Jews or who display no connection or involvement with Jewish matters. Our interest is the presence, not the absence, of Jewish themes. While such character types may play a role in influencing audience perceptions of the Jew for both Jewish and non–Jewish viewers, that is the subject for another study. There are more than enough shows with explicit Jewish themes to fill this volume; we believe such shows, which commentators largely ignored in favor of a few high-visibility ones with little Jewish content, to be of particular interest and significance.

We have sought to create as comprehensive a work as possible and have made every effort to identify and discuss the gamut of Jewish themes and characters that have been featured in popular prime-time network shows over the past fifty years. While we have included hundreds of programs to represent TV's depictions of Jewish themes and characters, the sheer volume of relevant programs, coupled with our continuing research in this field, ensures many updates and future studies on this subject.

Identification and analysis of the programs that we discuss in this book are the result of many years of original research and thousands of hours of viewing these programs. We watched every show in this book except in those rare cases where a show no longer exists due to the unfortunate history of haphazard preservation activity; in such instances we read a complete script or a detailed synopsis.

The book is arranged thematically — a structure we found to yield the most useful and interesting analysis and insights — rather than purely chronologically, although chronological trends and contexts are examined where relevant. The inclusion of such details as episode titles and dates is related to their availability and direct relevance to the subject at hand.

In our effort to do justice to this vast amount of previously uncharted material, we have been compelled to set aside for the moment other fascinating aspects of this topic. *The Chosen Image* is not, for instance, a behind-the-scenes book or a look at the possible influence of various groups in shaping Jewish TV images — issues we intend to explore in the future. Before such important topics can be thoughtfully addressed, an awareness and under-standing of the programs themselves — so long overlooked and overdue — is necessary.

The need for such work has inspired us in many ways, including acade-mic study. Jonathan Pearl, an ordained, practicing rabbi, received his Ph.D. from New York University's Department of Hebraic and Judaic Studies, writ-ing his dissertation on Jewish themes in prime-time network programming; Judith Pearl earned her master's degree from the Department of Television and Radio Studies at Brooklyn College, focusing on audience perceptions of Jew-ish images on television. Continuing need and widespread interest led to our founding of the Jewish Televimages Resource Center, dedicated to examining, evaluating, and enhancing popular television's Jewish themes and characters. This book is a natural outgrowth of our studies and of the national recogni-tion of our work as directors of the JTRC.

We have written this book for Jews and non–Jews, for students and schol-ars of communications and of Jewish studies, for observers of popular culture, for those in the television community, and for any of the millions of Ameri-cans for whom watching television is an integral part of life. It is our hope that *The Chosen Image* and our continuing explorations on this subject will add a new dimension to the fields of both Judaic studies and mass communications, and bring a fresh perspective to our understanding of television.

Introduction

By the end of his twelve years on prime-time television, Archie Bunker, America's best-known bigot, had come to raise a Jewish child in his home, befriend a black Jew, go into business with a Jewish partner, enroll as a member of Temple Beth Shalom, eulogize his close friend at a Jewish funeral, host a Sabbath dinner, participate in a *bat mitzvah* ceremony, and join a group to fight synagogue vandalism.

While the famed style of *All in the Family* (and its sequel, *Archie Bunker's Place*) was unique, its inclusion of Jews and Jewish issues was far from unusual. Since the inception of network television half a century ago, hundreds of popular TV shows have portrayed Jewish themes. Such topics as anti–Semitism, intermarriage, Jewish lore and traditions, Israel, the Holocaust, and questions of Jewish identity have been featured in a wide range of television genres. Situation comedies, Westerns, made-for-TV movies, miniseries, dramatic and supernatural anthologies, and medical, law, family, police, and science fiction dramas, all have portrayed Jewish issues as a central theme or story line.

What is the television image of Jews and Judaism that emerges from this fascinating wealth of programming? In nearly every instance, the Jewish issues have been portrayed with respect, relative depth, affection, and good intentions, and the Jewish characters who appear in these shows have, without any doubt, been Jewish — often depicted as deeply involved in their Judaism. The picture is not a monolithic one, nor for the most part stereotypical; the themes and characters portrayed are highly varied, both in terms of subject matter and manner of depiction.

These portrayals of significant Jewish issues and Jewishly involved characters belie the commonly held but erroneous view that television depicts Jewish issues only superficially, and Jewish characters as stereotypes or as homogenized ethnics without distinct identity. Such inaccurate conclusions were inevitably drawn by those who, dabbling in the subject and thus drawing only on a small group of well-known but hardly representative shows, remained neglectful or unaware of the vast body of programming that has gone unexplored until now.[1]

But an in-depth and careful exploration of these programs, which is the purpose of this book, is vital since television, it has been argued, "is without question the single most important source of information in the United States."[2] Ninety-eight percent of American households have at least one television, and the average American television set is on for some seven hours each day. According to George Gerbner, a leading authority on the social impact of television, "today, television tells most of the stories to most of the people most of the time.... No other medium reaches into every home or has comparable cradle-to-grave influence over what a society learns about itself."[3] Indeed, John E. O'Connor, an historian and television scholar, has stated that "for the vast majority of viewers, television is actuality."[4]

It follows, then, that most American television viewers, especially those who have little personal contact with Jews, gain a large portion of their ideas about Jews and Judaism from the small screen. As one study concluded, "those who watch more television exhibit ... a greater likelihood of accepting the medium's images of minorities as authentic."[5] Thus television's depictions of Jewish themes and characters, whether accurate or not, are often accepted by viewers as reality and have enormous potential to affect their real-life behaviors, attitudes, knowledge, and understanding.

The effect of these programs on Jewish viewers should also not be overlooked. Popular television's frequent attention to issues of Jewish identity, as Jewish characters grapple with such matters and manifest their Judaism in a variety of ways, have the potential to touch Jewish viewers, leading them toward their own Jewish searchings.

Considering the significant role television has played and continues to play in exposing Americans to the nature of Jews and Judaism, the importance of engaging in a serious study of the depiction of Jewish themes in television dramatic programs can hardly be overestimated. Television, which has been socially defined as "the culture of the masses,"[6] is clearly a medium whose contents cannot be ignored.

Images in Popular Culture

The exploration of Jewish television images falls within a broad and long-standing tradition of examining popular culture images for their reflection of the world and their impact upon it.

Popular culture has long been of interest to historians, sociologists, and other specialists of the humanities because it provides special insights into the nature of society. It has been defined as "mass media content,"[7] that is, material that appeals to the broadest and most diverse cross section of the population and which is transmitted through the mass media. These forms of media — books, periodicals, film, and television — are important sources for historical and social research, because they are what most people read, listen to, and watch.

Books, whether in the form of popular, classic, or dramatic literature, have long served as primary source material for studies of ethnic images. The image of the Jew in literature and theater has been well explored in works such as Montagu Frank Modder's *The Jew in the Literature of England,* Sol Liptzin's *The Jew in American Literature,* a doctoral dissertation by Rhoda Kachuck entitled "The Portrayal of the Jew in American Drama Since 1920," and articles such as Marc Lee Raphael's "From Marjorie to Tevye: The Image of the Jews in American Popular Literature, Theatre and Comedy, 1955–1965."

More recently, the periodical press has developed as an important historical source, not merely for its recording of events, but also for "the interpretations of the life and interests of a community, of a nation, of an age, as these are unconsciously revealed through the columns and pages of periodical literature."[8] As an example applicable to the study of Jewish images, Irving Weingarten explored and analyzed major issues in the American periodical press pertaining to Jewish immigration and immigrants in his doctoral dissertation, "The Image of the Jew in the American Periodical Press, 1881–1921."

While film is now widely recognized and respected as a medium of great value in historical and sociological studies, its acceptance as such by the academic community was a slow process. Sir Arthur Elton, a pioneer documentary filmmaker, is said to have pleaded for scholarly recognition of film as valuable source material.[9] This cause was taken up by many others[10] and was eventually heeded, as evidenced by the ever growing amount of research using film as a primary source. Indeed numerous cinema studies on both the scholarly and popular levels deal with ethnic, national, and religious images. The portrayals in feature films of Asians, blacks, Italians, Irish, Slavs, Australians, and Roman Catholics, for example, have been explored in numerous books and articles.[11] In his work *The Latin Image in American Film,* Allen Woll maintains that film has played a decisive role in shaping Americans' views of Latin America.[12] The editors of *The Pretend Indians: Images of Native Americans in the Movies* also acknowledge the importance of film "as a purveyor of national ideologies, values, and trends. This is especially true of our understanding of minorities...."[13]

Recognizing this, many writers have explored the depiction of Jewish themes and characters in cinema.[14] Lester Friedman wrote *Hollywood's Image of the Jew* "to provide readers with a starting point for thinking about images of Jews in the American cinema."[15] In *The Jew in American Cinema,* Patricia Erens sought to "establish an historical record of what films were actually produced, to indicate the number and types of characters who were identified as Jewish, and to chronicle the narrative context in which these characters appeared."[16] In a more narrow treatment of this subject, Holocaust-related films were the focus of Annette Insdorf's *Indelible Shadows: Film and the Holocaust,*

Judith Doneson's *The Holocaust in American Film*, and Ilan Avisar's *Screening the Holocaust: Cinema's Images of the Unimaginable*. These books demonstrate that film is an invaluable source of understanding events as they occurred, how these events were construed by different people and cultures, how they were depicted, and how their messages were conveyed to the audience.

Images on Television

The concern over ethnic images in cinema is a vital one. However, as UCLA professor Howard Suber points out, "The motion picture in America lost its mass base in the post-war period. In the process, it became a less reliable index of our pluralistic society. It fell to television to carry on — or to not carry on — the concern with ethnic groups which had risen during World War II."[17]

While television would indeed "carry on" a concern for ethnic images, it was destined to do so in a wholly different way: television's penetration was to be all-encompassing, its influence enormous. The new medium was unprecedented in its "sheer mass, in its rapid infiltration of everyday American life, and in the fact that its images ... have been transmitted, year after year into the consciousnesses of hundreds of millions of viewers."[18]

Indeed, it is this "infiltration of everyday American life" that renders TV's Jewish images far more significant and influential than those of feature films. Unlike feature films with their one-time exposure, television series have the unique characteristic of continuity, offering viewers a sense of familiarity and comfort through the ongoing characters whom they welcome, week after week, into their homes, their lives, and their thoughts. Already absorbed in the series and in the lives of their favorite TV heroes and characters, viewers can more receptively observe the Jewish theme or character within this recognizable and familiar context — one that has captured and maintains their long-term interest.

Even the made-for-TV movie, which like the cinematic feature is initially a one-time viewing event, has far greater exposure than the theatrical release; television movies immediately reach a much larger audience, and continue to do so for many years afterward through repeat broadcasts and syndication. Thus they have greater short-term and long-term opportunity to affect audiences. John Corty, who has been described as "a film director who prefers TV," doubtless had this in mind when he stated, "I wouldn't give up television movies. There is nothing like the response you get. Fifty million people saw 'Jane Pittman' in one night. That's very different from even the biggest hit movie."[19]

Because of its unique capacity to reach and influence a massive audience, television is gaining in prominence and stature as a resource for the study of popular culture and as a primary historical source. The significance of using television as a primary source lies in the need to know and understand what most people perceive. And a most effective way of gaining an awareness of people's perceptions is to tune in to their channels of communication. As a measure of television's central position in the lives of most Americans, consider that "what a series such as 'The Waltons' has to say about life in the Depression is likely to have a far more penetrating and long-lasting effect on the nation's consciousness than any number of carefully researched scholarly articles or books."[20]

In view of the fact that popular television programs reach into virtually all homes and "presumably influence our view of the world,"[21] researchers have become increasingly attentive to the medium and the images that it portrays. Numerous studies have documented and analyzed the portrayal of certain groups on television and how these portrayals have changed with time. In general, these studies have concluded that the television images are either stereotypical in nature or are composite pictures drawing on traits from a variety of ethnic groups.

In light of this, it is with a great sense of urgency that many groups in society have become concerned about how they are presented, and represented, on television. In 1975, when Chinese Americans reacted to the airing of a new television series, *Khan*, it was nothing new. As one contemporary observer noted, "Americans of Chinese descent are proving that they can be as concerned over ethnic stereotyping as any other group."[22] According to a number of Chinese American groups, the show presented a "misleading" image of life in Chinatown and of Chinese immigrants. Broadening the issue, a Korean American seized the opportunity to protest "an unspoken conspiracy in the mass media against the Asian American male. How else explain the dearth of Asian American men in attractive, positive roles, and the abundance of them in subservient, demeaning ones in movies, TV shows, commercials, and magazine ads?"[23] In contrast, Polish people reacted positively to the detective series *Banacek*; as one reviewer stated, "This will be the first time in television a Pole is portrayed as smart and shrewd."[24] Similarly, a study on the television image of Hispanic Americans found that characters like Victor Sifuentes on *L.A. Law* provide "the first real opportunity for a breakthrough for Hispanics on television."[25]

The image of Italian Americans was the focus of a 1982 study prepared for the Commission for Social Justice, which concluded that "television entertainment is lacking in portrayals of positive Italian American role models."[26] An earlier article on the same subject had noted that "Italian mothers, and less frequently, Italian fathers and maybe an Italian priest are dragged briefly in front of the camera.... That's about it for Italian-American culture."[27] Apparently, Italian ethnicity is projected merely through character stereotypes and has little to do with the plot, story line, or theme of the program.

Other television images that have been the subject of various studies include the handicapped, the elderly, and businessmen.[28] The concern for television stereotyping of Arabs was the subject of a book called *The TV Arab*.[29] In it the author reports what he perceives as television's "four basic myths about Arabs: they are all fabulously wealthy; they are barbaric and uncultured; they are sex maniacs with a penchant for white slavery; and they revel in acts of terrorism."[30]

The most widespread and publicized concern about television images has focused on portrayals of women and blacks. The United States Commission on Civil Rights called for research on this topic in a report titled "Window Dressing on the Set: Women and Minorities in Television," which stated that "television's portrayal of women and minorities and the potential impact of these portrayals are issues of critical importance to the American society. To the extent that the viewers' beliefs, attitudes, and behavior are affected by what they see on television, relations between the races and sexes may be affected by television's limited and often stereotyped portrayals of men and women, both white and nonwhite. There should be ongoing research to serve as a barometer of change, or the lack of it."[31] Indeed, numerous studies have researched the image of women in television. Topics have included the regularity with which women (both white and minority) appear on prime-time programs,[32] the images of nuns,[33] and the female in "traditional male roles" such as crime fighters.[34] A study that explored in depth the images of nurses on television was undertaken because "the future of the nursing profession depends to a large extent upon popular attitudes and assumptions about the contribution of nurses to the nation's welfare ... [and] no medium of communication comes close to matching television in its power and influence."[35] The study maintained that such research is necessary if popular perceptions and conceptions are to be understood and then corrected.

The portrayal of blacks on television has also received wide attention in research studies and articles. In the first book on the subject, J. Fred MacDonald stated in 1983 that "never have so many Blacks appeared on television, yet never has their image been more stereotyped."[36] Since then, the 1984 debut and subsequent success of *The Cosby Show* generated much spirited discussion over whether that show improved the black TV image or whether it is to be criticized for "being optimistic and upbeat"[37] and "divorced from the everyday experiences of most Blacks."[38]

While the various studies, including all those mentioned above, may differ in their subjects and methodologies, they do share a view of what would constitute a fair television portrayal of a minority or ethnic group. As expressed by Richard Koiner in "The Black Image on TV," the minority or ethnic image should extend "beyond mere comedy and past the limitations of absolute good or absolute bad, to include the shadings of gray which more truthfully reflect human behavior."[39]

Jewish Images on Television

As far back as 1959, the importance of analyzing Jewish topics on television was realized by Zev Zahavy, whose doctoral dissertation, "A History and Survey of Jewish Religious Broadcasting," was a pioneering effort in the field.[40] This detailed history of the origins of Jewish religious radio and television programs analyzed such shows as *The Eternal Light, Lamp unto My Feet,* and *Television Chapel.* Broadcast on Sunday mornings, this specialized religious programming employed sermons, services, discussions, and special plays to impart religious values; topics were related to Jewish holidays or to current events, such as World War II.

Although a valuable chronicle of these early religious programs, Zahavy's work does not deal with popular television, nor was the concern of his dissertation the message of Judaism as conveyed through popular programming to a mass audience. He focused on those people whose motivation for watching the religious programs was to learn about Judaism or to experience Judaism through the specialized programs on television. The viewers of these programs "expect to see or hear a presentation which reflects the good taste and high ideals of its specialized field. A person tuned to a Jewish religious broadcast knows in advance that he is foregoing the possibility of pure entertainment on another station so that he may share an emotional, spiritual experience of a religious nature."[41] Viewed by a small, highly self-selected audience and broadcast early on Sunday mornings when few people are awake, these programs could hardly affect mass popular perceptions of Jews and Judaism. It has even been suggested that the average American television viewer "is extremely unlikely to turn on serious and informative public affairs presentations, even if he is watching while they are on the air."[42]

In order to glean the picture of Jews being transmitted on television at the times when most people are awake and watching, one must study the popular programs to which the masses are attuned — namely, prime-time television dramatic programs.

Surprisingly, despite the importance of this subject and the many in-depth studies made by other ethnic and religious groups about how their members are portrayed on popular TV, until now there has been no comprehensive exploration of popular television's vast array of programs featuring Jewish themes. The importance of television, however, has not been completely ignored, and a few writers have dealt with some specific programs with Jewish content, primarily the Holocaust. In her cinema study *The Holocaust in American Film* Judith Doneson points out cinema's limited ability to disseminate information and acknowledges the impact of television, which "offers an all-encompassing world view that is available to an audience any time, day or night.... Often television's position on an issue will help shape the issue in the popular consciousness."[43] Doneson's recognition of television's ubiquitousness, powerful influence, and audience allure leads her to assert that "if we are to remember the Holocaust, it is chiefly through programs such as *Holocaust* that this task will be achieved."[44] Similarly, in *Indelible Shadows: Film and the Holocaust*, Annette Insdorf discusses, from the perspectives of cinematography and film criticism, several television programs about the Holocaust and acknowledges the importance of television presentations.[45] A few television programs about the Holocaust were also noted in an article by Professor Alvin Rosenfeld, who observed, "It is undeniable that in one manner or another very large numbers of people are being educated about the Holocaust via television."[46] Similarly, in a review of four television dramatic programs dealing with the Holocaust, historian John Toland concluded that "television has succeeded in bringing home to viewers the true horror of the 'Final Solution'."[47]

There have, of course, been other reviews of specific television programs with Jewish themes.[48] Such individual program reviews, limited by their narrow constraints and not necessarily focused on the "Jewishness" of the program, cannot analyze the larger picture of the portrayal of a specific theme in television; any attempt to do so would lead to equally narrow conclusions.

A few articles have attempted to address the broader issue of Jewish themes on television. Generally, however, these articles either assert that there have been few clearly identifiable Jewish themes on television, or acknowledge some Jewish thematic presence but present an all-too-brief and shallow picture of such.[49] Basing conclusions on only a few programs,[50] much of this material concentrates on character portrayals and states that Jewish characters are, for example, "rarely identified as [Jews] in television today,"[51] that "the TV Jew has been homogenized ... his religion [has] become a guessing game,"[52] and that "Jews are rarely portrayed on the small screen."[53] A professor of history at Millersville University posits, "If one were to make a composite of Jewish stereotypes as gleaned from watching ... television for the past 25 years, one would conclude that Jews were ... materially rather than culturally or religiously oriented."[54] Furthermore, he believes that the viewer is presented with characters who are "Jewish by name but with little else to connect them to Jewish tradition or culture. Non-Jews in the Midwest and South must think we ordain psychologists [referring to the psychiatrist Sidney Friedman in the series *M*A*S*H*] ... instead of rabbis."[55] Likewise, an article in the *Christian Science Monitor* states that "usually in series TV, a Jew is identifiable only by his name."[56] Commenting on results of a doctoral dissertation on TV's image of organized religion, a professor of religious sociology at Ohio State University wondered, "Why the drought as far as Jewish symbolism on TV?"[57]

The blatant lack of in-depth research in this heretofore uncharted field of study even misled a prominent writer, in reviewing the miniseries *Holocaust*, to state in colossal error that "this was the first time in 34 years that television acknowledged and presented to a wide audience this most painful chapter in history."[58]

The great number, fascinating variety, and at times astounding depth of the popular television programs that comprise this book clearly belie these earlier assessments. In fact, portrayals of Jewish tradition, culture, and history abound in television's dramatic programs, and the Jewish characters who appear in these shows are often portrayed as vitally concerned with their Jewish heritage.

While popular television programs were created to entertain, researchers would be remiss were they to neglect their deeper and more lasting value as unique historical and cultural records of American life. Indeed, because of popular television's role as a reflector of contemporary social values, an examination of its great kaleidoscopic picture of Jewish life provides fresh insights of both historic and contemporary significance. Varying, real-life attitudes about Jews and Jewish issues are reflected in TV portrayals, an analysis of which can reveal much about evolving perspectives and current realities.

As television executive Sergio Zavoli, president of RAI-Raddiotelevisione Italiana, has observed, if television programs are ignored by researchers and left to collect dust on archive or studio shelves, the vast amount of programming in existence would amount to no more than "a huge and shapeless mass with no use whatsoever, except in terms of immediate consumption ... unless someone takes the responsibility to screen, to select and to interpret."[59]

This book is our effort to begin fulfilling this responsibility for the hundreds of programs that have featured Jewish themes and characters over the history of popular television.

1

Rites and Rituals,
Lore and Traditions

High atop the Blue Ridge Mountains in rural Virginia during the 1940s, a Southern Baptist family celebrated a *bar mitzvah*, danced the *horah*, and heard *kaddish* recited over the grave of their family elder. The family was named the Waltons, and their participation in Jewish rituals and traditions took place on episodes of the hit series *The Waltons*, which ran on television for nearly a decade (1972–1981).

That so American and Christian a family as the Waltons embraced Jewish customs on a popular family show indicates just how diverse and widespread is the depiction of Jewish traditions and ceremonies on television. Hundreds of popular shows of every genre have woven into their story lines Jewish weddings and funerals, *bar* and *bat mitzvahs*,[1] circumcisions, the observance of *Shabbat* and Jewish holidays, Hebrew and Yiddish songs and conversations, blessings and prayers, and quotations from the Hebrew Bible, the *Talmud*, and the book of Jewish mysticism, the *Zohar*.

Indeed, among the many ways of portraying Jews and Judaism on popular TV shows, none is more frequent and direct as the depiction of Jewish rites and rituals, traditions and customs. As the most tangible form of religious expression and identity, ritual is a natural focus of television when it turns its attention to religious issues. Through the observance of Jewish rituals, TV Jews express their identity and, in turn, can be most readily and overtly identified as Jews to the viewing audience.

Owing to the universality of religious observance, television's dramatization of Jewish rituals holds the possibility of creating bridges between Jews and non–Jews. Overwhelmingly, Americans consider themselves a religious people, for whom religious identity, belief, and activity is an important part of life.[2] The observance of Jewish rituals seen on TV is therefore merely an extension of the already familiar idea of religious observance in general. Certainly television writers — attentive always to commercial considerations — must believe that the depiction of Jewish ceremonies will not turn off viewers but will be acceptable and understandable to them and that on some level they can identify with them.

While television depicts Jewish customs and ceremonies as a natural piece of the fabric of American religious and cultural life, it does not overlook their religious distinctiveness. When Jewish rituals are portrayed, they are almost invariably discussed and explained, sometimes in astounding detail.

In nearly every instance, non–Jews participate in the Jewish ceremony, respecting, enjoying, and learning from it. Their frequent presence and active involvement underscores the message that these things are a normal, acceptable part of America.

The notion of acceptability of Jewish ritual is an important message not only for gentiles but for Jews as well. For assimilated Jews, television's portrayals of religious observance may involve them in an aroused sense of identity, by stirring emotional ties or connections to their past. That their favorite TV characters do not hesitate to identify Jewishly — in open sight of millions of non–Jewish viewers — may provide a sense of security and a feeling that it is acceptable to do so.

Over the history of popular TV, virtually no Jewish ritual has gone undepicted, offering a fascinating look and opportunity for learning about a vast array of Jewish customs, traditions, and rituals.

Life Cycle Events

BAR AND BAT MITZVAH

Of all the Jewish rites of passage depicted on popular TV, none has received more attention than the *bar mitzvah*. (Depictions of *bat mitzvahs*, the first of which did not appear on a popular TV show until 1981, are discussed below.) Not only have more *bar mitzvahs* been depicted than any other life cycle event, but often great pains are taken to explain the meaning of the ceremony, its importance to the family, and its significance in Jewish life.

Television's emphasis on the *bar mitzvah* parallels the prominent role that the event has taken on in the lives of American Jews today. As one observer noted, "Few religious practices have been as widely accepted by American Jewry as the celebration of the *bar mitzvah*, which claims a place in their social and religious life that is unparalleled in Jewish history."[3] While scholars debate whether this centrality is part of a historical continuum or aberration, the fact is that for many American Jews, the focus of *bar mitzvah* has shifted from scholarly achievement to lavish partying. Indeed, "like most Americans, American Jews have enthusiastically embraced the cult of consumerism, and in *bar mitzvah* they demonstrate the depth of their commitment to it."[4] This focus on extravagance is all too well known in the popular conception and indeed has been the subject of parody in several feature films, most notably *The Apprenticeship of Duddy Kravitz.*

Markedly different is the television depiction of such events. Remarkably, refreshingly, and importantly, television has focused its attention and that of millions of viewers on the actual meaning and purpose behind *bar mitzvah*—namely study, maturity, and the beginning of moral understanding and religious responsibility. These aspects of the *bar mitzvah* are highlighted in nearly every popular TV show featuring this rite; and in fact a TV *bar mitzvah* usually serves as a catalyst for some great moral revelation that occurs during the course of the show.

This is often achieved under unusual or extraordinary circumstances, not surprisingly, given television's need as an entertainment medium for dramatic situations. In a 1969 episode of *Ironside* titled "L'chayim," the theft of a *Torah* scroll offers the thirteen-year-old grandson of a rabbi a chance to assume grown-up responsibilities and religious commitment as his *bar mitzvah* approaches. Thieves have vandalized the synagogue and stolen a *Torah* that had survived the Holocaust, and they are demanding that $5,000 in ransom money be delivered to them — by the young soon-to-be *bar mitzvah* boy, Eli. Although his grandfather, Rabbi Farber, refuses to send him, insisting "He's only a child!" young Eli declares, "Grandpa, I'm thirteen — that's when you said I'd be man. I *want* to go!" In stating this, Eli expresses that becoming a *bar mitzvah* means taking responsibility for the preservation of his heritage; and his sole demonstrated concern is for the recovery of the *Torah*— not over any disruption to a *bar mitzvah* party. His efforts are rewarded when the *Torah* is eventually rescued, and he dances with it proudly as he is shown celebrating his *bar mitzvah* in synagogue.

In another police show decades later, a different boy on the eve of his *bar mitzvah* also faced adult moral choices as he found himself in the vortex of a criminal investigation. In a two-part episode of *The Commish*, David Scali — son of a suburban police commissioner — discovers that his girlfriend's father is a dangerous gangster. David must decide whether to testify against him and doom his romance. The difficult choice is his. "This is all on you now, David," his father tells him. "You're old enough to make your own choices. Hopefully, your mother and I have done our job so you can make the right ones, but we can't make them for you." With the notion of responsibility and becoming an adult weighing heavy on David on the eve of his *bar mitzvah*, it is clear what decision he will make. He refers to the difficulty of it in a moving *bar mitzvah* speech that closes the episode and in which he praises his parents as "the models I choose to pattern myself after." At last, after all the difficulty and soul-searching this thirteen-year-old could muster, he can finally conclude his speech — proud that he made the right decision — by saying confidently, "... today I become a man," which are the final words of the show.

In its emphasis on the moral and ethical aspects of becoming a *bar* or *bat mitzvah, The Commish* is in keeping with several other TV programs that have emphasized this component of the Jewish rite of passage over the party aspects of the event that so often predominate in real life. In fact in a previous *Commish* episode, which introduced the subject of David's *bar mitzvah*, the boy's initial focus was on all the gifts and checks that he hoped to receive. But there too, the youngster — guided by his parents but left by them to make his own decision — concluded that these were not the focus of the event and chose to have a different kind of *bar mitzvah*.

Sometimes the passage into religious adulthood symbolized by the *bar mitzvah* takes place not when a boy is thirteen — the traditional age for a *bar mitzvah* ceremony — but at a later stage in life. There have been TV programs mirroring real life instances where, due to a variety of circumstances, a youngster did not have a *bar mitzvah* at thirteen and later, as an adult, desires to fulfill this obligation. Television first depicted such a situation in a 1962 story titled "The *Bar Mitzvah* of Major Orlovsky," presented as part of the dramatic anthology series *General Electric Theater*. Because Orlovsky, who was born in Russia, had run away from home at an early age and then fought in the Russian army until defecting to the West, he had never had a *bar mitzvah*. He had also run away from his religion, but suddenly his life is changed when he meets and falls in love with Miriam Raskin, a widow and a rabbi's daughter, who is about to celebrate her son's *bar mitzvah*. Orlovsky's involvement with Miriam and her family finally lead him back to Judaism and to the celebration of his own *bar mitzvah*.

In a similar vein, the very popular 1960s situation comedy *The Dick Van Dyke Show* presented an episode focusing on the assimilated Jewish character of Buddy Sorrell. Buddy, who is one of Rob's partners in a comedy-writing trio, begins behaving very strangely and secretively, leading his coworkers to suspect that he is either seeing a psychiatrist or having an affair. A series of comedic twists reveal that in fact Buddy has been studying for his *bar mitzvah* with his rabbi. He explains that as a youngster he had to work and was unable to celebrate his *bar mitzvah* but had promised himself and his mother that when circumstances allowed, he would do so. Later, in synagogue, his mother and his friends share his joy as he fulfills his promise.

At times, television portrays the *bar mitzvah* as a moral milestone not so much for the young celebrant as for his older relatives. An episode of the 1950s *Crossroads* anthology series[5] titled "The Rabbi Davis Story" depicts the story of a Jewish man who has abandoned his Jewish values to become a crooked politician. His nephew, who is in his guardianship, is about to become a *bar mitzvah* in the congregation of a rabbi who is determined to expose the politician's unsavory schemes. At the *bar mitzvah* ceremony, the rabbi addresses the young man about values and ethics, hoping to instill the uncle with a sense of shame for his actions at the same time. The strength of the rabbi's words and the power of the *bar mitzvah* ceremony have the desired effect: the politician is led to a newfound sense of morality, corrects his evil ways, and tells the rabbi, "It was the whole *bar mitzvah* service that got me. I don't know why I ever left the fold."

A similar theme was done in a humorous style in a 1963 episode of the comedy series *Car 54, Where Are You?* New York City police officers Toody and Muldoon are bumbling cops, but they have hearts of gold. Friendly to everyone and always trying to solve everybody's problems, they seek a solution to young Joey Pokrass's dilemma in an episode titled "See You at the *Bar Mitzvah*." Joey's father is a hated landlord, an overbearing, oafish man known and despised throughout the community for the atrocious condition of his buildings and his refusal to improve them for suffering tenants. No one, therefore, will attend his son's *bar mitzvah*, despite Toody and Muldoon's pleas that they not take out their wrath on the innocent boy. The officers are forced to resort to some comical efforts to spare Joey's feelings: they bring prisoners from night court to the *bar mitzvah* (and even *they* are unwilling to attend a Pokrass event!) so that there will be *someone* in attendance as Joey begins chanting in Hebrew. But it seems, after all, that Toody and Muldoon's personal appeal to the community has paid off. Everyone who had earlier refused to attend is seen filing into the *bar mitzvah*, having realized that Joey should not be made to suffer just because of his father. The elder Pokrass is so touched by the outpouring of goodness and affection for his son that he mends his ways, the next day repairing all his buildings to the delight of astonished tenants. To the officers, he reveals the reason: "Yesterday my son was *bar mitzvahed*,[6] but it was *me* who became a man."

For a number of young TV characters with disabilities, the celebration of a *bar mitzvah* marks a special turning point and major accomplishment in their lives. Overcoming feelings of inferiority, they are able, by virtue of their own abilities and desire, to attain a new status in life — that of being equal to those without disabilities in their religious obligations. One television drama that did not air during prime-time hours but as a 1987 *ABC Afterschool Special* dramatized the real-life story of Brad Silverman, a boy with Down's syndrome who was dissuaded by both rabbi and cantor from having a *bar mitzvah*. They were sure he could not master the prayers and *Torah* reading in Hebrew, but Brad's determination and relentless work on the material won out in the end. On the day of his *bar mitzvah*, he chants proudly from the *bimah* (synagogue pulpit), shushing the cantor who offers unsolicited and unneeded assistance.

Another boy who overcame disabilities to celebrate his *bar mitzvah* was featured in a 1981 made-for-TV movie called *Rivkin: Bounty Hunter*. Keith is a wheelchair-bound youngster whose mother has died and whose father's unusual occupation, bounty hunting, keeps him away from home for long stretches of time. Despite these difficulties, Keith studies hard for his *bar mitzvah*, with the help of a close friend and neighbor who happens to be a priest, and finally celebrates the occasion in synagogue.

The travails of another orphan preparing for his *bar mitzvah* were depicted years earlier on a 1962 episode of *The Dick Powell Show*. Young Davey Jacobs has lost both parents and, as the rabbi explains to him, will therefore celebrate his *bar mitzvah* at age twelve instead of thirteen.[7] Although proud to be having a *bar mitzvah*—he explains its meaning and rituals to his non–Jewish friend—Davey is consumed with anger and guilt over his mother's recent death and, unfairly blaming his older brother for her death, refuses to allow him to attend the event. Nothing can defuse this family crisis until a concerned adult friend makes a last-minute plea to Davey, urging him to understand that his own feelings of undeserved guilt are making him lash out and reminding him, "In a few minutes, you'll be taking your first step toward manhood, your first step toward understanding. Davey, make it the right step." A tearful epiphany follows, as Davey allows his waiting brother into the synagogue and they embrace. In this depiction, the occasion of his *bar mitzvah* has bestowed upon Davey new understanding and compassion and a self-awareness that leads to personal and familial healing.

The impact of a boy's *bar mitzvah* on his non–Jewish friends has been the subject of a number of TV programs. Sometimes the effect on a non–Jewish youngster is shallow and silly: on an episode of the 1970s comedy series *The Partridge Family*, young Danny Partridge says having a *bar mitzvah* would be fun because "I hear you get a lot of presents." Much more often, the effect is profound. In a 1984 episode of the situation comedy *Diff'rent Strokes*, the young African American main character of the show, Arnold, returns home from the *bar mitzvah* of a friend's brother and announces his decision to convert to Judaism. Arnold is obviously impressed by all the Jewish food ("a *knish*—that's a Jewish taco"), the presents ("he got a camera, a tape recorder—not to mention all the money"), and the prospect of becoming a man and "getting into X-rated movies at kid's prices." Arnold also glowingly describes how the *bar mitzvah* boy "rattled off the whole speech in Hebrew.... Then everybody thanked him and congratulated him and kissed him and shook his hand.... I've never seen so much love and warmth and affection—and it was fun too!" But Arnold's enthusiasm for conversion dims when a talk with the rabbi alerts him to Hebrew school, the need for much study to catch up, and the twenty-four-hour fast on *Yom Kippur*. This last point in particular sends the food-fixated Arnold into total confusion. "I like the idea of being Jewish," he muses, "but ... I'm not sure it's for me." Reminding him that religion is a complicated matter, Arnold's sympathetic adoptive father invites him to come back to their old church (which Arnold had sworn off in anticipation of his conversion). There Arnold joins in joyous hymn singing, seemingly with a strengthened sense of religious identity, as he completes a process of self-searching and spiritual questioning initiated by the *bar mitzvah*. Although he decides not to become Jewish, it was the Jewish ceremony that led him to a new level of spiritual awareness.

Such searching confronts another non–Jewish boy as his Jewish friend celebrates his *bar mitzvah*, but, unlike Arnold, this youngster can find no solace or answers in his own tradition. In a stirring 1989 episode of the acclaimed series *The Wonder Years*, set in 1960s suburbia, young Kevin watches his best friend Paul prepare for his *bar mitzvah* with a mixture of envy and longing. Joining Paul's family for dinner, Kevin waits with suspense as Paul's grandfather is about to give him his *bar mitzvah* gift. It turns out to be — not stock options or keys to a new car as Kevin had imagined — but a book from which Paul's grandfather had read his prayers on the day of his own *bar mitzvah*, which had been given to him, in turn, by his father. Given the pervasiveness of materialism in television and in the society that it mirrors, this scene of a simple gift of a book being handed down over four generations is striking. Even more powerful is Paul's reaction: rather than disappointment or a request for a "real" present, he responds with intense gratitude, emotion, and understanding. Even Kevin is caught up in the moment and is seemingly taken with the meaning and greatness of this gift and the sense of heritage and rootedness that it represents. As he sees Paul's family bound up in traditions, closeness, and warmth, he seeks out the same in his own family. He asks his mother about his ancestors, but the answers are unexciting; he tries to commune with his father by helping him fix the car, but he is shooed away after causing a mechanical disaster.

Angry over this void in his life that is underscored by Paul's impending *bar mitzvah*, Kevin refuses to attend on the pretext that since it is also *his* birthday that day, he is otherwise occupied. Paul is disappointed and confused, but the *bar mitzvah* goes on. In the midst of Paul's *Torah* reading in the synagogue, Kevin appears, having had a change of heart. Paul's face brightens, and at the reception that follows, the two clasp arms to dance a delirious *horah*. This is the final image of the show, as the voice of the narrator — the adult Kevin reminiscing from the perspective of twenty years later — says, "And so it turned out to be a great birthday after all. And in a funny way, when I look back on it, I sort of feel like it was my *bar mitzvah* too."

The impact of a *bar mitzvah* on others less directly involved was seen on an episode of the comedy *Roseanne*. When she and her husband crash a *bar mitzvah* party, it becomes an occasion for the couple to discover some deeper truths about life and to draw closer in their relationship.

Although America's first recorded real-life *bat mitzvah* took place in 1922,[8] no young woman celebrated this rite of passage on a popular TV show until 1981. And it was, of all people, the Jewish niece of Archie Bunker, star of the classic comedy series *All in the Family*, known later as *Archie Bunker's Place*. During the run of the latter series, a two-part episode portrayed the *bat mitzvah* of Stephanie Mills, whom Archie and his late wife Edith had raised since the girl's Jewish mother was killed in a car accident and father ran off. The story opens as Stephanie returns home announcing that she has just been at a friend's *bat mitzvah* ceremony and reception. When the confused housekeeper says that she thought the occasion was called a *bar mitzvah*, Stephanie explains that the *bar mitzvah* is for boys and the *bat mitzvah* is for girls and that "it's sort of like confirmation. According to Jewish Law, it means you become an adult." A satirical note of reality and a reflection on some current American *bar/bat mitzvah* mores is injected when Stephanie's Jewish grandmother becomes involved in planning the affair and insists that it be a lavish event. "This ceremony has a religious meaning," she tells Archie in all seriousness. "It's a sacred rite, deeply rooted in tradition and it requires a dignified setting — like my country club," which, she explains, has a ballroom, offers a five-course meal (choice of capon or prime rib), dancing, a sit-down dinner, a dessert buffet, and strolling violins. Stephanie, though, will have none of it, and insists that the party that follows the synagogue services be held at home — a far cry from her grandmother's envisioned elaborate affair.

When the *bat mitzvah* service finally takes place, Stephanie chants a portion of her *Torah* reading in Hebrew and recites various prayers, flanked by the rabbi and a woman cantor. Archie, head covered by a yarmulke, looks on proudly. In concluding her *bat mitzvah* speech, Stephanie says, "I want to thank all of you for the privilege of becoming an adult in your eyes." And indeed, this is to be a day of harsh revelation for Stephanie, as she later confronts some difficult realities during the reception that follows at home. Her estranged father — an unexpected and uninvited guest at her *bat mitzvah* who is out of work — sneaks up to her room, steals her *bat mitzvah* cash gifts, which have been carefully and lovingly arranged into a small tree design, and is caught and berated by Archie, who shames him into returning the money. But Stephanie, unnoticed, has witnessed the whole event and emerges to insist that her father take all the money, if he needs it that much. In this act of giving and compassion, she transforms the gifts of her *bat mitzvah* — its external and material aspects — into its moral essence.

This kind of sensitivity and responsibility characterize most of popular TV's *bar* and *bat mitzvah* youngsters. They do not plead for or even desire elaborate affairs, nor do they expect expensive gifts. Rather, their excitement and anticipation for *bar mitzvah* lies in their eagerness to become full-fledged members of their faith and to assume adult responsibilities and mature attitudes and concerns.

In contrast, there are some synagogues pejoratively nicknamed "*bar mitzvah* factories," meaning institutions that cater to the whims of marginally affiliated Jews whose only connection with Judaism is the *bar* or *bat mitzvah* of their children. Too often the event hardly represents the taking on of responsibilities and commitment associated with becoming a *bar* or *bat mitzvah*. In spite of this, these television depictions offer a valuable counterpoint in focusing on those aspects of the rite that matter most — the spiritual, the familial, the learning, and the sense of heritage and community.

WEDDINGS

While it is through the *bar* and *bat mitzvah* that television paints a picture of religious initiation, it is through its portrayal of Jewish weddings that it conveys a statement of reaffirmation of faith at a more mature stage of life. When Jewish TV couples marry in a religious ceremony, they demonstrate their desire to identify with and carry on their heritage. And indeed, although the rate of intermarriage is high — both in real life and on television (a subject discussed in Chapter 6) — several programs have depicted Jews marrying within the faith in Jewish wedding ceremonies, usually despite great obstacles or dire circumstances. These shows generally highlight the importance of a Jewish wedding, both for the couple and for the survival of the Jewish people, and depict the traditional elements of a religious ceremony: a rabbi conducting the ceremony under a wedding canopy, the singing of blessings and traditional songs, the bride and groom sipping wine and exchanging vows (and rings), and the groom breaking the glass.

One Jewish couple who faced many difficulties arranging their religious wedding was depicted in an episode of the popular late 1960s comedy series *The Flying Nun* titled "The Rabbi and the Nun." The young couple — and their rabbi — were determined to have a Jewish wedding ceremony even if this meant having it at a convent. It seems that Temple Beth Shalom, the only synagogue in San Tanco, Puerto Rico, is too small for the affair. When Sister Bertrille, the flying nun, learns about the couple's dilemma, she offers use of the convent to Rabbi Mendez, who replies, "There's nothing in the Old Testament[9] that forbids it." In preparation for the wedding, the rabbi sets up a *chuppah* in the convent garden, explaining to the nuns that it's "a canopy — it's a tradition for Jews to get married under a canopy." When the ceremony takes place, it is a fully Jewish event, as the rabbi recites blessings, the couple exchanges religious vows, and the groom breaks the glass. The exuberant nuns yelp *"mazel tov"* and then break into a chorus of *"Havah Nagila,"* the popular Israeli folk dance traditionally heard at Jewish celebrations.

Despite the unlikely scenario of a Jewish wedding at a convent and the comedic approach, this program dramatizes the importance of Jews marrying within their faith and holding a Jewish ceremony. Clearly, the Jewish community on the fictional San Tanco was very small — without any adequate site to accommodate a large group, like a bigger synagogue or a kosher catering hall. And yet, despite the paucity of Jews, the couple wanted to marry within their faith and to have a Jewish wedding, going to such lengths as to hold it at a convent, an ingenious, if unusual, adaptation. The vital communal aspect to Judaism is underscored in this depiction of the difficulties facing Jews where there are few coreligionists and limited communal facilities.

Such conditions faced Jews on the American frontier who were depicted on various TV Westerns, yet several of them managed to have Jewish weddings.

In a 1968 episode of *Here Come the Brides*, set in an 1870s Seattle logging camp, a young Jewish woman manages to find a Jewish groom, and in preparation for her wedding, goes through the ceremony of ritual immersion known as *mikveh*. It is explained that this is "a religious ceremony the bride goes through the night before a wedding," and an interpretation of its symbolism is offered. This detailed explanation of Jewish traditions and rituals continues during the wedding ceremony the next day: the couple is married by an Irish ship captain[10] who announces in his thick, lilting brogue that the ceremony is full of "all these symbols" and goes on to give interpretations of the meaning of the *chuppah*, the sipping of wine, and the breaking of the glass.

Another frontier Jewish wedding ceremony was featured on the popular Western *Have Gun, Will Travel*. In this 1961 episode, the wedding of Rivka Shotness, daughter of Russian-born peddler Nathan Shotness, and Faivel Melamed, is threatened by a gang of revenge-bent, murderous outlaws who have vowed to disrupt the event. At the insistence of the bride and groom, the wedding goes ahead as planned. Everything is set at Nathan's ranch for a proper Jewish wedding: there is a velvet *chuppah*, a silver wine goblet, a rabbi, and a fiddler. But as the rabbi begins to recite Hebrew wedding prayers, the outlaws arrive, wreaking havoc just outside the house where guests had gathered. Amidst the sounds of destruction and the outlaws' wild whoops the wedding continues, as the rabbi chants a traditional Jewish wedding song taken from the Hebrew Bible: "Once more shall it be heard in the cities of Judah and the courtyards of Jerusalem, the voice of gladness and the voice of joy, the voice of the bridegroom and bride."[11] Finally the thugs are routed through the combined efforts of Paladin, Nathan, and Faivel the groom, who returns to the *chuppah* to break the glass. As he does so, the rabbi explains the custom, saying, "In our moment of joy, let us also commemorate the destruction of our holy temple."[12] The now-festive occasion resumes with joyous dancing.

Another Jewish wedding proceeding amidst threats, here during the American Colonial period, was depicted in an episode of the *Crossroads* anthology series, which dramatized the lives of real-life clergy. In this 1956 segment, Rabbi Gershom Seixas, a rabbi who preached for independence during the Revolutionary War, is driven by British threats from his New York pulpit to Philadelphia. When summoned back to British-held New York to perform a wedding for an enemy soldier who is Jewish, he struggles to make a decision between risking his own life and fulfilling what he calls a "holy duty." He asks rhetorically of those who fear for his safety, "Can I refuse when he begs me to come to him as a rabbi?" The importance of performing a wedding compels the rabbi to journey to New York. There, at the Red Lion Tavern, as the ceremony is about to begin (complete with *chuppah*), renegade British soldiers burst in to capture the rabbi in violation of his guarantee of safe conduct for performing a "spiritual necessity." They are overcome, and the wedding takes place.

Jewish weddings occurring amidst the ultimate violence, the Holocaust, have also been depicted on popular TV shows. In the 1982 made-for-TV movie *The Wall*, for example, love manages to survive in the Warsaw ghetto, and although one character asks in desperation, "How long can love last inside a wall?" a Jewish wedding does take place within the ghetto. Outside the confines of a ghetto, the 1979 miniseries *Holocaust* depicted two young Jewish partisan fighters who fall in love and are married by a rabbi in an open field just before they are about to embark on a mission. Their *chuppah* is a prayer shawl held aloft by their comrades.

These TV weddings that proceed amidst the most extreme of circumstances display the importance to the Jewish character of marrying within his or her religion and the necessity of having a Jewish wedding ceremony. Because most of these characters are not depicted as otherwise very religiously observant, their insistence on marrying someone Jewish in a religious ceremony is shown not to be foreign or way-out. Simply, their devotion to their faith impels them to stay in that faith by marrying Jewishly.

Other Jewish TV characters display this need, even under more ordinary circumstances. Jewish wedding ceremonies have been depicted on many other programs, including the 1977 miniseries *Seventh Avenue* and episodes of the 1970s medical drama *Medical Center* and the short-lived 1988 series *Hot House*.

Television has depicted not only the beginning of a Jewish marriage but also its demise. In tackling the matter of a Jewish divorce (a *get*), *L.A. Law* addressed an important and controversial issue in the Jewish world. Because under Orthodox *halacha* (law) the husband grants his wife a *get*, women are sometimes held hostage by unscrupulous mates seeking more favorable divorce terms. (Within Orthodoxy, there are slight and slow efforts under way to redress this problem. The Reform, Reconstructionist, and Conservative movements have taken further steps to rework the Jewish divorce process to eliminate such situations). With its typical blending of satire and seriousness, *L.A. Law* featured a Jewish couple going through a *halachic* divorce, as a wife sought a *get* in order to remarry an Orthodox man. (*He* was refreshingly portrayed as a modern, regular person, while the rabbis later shown presiding over the *get* were cast in Hollywood's tiresome, near-universal vision of Orthodox rabbis: bearded, medieval-like characters in a darkened room.) Sniffing an opportunity, the greedy husband extracted assets of increasing worth, until she finally gave up all claims to their Pacific Palisades home. Her smug mate (even his lawyer Arnie Becker is disgusted by these tactics) seems to have won all — until the parties happen upon a newscast about the chance destruction of the disputed home by a fierce storm. Everyone is delighted except the erstwhile husband, and as the show's final camera shot pans on his distraught face, celestial music and rolling thunder is heard. While this "miraculous" ending through divine retribution was a humorous and superficially satisfying conclusion and *L.A. Law* is to be commended for exposing this difficult issue on popular TV for the first time, more realistic solutions are needed in real life.

RITES OF DEATH AND MOURNING

The abundance of television references to and depictions of Jewish funerals, mourning rituals, and unveilings — from the hit medical series *ER* and *Chicago Hope* to dramas like *Relativity*, *L.A. Law*, and *Picket Fences* — mirrors the inevitable necessity of these in real life. The natural human response to seek religious solace at times of bereavement finds expression among Jews as well: no matter what their degree of religious observance, affiliation, or identity, they will by and large turn to religious ritual at times of death and mourning. Partly because of superstition, fear, and genuine need and partly because it is an easy, "one-time" way of identifying religiously, even the most assimilated Jew will have a Jewish funeral.

This need for a Jewish funeral among even the most attenuated of Jews is reflected on several popular TV shows. One instance is the 1984 miniseries *Ellis Island*, which chronicled the life of a Russian immigrant in America. He de–Judaizes his name upon arriving in America, intermarries, and, throughout the entire seven-hour, three-part program, participates in no aspect of Jewish life. The one exception is when his young daughter dies and she is given a Jewish funeral, complete with the chanting of the memorial prayer *El Malei Rachamim*.

The Jewishness of an otherwise un–Jewish character emerging at the time of a funeral was demonstrated to an extreme on a 1977 episode of *All in the Family*. When Archie's best friend and coworker Stretch Cunningham dies, Archie is asked to deliver the eulogy (or, as Archie calls it, the "urology"). Only when he arrives at the funeral and sees everyone wearing *kippot* (*yarmulkes*) and a rabbi officiating does a stunned Archie learn that Stretch was in fact Jewish. Nothing, apparently, that Stretch ever said or did while he was alive gave Archie any inkling that he was Jewish.

Several other programs have revealed that a character was Jewish only through the presentation of a Jewish funeral. On the 1988 made-for-TV movie *Favorite Son*, viewers learn that a young FBI agent was Jewish when his funeral is shown after he is murdered. Two years earlier, a lawyer on an episode of *L.A. Law* (he even talks about Christmas in his final courtroom summation) is shown to be a Jew at the funeral held after he commits suicide.

Jewish funerals have been portrayed for people who were not only thoroughly assimilated but whose whole lives were antithetical to any religious values. With the rise of crime-busting gangster series in the early 1960s, a spate of Jewish mobsters reached the TV screen. One such ruthless character, appearing on an episode of *The Untouchables*, comes to rest in a religious setting after he is gunned down in a violent mob hit. The show does not depict the funeral ceremony itself, but the outside of what is clearly a synagogue is shown. In a similar vein, a Jewish mobster portrayed on another crime series, *The Lawless Years*, is actually gunned down on the steps of a synagogue while taking his first tentative steps there after renouncing his life of crime. Indeed, it was the death of his sister (her Jewish funeral *was* depicted) that led to this renunciation.

This picture of a Jewish funeral's serving as a point of religious awakening was a dramatic and key component of the 1974 miniseries *QB VII*. While his father was alive, the middle-aged TV scriptwriter Ben Cady rejected everything about him, particularly his religion. But when the elderly man suffers a heart attack in Israel, where he had settled, Ben immediately flies out to be by his bedside. Entering the small apartment where his father lies dying, Ben encounters a roomful of pious Jews intently praying around the frail man, creating a low, buzzlike din. Clearly, the Hollywood writer has entered a world that is utterly foreign to him. This notion is underscored at the subsequent funeral, after his father dies. (This scene also gives viewers an unusual look at an Israeli funeral, which is quite different from an American one: there is no coffin — the body is buried in a white shroud, and it all takes place graveside.) At the grave, while the Orthodox mourners are reciting *kaddish*, the Jewish mourners' prayer, Ben is shown stumbling through it in transliteration. A lingering camera shot on the printed English letters of a borrowed prayer book, with Ben's finger awkwardly following along, coupled with his cumbersome recitation in contrast to those around him, points up his total disengagement from anything Jewish and the gulf between his and his father's world. The stark realization of this sets Ben on a journey of rediscovering his heritage.

The *kaddish* prayer and the ritual of *shiva* (the seven-day formal mourning period) have served as points of rediscovery and reconciliation for several other Jewish characters, including one in as improbable a setting as a futuristic space station. On the science fiction series *Babylon 5*, set in a twenty-third century space station inhabited by earthlings and aliens, Commander Susan Ivanova eschewed any Jewish mourning rites or outward grief when her estranged father died. But an onboard visit from her uncle, a rabbi, forces her to confront her emotions and her past, and she decides to return to Earth to hold a proper *shiva* for her father. In a final scene, among family and friends she is depicted as having found peace amidst the Jewish mourning rituals and the reconnection and opportunities for healing that they represent.

On *thirtysomething*, recitation of the *kaddish* — for his father on his *yahrzeit*, anniversary of death — brings Michael Steadman back to a heritage from which he had grown distant. For the first time in years, he tentatively enters a synagogue, where he hears the *kaddish* described as a "solemn testimony to that unbroken faith which links the generations one to another." Along with the congregation, he recites the prayer, memorializing his father and linking himself to his people's history and destiny.

A similar theme in a very different setting prevailed on the detective series *Homicide: Life on the Streets*. While investigating the murder of a childhood friend, Baltimore's Detective Munch finds that his feelings about being Jewish are rekindled. Despite an initial reluctance to acknowledge and follow through on these stirrings, he ultimately attends the woman's *shiva*, booming out the words of the *kaddish* in the show's concluding lines.

The emotional pull for Jews of the *kaddish* prayer and the great need mourners feel to recite it when a relative passes on was the basis for a 1980 episode of *The Waltons*. Upon learning that his grandfather has just recently died in the Holocaust, Ted Lapinsky, an assimilated, young Jewish soldier, tells Jason Walton he would like to join a unit going to Europe so that he can locate his grandfather's grave and "say a special prayer to put his soul at peace — and mine too." Jason asks him to join his family on Walton's Mountain, where his own grandfather is buried, and there recite his prayer "for both grandpas — Lapinsky and Walton." Once on Walton's Mountain, Ted explains to the family gathered there that this prayer, the *kaddish*, is "our mourning prayer. It's over 5,000 years old, from Israel. It glorifies God and affirms our faith. And mostly, it asks for peace for our loved one, and everyone." Clearly moved by these words and their participation in this Jewish ritual, the Waltons say, "We could certainly use that kind of prayer."

The importance for Jewish characters of saying *kaddish* was echoed decades later in an episode of the popular series *Northern Exposure*. After Dr. Joel Fleischman learns that his Uncle Manny has died, he seeks to find ten Jews — from among the sparsely populated nearby Alaskan towns — to form a *minyan* so he can recite the *kaddish*. As he manages to slowly assemble a *minyan*, he expresses the viewpoint that these unfamiliar Jews are mere strangers — not his family nor his community. He turns instead to his townsfolk, declaring that they are his family and community and that it is with them that he wants to recite the *kaddish*, even though they are not Jewish. Although this is a favorable portrait of ecumenism and a demonstration of the modern notion that one can find family and community in different spheres, it was in a sense a negation of Jewish community, as it depicted Joel's inability to sense the inherent and deep connection that bonds all Jews over space and time. Such a notion, however, was clear to an ailing grandfather on an episode of *Touched by an Angel* who goes to great lengths both geographically and emotionally to overcome an estranged relationship with his grandson and forge the bond of continuity by asking his grandson to recite *kaddish* for him after he dies.

Like the explanation of the *kaddish* on *The Waltons*, which brought together a young Jew and a Baptist family, the description of other Jewish mourning rites often serves as a basis for inter-religious learning and interest between TV's Jewish and non–Jewish characters. Such explanations have been included on a number of shows, both dramas and comedies alike. A 1984 episode of the humorous series *Facts of Life*, chronicling the lives of teenaged girls at a prestigious boarding school, featured a house of *shiva*, a Jewish home in mourning. After the father of one of the students dies, the other girls join her on her trip home — and there learn about Jewish mourning customs. When the guests are taken aback that there are no flowers in the house, the headmistress explains, "*Shiva* is the Jewish period of mourning, and the family follows certain customs, like wearing that black ribbon." Another student volunteers that there is also "no music or TV allowed." When one of the girls notices the draped mirrors, the headmistress explains that "in a *shiva* house, all the mirrors are covered." An explanation of that symbolism is offered by another student, who says it's because "they're a symbol of vanity, and they're out of place in a house of mourning." On an early episode (1969) of the popular series *Marcus Welby, M.D.*, which included the depiction of a Jewish funeral and the chanting of *El Malei Rachamim*, Dr. Welby, a friend of the bereaved family, learns the meaning of an unveiling. It is explained to him that it is a religious ceremony in which the headstone is unveiled eleven months after the funeral.

On the hit comedy *Frasier*, it was at a house of *shiva* that the good doctor experienced a moment of transcendent insight and achieved a new level of consciousness. The sudden death of a friend — who was young, healthy, and fit — had sent Dr. Frasier Crane into a tailspin of anxiety and fear. How could an active jogger and health-food nut have passed on like this? At the *shiva* he pondered this, inquiring of the other mourners. Finally, he concluded that the answer was a simple and complete enjoyment of life.

In contrast to the more frequent depictions of assimilated Jewish characters involved in religious mourning rites, an Orthodox Jewish family was portrayed on an episode of the famed Western series *Gunsmoke* in 1973. When tragedy befalls with the death of a son, the family follows a whole range of Jewish mourning rituals, such as tearing the garment, reciting the *kaddish* following the boy's burial, and ritually washing their hands upon returning home. There the mirrors are covered, and they sit *shiva* on small wooden boxes.

When another Orthodox family was portrayed a few years later on an episode of *Lou Grant*, viewers learn about the folk custom of reciting *kaddish* over one who has not actually died but who has so turned on his people and his faith that he is rendered dead to his parents. When Billy Newman, an investigative journalist, learns that the leader of a neo–Nazi group was actually a Jew raised in an Orthodox home, she tries to interview his parents. They refuse to speak with her, revealing only that they "said *kaddish* for him years ago."[13]

Jewish mourning customs were both a catalyst for religious searching and the object of criticism on a 1988 episode of the short-lived series *Bronx Zoo*, about a tough New York City high school. When Matthew, one of the students, is confronted with the death of his Uncle Louis, he has a difficult time accepting the death and the way in which his uncle was mourned. Matthew tells a friend that the *shiva* did not seem very respectful to his memory: "All they did was complain about the deli.... They were stuffing their faces with pastrami and brisket." As a result, he questions his religious beliefs and undertakes a spiritual exploration that leads him to a church, among other places. Finally, in a dream sequence, Uncle Louis appears to him, saying that while he appreciates

Matthew's love, his concerns are misplaced: "When a person dies, he is dead —
it's the living who have to go on…. As long as you remember, I'll always be
there." Matthew is finally able to accept his uncle's death as the two of them
stand together and recite the *kaddish*. Ultimately, despite the inappropriate
excesses of the *shiva* that rightly disturbed him, it is in Judaism — as expressed
through his uncle's very Jewish philosophy on death, with its emphasis on life
and the living, and the recitation of the *kaddish*— that Matthew finds the solace
and comfort he sought.

While it may at first seem surprising that a prayer associated with death
has engendered so many TV story lines, the import of the *kaddish* is clear in
its drama and simplicity: it is a toneful, lilting link between past and present.
Its sonorous tones, with their strong emotional pull, hold a significant place in
Jewish life that is reflected on television. That several shows with Jewish themes
are woven around the prayer is logical, given Judaism's high level of respect
for a sense of history and for earlier generations who placed their mark upon
those living today. The sense of connecting to a past and carrying it on in some
form to the future is powerfully and hauntingly encapsulated in the *kaddish*
reclaimed by these Jewish TV characters.

BRIT MILAH AND BRIT BAT

The continuation of life and the passing of religious heritage from one generation to another is expressed in the ceremonies greeting newborns into the
Jewish faith. The traditional circumcision ceremony for male infants (known
as the *brit milah*, or *bris*) and the newer naming ceremony for a female infant
(known among other names as a *brit bat*)[14] are the festive occasions marking
the induction of the newcomers into the Covenant of Israel.

Perhaps TV's best known depiction of a circumcision took place on
M*A*S*H, the long-running hit series that took a wry look at military conflict
through the eyes of members of a medical unit during the Korean War. When,
in a 1974 episode, a Korean woman with a newborn infant and little command
of English approaches the surgeons with a request that a *bris* be performed,
they are taken aback until she hands them a note explaining that the father is
a Jewish soldier now at the front who has requested that the ceremony be performed. As Radar, the company clerk, explains, "It's like a christening performed on newborn male personnel who are Jewish Hebrews." When the
doctors' efforts to obtain a rabbi are unsuccessful, they enlist the services of
the only cleric nearby: Father Mulcahy. With the surgeons poised, the Korean
mother nearby, and the priest receiving radio signals from a rabbi on a ship
off the coast with instructions as to what prayers to say, the *brit milah* ceremony proceeds. Father Mulcahy admirably attempts the Hebrew prayers, wine
is given to the baby, and at the conclusion of the ceremony, everyone yells,
"*mazel tov*."

The *brit milah* ceremony, with its delicate medical aspect, has naturally been a source for much TV humor. When the Jewish magazine writer featured on *Anything but Love*, for instance, recites his list of maxims to live by, they include the directive to "Never yell 'Oops' at a *bris*." On *St. Elsewhere*, a Jewish doctor discusses with colleagues the medical procedure of restoring a foreskin and concludes, "My rabbi wouldn't be too thrilled."

Humor centered around a *brit milah* was the premise of entire episodes of several hit comedy series. When Frasier and Lilith Crane of *Cheers* had a baby boy on a 1989 episode, Frasier — who is not Jewish — is depicted as eager to raise the child in Lilith's Jewish faith. He wants to go through with the baby's *brit milah* but cannot overcome his emotional resistance. His comically exaggerated squeamishness and that of his burly bar buddies over the procedure along with his efforts to wrest the infant from the impending ceremony are the subject for humor. Such humor also prevailed on a slapstick-filled episode of *The Nanny*, where a home video made at a cousin's *brit milah* ends up being broadcast on *America's Wackiest Videos*.

Humor and poignancy were combined in an episode of *L.A. Law* that told the story of an elderly *mohel* (ritual circumciser) who was being sued for making a nick in an infant's genitals while performing a circumcision. The creators had some fun with the subject: the episode was titled "The Pay's Lousy, but the Tips Are Great," and when asked on the stand what he did after noticing that he made the nick the *mohel* testified, "I said 'Oops'." Nevertheless, this was a sensitive exploration of the plight of an elderly Jew forced to give up his profession due to aging, unsteady hands. As he reflects in despair on the judgment forbidding him from ever again performing circumcisions, he bemoans loosing not only his sole means of livelihood but also the deepest expression of his religious identity and the very essence of his life: "Nothing gives me greater pleasure than the *bris*. It's the only thing I do that makes me feel alive."

Quite a different attitude toward *brit milah* was presented on an episode of *Seinfeld*. Usually brimming with witty humor, the hit comedy series presented a tasteless, humorless, and embarrassingly bad episode about a *brit milah* that was replete with gross and offensive stereotypes. The story, which revolved around Jerry and Elaine's being asked to be the godparents for an infant boy and to find a *mohel* for the circumcision started off funny enough. Even its airing of various views on the subject of circumcision was in the realm of appropriate debate (although very little was said of a positive nature). Yet the program sank to sad depths when viewers met the *mohel* (ritual circumciser), a coarse, cold and uncaring, buffoonlike boor. The entire *brit milah* ceremony was presented in this light, with no nods to its meaning, importance, or spirituality. (If one could imagine the notorious wedding scene of *Goodbye Columbus* combined with a scene from Woody Allen at his self-disparaging worst, all transformed to a *brit milah*, this would be it.) The writers of the show made a weak attempt to balance this by later having Jerry and Elaine comment on how bad the *mohel* was, saying that he had to be "one in a million." But viewers met *only* him — a crude and unfunny character — and saw a ceremony presented as barbaric, cruel, and devoid of any meaning. In fact, the parents ultimately chose the wild character Kramer to be the godfather because he is the only one who really cared about the baby — he loudly protested a circumcision from the start! What emerged was an offensive and ugly picture.

Adults undergoing a *brit milah*, whether to connect with a neglected heritage or on the path to becoming Jewish, have been the subject of such shows as *Medicine Ball* and *Caroline in the City*.

An unusual program in that it depicted not a *brit milah* but a naming ceremony for a baby girl (in this show called a *brit bat*) appeared as part of the short-lived series *A Year in the Life*. In this 1987 episode, the naming of a baby girl takes place in synagogue as the rabbi says, "May the one who blessed our mothers and our fathers, Abraham and Sarah, Isaac and Rebecca, Jacob and Leah and Rachel, bless this child as she comes into the covenant of her people. Blessed is she who comes to be blessed."

In this positive reflection on welcome changes regarding the status of women within Judaism, it is noteworthy that the ceremony honoring the baby girl is presided over by a woman rabbi who not only invokes the patriarchs of Israel but adapts the traditional liturgy to include Israel's matriarchs as well, as she blesses this newest, female member of the Jewish people.

Holidays

Like rituals, which communicate religious distinctiveness and offer a sense of identity, the observance of holidays are a vital part of communal life and expression. Since every group — national, religious, social — has its holidays and commemorations that instill a sense of heritage, identity, and pride, the depiction of Jewish holidays on television is a common expression to which a broad spectrum of viewers can relate.

All major and nearly all minor Jewish holidays have been depicted on popular TV.

CHANUKAH

For Jews, Chanukah has always been a joyful time of flickering menorah lights, melodious songs, dreidel playing, gift giving, the gathering together of generations, the laughter of children, and the sheer celebration of history and culture, survival, and identity. But for most of television's history, Chanukah — the Jewish holiday of national redemption and religious freedom — went virtually unmentioned.

Not until the late 1960s and early 1970s did TV begin to take note of Chanukah, due to its proximity to Christmas and the attendant commercialization of the December "holiday season." At the same time, the growing rate of intermarriage brought celebrations of Chanukah into more and more American families and brought the holiday into the American lexicon.

As a result, Chanukah, a technically minor, post–Biblical holiday, has taken on enormous dimensions, out of proportion to its place in the Jewish calendar. Yet its rising visibility and prominence in contemporary life has been widely reflected on television.

For a long while, this newfound awareness of Chanukah was manifested merely through passing references on TV shows, which would offer a requisite mention of the Jewish holiday that found itself smack in the middle of the Christian holiday season. Christmas episodes or TV movies would almost invariably include references to Chanukah; nearly every such program now includes the utterance of a "Happy Chanukah," in an obligatory nod to religious pluralism. Somewhat more creative yet equally superficial references arise in a countless variety of circumstances. On a 1988 Christmas episode of *Day by Day*, a comedy series about a couple running a day-care center, the children are celebrating Christmas, but one toddler is shown costumed in a large Jewish star and a *chanukiah* (a Chanukah menorah) is seen hanging on the wall. There is no explanation of anything to do with Chanukah at all. A *Kate and Allie* episode had the two women baking Christmas cookies and announcing that some of them are in fact Chanukah cookies.

This linkage of the holidays is mirrored in nearly all of the many TV depictions of what is now known as, in reflection of this phenomenon, the Christmas-Chanukah season. Predominantly, these TV depictions suggest — if they do not openly state — that the two holidays bear the same messages of love, togetherness, and so forth, and are therefore to be equated in manner of celebration and religious (or, to be more precise, nonreligious) significance. This, however, is a distortion of the religious, historical and unique meanings of both Christmas and Chanukah, which a lack of background and context has created.[15] If this is accepted as reality, then Chanukah and Judaism are in danger of losing their uniqueness and identity.

These references, while perhaps inspired by well-meant efforts to recognize religious diversity or to provide American Jewish viewers with a sense of inclusion in television's celebration of the holiday season, are a far cry from the many depictions of other aspects of Jewish life, discussed above, which do expend the effort to enlighten, touch, and inform the audience about Jewish lore and traditions. Indeed, in promoting the sense that Christmas and Chanukah are comparable, similar, and equatable holidays, these images serve to exacerbate an already difficult time for many American Jews who lack a strong and proud religious identity. Many of these Jews, threatened by the ubiquitousness of Christmas tinsel, carols, ornaments, and the "Christmas spirit," either join in the secularized and popular celebration of Christmas or redefine the celebration of their "simple and pedestrian"[16] Chanukah to compete with Christmas.[17]

A program that went far beyond simply merging Christmas and Chanukah to in fact disparage the Jewish component of the "holiday season" was the 1989 Christmas episode of *The Famous Teddy Z*, a comedy series about the world of Hollywood agents. In this fantasy-like episode — a takeoff of Charles Dickens's *A Christmas Carol*— a Jewish character is cast in the role of Scrooge, as a selfish, bitter person who ruins Christmas for the Gentiles. Throughout the program, viewers see a world where Jews are expected to celebrate Christmas, where even the sympathetic Jewish character of elderly Abe Werkfinder (director of the agency) becomes a Ghost of Christmas Past, and where the celebration of Chanukah is a paltry disappointment compared to that of Christmas.

It seems that the Jewish Al Floss, the most disagreeable agent at Werkfinder's company, sinks to new depths when he orders a subordinate — young, likable Teddy, main character of the show — and his secretary to work on Christmas because a vital contract is arriving from overseas. Al, however, will be off in Hawaii, an itinerary that shocks Teddy. He asks, "Christmas in Hawaii?" as if the holiday should have any religious and familial significance to the Jewish Al, which it naturally does to the Christian Teddy. Al's snide retorts to Teddy express no sense that as a Jew he has no reason to celebrate Christmas.

The plot thickens when that night, Al dreams that he is visited by three Christmas ghosts, each of them represented by a coworker. Abe, the Ghost of Christmas Past, takes Al back to his childhood, where viewers learn why he hates the holiday. His mother tells him "We're Jewish, Albert, Santa Claus doesn't come here," to which he says "I'm not buying that." Still, she goes on to explain that he cannot have the bicycle he so desperately wants and which all his Christian friends are receiving because "we just can't afford it now, we just don't have the money, sweetheart." The next revelation comes to Al through the Ghost of Christmas Present, who takes him to a present-day scene of Teddy's family where he learns how miserable he has made Teddy's elderly grandmother, as she must spend Christmas without him. A final revelation comes from the Ghost of Christmas Future (in the person of Teddy), who foretells of Al's death a few years hence and of no one visiting his grave, but says that "Everybody's given a chance to change. And when people change, their futures change as well."

Finally Al awakens and, momentarily wracked with guilt, cries out, "I have been blind to things like thoughtfulness and gratitude." This notion quickly passes, however, and after wishing Tiffany — his date for Hawaii — a "Merry Christmas" over the phone, he dashes off to the tropics. Feeling unsuccessful, the three ghosts appear dejectedly in Al's apartment. But Teddy has a thought and zaps into sudden existence a beautiful, large Christmas tree. A puzzled Abe asks Teddy, "What are you giving him a Christmas tree for? He's Jewish." Teddy, in a comment suggesting that perhaps some contact with Christmas will repair the Jew's evil ways, says "At least he'll have to take it down." Even Abe agrees that "that's a great idea," and upon leaving, he zaps a shiny new bicycle under the tree — the present for lack of which Al was made so bitter — saying, "God bless everyone, even Al Floss."

That the Jewish Al Floss at last receives, through the magic of Christmas, via a Christmas ghost, under a Christmas tree, the gift that Chanukah was unable to provide him is a negation of any possible role of Judaism in the life of a Jew and the promotion of such a role for Christianity. In an unremitting barrage throughout the show, Al is described as being blind to the light of warmth, thoughtfulness, and gratitude and as responsible for Christmases ruined; while the positively portrayed Jew (Abe, the Christmas ghost) shines brightly only because he is an agent of the wonderful Christmas holiday. In an unusually negative and offensive television depiction, it is as if Judaism is here deemed nonexistent and Jews as redeemable only by virtue of Christianity.

While the predominant Chanukah image has been as a Jewish adjunct to Christmas, in recent years several programs have depicted the celebration of Chanukah on its own merit rather than as a decorative bauble to a Christmas scene. Viewers have seen an unraveling of the TV-melded Christmas-Chanukah holiday, as a clearer picture of the Jewish holiday, celebrated by Jewish characters, has emerged. As it was stated simply by the infant Max on the short-lived *Baby Talk*, a comedy where babies talked through adult voice-overs, "I'm Jewish. We don't celebrate Christmas; we celebrate Chanukah."

The celebration of Chanukah was a main theme, for example, on an episode of the critically acclaimed 1988 series *Frank's Place*, about the comic doings of the quirky characters at a New Orleans restaurant. When Frank Parrish, the black owner of the restaurant, is invited by his Jewish lawyer, Bubba Weisberger, to spend an evening of Chanukah with his family, it is an opportunity for Frank and viewers to learn about the holiday. Seated at the festive table, wearing a yarmulke, Frank is enlightened about potato pancakes, playing dreidel, Chanukah *gelt*, and — when the children light the Chanukah candles, after the appropriate Hebrew blessings — the story of Chanukah itself. In beguiling Southern accents, a Jewish little boy and girl earnestly explain to all assembled, "We light a candle each night to remember when Judah Maccabee and his men recaptured the Temple from all the bad guys. There was only enough oil for the eternal flame to burn for one night, but then a miracle happened, and the light burned for eight nights — the eight nights of Chanukah. And it never went out, and that light still shines for the whole world." Within the confines of a half-hour sit-com, this simple yet inspiring description of Chanukah elegantly conveys the holiday's message of strength, survival, and unity of the Jewish people. Although the evening quickly and comically disintegrates when Bubba's Jewish mother entangles him in a family argument, this picture of a Jewish family's coming together to celebrate Chanukah and delighting in its meaning and traditions — without any thought of Christmas — is an unusual and welcome depiction.

Chanukah celebrations infused an episode of *Big Brother Jake*, a program produced by the Family Channel (formerly the Christian Broadcasting Network) about a multicultural group of children being raised by a foster mother in Brooklyn, with the help of an adult "big brother" Jake. Jake, who is Jewish, uses the occasion of Chanukah to help one of the foster children, who is also Jewish, learn about his own identity and heritage, first tentatively, then with a great sense of pride and self-worth. In the process, Jake himself reclaims a lost part of his heritage and in the final scene gathers the family around to light the Chanukah candles, while he recites the blessings in flawless Hebrew, an accomplishment that makes him very proud.

Joyous scenes of Chanukah also found their way onto several TV movies and miniseries whose main theme was decidedly not joy. On both *The Diary of Anne Frank* (1967 and 1980 versions) and *Wallenberg* (1985),[18] viewers see scenes of gift giving, candle lighting, singing and feasting on latkes. There is a sense in these programs that the celebration of a holiday commemorating the victory of Jewish forces over a much greater military might lends spiritual encouragement and a sense of historical confidence to these Jews seeking to survive the Holocaust.

But for many Jews in contemporary America, Chanukah is a time when identity is sorely tested, when the symbols, sights, and sounds of a different and dominant culture are pervasive. It is a time when Christmas is in the air — and *on* the air, as Christmas remains America's and popular TV's predominant holiday. Many shows, in further developing the image of Chanukah as clearly distinct from Christmas, also delved into its role as a lightning rod for exploration of religious, ethnic, and cultural identity that takes on heightened urgency and often anxiety at this time of year. In recent seasons, TV programs have painted a more realistic and inclusive view of some of the difficulties and resolutions brought on by a holiday season that is increasingly complex for so many. Indeed, for the many Jews in real life who may have difficulty choosing to focus on and celebrate their own faith and identity at this time of year, such shows may help provide them the sense of validity and encouragement they sorely lack.

In *Northern Exposure*, the popular, off-beat drama about life in Cicely, Alaska, the season's spiritual conflicts are epitomized by the Christmas tree, which is often an emotion-laden symbol. Dr. Joel Fleischman, the town's lone Jew, grapples with feelings of isolation and identity as everyone around him celebrates Christmas or the traditional Indian raven festival. Fleischman correctly notes that the Christmas tree "is a Christian symbol" and rejects it for himself since he is Jewish. But unmoored from all that is familiar and unfettered by parental disapproval that he well remembers, Fleischman harbors second thoughts about his rejection of what he considers to be an aesthetic and alluring object. After taking one into his home, however, he ultimately removes it, bringing it to a non–Jewish friend whom he tells, "It belongs to you. Scratch the plum pudding, there's a matzah ball underneath. I'm a Jew. That's all there is to it."

The 1992 series *WIOU*, set in a television newsroom, aired an unusual holiday episode in which the story of Chanukah held center stage. The defacing of a Chanukah menorah in a public park by anti–Semitic thugs became the occasion for series regular Willis Teitlebaum — a young Jew who admits to knowing little about his Jewish heritage — to be overwhelmed by a mixture of feelings: anger at the vandalism, guilt at having denied his Jewishness when confronted by the threatening hoodlums, and a vague yearning to understand and be a part of his religion and people. To sort out his emotional turmoil, Willis turns to an older colleague, news anchorman Neal Frazier, who delivers a stirring on-air editorial that denounces the vandalism and eloquently recounts the story of Chanukah, addressing its sense of grandeur and relevance. The story's final scene finds Willis and Frazier back in the park, reading the candle-lighting blessings as they kindle a small Chanukah menorah they have brought there. Within the space of an hour, *WIOU* managed to include a moving retelling of the Chanukah story and to accord the holiday an unusual and elegant treatment. By presenting Chanukah as a holiday with its own singular importance and message (rather than submerged by and erroneously equated with Christmas, as so many TV shows routinely have) and by projecting the significance of the holiday for Jewish identity and its message of abhorrence of religious bigotry, *WIOU* offered a powerful and unusual message indeed.

Another major issue arising during the holiday season concerns intermarried couples and the questions of whether, which, and how they will celebrate the holidays. The intersection of Christmas and Chanukah has led to explosive situations on such programs as *Bridget Loves Bernie* and *thirtysomething*, where the emotionally laden matter of holiday celebrations raises a host of related issues. These may be simplistically glossed over, as they were in *Bridget Loves Bernie*, or the subject of endless angst, as on *thirtysomething*. In any case, with the juxtaposition of Christmas and Chanukah, questions of religious identity arise, leading to an array of conflicts and compromises. (These are explored in Chapter 6, "Intermarriage.")

As more attention is paid to some of the issues Jews face during this holiday season, inevitably the results are sometimes less than satisfying. Marty Gold, on the erstwhile *Anything but Love*, jumped headlong into Christmas celebrations, spending a romantic first Christmas with his non–Jewish girlfriend decorating a tree and exchanging Christmas presents, seeming to leave his Jewish identity aside. On an episode of *L.A. Law*, Stuart Markowitz was noticeably out of town for the holidays, obviating a display of any holiday angst on his part. And on an episode of the popular series *Cheers*, Dr. Frasier Crane, intermarried to the Jewish Dr. Lilith Sternin, angrily asserts, "A Christmas tree isn't even symbolic of Christianity, but apparently it threatens Lilith's Jewish faith: look out everybody, a fir tree! Five-thousand-year-old religion, and Frasier Crane's going to bring it down with a four-foot tree and some tinsel!" This supposedly humorous remark is not only incorrect, but it derides Judaism's need, right, and efforts to maintain its own distinct symbols and uniqueness in the face of a dominant culture and religion. While Judaism has always adapted to new situations, the adoption of a symbol antithetical to its own beliefs and the dilution of its own symbols is indeed cause for concern on the part of this five-thousand-year-old religion.

Yet such anomalies are fortunately vastly overshadowed by the predominant images of Jewish self-respect. A striking example was an outstanding Chanukah depiction on an episode of *Sisters,* a drama series chronicling the lives and loves of four adult female siblings — one of whom, Frankie, has converted to Judaism. What makes the story unusual is its direct focus on the holiday of Chanukah and its exploration of both the history of the celebration and its contemporary significance on a number of levels. The story follows Frankie as she — eager to share with her extended family the excitement, familiarity, and pride she has for her new life as a Jew — invites them all to a Chanukah dinner at her home. But a somber specter intrudes upon her Chanukah cheer: while out preparing for the festivities and doing holiday shopping, she is mortified to see that the restaurant owned by her husband, who is Jewish, has been the target of anti–Semitic vandalism and graffiti. Frankie takes this deeply to heart and presses the Jewish community, particularly the neighborhood Jewish merchants, to act decisively to defend and protect themselves by forming a neighborhood watch group. Some among them object to her advocacy, belittling her allegiance as one who was not born Jewish. Despite this disgraceful show of prejudice, Frankie persists in her efforts. The threads of the story are woven together in the episode's final scene, where, at the Chanukah dinner at last, Frankie and her husband recount the tale of Chanukah and explain that the holiday is "all about standing up against oppression and hatred and being proud of who we are."

It is not far-fetched to characterize Frankie as a modern-day Maccabee. Fighting for her religion, her rights, and her freedom — as did the ancient Jews — she cuts a heroic figure on many counts. By the very fact of her inviting her non–Jewish family to celebrate her Jewish holiday in her home, she asserts the right to unabashedly celebrate a minority holiday, with joy and commitment, within a majority culture. And by rallying a small group of Jews to fight against anti–Semitism and bigotry, she personifies a central tenet of the heroic story of Chanukah, in which the few stand up against the many and triumph. Finally, even when facing a particular bias from within her own community, Frankie remains unflinchingly committed to her cause and proud to assert her Jewish identity within the community. Like the Maccabees, Frankie and this *Sisters* episode triumph.

Of all times for Jews to express pride in their identity, Chanukah is surely one of the most historically appropriate and significant. Due to the maturing of the television medium and the nation's growing recognition of different modes of religious observance and belief, TV has to its credit made strides in unraveling the Christmas-Chanukah myth and offering up Jewish characters who can revel in their own holiday. By depicting the celebration of one holiday without an obligatory and superficial nod to the other, television has come to acknowledge and respect the unique spiritual messages of each. At last the small screen has accorded the ancient holiday of Chanukah the contemporary significance and the distinctiveness denied it throughout most of television's history.

This new attention to Chanukah on its own terms has also found welcome expression in a spurt of children's programs devoted to the holiday. In recent years, the younger set have been treated to stories, lore, and fun treatments of Chanukah on such popular children's vehicles as Shari Lewis's *Lamb Chop's Special Chanukah* and Nickelodeon's *Weinerville Chanukah Special* and *Rugrats Chanukah Special*. An episode of public television's *The Puzzle Place* had one of the Jewish youngsters of a multiethnic ensemble declaring that she doesn't celebrate Christmas "because it's not my holiday. This time of year I celebrate Chanukah." She went on to explain all that that entails. At one time, children's fare in December was awash solely in Christmas images; the diversity of observance that these newer shows present is a healthy and refreshing development.

THE HIGH HOLIDAYS AND PASSOVER

The holidays of *Rosh Hashanah* and *Yom Kippur*, known as the High Holidays, and the celebration of Passover are among the most observed of all Jewish customs among American Jews. Despite this, they have received far less attention on popular TV than has Chanukah. Chanukah, obviously, has the unnatural boost of Christmas, but there may be other reasons why the more major holidays in Judaism have been less examined. Generally, the High Holidays fall in early to mid–September, before the new TV season is fully underway. Passover, too, coming out in the spring, when repeats may start running and the height of the TV season is past, may suffer from the draw of the calendar. Doubtless it has also received less attention because the Christian holiday that falls near it, Easter, is far less the subject of popular and commercial attention than Christmas.

Still, while timing inhibits contemporaneous dramas relating to the High Holidays and Passover, due to their importance on the Jewish calendar they are described and explained in a number of programs. On the wedding episode of *Here Come the Brides*, for example, the Jewish Will Sullivan explains to

Gentile loggers that "The Day of Atonement … is a sacred holiday when Jews fast and pray for forgiveness of past sins." That same aspect of *Yom Kippur* is brought out on the *Diff'rent Strokes bar mitzvah* episode, when the rabbi counsels Arnold about conversion, saying, "On that holy day, you must fast for twenty-four hours to atone for your sins." And Archie Bunker, in his inimitable style, points to *Yom Kippur* as proof that Jews "don't need to eat," explaining to his wife Edith, "They even made a holiday out of it. They starve themselves a whole day, then they fill up on young kippers." Other High Holiday allusions have been made in shows like the 1980s family drama *Our House* and the 1981 made-for-TV movie *Skokie*.

One program that mentioned *Yom Kippur* and demonstrated an unusual awareness of its significance by equating it — rather than Chanukah — with Christmas was a *Hallmark Hall of Fame* presentation titled "Have I Got a Christmas for You," broadcast in 1977. When Christmas arrives, Jewish postal workers offer to fill in for their Christian colleagues so that the latter can celebrate the holiday at home with their families. It is recalled that the Christian workers had extended a similar kindness to their Jewish colleagues — on the eve of *Yom Kippur* when workers had to be on duty until 6 P.M. The Christian postal workers came up with the idea of filling in for their Jewish coworkers and sending them home to be with their families for the holy day. This expressed comparison between the centrality and solemnity of Christmas with that of *Yom Kippur* and the portrayal of Christians recognizing the importance to Jews of *Yom Kippur* is striking, since on television — as in real life — this juxtaposition is highly unusual, given the typical linking of Christmas with *Chanukah*.

The High Holidays as a main story line characterized a number of TV programs in the 1950s. Significantly, all of these focused on the cantor, with the music of the holidays as a central motif. This is hardly remarkable, since these holidays are strongly associated with cantorial melodies, particularly the *Kol Nidre*, the well-known plaintive prayer that is an emotional high point of *Yom Kippur*.

One program dealt directly with the pivotal and emotional role the cantor plays in these holidays, as the allegorical representative of the congregation petitioning God. In a famed TV drama, "Holiday Song," which aired as part of the *Philco Television Playhouse* in 1953, a cantor encapsulates the intense spiritual tenor of the High Holidays as he undergoes a crisis of faith brought on by consideration of all the misery in the world. Suddenly bereft of spiritual certainty, he feels he cannot justly sing on behalf of the congregation. With the holidays quickly approaching, this dilemma takes on a great urgency. Soul searching, the cantor journeys by subway to consult with a renowned sage but loses his way on repeated trips. Instead he meets first the wife, then the husband of a couple who had been separated by World War II and who each thought the other to be dead. By reuniting the couple, through what he perceives to be a miracle, he restores his faith and is able to sing.

Another story about a cantor and the High Holidays was a 1959 TV version of *The Jazz Singer*, recounting the well-known tale of a cantor's son who, to the great chagrin of his father, is drawn to the world of show business. Ultimately, the son returns to his roots and tradition at the time of *Yom Kippur* and chants *Kol Nidre* in a demonstration of his continuing attachment to that tradition.

During the run of the series *The Goldbergs*, several Septembers saw the presentation of a *Yom Kippur* episode in which the Goldberg family would attend synagogue services and viewers would be treated to an elaborate liturgical service.

A troubling aspect of some synagogue services during the High Holidays was displayed in a made-for-television movie about Joan Rivers and her daughter, as they cope with the suicide-death of Joan's husband. In one scene, despite their desperate pleading with a guard, they are refused admission to a synagogue for *Yom Kippur* services as they have no tickets.

On a 1989 episode of the short-lived comedy series *Doctor, Doctor*, Grant Linowitz, a Jewish physician at a Rhode Island group practice, asks his Gentile colleagues to spend *Yom Kippur* with him, explaining that his family is away and he's never been alone on this holiday before. When they ask to learn more about the day, Grant explains that it's a family time, that Jews fast, and that they gather with friends and family at its conclusion to have a festive break-the-fast meal. One of the doctors goes to synagogue with him, and all the others join in the break-the-fast, held at the home of Mike, star of the series. Mike's parents and brother are also in attendance, and Grant leads them all in Hebrew blessings.

It was perhaps in a *Northern Exposure* episode that the sense and significance of *Yom Kippur*—on emotional, psychological, religious, and spiritual levels—reached a pinnacle for television depictions. In a powerful tale that aired in the fall of 1994, Dr. Joel Fleischman, the only Jew in the Alaskan town of Cicely, seeks to observe *Yom Kippur* and ends up going on a deep inward journey to repair the harsh edges of his soul. The episode starts off mundanely enough, with Joel at a local eats place "loading up on carbohydrates" in preparation for his fasting on *Yom Kippur* to begin that evening while explaining to a friend the meaning, purpose, and background of the holiday. Later, during the night, Joel is awakened and startled to find his rabbi, who has appeared suddenly in his room, arousing him and coaxing him in an avuncular but no-nonsense way, "Come on, Joel, we have work to do." The episode takes on the veneer of Charles Dickens's *A Christmas Carol*, as Rabbi Schulman advises Joel to "think of me as the spirit of *Yom Kippur* past." He proceeds to load videotapes into the VCR, and a growingly uncomfortable Joel is compelled to watch video vignettes of his past behavior to other people — all of it embarrassingly unflattering. He sees himself brusquely firing a trusted receptionist with little cause, coarsely insulting a lover, crudely berating and mocking colleagues and friends, and displaying all manner of unpleasant behavior for which his character was well known. He is clearly shocked and chagrined. "Don't worry," Rabbi Schulman comforts him. "You're not on trial," he says but adds, "Well, you are in a way."

When next they meet, the rabbi declares himself "the spirit of *Yom Kippur* present." He explains to Joel almost apologetically, "Repentance is not like washing your hands, you know. It takes time, devotion, pain even." Out they go into a freezing Alaska night, where Rabbi Schulman leads him to the cold scene of a homeless person foraging for shelter and food. This is Hayden, an impoverished townperson whose home had burned down due to his smoking in bed. Earlier in the episode, Joel had refused friends' solicitations to help rebuild Hayden's home for him; Joel declared that Hayden was responsible for his own misfortune and that he didn't want to encourage such behavior. Now, faced with the vision of Hayden shivering in the cold, Joel protests that "I didn't mean it literally." The rabbi takes Joel to another scene of the results of his thoughtlessness: now Joel sees his fired receptionist eating a paltry meal, and he learns that her salary had been supporting distant relatives.

Joel's regret is deepening, but it is the third appearance of the rabbi as "the spirit of *Yom Kippur* future" that completes his journey. He is treated this time to a scene in the future of himself leaving Cicely, his term of obligatory medical duty there completed. He sees himself departing on the bus, but with him gone, no one has a good word to say to him. Observing all this as a third party, Joel is shattered and incredulous. At last the rabbi takes Joel to the final stop on the tour, transporting him instantaneously to a dark and howling cemetery, where Joel is confronted by Hayden's tombstone. Contemplating the man's death from exposure and starvation, a distraught Joel begs of Rabbi Schulman, "Is this the *Yom Kippur* that *has* to be, or the *Yom Kippur* that just *may* be? Can I change this judgment, please?" The rabbi is silent but points off to the distance to massive wrought-iron gates beyond which is an orange-yellow brightness. "What is that? The gates of prayer. Can I still get in?" As the rabbi sounds the *shofar*, the massive gates begin to close. In this chilling scene, Joel runs frantically, screaming, "Wait! Let me in! Don't close! Wait — I'll change!" Reaching them as they are closing, he clings to them wildly, yelling.

He awakes from this dream clinging to his bed, then rises frantically to ask what day it is. Told that it is *Yom Kippur*, he says, "Great! I haven't missed it!" and goes about righting his wrongs. He rehires his receptionist and promises better communication with her, then signs up for extra duty to rebuild Hayden's house. In the final scene, he sits alone atop a hilltop contemplating *Yom Kippur's* setting sun and peels an orange to conclude his fast.

Draping a Dickens story in the imagery of *Yom Kippur* could have gone off base, but here it is done so skillfully that the result is a unique and stirring episode that plumbs the core of *Yom Kippur*. The show explains some basic information about the holiday, then draws on its powerful metaphors and symbols — notions of repentance, the books of life and death, the *shofar* to arouse us out of our "sleep" and indifference, and the liturgical imagery of the closing gates of repentance as *Yom Kippur* draws to a close — to give a taste of the grandeur of the holiday and to demonstrate its potential for affecting someone on spiritual and practical levels. Indeed, Joel's change of heart through personal contemplation and struggle is an inspiring example of what *Yom Kippur* is supposed to achieve. In portraying his struggle and the ideas that characterize *Yom Kippur*— the difficulty of confronting our shortcomings, the challenge of being kind, the perception of ourselves as sometimes so different from that held by others, taking stock of ourselves, the notion of consequences to our actions, and the ability to change — this show is a grand paean to *Yom Kippur* and all that it stands for. It may not be a Christmas carol, but it is a modern-day *Yom Kippur* prayer.

As the most observed ritual in Jewish life, the Passover *seder*, at which Jewish families gather to recount the story of the Exodus of the Jews from Egyptian slavery, is a towering event in the Jewish calendar. On popular TV, it has been less conspicuous, a situation wryly noted in a TV program itself. When a non–Jewish character in *Anything but Love* comments that "I never know when it's Passover. I mean, every other holiday gets at least a couple of good TV specials," the Jewish Marty Gold retorts, "What? You mean you've never seen that perennial holiday classic, *Let My People Go, Charlie Brown?*" While such a comment acknowledges the paucity of Passover shows, interestingly it presumes some familiarity with the story of Passover among viewers. The irony is greater than Gold knew: the holiday that is celebrated by more Jews than any other (94 percent of Jews attend a *seder* on the first night of Passover), has received scant attention on popular TV. Untethered by the calendar to a media-grabbing Christian holiday (as is Chanukah to Christmas; America's and television's celebration of Easter is much more subdued), the holiday has received a far less visible role on TV.

While indeed Passover has not received attention on popular TV commensurate with its observance among Jews, the holiday has been depicted on several shows in some interesting settings. A *seder* in the Dakota territories of the 1860s was portrayed on a *Philco Television Playhouse* segment that aired in 1954. In attendance were Hungarian Jewish immigrants, Swedish greenhorns, and American Indians. The Jewish family briefly explained to all present the meaning of the holiday as a celebration of freedom and the symbolism of the special food. Despite bitter winter months of seclusion and despair, the family finds hope and renewal in the Passover *seder*.

This theme of sharing the Passover *seder* with non–Jews and utilizing it to teach about Jewish history and customs is one that runs throughout TV's Passover depictions. In a 1962 episode of the famed medical series *Dr. Kildare*, not only were extensive portions of the *Haggadah* read and various parts of the *seder* dramatized, but the presence of the non–Jewish Dr. Kildare at the home of his Jewish intern provided the intern's father with the opportunity to teach about the meaning of Passover and the rituals of the *seder*.

Seders have been depicted in diverse settings on shows such as *St. Elsewhere, The Goldbergs,* and *The Nanny.* In a 1982 made-for-TV movie, *The Wall,* the depiction of a *seder* by Jews in the Warsaw ghetto, intercut with scenes of Nazi tanks storming the ghetto, made the connection between the ancient story of Jewish freedom from Egyptian bondage and the ultimate ability of Jews to survive modern-day oppression.

Northern Exposure contributed not one but two episodes that featured Passover story lines. In the first, Joel Fleischman is transported in a dream sequence to a Polish *shtetl* where a *seder* meeting with Elijah the Prophet provokes a change in him. A few seasons later, when his non–Jewish girlfriend offers to make a *seder* for him, Fleischman rejects the idea, as he is conflicted about the course of his relationship with her and with his heritage. In a play on the story of Jonah, Fleischman flees from reality and in a dreamlike sequence is launched into a bizarre journey, where he finds himself in the belly of a fish conversing with his rabbi about these matters. He eventually returns to land, to his girlfriend, and to the observance of Passover, as he accepts her efforts and leads a *seder*.

A television character's reconnecting with his heritage against the backdrop of Passover was also the theme more recently of a *Sisters* episode. Big Al Barker, intermarried and assimilated, is spurred by anti–Semitism to reassert his Jewish identity and conduct a Passover *seder*.

An involved explanation of matzah appeared not during a dramatized *seder* but on a non–Passover episode of *Chicken Soup* (the short-lived 1989 series). When Jackie Fisher arrives for dinner at the family of his Irish Catholic girlfriend, Maddie, he is served matzah with the meal. In the ensuing exchange, Maddie's young nephew expresses interest in learning why Jews eat matzah on Passover (after hearing from Jackie, "To tell you the truth, we eat them mostly on Passover"), and, in a departure from other Passover depictions, the explanation comes not from the Jewish character but the non–Jewish. Maddie explains, "You see, Brecken, when the Jews were fleeing from Egypt, they didn't have time to bake bread in the normal way, so it came out like this." The matzah becomes a subject for humor when Jackie pipes in, "Hopefully, tonight I won't have to flee so much, so I can eat the regular bread." When Maddie's unsettled sister-in-law asks, "Did I do something wrong?" Jackie replies, "No! As a matter of fact, I eat this all year round now. This way I stay in shape for fleeing."

The Passover humor was much less gentle later that season on an episode of *Anything but Love* that depicted the *seder*—normally a joyous and lively event—as dreary and lifeless. The program started on a brighter note when the non–Jewish Hannah Miller asks coworker Marty Gold if she can join him at his family's *seder*. She explains, "I've been to a Roman Catholic midnight mass, a Shinto service, and I've always wanted to see what Passover was all about." What she finds at Marty's *seder* are whiny, stereotypical characters and little enlightening explanation of anything (except a word about the Hebrew prophet Elijah).[19] As the participants recite the ten plagues, to a laugh track through all ten of them,[20] Marty notes, "This is historically where our cheerful disposition comes from." He thereby perpetuates the "centuries-old accusation of Jews being a cheerless group of refugee-conditioned people with bent backs having little time dedicated to the joy of life," when in fact, "our religion is the one most filled with the joy of song."[21] Hannah is mocked by another *seder* guest who first tells her to eat parsley in salt water (Hannah dutifully does so) and then, presumably as another *seder* custom, to pick up a piece of matzah and throw it against the wall. Hannah does so, and she is greatly embarrassed when she finds she is the only one hurling matzah and that this was supposed to be a good-natured joke. Normally brimming with a high level of witty and off-beat humor, this *Anything but Love* episode — with thoughtless, dreary characters; a stilted, joyless, songless *seder*; and virtually no explanations of the glorious ideals of Passover — was disappointing, as an opportunity was missed for what could have been a clever juxtaposition of comedy with an important Jewish theme.

With families gathered around the *seder*, the opportunity exists — in both TV and real life — for the eruption of family tensions. In an episode of the HBO comedy series *Dream On*, the *seder* becomes a battleground between divorced parents of different faiths vying for their son's religious allegiance. In a tragicomic scene, family members take sides in a cultural-religious face-off, as gefilte fish and ham vie for space on the festive table that is half *seder* and half Easter dinner. This marks, in a sense, the arrival of Passover on TV, as it here assumes a role traditionally monopolized by the Chanukah/Christmas season as a new minefield between television's interfaith couples facing difficulties about their religious differences.

SUKKOT, SHAVUOT, AND PURIM

The holidays of *Sukkot* and *Shavuot*, which are actually two of the three major biblical holidays of Judaism[22] (along with Passover), have been denied popular attention both in contemporary Jewish life and on popular television. There have been a very few depictions of some aspects of *Sukkot* and only a few humorous references to *Shavuot*.

An interesting setting for *Sukkot* was the pilot movie for the detective series *Cagney and Lacey*, which aired in 1981. When investigating the murder of a diamond dealer, the policewomen plunge into the world of New York's Forty-Seventh Street diamond district, peopled by Orthodox Jews. A clue to the crime may lie in the differences between the black, fur-lined hats of various Hasidic sects. In trying to learn something about this, Detective Christine Cagney hops into a Lubavitch "mitzvah-mobile,"[23] which is parked on Forty-Seventh Street and decorated with the sign "Sukkah on Wheels." There the

Irish American officer is told by a young Hasid, "*Sukkos*[24] is a Jewish holiday —
we could send you information." She learns more about the holiday when the
trail leads her to Borough Park and a helpful tipster whispers that she can capture the murderer (a Nazi impersonating a Jew) at the synagogue that night.
The tipster explains, "Everyone will be there…. Tonight is *Hoshanah Rabbah* —
the eighth day of the holiday. The *Torahs* are brought to the *bima*, the reading
desk of the synagogue." The culprit is caught, however, before viewers have a
chance to see this event.

The aspect of building a *sukkah* — the temporary, outdoor booth that is
the central symbol of *Sukkot* — and inviting friends and family to share meals
and festivities there was alluded to on the detective series *Wiseguy*. In a 1988
episode, a well-to-do garment industry executive invites all his colleagues to
a *Sukkot* party. A nighttime scene of the basically outdoor party suggests a
spirit of *Sukkot*, but no explanations are offered.

Questions of particular ritual observance on *Sukkot* were highlighted in
an episode of *Brooklyn Bridge*, about a Jewish family in 1950s Brooklyn, when
the young boys and their mother argue over the appropriateness of watching
TV on *Sukkot* night during a family holiday meal. As the older boy advances
his argument for watching TV — a source of enjoyment for him — he asks why
it should not be permitted on *Sukkot*, since it is a "festive occasion." His characterization of *Sukkot* is on the mark, but why does he then go on to make the
disparaging and quite erroneous remark that it is "one of the rare up Jewish
holidays"? Such a statement, reflecting an ignorance of Judaism and perpetuating a false and insidious notion that Jewish religious life is doleful, diminished a series that for the most part was otherwise beautifully crafted, enjoyable,
moving, and refreshing for its distinctive ethnicity.

The holiday of *Shavuot* gained some exposure whenever *Anything But
Love's* Marty Gold repeatedly used a pet phrase of his to express a long delay:
"You could wait from now until *Shavuos*."

Although a minor holiday in the Jewish calendar, *Purim* has been depicted
on two prime-time shows. In an episode of the detective series *Lanigan's Rabbi*,
which had a brief run in 1977, Rabbi Small is seen at the synagogue preparing
the children to perform a *Purim* play. He offers a concise history of the holiday and tells the youngsters that the "*Purim* story is a good detective story
without the chases and violence."

An episode of the 1970s comedy series *The Partridge Family* also touched
on some aspect of *Purim*. Public school student Danny Partridge pretends to
be Jewish so that he can join a classmate — on whom he has a crush — who is
given permission to take off for *Purim*. While not explaining the holiday (and
while presenting some misconceptions about it, such as having to take the day
off from school),[25] the program shows Danny joining in a *Purim* carnival,
throwing bean bags at Haman, and enjoying *Purim* costumes in the atmosphere
of this joyous holiday.

SHABBAT

Shabbat, the Jewish day of rest and the word from which Sabbath derives, is a time of spiritual elevation, of separation from the mundane achieved by shutting out worldly matters and celebrated with singing, festive meals, prayer and study, family gatherings, and a cessation of work. That *Shabbat* has been featured in numerous popular TV shows is highly appropriate, since it is considered the most important and prominent holiday of the Jewish calendar.[26] Still, the majority of American Jews are less attentive to *Shabbat* and more likely aware and observant of such holidays as Chanukah, *Rosh Hashanah*, *Yom Kippur*, and Passover. If TV depictions can have any impact on popular conceptions about the priorities of the Jewish holidays, the significant presence of *Shabbat* depictions on TV is welcome, as it accords this important day some of the respect and prominence it is due but which it may, in real life, rarely receive.

The depictions of *Shabbat* touch on various aspects of the day. One of the most joyous manifestations of *Shabbat* and the one that has received the greatest attention on TV is the Friday evening *Shabbat* meal. Its festivity is shown through such rituals as the lighting of candles and the recitation of blessings over the wine and *challah* (often in Hebrew), along with exuberant singing, family warmth and closeness, and a lavish meal replete with Jewish foods.

As is the case with the presentation of most other Jewish rituals, the Friday evening *Shabbat* meal is almost never depicted without the presence of non–Jews; they appear either as guests in a Jewish home or as hosts who make the effort to prepare such a meal for Jewish guests. In perhaps the most striking example of this, the famed Western hero Paladin of *Have Gun, Will Travel* turns out to be an exemplary guest at a *Shabbat* dinner with his Jewish friends and clients, the Shotnesses. He seems completely at home and comfortable participating in the *Shabbat* rituals; he even recites the blessing over the wine in Hebrew and later quotes from the *Zohar*, the esoteric book of Jewish mysticism. Such a depiction is no less than inspiring as it demonstrates to viewers the beauty of Jewish traditions, the respect that a heroic non–Jew has for these traditions, and the importance of being aware and knowledgeable of other people's heritages without bias or prejudice.

While such intimate knowledge of Jewish lore by a non–Jew has been rare, respect, interest, and enthusiasm by non–Jews has not. In a 1979 episode of *The White Shadow*, a non–Jewish high school basketball coach participates in a student's *Shabbat* dinner when Abner Goldstein, an orphan who lives with his grandparents, invites him for a *Shabbat* dinner.

Another *Shabbat* dinner appeared on the medical series *Buck James*, which aired briefly in 1988 and featured the Jewish doctor Rebecca Meyers. When Rebecca's grandparents come to town to visit her, they meet chief surgeon Buck James, a strapping cowboy-doctor and invite him to join the family for a Friday night meal, explaining that "Friday night is the beginning of our Sabbath.

We say a few prayers; we have dinner." Buck arrives at the Meyerses' soon after his own daughter has experienced a miscarriage, but the *Shabbat* mood there, as Rebecca and grandmother, heads kerchiefed, light the candles, seems to be a balm to him, as he appears to be very much moved by it all.

Sometimes the *Shabbat* dinner takes place in a program that also portrays other Jewish holidays. The *Purim* episode of *The Partridge Family* also includes a *Shabbat* dinner. With Danny Partridge courting the rabbi's daughter, Rachel — and pretending to be Jewish — the Partridges find themselves invited guests at Rachel and her family's *Shabbat* dinner. They all sit around the festively set table, the men wearing yarmulkes, and the rabbi recites the *kiddush*. The situation becomes most embarrassing when Rabbi Stern tells them that they will start with *Hamotzi* and Danny asks him to "please pass the *Hamotzi*."[27] The rabbi explains that *Hamotzi* is the prayer over the bread and then asks Mrs. Partridge to recite the blessing. The awkward moment impels Danny to confess. In a similar vein, the Chanukah episode of *Frank's Place* happens to take place on a Friday evening, leading to some discussion about *Shabbat*.

In some programs, non–Jews not only participate in a *Shabbat* meal but take the initiative to prepare one for their Jewish friends, or even family — as in the case of *Archie Bunker's Place*. In the 1979 episode "The *Shabbat* Dinner," Edith cooks chicken soup and matzah balls in preparation for a *Shabbat* meal that the Bunkers are preparing for their Jewish niece, Stephanie. The youngster instructs Edith in the correct pronunciation of *Shabbat*, makes sure that Archie puts on a yarmulke, guides everyone in the premeal rituals, and leads them in singing a *Shabbat* song in Hebrew. Archie's Jewish business partner, Murray Klein, along with his mother and non–Jewish girlfriend, are also present and participate in the *Shabbat* festivities.

In a 1978 episode of the humorous family drama *Eight Is Enough*, a non–Jewish girl is pursuing a man she believes to be Jewish and seeks to win his heart by demonstrating her interest in his faith — so she prepares a *Shabbat* meal. The day-long preparations include cooking Jewish delicacies and setting out an ornate *Shabbat* table.

Often, faithful Jews will carry out traditions even under the most difficult of circumstances. *Shabbat* is no exception to this. In the 1976 made-for-television movie *Victory at Entebbe*, for instance, the Jewish hostages under Arab attack nevertheless manage to find makeshift *Shabbat* candles and wine, make the appropriate blessings over them, and sing Hebrew *Shabbat* songs to fulfill their religious obligation and reaffirm their commitment.

Adversity is not a requirement, however, in the portrayal of observant Jews celebrating *Shabbat*, just simple pride in and comfort with one's religious identity. A prominent example of more recent vintage appeared on *The Trials of Rosie O'Neill*, in which the *kippah*-wearing public defender Ben Meyer is shown at home welcoming the Sabbath in prayer and song with his family and guest at the *Shabbat* table.

This picture of *Shabbat* bringing family together and ushering in a respite of harmony amidst tumultuous times found poignant expression on an episode of *Sisters*. The series included an intermarriage — between the Jewish Mitch Margolis and one of the four sisters, Frankie. When Mitch is out of town and his outgoing, assertive mother arrives unexpectedly and meets his new bride for the first time, the stage is set for a clash of personalities and cultures. It is hardly a surprising plot twist that the two women inevitably and gradually become closer and more understanding of one another during the course of her visit. But it *is* unexpected that their point of connecting to one another is through Judaism and *Shabbat*.

The mother has brought the couple a wedding gift: a pair of silver *Shabbat* candlesticks from Russia, passed down from her own grandmother. Although, she says, they would mean little to her own son Mitch, she lovingly tells Frankie what memories the candlesticks evoke for her. She recalls frantic preparations to clean and prepare the house for *Shabbat*, when a peace and quiet would descend — a time when the family gathered to light candles and eat a *Shabbat* meal, a time of talking and laughing together when "all troubles would be put aside." Bemoaning that her family is now spread out all over the country the mother concludes, "You knew you were a part of something." This story line concludes with Frankie surprising her mother-in-law with a *Shabbat* dinner, and the two say the *bracha* (Hebrew blessing) over the *Shabbat* candles.

While one could take issue with *Sisters'* depiction of yet another TV intermarriage, its evocation of the beauty of the traditional Jewish *Shabbat* and the day's incomparable benefit for so many aspects of life was both very incisive and moving. Clearly, Jewish life is approached here with a significant degree of warmth, knowledge, and affection.

Another nostalgic look at *Shabbat* was recounted by the grandmother on *Brooklyn Bridge*. At the close of a busy Saturday during which various family members spent the day at the movies or at Coney Island (their intended assignments were to do laundry and to shop at A&S department store's once-a-year underwear sale), Grandma Silver fondly describes what *Shabbat* was like in her hometown in Europe. "Our whole village would stop on *Shabbos*," she tells her attentive children and grandchildren. "No one would work. The men would not plow; the women would not sew. From sundown Friday, all day Saturday, a whole village — praying, thinking, singing. My mother, my father — they forgot all their troubles. Life was hard for six days. Then for one, it was beautiful." The comforting picture she weaves evokes a world far from the path this busy first-generation family now treads as it struggles to succeed in America and become Americanized. The contrasting approaches to the day point up the difference between Saturday for many families, a day of frantic chores, and *Shabbat*, a day of respite, contemplation and study, family meals and togetherness. Still, on this particular Saturday, the family seems to be savoring the

fact that the day was special: they threw off their assigned tasks and drudgery
in a sort of stitching together of a new kind of day. As the grandmother said,
whether questioningly or convincingly, at the close of her description of *Shabbat*, "The world has changed now, but as long as we are together, Saturday is
still special, right?"

While nostalgic descriptions of bygone *Shabbat* days would seem to create a sense that the day is the province of only older generations, many of TV's
young characters also have fond notions of *Shabbat*. On *Reasonable Doubts*,
attorney Tess Kaufman expressed a connection to Jewish life and traditions
under unlikely circumstances: a property dispute during a divorce from her
husband. Returning home one evening, Tess finds her home in shambles, with
TV and VCR missing. But only the loss of a pair of candlesticks upsets her.
"They were my grandmother's," she explains. "When I was a little girl she'd let
me light the candles on Friday night, and she'd say a blessing." When it is
revealed that her husband's lawyers took the property, he — otherwise depicted
as a quintessential cad — is softly apologetic that the candlesticks were taken
by mistake and returns them. It seems that the aura of *Shabbat* and its candlesticks mollified even his abrasive manner.

Shabbat has been portrayed in such detail that even the prohibition of
specific activities on *Shabbat*— prohibitions observed by more traditional
Jews — has been explored in various shows and was even the central story line
of one. An episode of *Magnum, P.I.*, for example, which aired in 1985, depicts
a Rabbi Solomon who demands that the car in which he is riding on a late Friday afternoon be stopped. He exits the car to walk the rest of the way, explaining that it is against his tradition to ride on *Shabbat*. The car explodes seconds
after he exits it, suggesting divine approval for his observance. Similarly, when
Nathan Shotness is introduced on *Have Gun, Will Travel*, his wagon describes
the services he offers: peddler, mail carrier — but concludes with the admoni-
tion "never on Saturday."

Of course, these prohibitions may be broken under certain circumstances.
This was shown in an episode of the comedy series *Barney Miller*, when a
Hasidic Jew tells of a woman who witnessed a mugging and "broke her Sabbath and telephoned for help." Another episode of *Barney Miller* included a
humorous reference to *Shabbat* prohibitions. A rabbi who learns that a Jewish boy robbed a liquor store says to him "I hope at least you don't rob on the
Sabbath," to which the boy quips, "I usually wait for sundown."

At times, these prohibitions cause conflict, symbolizing a whole attitude
toward observance and mode of attachment to Judaism. A 1971 episode of *The
Bill Cosby Show*[28] was devoted to exploring a struggle related to this problem.
In "The Saturday Game," a young Hasidic boy is torn between a strong allegiance to his faith, which prohibits his participation in a very important base-
ball game to be held on Saturday, and his desire to fulfill his other responsibility,
to his teammates who rely on him for his unmatched pitching abilities.

Similar conflicts beset Jewish immigrants on the Lower East Side when the survival imperatives of working on *Shabbat* cause strife between a father and his daughter who toils at a garment factory on the miniseries *The Triangle Factory Fire Scandal* (1979). And when she wants to spend Friday evenings not at synagogue but at parties, the conflict continues. Likewise, another immigrant father, on the miniseries *Evergreen* (1985), becomes incensed that his son insists on going roller-skating on *Shabbat* morning instead of to synagogue and seeks to impart to him to importance of Jewish tradition.

Another instance where *Shabbat*, as a quintessential embodiment of Jewish religious values and observance, evokes conflict is between in-laws of an intermarried couple on *Little House on the Prairie*. When they all join together for a *Shabbat* meal, the Jewish father-in-law, Mr. Cohen, tells his Gentile in-laws, "No doubt you will share many Sabbath meals with our children in the future." The non–Jewish mother-in-law quickly retorts, "No doubt about it — every Sunday," and a shouting match ensues between them. The fighting eventually drives Mr. Cohen from the table declaring, "The Sabbath is a celebration. A Jew does not eat at a table filled with anger."

The intrusion of acrimony and rancor is underscored by its juxtaposition with *Shabbat*, the quintessence of harmony and peace. Indeed, it is the *Shabbat* sense of delight in family and spiritual tranquillity and elevation that has been the central aspect of the TV image of this most-depicted Jewish holy day.

Other Customs

Many other manifestations of Judaism that are prominent in Jewish life have also found their way onto popular TV and while not always depicted as major themes do appear countless times in a variety of ways. A whole panoply of descriptions and depictions of aspects of Jewish worship, sacred symbols and objects, books, languages, and literature enter into all kinds of programs with great frequency and diversity.

Synagogue and Prayer

The portrayal and presence of synagogues on television programs are too numerous to itemize. The settings have been quite varied, ranging from the burning and destruction of synagogues in Europe during the Holocaust to more tranquil scenes in America, where the synagogue is shown as a place of worship, as a meeting place for discussing issues of concern to the Jewish community, and of course as site of *bar* and *bat mitzvah* celebrations. Sometimes it is merely a background setting to identify a character as Jewish. In an unusual twist, it served as a place of refuge for a hunted Nazi. A major theme relating to synagogues on TV has been synagogue vandalism as a manifestation of anti–Semitism and neo–Nazism (see Chapter 3, "Anti-Semitism").

Much could be done to improve the TV image of synagogue services so that it would more fairly reflect the lively atmosphere that is in fact found in many synagogues today. Unfortunately, except when *bar* and *bat mitzvah* celebrations are shown to be held there, synagogues services are generally depicted as dark and cheerless, devoid of singing or dancing, and peopled by a scattering of moribund, elderly devotioners. An extreme of this appeared on an episode of the series *Men*, where a Jewish yuppie type descends some stairs to a room enveloped in a gauzelike haze with ghoulish old men praying.

For the most part, however, programs that include Jews praying or reciting particular Jewish blessings or prayers — whether the program is comedy or drama — depict this as something sacred and treat it with dignity and respect. Blessings and prayers are uttered frequently, appearing, for instance, as parts of a wedding ceremony, a *bar* or *bat mitzvah*, or a circumcision; when mourners recite the *kaddish*; during celebrations of holidays or recitation of daily prayers; the saying of *shema* when one is about to die; or a family offering a blessing of thanksgiving for a safe arrival at their destination after a grueling journey.

The importance of prayer and attending houses of worship to these Jewish characters is not alien to the American public because of the significant part these activities play in their own lives. While the prayers themselves are quite different from one religion to another, there exists no doubt a common concern for the act of praying, as reflected on TV in its abundant depictions of Jewish prayers. Indeed, the universality of this concern, and the recognition of diversity of expression was demonstrated in a telling moment on an episode of *Father Dowling Mysteries*, a series about a sleuthing Catholic clergyman. As Father Dowling is about to offer Catholic prayers over a vagrant's dead body that he has just stumbled upon, he is informed that the deceased was Jewish, and he immediately recites the *shema* in Hebrew for the memory of this Jewish stranger. In a moment underscoring the importance of prayer, whatever one's religion, and conveying a message of interfaith harmony, Father Dowling reveals that he learned this prayer from his best friend — who is a rabbi.

SYMBOLS, OBJECTS, AND FOLKLORE

Many Jewish symbols and objects are likely recognizable to a whole range of viewers. In the eye of the viewer, authenticity, identification, and even some sense of familiarity is evoked when characters don such items as yarmulkes or prayer shawls — religious articles frequently depicted. Often a *menorah* on a bookshelf is the tip-off to a Jewish home.

Related to the *menorah* are Sabbath candlesticks, which have been depicted as symbolic of attachment to heritage and bringing peace and harmony to situations of strife. This effect of *Shabbat* candlesticks was beautifully illustrated on the episodes of *Sisters* and *Reasonable Doubts* mentioned above.

The Jewish Star of David is doubtless also highly recognizable and has been a prominently featured symbol in several shows. In *The Flying Nun*, for instance, airborne Sister Bertrille skywrites a huge white Jewish star in the blue skies in honor of the Jewish wedding taking place below as all look up in delighted amazement.

Sometimes these symbols, which lend a Jewish flavor to the show, take on even greater significance. An episode of *All in the Family* culminates in the symbolism of the Jewish star: after Archie Bunker discovers that his niece Stephanie is Jewish, he expresses his continuing love for her by giving her a necklace with a Jewish star, saying that "you gotta love somebody to give them one of these. I mean, you gotta love everything about them." Thus for Archie, Stephanie's Jewishness is embodied in the Jewish star, and in his giving her this gift it becomes the supreme symbol of his acceptance of her Jewishness.

The *Torah* also plays a central role in a number of programs. On the *bar mitzvah* episode of *Ironside*, in which a *Torah* scroll is stolen, the stage is set for discussion about the meaning of the *Torah*, its history, and its significance to the Jewish people. Most of the explanations are relayed by an African American police officer, Ironside's assistant, who reports in detail to his boss: "They call *Torah* the Sacred Scroll of the Law — the Five Books of Moses.... Anything else you want to know, just ask me — I'm the expert! ... A *Torah* is made of parchment, the skin of a kosher ram or goat. Each letter is artistically inscribed by artisans called *sofrim* and hand sewn in sections."

An added urgency to recovering the *Ironside Torah* is the fact that it had survived the Holocaust, a time when innumerable *Torah* scrolls were destroyed. A similar such *Torah* played a key role in a story on *Magnum, P.I.*, the 1980s detective series set in Hawaii. The episode opens in 1945 in Shanghai, which served as a refuge for those fleeing from Nazi Europe.[29] As a synagogue there endures the ravaging effects of wartime bombing, its members wrap their *Torah* in a prayer shawl in order to save it, but it is buried in the rubble. Some forty years later, Rabbi Asher Solomon arrives in Hawaii for a reunion with the many Jewish families who came from Shanghai.[30] The "Shanghai *Torah*," buried under the rubble and presumed lost for years, had just been returned to the Jewish community by the Taiwanese Department of Antiquities, and Rabbi Solomon was bringing it to the reunion.

When the *Torah* is subsequently stolen, the rabbi explains to private investigator Thomas Magnum how important it is to him: "This piece of parchment is something that I would risk anything for. It is a tangible reminder of where we come from and what we have lived through. My wife and son were killed in Poland before we could escape; the temple in Shanghai has long been in ruins. But this *Torah* has been reborn — it has been resurrected." Rabbi Solomon also explains to the police that "the sacred *Torah* [is a] symbol of faith and courage of countless generations of my people." When the *Torah* is finally recovered, Rabbi Solomon sings as he restores it and then takes it to the grave of Avraham Pressman, where he has invited Higgins, Magnum's associate, to join him. The rabbi explains that Avraham had been in the Shanghai congregation but had died before the *Torah* was recovered. Higgins is touched but questions the rabbi about the permissibility of bringing a *Torah* into the cemetery. Rabbi Solomon replies, "I know it's against the highest tradition. But after all this *Torah* has been through I think the good Lord above will forgive us ... and now we will take this *Torah* to the living — *L'chayim!*" That this and the *Ironside Torah* are both survivors of the Holocaust underscores the symbolism of the *Torah* as the foundation of the survival of the Jewish people.

With the recent surge of popularity in shows dealing with unexplained phenomena, known in the parlance as "the paranormal," the trove of Jewish folklore and mysticism is being mined for novel story lines. The wildly popular series *The X-Files*, about a male-female pair of FBI agents on the trail of cases offering no rational explanation, recently drew upon the legend of the *golem* found in Jewish mystic writings.

The *golem* legend dates back some sixteen hundred years, with early rabbinic writings and Talmudic passages referring to the ability to animate lifeless beings fashioned from clay or dirt through the incantation of magic combinations of Hebrew letters. The resulting *golem*, without a mind of its own, does the bidding of its creator — generally a mission of protection for Jewish communities besieged by anti–Semitic attacks. The legend gained popularity in the sixteenth century with the circulation of a tale of Rabbi Judah Loew of Prague (known as the Maharal) who was said to have fashioned a *golem* using the Hebrew word *emet*, meaning "truth." This *golem* was created to protect Prague's Jewish community from the fury provoked by the blood libel that it killed Christian children to use their blood to bake Passover matzah.

The *X-Files* episode goes into great detail in laying out the background and details of the *golem* legend. The figure comes into play following the brutal shooting murder of a young Hasidic store owner, Isaac Luria (a nod to the actual sixteenth-century Jewish mystic of the same name), in his grocery in Williamsburg, Brooklyn. After his suspected killers are themselves killed off one by one — with the fingerprints of the murdered Hasid upon them — the agents are brought in to investigate. One of them, Fox Mulder, finds a Jewish mystic book in Luria's grave, which prompts him to contact a Jewish researcher who elucidates the *golem* legends and incantations found therein. When it becomes clear through a parallel investigation that Luria was killed by anti–Semitic youths backed by a neo–Nazi operation, Mulder comes up with an explanation for the apparent revenge murders: a modern-day *golem* has been fashioned by someone to avenge the hate killing of this young Hasid, murdered just days before his wedding day.

Other issues arise during the investigation: the would-be groom's intended father-in-law is a Holocaust survivor who sees anti–Semitism as permeating society; the neo–Nazis distribute Goebbelsesque flyers blaming the Jews for

AIDS; Mulder and his partner debate issues of free speech, even if it is hateful, versus the dangerous realities of its effects.

Mulder learns more details about the *golem* legend that aid in his investigation, including arcane explanations regarding the letters on the creature's hand that have brought it to life: the three Hebrew letters *aleph, mem, tav*— spelling out the word *emet*, "truth" in Hebrew. But when the first letter is erased, leaving just *mem* and *tav* to spell out *mayt* "dead," the *golem* is destroyed. "Therein lies the paradox," the researcher explains to Mulder, "because the danger of the truth is contained in the word *golem* itself—which means matter without form, body without soul. In the legends, it runs amok and has to be destroyed by its creator. Again, Mr. Mulder, the power of letters not just to create, but to kill."

In the show's final scenes set in a *Hasidic* synagogue, it becomes clear that the creator of this *golem* was Luria's bereaved fiancée Arielle, who could not bear the grief of his death and craved to see him again even in a distorted, inhuman, and destructive form. In her wedding dress, she greets the horrific creature with a grotesque resemblance to Isaac, reciting in English and Hebrew the Jewish wedding vow. He places on her finger a silver ring that her father had kept hidden since his escape from the Holocaust and that represented to him the loss of his Czech hometown in which nine thousand Jews were killed on one day in the spring of 1943. But the *golem* has indeed run amok, seeking to kill Arielle's father because he opposes him and overcoming the FBI agents with his super-human strength.

At last it is Arielle, content that she has seen a form of Isaac one last time, who, after caressing his hand, erases from it the initial *aleph*, thereby ensuring the creature's destruction. Huddled over his melting, muddied form, she recites the *kaddish* as Mulder explains to his bewildered partner, "She's saying goodbye."

Another popular legend of Jewish folklore received an airing on *Psi Factor*, a series subtitled *Chronicles of the Paranormal*. One episode revolved around the notion of a dybbuk, a demon that invades the souls of the innocent, made known by the stories of Isaac Bashevis Singer. The show included an adaptation of the ancient Jewish ritual to stop the dybbuk, in a sort of Jewish version of *The Exorcist*.

JEWISH FOOD AND KASHRUT

The most prominently featured "Jewish symbol" on television has been Jewish food. It is included — usually with much commentary — in nearly every depiction of a Jewish ritual. Much of the banter about it is humorous, such as the rabbi's comment on *Diff'rent Strokes* that "a bris is a medical procedure which my people have turned into a catered affair." The sometimes exaggerated attention to Jewish food, however, fairly reflects the importance of food in Jewish life, rituals, and tradition.

While the very mention of Jewish food often tends to evoke laughter, there is a more sobering side to food in its symbolism of the sustenance of life. For all people, food is and has been a symbol of survival, and all ethnic groups have food-related occasions, as well as humor. Without a doubt, though, Jews are particularly spotlighted for their affinity for special ethnic delicacies and for enjoying food. The existence of a prime-time program featuring Jewish characters in leading roles that is named after what is arguably the most Jewishly associated food on record — chicken soup — is no accident. Jews and food are associated. In many programs over the past fifty years, Jewish food is eaten, described, hated, and enjoyed.

One program where Jewish food is delightfully devoured by non–Jews was a 1968 episode of *Gomer Pyle, U.S.M.C.* The show focuses on Jewish grandmother Molly Gordon cooking Jewish food for Gomer, his sergeant, and the entire troop, who consume it all with gusto. The army men are introduced to such delicacies as *tzimmes*, chopped liver, and *gedempte flanken*.

Television's *Shabbat* dinner scenes often include elaborate descriptions of the Jewish food, usually within some humorous context. On *The White Shadow*, for instance, the basketball coach invited for a *Shabbat* dinner passes with flying colors the Jewish food quiz that the grandmother administers. Of his ability to identify every dish she puts before him, including gefilte fish, matzah ball soup, and *kreplach*, he explains "Bayside, Queens, where I come from, has more Jewish delis than bowling alleys — I know all the dishes."

The strong association of Jews with food was humorously underlined in an episode of *Sanford and Son*, the 1970s comedy series. When Fred suddenly believes himself to be Jewish, he quickly loads up on corned beef and chopped liver and proudly identifies himself as "Frederick G. Sanford — the g stands for gefilte fish."

Sometimes Jewish food, with an apparent reputation for heaviness, is an object of ridicule, and non–Jews approach it with an attitude of blatant fear, distaste, and trepidation, as if it were some strange, repelling foreign entity. Such was the case on *Eight Is Enough*, when the young woman spent all day preparing a *Shabbat* meal, and her family would barely touch it, practically gagging on it when they did try some. At the *shiva* on *Facts of Life*, few of the girls wanted to taste the food that seemed to emerge endlessly, as a new casserole dish arrived with every additional guest.

On *The Partridge Family*'s *Purim* episode, Jewish food has the opposite effect: having tasted and greatly enjoyed the *Shabbat* dinner at the rabbi's home, the Partridges resolve as a result to try foods from a different culture each week. Their exposure to Jewish food led to a new openness and curiosity about other ethnic dishes.

Perhaps the most well known aspect of Jewish food is the concept of kosher or the observance of dietary laws known as *kashrut*. The word kosher itself appears on innumerable programs in the most offhand way to denote that something is — OK, above/board, correct, or even pure. The ubiquitousness of the word on popular TV indicates just how thoroughly it has come into common usage. Indeed, it is uttered not only by Jewish characters but by all types, often with the intent of evoking humor in the odd juxtaposition of its utterance by, say, a priest.

Even Archie Bunker has heard about Jewish dietary laws, although his understanding, as usual, is hilariously off-kilter. On an episode where he is expecting a Jewish dinner guest, he loads up on Jewish food and instructs Edith, when putting it in the refrigerator, to "keep the Jewish food to one side so it don't lose its kosher."

At times, the word kosher is used in a derogatory way to identify a character as Jewish. When, on the pilot episode of *Hill Street Blues*, Lieutenant Howard Hunter curtly remarks — in discussing riot control — that fellow officer Henry Goldblume "couldn't diffuse a roll of kosher toilet paper," viewers are tipped off that Goldblume is Jewish, and one whose Jewishness is to be a factor in the squad room and the streets.

Seinfeld's apparent love-hate relationship with matters Jewish extends to issues of *kashrut* as well. Assorted references to Jewish dietary laws have found their way onto the show to varying effect. In one episode, an offensive bit of dialogue takes place in a scene on an airplane. When regular character Elaine is served a kosher meal by mistake and protests that she doesn't even know what a kosher meal is, two fellow passengers seek to enlighten her through this ghastly conversation: "I think it means when a rabbi has inspected it." "No, no, it all has to do with the way they kill the pig." "They don't eat pigs." "They do if it's killed right — under a rabbi's supervision!" The notion that Jewish dietary laws permit the eating of pork is, of course, erroneous, and the whole conversation conjures up and perpetuates an anti–Semitic view of Jewish laws as arcane and ghoulish. In addition, when another passenger who *did* order the kosher meal comes forward and is asked why he didn't claim it earlier, he declares (with a clearly Yiddish accent), "I ordered it six weeks ago," as if the observance of *kashrut* is a fleeting and easily forgotten matter. A more positive treatment of the subject was included on a different *Seinfeld* episode, when character George Costanza was thrilled with friend Jerry Seinfeld's offer to take him on an all-expense-paid trip to L.A. (comic Jerry was to appear on *The Tonight Show*). Ecstatic over the upcoming flight, George delightedly implored, "Can I order the kosher meal? I heard it's great!" While the line might be interpreted as a reflection of George's nebbishy character, this was nonetheless a rare-for-TV compliment of kosher food — a cuisine often the target of disparaging and tasteless TV humor.

Kashrut also played center stage in the life of Jerry's Jewish girlfriend, in an episode in which they spend the weekend in the Hamptons with a number of friends. As all sit around the table eating lobster, Kramer offers her some, which she refuses, explaining that she can't because she keeps kosher. Unfazed by the question, "You mean you've never tasted lobster before?" she matter-of-factly responds, "No." Kramer comments, "Wow! You're so pious — I really respect that. You know, when you die you're going to get some special attention." When later that night she succumbs to the pressure and sneaks into a dark kitchen to snatch a taste of the lobster, Kramer flicks on the light, holding up the lobster. "Is this what you're looking for?" She demands the delicacy, but he refuses, telling her he cannot let her have it. In the clarity of daylight, she thanks Kramer the next morning for withholding the taboo food from her, adding sincerely, "You really saved me." While this story could be perceived either as a mockery of someone trying to keep *kashrut* or as an acknowledgment of the pressures of temptation — averted by a concerned friend — Kramer's apparently sincere response to her gratitude seems to stem from genuine concern: "Well, I knew you'd regret it for the rest of your life." It was disturbing that such a depiction had to end with a mean-spirited George tricking her into eating the lobster, causing her to hastily take leave of them, utterly devastated.

Jewish food got another chance on *Seinfeld* when an episode aired about a Jewish singles dance in which George's father attempts to perfect the challenges of cooking good Jewish food.

The observance of *kashrut* by traditional Jews has been explored on several shows. TV's Jewish characters of the Old West and frontier America had a particularly difficult time observing such strictures but determinedly sought to do so as a means of upholding religious identity and principles. In an episode of *Little House on the Prairie*, the Jewish Mr. Cohen, dining at the home of his non–Jewish in-laws, is upset to see milk and meat on the same table, a combination proscribed by the laws of *kashrut*. He also refuses the meat itself, politely explaining, "There's nothing wrong with it, I'm sure, but Jewish law forbids me to eat non-kosher meat," and asks for a plate of vegetables.

In contrast to this, immigrant Jews at the Dakota *seder* featured in the *Philco TV Playhouse* seem compelled to adjust their observance of *kashrut* in the face of barren land, harsh conditions, the death of the family patriarch, and the scarcity of food. When American Indians bring meat for the festive occasion, the family accepts the gift with gratitude, even stating that they think the meat is kosher.

In very different circumstances, a rabbi in the Warsaw ghetto addresses issues of *kashrut* in the 1982 made-for-TV movie *The Wall*. With starvation raging in the ghetto, he offers a lengthy explanation of why Jews there may eat the horse meat (normally forbidden) that someone has brought them.[31]

From TV's abundant attention to Jewish food emerges the picture that in Judaism, food — which is the sustenance of life — is not taken for granted but is the subject of very particular care and thought through rituals and traditions. It is a focus not only of day-to-day life and enjoyment but is an integral part of Jewish religious observance and Judaism's notions about the sanctity of life and the cherishing of the good things before us. Given food's exalted place in Jewish life, it is no wonder that popular television depicts it as an expression of Jewish identity and religious attachment and as another distinctive quality on the part of TV's Jewish characters and the Judaism they bear.

JEWISH WISDOM AND LANGUAGES

Judaism is rich in wisdom literature such as the Hebrew Bible, the *Talmud*, and the *Zohar*. These abound with moral and ethical lessons that have been adapted and popularized throughout the ages and that have found their way onto popular TV. The presence of such Jewish wisdom can enhance the depiction of a larger Jewish theme in a program. A number of programs have included Jewish characters quoting from such sources or specific sages to make a particular point. One such character, Rabbi Small, the sleuthing rabbi of *Lanigan's Rabbi*, regularly cited Jewish wisdom in offering advice, solace, and insights to his congregants, his wife, the community at large, police chief Lanigan, and even crime suspects.

Even more interesting and with greater potential for impacting non–Jewish viewers are the non–Jewish characters — often the series star — who manifest a familiarity with and knowledge of Jewish sources. In episodes of *Have Gun, Will Travel*, for instance, Paladin, the program's erudite gunslinger, quotes from the Hebrew Bible, the *Talmud*, the *Zohar*, and ancient rabbinic sages. Often, he utters these in Hebrew and then goes on to translate them, as when he employs an adage from the sage Hillel[32] to lend some advice to Nathan Shotness: " '*Al tifrosh min ha-tzee-bur.*' Don't separate yourself from the community."[33]

Rabbi Hillel's popularity as disseminator of wisdom extended to a 1973 episode of *Medical Center*, where series star Dr. Gannon appears to be an admirer of him as well. When a patient tells Gannon, "Hillel says, 'If I am not for myself, who will be for me?'" the doctor retorts, "He also said, 'If I am for myself alone, what am I?'" Surprised, the patient asks, "Do they teach Hillel in medical school?" and Dr. Gannon, years before the question of teaching ethics in medical school became a hot topic, replies, "No—but they should."

Jewish wisdom was drawn upon to bring a family together in an episode of the popular animated series *The Simpsons*, when it is revealed that Krusty the Clown is Jewish. The episode focused on his estrangement from his father, a rabbi, and efforts by the Simpson children to reconcile father and son — by finding and quoting to the rabbi relevant *Talmudic* passages. They log hours upon hours at the library poring over Jewish texts, and they confront the rabbi with such gems as, "Does it not say in the Babylonian *Talmud* 'A child shall be pushed aside with the left hand and drawn closer with the right'?"

The Jewish languages of Hebrew and Yiddish have also been heard on popular TV in a variety of circumstances. In addition to Hebrew quotations from Jewish sources, the language appears most frequently in scenes of prayer, as during depictions of synagogue worship, chanting of the *Torah* and *haftarah*,[34] singing of such well-known blessings as those over wine and over bread, and recitation of such prayers as the *kaddish*. In many programs, familiar Hebrew words like *l'chayim* and *shalom* are spoken by both Jewish and non–Jewish characters. However, one program took the theme of cultural similarities and cooperation quite far when explaining that *shalom* means "Merry Christmas."[35]

The singing of songs is a universal form of expressing one's feelings and emotions. Although the words may be in Hebrew, when Jewish characters are depicted singing Jewish songs — in times of joy and times of sorrow and strife — they tap into a range of emotions. In the miniseries *Holocaust*, for instance, Berta Weiss, a music teacher in the Warsaw ghetto, teaches her students to sing "*Hatikvah*" (meaning "the hope"), Israel's soon-to-be national anthem, thereby relaying Jewish hope for the future even amidst the depths of the Holocaust. The changing moods during a terrorist hijacking were punctuated by Hebrew songs in the Entebbe movies. Hebrew *Shabbat* songs were sung by the hostages during their *Shabbat* in captivity, Israeli folk songs by Israeli commandos on the way to Entebbe, and songs of joy by the rescued hostages on their way home. Indeed, depictions of Israel are generally accompanied by Israeli-sounding music and much singing of folk songs and dancing of *horahs*, which add an element of buoyant energy.

Just as many Yiddishisms have made their way into the English language and dictionaries and have gained widespread popularity in everyday usage, so too have numerous Yiddish words and phrases frequented the prime-time television scene. Many of these words might be familiar to the general viewer — words such as *meshugenneh*, *oy vay*, and *mazel tov*.[36]

Besides these isolated words, some of the sounds of Yiddish — the nuances, music, inflections, and mannerisms — have been transmitted through more lengthy conversations in a number of programs. It was no surprise to hear a Yiddish conversation in the 1983 miniseries *The Winds of War* among a group of Polish Jews, for example. Of greater interest and significance, however, due to their unexpected and seemingly incongruous setting, were the frequent Yiddish conversations in episodes of the police drama series *Cagney & Lacey*. Such conversations often took place between Lieutenant Samuels and Officer Coleman, two middle-aged men who seemed unlikely to speak fluent Yiddish. The significance of such portrayals lies in their potential for dispelling preconceived stereotypical notions about Jewish characters and characteristics. As evidenced by their conversations — on such topics as the lamentable decline in the quality of *challah* these days — these ordinary-looking American men, in a profession not widely associated with Jews, nonetheless display affectionate ties to their heritage, their language, and their history.

A renowned and colorful aspect of Yiddish was brought out on a number of shows: Yiddish curses, which are not expletives but are picturesque aphorisms of stinging wit and originality. On *The Waltons*, Ted Lapinsky recalls how his grandfather protected him from neighborhood bullies — frightening them by vehemently hurling such favorites as, "May you grow like an onion — with your head in the ground"; "If you were twice as smart, you'd still be an idiot"; "You should inherit a hotel with a thousand rooms and be found dead in every room." On an episode of *Little House on the Prairie*, an elderly craftsman wishes on an outspoken anti–Semite, "May all his teeth fall out, except one — and in that one he should get a toothache."

Yiddish songs also made their way to the small screen in prime-time on two comedies of the 1960s. In an episode of *Gomer Pyle, U.S.M.C.*, a Jewish grandmother teaches Gomer the old Yiddish theater song *"Di Grineh Kuzine"* by singing it for him; they then sing it together in Yiddish. More Yiddish singing lessons take place in an episode of *Car 54, Where Are You?* where a non–Jewish, formerly stodgy architect learns and sings *"Oyf'n Pripetchik."*

Yiddish language and culture were central characters on PBS's *American Playhouse* in "Yiddish," a segment of a dramatic trilogy, *The Sunset Gang*, about the lives of elderly Jews in a Florida retirement community. Based on the short stories of Warren Adler and airing in 1991, "Yiddish" told with poignancy and humor the story of a man and a woman, long married to others, who meet at the Sunset Village Yiddish Club. Drawn together by their shared, burgeoning love for Yiddish, they find themselves falling in love — as they exchange playful and romantic *bon mots* in the language. In a dignified and unusual portrait of older American Jews, the two must decide whether to leave their respective mates and respectable lives to forge a new, exciting life together.

While this program was uncommon in many regards, its nod to Yiddish was not. Through the speaking and singing of Hebrew and Yiddish, and the quoting of biblical, Talmudic, and other Jewish texts — by Jewish and non–Jewish characters alike — television viewers have been exposed to the sounds of Jewish wisdom and languages.

* * *

The depiction on popular TV of just about every Jewish rite and ritual, lore and tradition bespeaks a broad-based and ongoing American interest in questions of religious identity and observance. For given the inherent constraints of TV as a mass medium to appeal to a broad-spectrum audience, the inclusion of so many aspects of a religious — indeed Jewish — nature, must tap into a sense of familiarity, recognition, and acceptance on the part of viewers.

Perhaps a part of this acceptance lies in the way these rites and rituals are portrayed. In nearly every case, they are presented as pleasant and ennobling, and they bestow strength, harmony, fulfillment, and sense of identity upon those who observe them. Even when it is the root of conflict — between the generations, for instance — the sense of a fundamental need for some kind of religious identity is not undermined.

If Americans can relate to the broad notion of religion as a normal and beneficent part of life, the particular aspect of Jewish rituals is brought into that larger framework in a variety of ways. For one thing, non–Jews nearly always participate in the portrayed ceremonies, usually learning and respecting, frequently joining in or even leading. Often, Jewish rituals are explained in Christian terms, so they seem less foreign and more understandable. In *The Partridge Family*, for instance, the Jewish blessing over the bread, *Hamotzi*, is explained by the comment, "It's like grace." And on *Archie Bunker's Place*, Stephanie tells non–Jews that her *bat mitzvah* "is like confirmation."

While at times preliminary explanations are couched in Christian terms, the depictions of the ceremonies unabashedly display their distinctively Jewish character. More often than not, this is accompanied with detailed explanation — as in the *Dr. Kildare seder*. There are times, not surprisingly, when dramatic license rides roughshod with accuracy and authenticity. This is particularly regrettable when alterations could be made without any diminution of dramatic effect.

By placing Jewish religious expressions within a familiar context and then explaining them with more specificity and detail, these programs offer an opportunity for learning about a way of life with which most Americans have little direct contact. Or, by linking a tangible, familiar symbol of Judaism to a larger Jewish theme in the program, it is possible for new information and knowledge to be transmitted to the viewer.

The presence of non–Jews observing, participating in, and learning about the wide spectrum of Jewish life and practices aids in that transmission, providing viewers with a strong message about the acceptance of Jews and Jewish customs. Popular TV heroes Dr. Kildare, Archie Bunker, Paladin, the Flying Nun, Gomer Pyle, and Hawkeye Pierce all exuberantly taking part in Jewish rituals, comprise a picture of America at its self-envisioned ideal, redolent with genuine interfaith interest, tolerance, and openness.

The palette of Jewish rites and rituals presented on popular TV provides an encompassing glimpse of Jewish life. In this kaleidoscope of depictions, with only a few exceptions, the Jewish rites and holidays are portrayed with respect and sincerity, and the character involved in it displays an attachment and affection for it. Indeed, Jewish rites and rituals, lore and traditions, inform the lives of a great variety of Jewish characters in such diverse ways: Jewish police speaking Yiddish, a young girl celebrating her *bat mitzvah*, a Jewish peddler quoting *Talmud*, a woman rabbi conducting a *brit bat*, Jews in the Warsaw Ghetto concerned about *kashrut*, a bride explaining *mikveh*, and on and on. It has been shown to touch on every aspect of life: food, clothing, speech, the calendar, birth, death, knowledge, and identity.

That religion and religious observance is a good and natural part of American life is presented as axiomatic. That Jewish rites, rituals, lore and traditions are presented so positively within this framework attests to television's recognition of religious pluralism and respect for ethnic diversity, as it acknowledges Judaism both for its distinctiveness and for the universal messages that it imparts.

2

Encountering America

The picture of diversity that television offers of religious practices and expression extends to its view of the human fabric of America as well. Mirroring the nation's ethnic mosaic, TV programs have portrayed characters from a panoply of backgrounds and cultures. Within this diversity, Americans are nearly always shown to be pursuing together (with the exception of the show's villains) the common good.

This balancing act between diversity and unity is the paradox and challenge of America and is reflected on its TV shows. Here, scenarios and plotlines allow for the possibility of both commonality and distinctiveness, tolerance and limits, tribal and national affinities. Within this picture, Jewish characters — as a distinctive minority with a rich heritage, culture, and religion — are key players. The Jewish experience in America, while in some sense unique, serves as a paradigm for the dynamic and delicate process of encountering America.

The active, long-standing involvement of Jews in American life has been a source of real-life dramas and, naturally it follows, those that imbue popular TV. It was centuries ago that the rendezvous of America and its Jewish population began, something to which television has paid significant attention.

The Jewish Experience in Early America

Prime-time television's portrayal of the Jewish experience in early America has covered nearly two centuries of Jewish immigration, involvement, history, adjustment, and integration in this country — ranging from Revolutionary War times through the era of mass immigration to the United States in the early twentieth century.

In most of these depictions, the focus is on the immigrant's struggle to maintain Jewish traditions and identity in the face of a new, expansive culture; the importance and difficult challenge of finding a Jewish mate among the paucity of Jews in early America; and the immigrant's struggle to survive amidst the harsh and sometimes violent conditions encountered in the new land.

Some of the earliest TV depictions of Jews in American history spotlighted their part in the spiritual growth of America and their role as patriots contributing to the birth and both the unity and diversity of the nation. Although the Jewish presence in America predated the Revolutionary War period by more than a century,[1] this era was to be the earliest setting of television's depictions of the Jewish experience in America. A 1956 episode of the anthology series *Crossroads*, which presented dramatized biographies of real-life clergy, chronicles the story of Rabbi Gershom Seixas,[2] whose outspoken sermons against the British during the Colonial period incurred their wrath and endangered his life. In this dramatized version of his story, taking place in 1776, Rabbi Seixas quotes Jewish sources in his sermons in support of his anti–British stance[3]; he is praised by the narrator as "a man of God" and "a patriot of freedom." Under constant threat of capture and hanging, Seixas flees from his temple in New York to a congregation in Philadelphia. Impelled by his strong sense of rabbinic obligation, he later returns to New York under great personal danger to perform a Jewish wedding.

Religious obligation and convictions guided the actions of another rabbi whose role in American history was portrayed in a different *Crossroads* segment that aired the same year. Here the setting was the Civil War, and the story was of the real-life Rabbi Arnold Fischel. A young Jewish soldier named Dan, fighting for the Union Army, is mortally wounded while saving the life of Cable, his Christian comrade-in-arms. When Dan utters his last request — to have a Jewish chaplain pray with him and comfort him — his brother Nathan, also a Union soldier, searches for one in vain. With only a Catholic chaplain in sight, Dan dies without such spiritual comfort.

Terribly upset over "why there was no Jewish chaplain to pray with Dan," Cable sends a letter that reaches Rabbi Fischel. Cable explains his distress and that of Dan's brother Nathan, who "figured he was fighting for freedom and equal rights. Only if that's true he can't see why there weren't any Jewish chaplains around."

Fischel requests a chaplaincy assignment from the secretary of war, who turns it down citing an Act of Congress that states, "Chaplains appointed by vote of field officers or company commanders must be ordained ministers of the Christian denominations." After much effort, the rabbi successfully brings the matter to the attention of President Lincoln, who expresses his "grave concern" and agrees to "do everything possible to expedite a new law that includes all faiths."

In a melodramatic ending but one that tries to underscore the need for Jewish chaplains and the historic importance of Fischel's efforts, the rabbi goes off to the front, arriving just in time to comfort Nathan, who has been shot. The narrator's voice explains that eventually there came official word from the

War Department "authorizing the appointment of Brigade Chaplains of Protestant, Catholic, and Jewish faith."[4] The program's intent to depict Jews as part of the normal fabric of America was underscored by the narrator's final words, lauding those "men who believed that freedom was good only when it belonged to everyone, regardless of his faith."

Jews on the American Frontier

These portraits of Jews participating in the spiritual growth of a new nation have not been the only picture of Jews in early America; several programs portrayed their role in the physical growth of the nation through the settling of the American frontier. A 1954 episode of the *Philco TV Playhouse* told the story of one Jewish family's struggles with frontier life after seizing upon a government land grant program in the Dakotas.[5] The show portrayed Hungarian immigrants Lanie and Bela Kleinfeld of Chicago, who decide to adopt this pioneering spirit, driven in part to be with Americans, "not only with greenhorns."[6] The Kleinfelds give up their home; take their three children, Ilanka, Yanushka, and Rachel; and go to Dakota to settle the land. Although they were promised land rich for planting, they find bitterly harsh conditions[7] alleviated only by the kindness of a distant neighbor, Sven Andersen, who happens by and helps them build their home.

After a long winter of seclusion, Sven comes to greet his neighbors in the spring and declares his love for Ilanka. But when their parents meet at the Kleinfeld home, Lanie — who longs to meet "real Americans" — is bitterly disappointed when Sven's parents turn out to be greenhorns from Norway. Her hysterical outburst drives the Andersens from her home. Bela, outraged and ashamed of his wife's behavior, runs out of the house to spend the night in a shed, which catches fire during a storm, killing him. In a representation of the various elements mingling on the frontier, his grave is marked with a tombstone made from a buffalo's skull that is engraved with a Jewish star and the letters BK and a tree from Norway that Sven plants.

Soon after, Lanie invites Sven to join them in the celebration of Passover even though, as she explains in her broken English, "it won't be great feast because we have no food, but will be a celebration." She goes on to tell him that Passover is a "celebration of Jews going free from long time suffering in Egypt. Is time when all our people come together for feast of Thanksgiving for coming safe to the promised land." When Sven arrives for the festive meal, the three children greet him in Yiddish, saying *"Gut Yuntif,"* he dons a yarmulke (seeing Yanushka wearing one), and the family explains the Passover symbols to him. An American Indian family arrives and joins in the celebration; Lanie had helped the wife give birth.

This picture of diversity — American Indians, Norwegian newcomers, and

Hungarian Jewish immigrants — seems to encapsulate a vision of the American melting pot, as various cultures come harmoniously together. (Indeed, the very title of this episode, "And Crown Thy Good," evokes a sense of American community, taken as it is from the hymn "America the Beautiful," in which it is followed by the words "with brotherhood.") Yet, it all takes place within the setting of a Jewish ritual. The Jewish family has, despite great hardships and dangers throughout the show, unremittingly maintained its own laws and traditions, reciting Hebrew prayers, speaking Yiddish, wearing yarmulkes, and celebrating Jewish holidays. At a time in the 1950s when assimilation was an overriding impulse, this television show seems to reject the concept of a melting pot and argues for maintaining diversity while accepting the differences of others — a notion more attuned to the 1990s than the 1950s. Indeed, Yanushka seems to express this very idea when he lauds his mother for partaking in this multicultural gathering and for at last accepting the cultures of others while not abandoning her own. She earns from him what is for her the ultimate compliment: "Now you're really an American."

Jewish characters maintaining their Jewish identity and observances continued to be depicted in the 1960s, when Western series became the predominant genre of popular TV. A plethora of TV Westerns provided an opportunity to depict yet another aspect of the Jewish experience in early America, namely the Old West.

Amidst depictions of the rough and sometimes violent conditions of pioneer America emerged a picture of the Jew as the personification of lawfulness and civilization, fighting anarchy and lawlessness at every turn. In these shows, the Jewish characters draw on their heritage, beliefs, and memories of past persecutions in Europe to attempt to bring a modicum of civility and lawful behavior to the wild new land.

This theme infused the earliest depiction of a Jewish character on a Western series. The series was *Have Gun, Will Travel*, which featured the kindly and erudite gunslinger Paladin, and the 1960 episode portrayed Russian Jewish immigrants, Nathan and Rivka Shotness, father and daughter, he a peddler and mail carrier, she a nineteen-year-old. Trouble begins when Nathan witnesses a murder; he is determined to testify against the murderer despite threats against his life. Fearing for his safety and unbeknownst to him, Rivka hires Paladin to protect him. But Nathan, denouncing vigilante justice, is angry when he learns of this, and in the mistaken belief that Paladin is a hired killer rails at him, "For this, we come to Columbus' country — to hire killers and become as bad as they are?" His confidence in the law and its procedures is underlined when he quotes *Mishnah* to Paladin, "Pray for the welfare of the authorities; if not for the fear thereof, men would swallow each other alive."[8]

Despite warnings from Paladin to stay at home for reasons of safety, Nathan refuses to be intimidated, recalling past persecutions as a source of strength and warning. "In Kishinev,[9] when the Cossaks slaughtered my wife, she was also sitting home behind locked doors," he tells Paladin. "The Angel of Death doesn't need an excuse. When your time comes, either you meet him or he meets you." Nathan is confident in his approach; he even seems to enjoy toying with the bandits, setting up a decoy to set them on a false trail in what he calls a "game of chess."

But when the surrounding lawlessness becomes so overwhelming — the bandits kidnap Rivka and threaten to kill her if he testifies — Nathan begins to doubt his reliance on the law and bitterly questions his own approach. He acridly suggests to Paladin, employing imagery of the Hebrew Bible in which he is steeped, that they should have finished off the bandits when they had the chance. "Maybe *their* way is the right one. Maybe our father Jacob was a fool. When Esau came after him he should have met him in ambush, eh, instead of going out to meet him alone?" It is then Paladin who lends Nathan the courage of his earlier and fundamental convictions by replying, "You know Jacob could never step into Esau's skin. Didn't he try it once? And what did his father say? '*Ha-kol kol Ya'acov, v'hayadayim y'dei Esav.*' 'The hands are the hands of Esau. But the voice, the voice is Jacob's'."[10] With Paladin's help, Nathan testifies, Rivka is rescued, the bandits are routed, and the murderer is sent to jail.

All this takes place amidst a setting of a rich tapestry of Jewish life, which demonstrates the Shotnesses' continued adherence to tradition, even in their new land. Rivka tells Paladin she hired him because his name gave her confidence: "In the holy tongue it has a very favorable meaning: *Pala*, 'wonder'; *Din*, 'judgement.'" Nathan and Paladin repeatedly discuss various references to the Hebrew Bible and the *Talmud*, demonstrating both Nathan's depth of Judaic knowledge and affiliation and Paladin's familiarity with things Jewish.

The travails of the Shotnesses were revisited in a *Have Gun, Will Travel* episode that aired the following season, in which Rivka is about to marry a meek scholar, Russian immigrant Faivel Melamed. Paladin is invited but learns that the wedding is severely threatened by a gang headed by the murderer who had been convicted on Nathan's testimony (a corrupt judge was bribed for his release). In this episode, it is Rivka who is most adamant about not succumbing to the threats of outlaws. Although Nathan, fearful for his daughter and the wedding ceremony, advises the couple to go off to be married somewhere else, the bride and groom are determined to proceed with the ceremony at home. When the outlaws arrive with their destructive force, shattering windows and disrupting the wedding, Paladin, Nathan, and Faivel fight them off and the wedding proceeds.

In fighting off the bandits, Nathan and Faivel demonstrate that the Jew's oft-depicted advocacy of law and reason has its limits when faced with utter anarchy. This dual aspect of television's frontier Jews was projected in an episode of another popular Western of the 1960s, *Wagon Train*. Jewish immigrant Simon Levy and his family join the wagon train, and Simon enters into a not-so-friendly rivalry over checkers with another aficionado of the game and member of the westward caravan, Patrick McGowan. Their quarreling is abruptly set aside when a band of gunmen informs the wagon train they must pay heavily in order to cross through an important pass. McGowan says the wagon train should forge ahead and confront the gunmen. Levy, however, advises that the matter be discussed and is publicly branded a coward and shunned by the others. Their stances are reversed after they witness one of the gunmen set fire to a settler's wagon and then shoot him down. At a meeting, McGowan urges that payment be made. Levy, on the other hand, passionately expresses his revulsion at seeing this type of violence in a free country. Like Nathan Shotness, he calls up memories of the old country as a source of courage and determination in his new one, telling everyone about his life as a Jew there and declaring that he will now fight for his rights and freedom in his new, free country. Warning the group that if they pay the gunmen now, they will be paying people like them for the rest of their lives, Simon convinces the wagon train to forge ahead and take on the gunmen. He takes an active role in the subsequent shootout that vanquishes the would-be extortionists.

This theme has been explored in the context of generations, where the older authority figures insist on law and religious custom but their children are driven by the surroundings to different reactions. Such a clash, as TV's Jewish frontier families seek to reconcile faithfulness to tradition with response to threats in a dangerous young America, was the basis for an episode of the long-running Western series *Bonanza*. In this 1963 episode, peddler Aaron Kaufman and his daughter Rebecca stop to sell some wares at the Ponderosa, the sprawling ranch on which the Cartwrights — the show's central characters — live. While Aaron is discussing some purchases with Ben Cartwright, the patriarch of the family, his son Adam, who has taken a liking to Rebecca, shows her around the ranch. Observers of *Shabbat*, the Kaufmans hurriedly leave as Friday evening approaches but find that they cannot make it home in time and must pull off the road midway. Adam, who has come after them to extend an invitation to a Cartwright party in their honor, learns of their plan to spend the Sabbath in the middle of nowhere and decides to watch over them from a short distance. Two bandits, however, knock Adam unconscious and disrupt the Kaufmans in the middle of prayers and rob them, as Rebecca perturbedly watches her father take no action to interfere. Assuming Aaron has a great deal more money hidden, the gunmen tie up all three in the sun hoping that the torture will lead Aaron to speak up. When Adam suggests to Aaron a way of subduing their captors by telling them that he will get them the money from a place where there is actually a gun hidden, Aaron declines, saying that he is opposed to any form of violence. But when the bandits threaten Rebecca, Aaron is moved to go along with the plan, and he shoots the bandits in self-defense. The generations are reconciled when Rebecca expresses appreciation of her father's courageous attitudes and value for their Judaic heritage.

The theme of Old West Jews adhering to tradition amidst challenges of brutal lawlessness continued into the 1970s on an episode of TV's longest-running Western series, *Gunsmoke*, set in 1880s Dodge City, Kansas. Here, too, the story involves a generational conflict, as the Gorofsky family, immigrants from Russia, are trekking west to make a new home on a farm. When Moshe Gorofsky, his wife, and three sons stop by the roadside for prayers, they are set upon by three drunk thugs, brothers, who lasso one of the sons, drag him a distance, and leave him. The boy is later found badly injured, and just before dying, tells his father, "Moses smote the rock and wasn't allowed to see the promised land[11] ... Papa, I'm never going to see the farm." The family's adherence to Jewish tradition and law is again demonstrated through their full observance of mourning rituals.

This adherence leads to dramatic conflict when series hero Marshal Matt Dillon asks Moshe to testify that the three men murdered his son. Moshe insists that he cannot do so and offers a lengthy explanation of why he cannot: "This is the *Talmud*. All of the rules governing the lives of our people are in here. It has survived for thousands of years, and much of it has been used by nations throughout the ages as the basis of law in every land. The *Talmud* teaches us that if a man sees his friend enter a house, and in his hand his friend holds a knife, then when this same friend comes out — the knife bloodied and in the house five dead people — the man who saw his friend come and go is not a witness to murder.... In order to accuse a human being of murder, you must see the knife strike."[12] Moshe is steadfast that what he witnessed — "My son was pulled away with a rope around his neck ... a few minutes later he is found, the rope still around his neck, his head crushed.... Then he dies" — was circumstantial evidence. His refusal to testify is hotly disputed by another son, Gearshon, but Moshe replies, "The law of the *Talmud* is the law of our people. There are no exceptions. No one is above that law. It has kept us alive for thousands of years. And it applies to us as if the boy who was killed was another man's child. And we will obey that law." Father and son continue to argue opposing philosophies until the family breaks up over the clash. Moshe remains unshaken by the consequences, explaining that he does not fear offending the men who killed his son but fears "offending ourselves, our traditions, our Lord."

In its exposition of these divergent views, *Gunsmoke* engages in a colloquy on the proper response to violence and lawlessness. The father's way is by adhering to the strict letter of the law, the son's by fighting back. They are not that different in their goals: both have a determination to maintain identity and pride, and both want justice. Gearshon's view is aired when he recalls the pogroms in Russia in which Jews were killed, saying, "I never understood why we let them.... They killed us anyway. What could they have done if we fought back?" When his mother reminds him that her brother fought back and was killed, Gearshon says at least "he died with dignity.... They knew he lived. He made them know." Gearshon goes on to express a concern representative of a view held by many Jews today the world over, namely that it is imperative to let those who would harm them "know that these things cannot happen here for *any* reason — because we will not let it."

Without diminishing the validity of this view, the program ultimately comes down on the side of Moshe. His stance is vindicated when the thugs who attacked the family confess that they had indeed roped and dragged the boy but then had dropped the rope and ran away. The boy had then apparently gotten up and ran. The rope became entangled between two rocks, pulled him down, and crushed his head. Although Moshe's *Talmudic* analogy may be imprecise (the thugs who roped and dragged Semel clearly contributed to his death), his very use of Jewish law in the wild Old West parallels its age-old and lasting civilizing influence on Western civilization.[13] That Jewish characters draw on this heritage in the lawless setting of TV Westerns underscores both the ongoing Jewish connection to that heritage and its adaptability and usefulness in a new American setting.

The Search for a Jewish Mate in the Old West

Rivka Shotness had troubles at her wedding but none, apparently, in finding a Jewish husband in the Old West. In a frontier setting, on *Have Gun, Will Travel*, she wed a Jewish man in a full, traditional Jewish ceremony. Other Jewish characters were not so fortunate, and their efforts to find Jewish mates where Jews were few and far between were the subject of some attention on popular TV. Their demonstrated determination to do so adds to the TV picture of frontier Jews as being devoted to their religious heritage and concerned about its survival.

Perhaps the most resolute was Rachel Miller, who appeared on an episode of *Here Come the Brides*, a Western series with a comic tinge that aired from 1968 to 1970. The show's premise, which took place in a Seattle logging camp in the 1870s, was the continuing happiness of one hundred prospective brides who had been sent from New Bedford, Massachusetts, to quell the loggers' rebellion over the dearth of women. If any one of the young women became unhappy and returned home during the first year, landowner and camp operator Jason Bolt would loose his land to a debtor with whom he had entered an intricate arrangement. Thus the camp is sent into an uproar when it is discovered that one of the brides, a Miss Rachel Miller, is a Jew who insists on marrying only a Jewish man — and there are none in Seattle. Everyone is fearful that the camp will be lost, and Rachel suffers the abuse of some former friends who recoil at her now-revealed Jewishness. Others in the camp, although not bigoted, are miffed at Rachel's insistence on find a Jewish mate, which jeopardizes the whole setup. But Jason's brother defends her stance saying, "She's a Jewish woman who wants to marry a Jewish man, and there's nothing wrong with that." To the rescue comes the discovery that the camp carpenter, with the unlikely name of Will Sullivan, is a Jew. Because the pool of Jewish men is limited to one, desperate matchmaking efforts ensue to pair Will and Rachel. All end in comic disasters, until the two finally fall in love and wed.

The search for Jewish mates in frontier America was depicted even in the late 1970s, on an episode of *Little House on the Prairie*, set in 1870s Minnesota. Here, the son of a widowed and ailing coffin maker explains to his father that "there isn't a Jewish girl for five hundred miles." Although the son does not want to leave his father (who insists on remaining near his wife's grave), he is impelled to return to New York City, where an aunt and uncle have found him a Jewish girl. While the father, too, does not want to be separated from his son, he insists that the son go so that he can marry a Jewish woman. The alternative of remaining and intermarrying is not even raised as a possibility.

This is quite a different picture from another episode of *Little House on the Prairie* that aired two years later. In the same setting, from the same departure point of the paucity of Jews on the frontier, a different young man takes a non–Jewish wife. Indeed, he defends his having done so to his disapproving father by explaining the predicament of young Jewish men on the frontier, saying, "What choice do we have? Jewish women can't travel alone; they stay in the cities." This situation doubtless contributed to the intermarriages of other of TV's frontier Jews, with Old West intermarriages depicted on such shows as *Rawhide, Wagon Train, Bonanza,* and *Philco TV Playhouse.*

The intermarriage depicted on *Rawhide* in 1962 stemmed less from any desire to assimilate than from the delight at finding another "outsider." Mendel Sorkin, an observant Jew who is vocally proud of his heritage, demonstrably observes *Shabbat* and *kashrut,* and attends regularly to prayers, falls in love with an American Indian woman, Wahkshum. She, separated from her Cheyenne tribe early in life and reared among white people who mistreat and abuse her, feels at home in neither the white nor the Indian world. This feeling of unbelonging is shared by Mendel, who came from Holland and tells Wahkshum, "I love this country. It's been very good to me. But I'm a stranger. Do you know what I mean? I'm an outsider. My ways are different.... My prayers are different." The suggested sense of kinship between these two outsiders is underscored when they decide to marry — and purchase "a little land of our own" on which to settle that is halfway between Cheyenne land and the white village.

Sometimes the differentness of the immigrant Jew in the Old West led to less harmonious conclusions. A number of TV shows dealt with anti–Semitism in frontier America and the efforts of Jews and supportive non–Jews to fight it. In another *Rawhide* episode that aired two years later, a character similar to Mendel is featured: an observant Jewish immigrant peddler, here named

Michob. The declarations of Michob's differentness come not so much from him as from those around him who resent it and react with angry bigotry.

Comparable reactions face the Jewish coffin maker whose son journeys to New York for a Jewish wife on *Little House on the Prairie*. Even a future Nobel laureate whose youth is fictionalized on an episode of *Bonanza* faces harassment from a bigoted teacher. With the help of series hero Ben Cartwright the student overcomes these obstacles, and the program informs viewers that Albert Michaelson grew up to become the first American to ever win a Nobel prize in science.

The contribution to American life made by a different Jewish immigrant was the subject of another *Bonanza* episode, which dramatized the life of Phillip Deidesheimer, the German-born mining engineer whose invention enabled miners to work farther into the earth and with greater safety.

One Old West Jewish immigrant who is neither a historical figure nor a victim of bigotry but provides guidance, strength, and optimism to a troubled youth appeared in a 1966 episode of *The Virginian*. Jake is a former rabbi, now owner of a tailor shop on a Wyoming Territory town called Shiloh. He befriends a teenage boy, Johnny Younce, who had previously smashed the window of his shop and set fires to other stores. Johnny explains his frustration to Jake, saying that since he is poor and his girlfriend Susan McDevitt is of a high social standing, her father will not let them see each other, despite the fact that they love each other. When the young couple learns that Susan is pregnant and have nowhere else to turn, they go to Jake, who marries them. Jake's compassion influences the others, as they come to accept the couple and the boy improves his ways.

That this rabbi alone was able to bring reconciliation and understanding to a torn and troubled frontier family, even to a non–Jewish family, bespeaks his ability to bring old wisdom to very new circumstances. He is yet one more facet of TV's Old West Jewish characters, who—armed with Jewish tradition, knowledge, and heritage—seek to bring lawfulness, justice, and compassion to the American Frontier.

Ellis Island and the Lower East Side

While television has portrayed the less well known phenomenon of Jews in the Old West, it has also depicted what is perhaps most commonly associated with the Jewish immigrant experience in America: the early twentieth-century arrivals at Ellis Island and life on New York City's Lower East Side.

The great waves of immigration of this era brought large numbers of Jews, mostly from Eastern Europe, as well as, of course, many other ethnic groups. This was the era of the melting pot, and for Jewish immigrants, a whole different set of circumstances awaited them from those depicted on shows about the early frontier. While Old West Jews faced a rural setting, where they were at times viewed askance for being different but were able to maintain their customs, the Lower East Side thrust Jewish immigrants into the urban, industrialized world, where the imperatives to survive and achieve the American Dream often overrode attachments to religious traditions.

Thus, while TV has depicted frontier Jews as observant and often meek, peddler types, the TV immigrant Jew emerging from the Lower East Side is cast quite differently. For most of these characters, particularly those of the younger generation, the primary concern is not the maintaining of religious tradition amidst difficult circumstances but its virtual casting aside, as they strive to ascend the social ladder and become Americans. Indeed, among these families, conflict between the generations is heightened and more extreme amidst the strong assimilationist pressures and the sudden proximity of a host of other ethnic groups.

This picture of assimilation at an extreme, along with the portrayal of a potpourri of various ethnic groups interacting in early twentieth-century New York, was featured in the 1984 miniseries *Ellis Island*. The program focuses on four immigrants — a Russian Jew, an Italian, and two Irish sisters — who meet on a ship bound for America. Jacob Rubenstein, the Russian Jew, has managed to escape the pogroms of Russia that claimed the lives of other family members and is determined to make the best of his new, free life in America by putting his past behind him. Propelled by great ambitions for success and an innate musical talent, he succeeds in becoming a famous, sought-after, and wealthy songwriter. He also engineers a fairly full detachment from his heritage, changing his name to Jake Rubin, marrying a Gentile woman, and generally disregarding his history and roots. This TV character has a strong basis in reality, representing the route taken by a number of Jewish musicians who came to America via Ellis Island and went on to fame and fortune while neglecting and often forgetting their Judaic heritage and ties[14] — except perhaps for an occasional life-cycle event: in this program a Jewish funeral briefly shown when Jake's daughter dies.

Jake Rubin was a more recent and less amiable incarnation of the striving-to–Americanize immigrant who appeared in the form of the character Hyman Kaplan, first brought to TV in 1954 on a segment of the *Studio One* anthology series, in the television play *The Education of H*Y*M*A*N* K*A*P*L*A*N**. Although widely assumed to be Jewish, Hyman displays no ostensible act of religious observance or identification throughout the entire program, though he abounds in "Jewishisms": he bears a Jewish-sounding name, has a distinct Yiddish accent, and is employed as a garment worker. The story depicts Hyman's quaint, earnest, although sometimes bumbling and comical efforts to learn about his new country and its ways and history and to become a successful part of it. When he asks his boss (a cousin) for a raise, he receives a reproach instead. "Why haven't you become an American in the

three years you've been here?" rails the cousin, insisting that he "go to school
and learn American" before any raise is considered. Hyman takes off to night
school, studying civics and English in a classroom full of appropriately appor-
tioned ethnics. His consuming pursuit of America and complete lack of any
expressed interest in his own religion and background paints a strong picture
of assimilation. But Hyman's throttling toward Americanization raises questions even in his own mind, and these are telescoped in a story he tells in class
as part of a recitation assignment. After paying homage to Washington and
Lincoln, whom he much admires, Hyman tells of another whom he considers
to be a great American — his dear friend Jake, the hardworking delicatessen
owner, who recently got sick and died. The funeral was on Wednesday, a working day, and Hyman expresses his dilemma: "In the old country, this wouldn't
be a problem; I would go. But in America, they always say business before
pleasure, so I don't go to Jake Popper's funeral, with regret." Although he ultimately fails the class, he is undeterred in his determination to succeed, expressing delight at having learned for the sake of learning. In a final gift to the class,
Hyman presents them with a picture of Jake Popper, which he hangs in the
classroom between portraits of Washington and Lincoln, elevating the deli
owner to the pantheon of American heroes in a gesture meant to reconcile old
and new values.

An even more explicit presentation of the push and pull faced by Jewish
newcomers devoted to tradition but compelled to make a living under the harsh
conditions of immigrant America was portrayed in the 1979 made-for-TV
movie *The Triangle Factory Fire Scandal*. Dramatizing the infamous 1911 fire
in the New York City garment factory, which claimed the lives of scores of
young immigrant women, the program focuses on a generational conflict
within a Jewish family that encapsulates these opposing strains. Sonya, a young
Jewish woman, incurs her father's wrath when she leaves synagogue on a Friday night under the pretext of being sick and is then seen dancing at the wedding of a Catholic friend. In the ensuing explosive discussion, they argue over
the changes that life in America is bringing, including Sonya's working at the
Triangle Factory on *Shabbat*. She reminds her father, "You said yourself it's
work or starve." Still, he laments the changes, and expressing the immigrant's
fear of loss of heritage, states, "Work or starve — it's the *goyim's* country. In the
old country, it was different — everybody was like a family. The proper ways
were obeyed. But here, all kinds of people, each with their different ways —
and what is happening to ours?" Sonya, voicing the divergent view, which
embraces the immigrant's hope that hard work will lead to success and achievement and all its envisioned possibilities, replies, "We can dream. We can be
anything we want." In this dialectic pull between allegiance to heritage and the
magnetism and attraction of a new world, Sonya and her father squabble over
degree of observance, but questions of leaving the faith or of intermarrying do
not even enter the picture.

2. *Encountering America*

Yet other of TV's immigrant families faced these issues. The 1985 mini-series *Evergreen*, a family saga beginning in 1909 and spanning several decades, traced the lives and loves of Joseph and Anna Friedman from their years of poverty as children on the Lower East Side through their marriage (along with Anna's affair and its consequences), Joseph's stunning success in business, their subsequent opulent life, and the lives of their children and grandchildren. Joseph is a deeply religious man and very observant Jew, but his greatest hope is to send his son to an Ivy League school. Once there, the son meets and marries a non–Jewish woman, to the supreme chagrin of his infuriated father. The son's abandonment of Judaism stands in sharp contrast to Joseph's continued fervent observance, even after his beloved — although disowned — son is killed in a car accident. *Evergreen*'s presentation of an immigrant who, while striving for and achieving great business success and enduring family tragedy, holds fast to his religious beliefs and traditions and resists assimilation represents the opposite of what many immigrants believed they had to give up in order to succeed. Joseph's way, however, is not emulated by the next generation, and his son's intermarriage and break with the past suggests that relentless assimilationist forces will have their day. Only when the grandson — who was raised in early childhood by his non–Jewish and anti–Semitic grandparents and later by the Friedmans — decides enthusiastically to go to Israel upon graduating from college is there a sense that a kind of ethnic pride and attachment can emerge unexpectedly and exist within the American milieu.

The intermarrying son on *Evergreen* was surpassed in his flight from Judaism by another child of immigrants portrayed in the 1979 miniseries *Studs Lonigan*. Chronicling immigrant life in Chicago from 1916 to 1930, the program tells the tale of a Jewish and an Irish family, focusing a great deal on the ethnic hatred between the two groups. Here a young Jewish man, to the extreme distress of his parents, converts to Catholicism and weds a Catholic woman, saying both actions are the best thing that ever happened to him.

It is not love but violence that drives a young Jewish immigrant to abandon Judaism in a 1961 program about crime solving on the Lower East Side of the 1920s, *The Lawless Years*. (This was a short-lived series that predated by six months the well-known, long-running hit *The Untouchables*). In a four-episode arc,[15] a Russian immigrant swears vengeance after his sister is brutally attacked and then goes mad, turning him from the life of a rabbinical student to the world of organized crime, where he becomes an underworld kingpin. Thus, Louis Kassofsky becomes Louy K and achieves Americanization in a less conventional way but one that some real-life immigrant Jews chose: forming within organized crime what came to be known as the "kosher nostra."[16] Louy's actions are shown to be a disgrace to the Jewish community and are uniformly denounced by its members, including series hero Barney Ruditsky, veteran detective of the New York City Gangster Squad and coreligionist, who angrily tells Louy, "You're a disgrace, to your family, your race, and to anyone that ever was your friend." His sister's fate shapes his own, once again, when she dies (her Jewish funeral is depicted) and Louy is crushed, leading him to question his life in the crime world. After deciding to leave the life of crime and give his $10 million to charity, Louy revisits the old neighborhood, wanders amidst the pushcarts of Orchard street, and encounters an old family acquaintance, a fish peddler, who urges him to "go into the old *shul*. For old time's sake.... It would make a lot of people happy." As Louy climbs the synagogue steps, he is gunned down by a burst of machine-gun fire in a gangland hit, and as he lies bleeding on the steps, the worshippers within emerge to carry his dying body into the synagogue. Although Louy dies upon his return to the synagogue, this may be more a function of dramatic imperatives of early TV crime dramas compelled to show the punishment of crime than of any philosophical statement. In fact, this final scene of Louy's approaching the synagogue seems to suggest that he was able to find a way back to his heritage, despite his having gone far from it in a life wholly antithetical to its values. The role of both communal censure in the voice of Detective Ruditsky and disapproving family members, and of communal encouragement in the words of the fish peddler in effecting such a return is shown to be an important factor of Jewish immigrant life.

The Early Picture as Prelude

Indeed, while this strand — the call to tradition — has been amply depicted, a whole variety of immigrants' reactions to American life has been shown, as newcomers seek to strike a balance between life in the old country and their future in America. Assimilation, intermarriage, fright, and the seeking after adventure, fame, and fortune have all been part of that picture.

In presenting these approaches, television has often proclaimed the virtues of assimilation and sympathetically portrayed the Jewish immigrant's Americanization and striving toward the opportunities of America that Europe lacked. The overriding depiction of America is of a golden land of countless opportunities, as it indeed was for these immigrants, in which they could take full advantage of its openness and freedoms — religious, economic, political, social — to achieve things they never could in their countries of origin. For many, the most prudent and expeditious means of achieving their goals was to assimilate into the melting pot of immigrant life in America, with a concomitant departure from religious heritage.

Television has presented many such examples of the strong pull toward assimilating into the melting pot of America. This is hardly surprising, given that television is often considered to be a prime agent of that very process, a medium that — in its need to appeal to a mass audience — stresses familiarity and unifying American values. Owing to its ubiquitousness and pervasiveness, permeating the entire nation and exposing audiences to the same programs and thus the same messages and images, television can be called the ultimate symbol of a melting pot society.

At the same time, the immigrant's path has not been shown to be a simple or one-sided dash to Americanization. Conflicts, both within families and within the individual, over allegiance to tradition, heritage, and a sometimes opposing set of values have been shown to comprise a dialectic pull that faced Jewish immigrants. Varying levels of observance are an oft-depicted bone of contention. While there were indeed many immigrants who saw the need to abandon any ties to religious observance in order to be part of the American melting pot, others have been portrayed as believing that severing such ties was not a condition upon which integration into American society depended. In a number of programs, characters exhibited varying degrees of religious ties to Judaism, and some maintained a strong connection to their roots and heritage while expressing the importance of adhering to one's own religious beliefs.

Whether peopling the pushcart-filled streets of the Lower East Side or the towns and prairies of Colonial and frontier America, television's Jewish immigrant characters comprise a fascinating and diverse picture of the Jewish experience in an earlier America. (Indeed, an often overlooked aspect of American history — Jews in frontier America — was repeatedly explored on TV Westerns long before the popular film *The Frisco Kid*, a touching comedy about a Jewish peddler heading West.) Their involvement in so many diverse aspects of American life — providing rabbinic assistance for the Revolutionary War, homesteading in the Dakotas, inventing scientific innovations, being responsible for chaplains of all faiths being allowed to serve in the military — reflect the extended Jewish roots in this country. Their presence reflects a picture of an America open to religious pluralism; their depicted problems suggest the conflicts arising when cultures clash, when new challenges and opportunities face old traditions.

While facing such challenges, TV's Jewish immigrants, for the most part, maintained a sense of connection to their traditions and heritage, while adapting to and succeeding in America — an America ultimately shown to be hospitable to Jews and Judaism and in turn built up by the presence, values, and actions of its early Jewish citizens.

Jews in the South

In tandem with America's hospitality to Jews and Judaism has been popular television's receptivity to a diverse and wide ranging cast of Jewish characters and sensibilities. Over the course of its history, TV has portrayed Jews of nearly every background, political leaning, economic status, age, sexual orientation, and profession.

Such a vast scope extends not just to character types but to geographical moorings as well. Jews portrayed on television have hailed from every corner of the nation, despite some ingrained notions about Jews hailing predominantly from Northeastern urban centers. So prevalent is this myopic view — of Jews only as urbanites — that it was satirized on an episode of *Murphy Brown*. Miles Silverberg, executive producer of the fictional *FYI* news magazine show, is introduced to visitors from a small town in Middle America, who after exclaiming that Silverberg is a Jewish name, explain to their children "This man is Jewish. It's a wonderful and rare religion practiced in big cities." As well as in myriad small towns across the landscape of television's America.

Indeed, in one small Mississippi town, a synagogue was vandalized. Charges of anti–Semitism and cover-ups embroiled the local police force. Violence from the past is dredged up as issues of racism and tolerance confront the town's Christian and Jewish, black and white citizens. Sounding like the subject of a major newspaper exposé, this was actually the story line of an episode of *In the Heat of the Night*.

Situated in the fictional Mississippi town of Sparta, the program sets at odds the town sheriff and the local rabbi, Hillel Feldman. When the two confront each other over transgressions past and present — revolving around the desecration of the synagogue — the stage is set for an unusual exploration of human feelings relating to these issues. In particular, the show provides a gripping angle on the life of Jews in America's South and the question of their grappling with a particular form of indigenous, sub-rosa anti–Semitism.

While this episode brought TV's picture of Jews in the South to new dramatic heights, the subject has had an interesting history on American television. A three-part arc on *I'll Fly Away*, a critically acclaimed but short-lived series set in the fictional Southern town of Bryland, follows the story as one of its lead characters, a teen-aged boy, dates a Jewish girl. This subjects both of them to anti–Semitic harassment.

Similar prejudices, with more lethal results, infused the TV movie titled *The Murder of Mary Phagan*, which dramatized the real-life story of the 1913 Atlanta lynching of Leo Frank, falsely accused of the murder of a young girl. Frank's status as a Jew from the North — he was born in Brooklyn — was depicted as a factor that further aroused and fueled the natives' fear and wrath.

A similar hint of the notion of Jew as "outside Northerner" informed the medical series *Buck James*, in which a Texas hospital hires a top-notch surgeon — with several strikes against her. She is a woman, she's Jewish, and she hails from the East Coast. Part of the series' drama arose from her struggling to overcome these obstacles.

A more benign picture of life for Jews in the South appeared in the wonderfully unconventional comedy series *Frank's Place*. Set in New Orleans, the show featured an ensemble of marvelous characters, including Jewish lawyer Bubba Weisberger, a close friend and confidante of the show's African

American main character (who was in fact shown spending a *Shabbat* and Chanukah celebration with Bubba). The show even touched on issues of assimilation (as did *I'll Fly Away*) and of differences between Sephardic and Ashkenazic Jews — with some characters raising arguments about who settled in the South first.

One more TV movie that portrayed both the belonging and the precariousness of Jews in the South was *Summer of My German Soldier*. Here a Jewish family — with problems of its own — runs a small goods store and, dependent upon a healthy flow of customers, must politely swallow small anti–Semitic insults that later erupt into open hostility for other reasons. In this show, as in several others depicting Jews in the South, there is a decided linking of blacks and Jews as outsiders who are supportive of each other in a hostile environment.

While such shows cannot, of course, provide a detailed and scholarly picture of Jews in the South, they do hint at the interesting and particular lives of Jews in a region not conventionally associated with Jewish population centers. Whether the Jewish characters are — as the range of depictions have portrayed them — small shopkeepers, highly skilled professionals, or religious leaders; whether they drive once a month to a distant synagogue to attend Sabbath services or have their own form of observance at home; and whether they celebrate Chanukah or are said to have a Christmas tree; they are shown to be part of a particular and fascinating component of America, with its own rewards and challenges. Their appearance on popular television adds to the textured picture of Jewish life in its diversity and underscores that television's view of Jews has not been monolithic.

Jews and Other Ethnic Groups

The ability of Jews and non–Jews to come together and overcome such potentially divisive issues as anti–Semitism is a frequent TV portrayal. Ultimately, everyone gets along with each other, as positive ties are fostered, knowledge is shared, and commonality among groups is stressed.

One way of stressing such commonality is by delving into similarities between Jews and other ethnic minorities, as several popular TV shows have done. On an episode of the detective series *Magnum, P.I.*, for example, a Chinese woman and a rabbi come to discover that they share a great veneration for the past and its symbols. Comparing quotes from their respective sages, they find similar words of wisdom in both.

On "Avenue Z Afternoon," a 1992 presentation of the *General Motors Playwrights Theater*, an elderly Jewish woman is held hostage in her Brooklyn apartment by an inept Puerto Rican street punk. Although she cannot understand why this boy would break into her house, why he doesn't get a job, or what he's saying about the *barrio,* as the drama unfolds the two begin to surmount their mutual dislike and distrust. He stops looking at her as some cute old Jewish lady or the enemy, and she stops looking at him as some crazed Puerto Rican who was just going to kill her. They slowly start to perceive each other as people and through this crisis develop a relationship with another human being — something hitherto lacking in both their lives.

Interactions between Jews and American Indians are not relegated only to bygone eras — with portrayals of Jewish peddlers and immigrants fanning out across early America, as described above — but are part and parcel of the modern idiom as well. An entire TV movie, *Isaac Littlefeathers,* was devoted to the story of a Native American boy who is abandoned by his parents and raised by an elderly Jewish widower. A Canadian production, the film was later shown as part of the PBS children's series *Wonderworks.*

Well-known drama series have also included social and cultural interactions between these two groups. *Northern Exposure*'s Dr. Joel Fleischman, a New York City transplant to the small town of Cicely, Alaska, often engaged in cultural exchanges with the Native Americans who were among his neighbors. In one episode, Fleischman expended great efforts to investigate Jewish influences on the Indian language. On the short-lived series *Buck James,* a Jew and an American Indian find theological affinities when Dr. Rebecca Meyers's grandfather, visiting her in the Southwest from New York City, begins a conversation with an American Indian. They compare various aspects of their religious beliefs and practices and find that they have a great deal in common. As the American Indian reveals that Mr. Meyers is the first Jew he has ever met and Mr. Meyers calls him "my first Indian gentleman," they befriend each other.

Needless to say, these positive messages do not always represent the world as it is in reality. In fact, television dramatic programs often depict relationships, events, and the behavior of characters as being of a better and higher moral character than in real life. But, in one hopeful assessment, a writer on ethnic images in film and television has stated, "Positive images will foster positive feelings and understanding. In that way, the hours Americans spend involved with visual media will not be wasted."[17]

Jews and Blacks

Perhaps nowhere is there more need for such lofty and worthy aspirations than in the relations between blacks and Jews. Especially relevant in light of current tensions, it was a noteworthy episode of *Sanford and Son* that emphasized those aspects of history, heritage and purpose that the two groups have in common. The segment, titled "Funny, You Don't Look It," has Fred Sanford, an African American, exploring what he believes to be are his Jewish roots after a family-tracing company tells him he is descended from Falashas. At first, his identification is comic, playing on stereotypical notions about Jews: he gushes about chicken soup, matzah balls, and gefilte fish; he tells of his hopes for his adult son to have a *bar mitzvah* and "become a doctor." As his search progresses, it becomes more substantive: he learns about *Shabbat* and reads books about Judaism. Even after Fred discovers that the company that traced his lineage was a scam operation, he is not upset. Instead, he is pleased that he learned much about Judaism, about a community of black Jews, and about similarities between Jews and blacks. As one of Fred's Jewish teachers tells the Sanford family, "The Jews and blacks do have a lot in common. I hope the similarities will bring us closer together."

Yet, as headlines of recent years point up, many Jews and blacks have not been brought closer together and relations between the two communities have at times been acrimonious and explosive. Needless to say, such issues were bound to find their way onto television entertainment shows.

One show that tackled black–Jewish relations was an episode of *Beverly Hills 90210*. This popular series from the prolific Aaron Spelling production stable is often criticized for being fluff entertainment with no substance. In fact, the show deals periodically with serious issues confronting young people, and among its Jewish themes have been such matters as anti–Semitism on college campuses and Holocaust survivors. One such episode dealt with the controversies engendered by a fictional demagogue who is black and anti–Jewish — clearly meant to be a Louis Farrakhan–Leonard Jeffries type. When he is invited to speak on campus by the black student senate, an ethnic battle erupts between the black students, who cite the First Amendment, and the Jewish students, who decry the speaker's anti–Semitism. The campus erupts with bomb threats, rallies, and counterrallies.

Enter the Jewish Andrea Zuckerman, who becomes involved in Jewish student politics as a result of the controversy. She tries to influence a friend who sits on the student senate to vote to bar the speaker from campus. She bemoans the thriving of anti–Semitism and ignorance on the eve of the twenty-first century.

Then she speaks to her grandmother, a Holocaust survivor. In a highly unlikely and odd response, the grandmother urges Andrea to go and listen to what the speaker has to say (even though the anti–Semitic nature of his rhetoric has been emphasized throughout the show). Andrea does so, abandoning her plans to march with the Jewish students in a candlelight vigil protesting his appearance. While an effort, perhaps, to soothe very some real tensions that exist between the communities, this denouement is nonetheless highly troubling, as it seems to undermine legitimate concerns about anti–Semitic demagoguery by having a Holocaust survivor urge a calm hearing of such views and having Andrea standing ultimately aloof from the acts meant to counter such views.

Another look at race relations appeared on *Picket Fences*, as the series took on the issue of busing and integration. Through an ongoing story line that continued across several episodes, high-tension feelings, emotions, and reactions were explored in an ever revolving way. Apparent bigots turned out to be human and complex; staunch heroes revealed hobbling flaws.

In one episode, young Zachary Brock writes a school report that is highly derogatory to blacks. After much soul-searching by his parents over how he could harbor such racist notions, it turns out that Zach obtained the offensive material from an outdated school encyclopedia. While this discovery in a sense exonerates him, Zach's Jewish connection (he had earlier considered converting to Judaism) could unfavorably and unfairly be attributed to his holding racist attitudes toward blacks.

A similar concern applies to the 1992 summer pilot *Driving Miss Daisy*, based on the hit movie. In this TV rendition, the association of Miss Daisy with what was widely perceived as an offensive depiction of a black character was not a particularly elevating image. It is possible, however, that few viewers associated Miss Daisy with Judaism, since her religion — a significant ingredient of the play and movie of the same name — was not even mentioned in the television pilot.

The drama series *Law and Order*, which mines daily headlines for topical issues that it addresses in thoughtful and unusual ways, has presented several episodes touching on black–Jewish relations. One segment brought the groups together when a prominent black political leader was shot and killed at a rally, and a Jewish liberal seen there with a gun is charged with his murder. A similar theme infused an episode of *N.Y. Undercover*, when a leader of a black Muslim group (clearly paralleling Farakkhan's Nation of Islam) is assassinated and everyone believes it to be the work of Jewish extremists. Recriminations and insults escalate between the two groups until a "war" breaks out that takes more lives. Although it is ultimately revealed that the assassin was not a Jew but an African American woman who held the victim responsible for her own father's assassination years earlier, the two groups — each portrayed as suffering from injustices and persecution — are shown to be worlds apart with little hope of reconciliation.

Another *Law and Order* episode chronicled the racial and ethnic tensions ignited during the investigation of the murder of an Orthodox Jew in New York City's diamond district. And the tragic events of Crown Heights in 1992 — when the accidental death of a black child was followed by anti–Jewish riots and murder — found their way into a 1994 episode of the same series. Picking up on these themes, through heated, realistic and no-punches-pulled dialogue rare for television, the show explored such issues as racism, anti–Semitism, urban conflict, and, ultimately, personal responsibility in an age that offers every avenue for avoiding such responsibility.

Littered among quality depictions like these are such shows as *In Living*

Color, a half-hour program of comedy skits where the Crown Heights issue appeared in the form of a *West Side Story* parody. The skit opens on a group of dancing Hasidic Jews who sing to the tune of "Jet Song," "When you're a Jew, you're a Jew all the way, from your first clearance sale to your *bar mitzvah* day;

> You never pay cost;
> you always get a bargain
> You learn in the crib
> to speak in legal jargon."

Although a backhanded compliment to Jews could be inferred when the Hasidim sing that when the blacks bring knives and guns "we bring lawyers" (projecting an image of black violence being met with Jewish brain power), the disparagement of either group with destructive stereotypes is harmful and in this case, totally devoid of humor.

Conflict has not been the only trait that has marked popular television's version of black–Jewish relations on the political front. A number of shows have depicted the two groups bound by a history of persecution, working shoulder to shoulder to fight injustice. Their combined efforts during the days of the Civil Rights movements were noted in a number of programs, including the TV movie *Murder in Mississippi.*

While headline-grabbing events such as those in Crown Heights garner the prominence that controversy routinely does, left unnoticed are those many story lines that matter-of-factly depict utterly normal and congenial relationships between blacks and Jews. Episodes of 1960s series such as *The Cosby Show, Mod Squad,* and *Ironside* depicted blacks and Jews as friends, allies, and caring and responsible human beings who share much. Such shows as *Facts of Life, The Trials of Rosie O'Neill, Hill Street Blues, Chicago Hope* and *704 Hauser* (which depicted a black family living in Archie Bunker's old house with a son whose girlfriend is white and Jewish) featured ongoing black and Jewish characters living life as most people do—not out of the headlines but negotiating a tangle of relationships and life's daily pleasures and tribulations.

Jewish Women

Jewish women are a vital and visible part of popular TV's Jewish images.[18] Indeed, Jewish female characters have graced the small screen since television's earliest days until today. Among these diverse characters have been Jewish mothers, grandmothers, teenagers, physicians, army personnel, lawyers, housewives, police officers, psychiatrists, fashion designers, business executives, teachers, and *rebbetzins* (rabbis' wives). This list is but a sampling of Jewish women characters who were all *regularly featured* Jewish female characters in various comedy and drama series over the years. By including miniseries, made-for-TV movies, and guest appearances on series' episodes, this eclectic grouping expands to include such additional Jewish female characters as rabbis, cantors, Holocaust survivors, organization directors, politicians, Mossad agents, journalists, shopkeepers, Nazi hunters, and countless others.

Even a mere glance at a cross section of the historic presence of popular television's Jewish women yields impressive results: *The Goldbergs'* Molly Goldberg, the all–American Jewish mother; Stephanie Mills, Archie Bunker's adopted Jewish daughter who celebrated her *bat mitzvah* on *All in the Family*; Helena Slomova, heroine partisan fighter in *Holocaust*; Anne Frank in *The Diary of Anne Frank*; Toni Hazelton, a World War II WAC who rediscovers and asserts her Jewish identity in an overwhelmingly non–Jewish milieu on *The Waltons*; Sofia Koslow, an Israeli Mossad agent in pursuit of a Nazi war criminal on *Trapper John, M.D.*; *Lanigan's Rabbi's* Miriam Small, the longest running *rebbetzin* character on popular television; Dr. Lilith Sternin, psychiatrist extraordinaire on *Cheers*; *Reasonable Doubts'* assistant district attorney Tess Kaufman, a role model of the highest ethical standards; *Beverly Hills, 90210's* Andrea Zuckerman, a high school student who debated issues of the Holocaust with her grandmother, a survivor, and who fought campus anti–Semitism; *Sisters'* Frankie Margolis, a high-powered advertising executive who has taken her conversion to Judaism very seriously; *The Commish's* Rachel Scali, a teacher who is intermarried yet with her husband is raising their child Jewishly; Dr. Deena Hertz, Orthodox Jewish psychiatrist on the series *Maria*; *Homefront's* Gina Sloan, a Holocaust survivor and single mother seeking a Jewish mate; and Fran Fine, nanny par excellence in *The Nanny*. Most important, the Jewishness of all these characters has been a featured element, not a mere label, and very relevant to the development of the series and the characters' places within them.

Television's Jewish women are as varied as one can imagine. They range from the motherly to the manic, from judges to JAPs, from rogues to rabbis.

As one of television's earliest and arguably best known Jewish mothers, Molly Goldberg possessed many of the traits that are traditionally associated with the Jewish mother: being warm, motherly, resourceful, nurturing, and problem-solving and on the flip side of this picture, being overbearing and inescapable. In fact, it was the joining of all these characteristics that made Molly the strength and backbone of her family. Many of television's Jewish mothers would conform to her role model in the years that followed.

One especially endearing one was Mrs. Bronson (played by the incomparable Molly Picon), who appeared on several episodes of *Car 54, Where Are You?* A diminutive grandmother, she has New York City's police department and its top politicians wrapped around her little finger. She lives in a Bronx apartment building that is slated for demolition to make way for a highway — but she's not going anywhere. Though only a scaffolding of a high-rise remains around her, she stands her ground, staying put in her now open-air apartment to which a parade of officialdom comes streaming. Though they plead with her to move out, she'll have none of it, instead beguiling them (to their stunned amazement) with servings of tea and honey cake, games of bingo, and her Jewish motherly charm.

A few years later, on *Gomer Pyle, U.S.M.C.*, another Molly Picon character appeared, this time taking on none other than the U.S. Marines. In a poignant morality tale about according respect and a sense of worth to the elderly, she teaches her son — as well as Private Gomer Pyle — that he must allow her to be busy and active in her life doing those things that are important to her despite their well-intentioned but unfounded concerns for her well-being.

Many other Jewish mothers have graced the small screen, often exhibiting what are considered traditional Jewish values: pressing their children to be educated, wanting them to succeed, and above all, wanting them to be married. Often these desires are expressed as a source of humor, as in the case of one Jewish mother on *Sister Kate* who encountered an attractive young woman during a game of bingo. She strikes up a conversation with her in the hopes of nabbing a suitable mate for her still-single adult son. Finally, the young woman demurs, saying, "I'm a nun." The ever-hopeful Jewish mother replies beamingly, "So I take it you're *single*?"

At times the intense involvement in their children's lives often attributed to Jewish mothers is portrayed as a none-too-welcome overbearingness in which they wield undue influence in their children's lives and psyches. In some shows, this leads to conflict and family tension or even breakup. In other instances, it is shown in a more affectionate light. Such was the case on *Chicken Soup*, in which 52-year-old, unmarried Jackie Fisher lives with his mother, who is still trying to find him nice Jewish girls to date. On the episode in which he took her in when she needed housing, he insisted over her protestations that that was the right thing to do, that he didn't care what other people might think. Despite her close involvement in his life and disagreements the two had about some important issues, their relationship was depicted as a warm and affectionate one.

Of course, not all of television's Jewish mothers have been portrayed in a positive light. Some have suffered from negative stereotyping and appear as anti–Semitic caricatures or misogynistic foils. These, however, have fortunately been more the exception than the rule, receiving, perhaps, more attention because of their negativity but in fact being but a small portion of the varied and mostly admirable Jewish mothers portrayed on TV. Nor are all of TV's mothers, of course, of the Molly Goldberg/Molly Picon variety. Many modern Jewish women with families and careers have filled TV screens over the years, all varying in profession, family situation, age, and level of involvement with their Judaism.

With this diversity, popular television has mostly avoided the "Jewish American princess," or JAP, stereotype which is so unsavory and so harmful to Jewish women. Indeed an entire episode of a youth-oriented drama series,

Class of '96, was devoted to displaying the harm of such images and had a Jewish college student leading the fight against JAP humor on campus. Because it portrayed a young Jewish woman in the forefront of confronting and ultimately repudiating — with the assistance of a woman rabbi and a female college dean — such images, rather than men holding the positions of authority and leading the fight to take care of the women, this show was particularly refreshing and important. It also had the courage to focus solely on the question of JAP jokes and bigotry against Jewish women, addressing it as a specific issue rather than watering it down to present viewers with a preachy discourse on all forms of hatred. Ordinarily, popular television explains a problem by universalizing it, with the supposed aim of making it more understandable. But inappropriate and forced comparisons serve only to diminish the importance of events or matters at hand — and the effectiveness of a show. Those who are battling the JAP jokes stick to that issue. The show, its message, and ultimately a rejection of all bigotry comes across more strongly as a result.

The mention of JAP images raises in the minds of many the picture of today's best known Jewish woman on TV, "the nanny named Fran." The "New Yawk"–accented, outrageously outfitted, *yenta* par excellence Miss Fran Fine has gained high visibility for her role in the hit comedy *The Nanny.* There she is ensconced as nanny to three sprouting children in an upper-class Manhattan townhouse and flirts with their British Broadway-producer father, Maxwell Sheffield.

The show's humor is based on the contrast between the earthy and direct Miss Fine and the endearing but tiptoeing Mr. Sheffield, and on the sub-rosa, ever-on-the-edge-of-blossoming romance between them. Fran Drescher has taken her share of criticism for her perceived perpetuation of negative stereotypes of Jewish women. Certainly Fran Fine has her own, unique style that not everyone may share. Yet week after week, she displays a personality that is warm, resourceful, giving, problem solving, and peace making. If her manner and accent (which is not put on — the actress, Fran Drescher, actually speaks that way) are a turn-off to some, who is bringing stereotypes to the table? (In fact, Drescher presented a prototype of the nanny character on a brief-lived comedy called *Princesses,* about three woman from vastly different backgrounds sharing a New York City apartment. On the show, which lasted for just a few weeks in the fall of 1991, Drescher played — what else? — the Jewish New Yorker Melissa Kirschner.)

Still, a number of *Nanny* episodes do include some distasteful Jewish depictions: Miss Fine seems to flaunt her delight in blatantly nonkosher food; her in-your-face love affair with shrimp graces nearly every episode. (She is certainly entitled to her personal practices, which are probably not out of line with that of many other American Jews on this matter.) But her character should not be judged with a knee-jerk negativism.

Among Fran Fine's positive traits, presumably valued by the Jewish community, is her oft-stated requirement that her future husband be Jewish. ("If he were Jewish, I'd marry him," she said of one appealing prospect.) Even her fantasized wedding to employer Maxwell Sheffield was under a *chuppah*, with a rabbi officiating. Clearly, whatever her faults, this Jewish woman is not a one-dimensional stereotype.

Nor does she hide her Jewishness, however much one may disagree with her expression of it. This stands in sharp contrast to another very popular female Jewish character on TV of an earlier era: Rhoda. Like Fran Fine, Rhoda was the subject of much attention and some criticism, as she was looked at as the supposed personification of Jewish womanhood. But unlike on *The Nanny*, on the *Rhoda* series there was little, if anything, to identify Rhoda as Jewish or to connect her to her supposed identity. Even her much-heralded wedding was devoid of any Jewish component, with a justice of the peace officiating.

While being open about her Jewishness, Fran Fine's particular strain of style may also have ushered in an era of greater attractiveness for TV's Jewish woman. In the past, some shows were criticized for consistently portraying Jewish women as less than alluring. One TV movie of 1991, *For the Very First Time*, had a Jewish teen who was dating a Catholic girl and beset by parental pressure, throw off the comment that "there's no such thing as a good-looking, nice Jewish girl." On *The Home Court*, a Jewish father greets his "Waspified" daughter whom he hasn't seen for some time saying delightedly, "You look great. You look like a *shiksa*!" "Thanks!" she gushes. (Although this might have been less an insult to Jewish women than an attempt to poke fun at her efforts to assume to a Waspish veneer.) Such images were considered a derogation of Jewish women and a perpetuation of a false notion of their unattractiveness, contributing — some argued — to the rise in intermarriages, as Jewish men sought mates elsewhere in part because of the negative popular media image of Jewish women.

If that is the case, then Fran Fine has perhaps served a positive role, as Jewish women in recent shows have been portrayed as the object of many men's desire. On the comedy *Caroline in the City*, a Gentile man is so wild for a Jewish woman who only dates Jewish men that he immediately and impulsively decides to convert to Judaism for that reason alone. That same TV season, 1996–97, a high school boy on *Mr. Rhodes* falls for a Jewish girl and is determined to learn everything he can about Chanukah to win her heart.

As well as being passive objects of desire, more interesting is that television's Jewish women are frequently shown to be actively protecting their people, defending their religion, or rejoicing in their heritage. On many shows, women Mossad agents are working to capture Nazi war criminals. On a beautiful TV movie, *Lena: My One Hundred Children* set post–World War II, a Jewish woman courageously toils to protect children who survived the Holocaust from further European anti–Semitism and to lead them to Israel.

Many modern-day women are shown to be reclaiming their Jewish heritage and gathering strength from it — ranging from the spunky, interesting, and blessedly normal Melissa Steadman on *thirtysomething,* who urges cousin Michael to try going to synagogue ("It's not like Hebrew school anymore," she assures him), to Andrea Zuckerman of *Beverly Hills 90210,* whose fight against sorority anti–Semitism encourages another young woman to "come out" as a Jew.

Even television's Jewish women in intermarriages often display a strong attachment to their background and are willing to express it in forceful ways. On *The Five Mrs. Buchanans,* after accidentally breaking her mother-in-law's plaster figure of baby Jesus and being berated by her for "destroying Christmas," Alexandra Buchanan stands up to the dour and dominating woman. When the mother-in-law scolds Alexandra for not respecting "this family's religious traditions," Alexandra explodes. "*This family?*" she says. "This family means what? All of you except me, the non–Christian? I *am* part of this family, and this is a fine time for you to tell me I don't respect *this family's* religious traditions."

She reminds Mother Buchanan of her twenty years of decorating Christmas trees and Easter baskets and then says, "And as long as we're on the subject of religious beliefs, what about mine? I don't remember you ever coming over here for the big Chanukah celebration. How do you think that makes me feel?" Then she brings out a large Chanukah menorah. "This is one of my symbols — not that you ever cared."

Another Jewish woman seeking to sort out a relationship — one with her Jewish boyfriend — was depicted in a gem of an episode of the 1993 anthology series *TriBeCa,* entitled "Stepping Back." Deftly character-driven, this show explored issues of life, love, and relationships as Maggie Miller, New York City architect, deals with life's trials and tribulations: the demands for commitment from her boyfriend, her grandmother's moving in with her (because *Grandma* has dumped *her* live-in boyfriend), a job move to the wilds of New Jersey, and blind dates arranged by friends. The show was notable for depicting not only one but two couples involved in Jewish-Jewish relationships in parallel romances (Maggie's and her grandmother's) and for portraying a warm granddaughter-grandmother relationship without the intrusion of easy stereotypes or sentimentality. Their Jewishness exuded naturally from them as an integral, natural, and unabashed part of their lives.

This has not been the case for all of popular TV's Jewish women. Some have been Jewish in name or mannerism only — as opposed to any explicit identification and Judaic manifestation; others have indeed fallen into stereotypes. Most, however, have been proud, heroic, and accomplished characters, and it would be a misreading of the history of Jewish images on TV to profess the nonexistence of the many Jewish women who constitute an important part of the television landscape — and thus obliterate their vibrant picture.

Rabbis and Cantors

In television's early years, rabbis were universally depicted as aged men with beards. That this was the way rabbis were supposed to look was noted in the made-for-TV movie *Skokie*. When Holocaust survivor Max Feldman wants to get involved in preventing the Nazis from marching in Skokie, his wife implores him not to, but to rather "leave it to people whose job it is to handle it — like the rabbi." Max retorts, "What kind of rabbi is that? He's a kid. He plays tennis. He doesn't even look like a rabbi."

This perception of what a rabbi should look like permeated non–Jewish circles as well, as in the instance when Archie Bunker went to see the rabbi of the synagogue where his niece attends Hebrew school. The patiently waiting Archie and Edith behold a sweaty and running-suit-attired young man enter the rabbi's study. When he offers to help them, Archie brushes him off, telling him, "We're waiting for the rabbi, kiddo." When the young man responds "I'm Rabbi Jacobs," Archie is incredulous.

But the evolution of what a TV rabbi looks like has mirrored a similar real-life transformation, with the most stark change being the appearance of women rabbis, both on screen and off. The first of several women rabbis to be depicted in popular television programs appeared on a 1987 episode of *A Year in the Life*, in which the rabbi officiates at a *brit bat* ceremony (baby naming ceremony for a girl). Women rabbis, once novel and controversial, have become so accepted that they are now matter-of-factly portrayed, whether dispensing advice as on *Dream On* or helping to solve a criminal case involving a Jewish embezzler on *The Marshall*. On the *Class of '96* episode about JAP jokes, the college student working against them is so impressed with her campus rabbi, who is a woman, that she says admiringly "I've never known a rabbi like that."

Women rabbis on TV have opened the door for a new dramatic complication, when they become the object of someone's love interest. When men on *Platypus Man* and *The Larry Sanders Show* fell in love with women rabbis, the stage was set for humorous complications that gave substance to entire episodes.[19]

Tongue-in-cheek portrayals of rabbis have also been fodder for humor, as on the short-lived summer series titled *Down and Out in Beverly Hills*, an episode of which featured a Jewish wedding Hollywood style — performed by a Hollywood-style rabbi referred to as "Rabbi Bob."

Even in television's early years, the typical rabbi was not the only rabbinic portrayal on TV. A number of segments of the anthology series *Crossroads*— a series dedicated entirely to the stories of clergymen — were about rabbis who were rather atypical. These dramatizations focused on the lives of outstanding historical figures, including such real-life rabbis as Saul Applebaum, Avraham Soltes, Arnold Fishel, and Gershom Medes Seixas.

While the old-style rabbis still make their appearances on TV in such series as *Chicago Hope*, more often than not the last two decades have seen a younger generation of rabbis without accents and without beards (or with just a trim goatee). Such rabbis have made their mark in numerous programs: *Hallmark Hall of Fame's* "Have I Got a Christmas for You," *Diff'rent Strokes*, *thirtysomething*, *The Waltons*, *The Partridge Family*, *Keep the Faith*, *Eight Is Enough*, and *Picket Fences*, to name a few. Another such rabbi was actually the lead character in a show the very name of which highlighted its major rabbinic presence: *Lanigan's Rabbi*. The series, which aired several episodes in 1977, was based on the Harry Kemelman novels (the first of which was *Friday the Rabbi Slept Late*) about a practicing, congregational rabbi with a hobby — he is an amateur detective who works with local police chief Lanigan to solve crimes.

The changing face of television's rabbis mirrors developments in real life. In fact, the very tension that exists between the old and the new was articulated and bemoaned by Rabbi Schulman on an episode of *Northern Exposure*, in which he wryly laments the fact that his synagogue board wants "someone more on the cutting edge to lead the community. 'Cutting edge' — when I was going to the seminary, believe me this was not a major consideration." (Rabbi Schulman was a recurring character in *Northern Exposure*, mystically appearing when Joel Fleischman needed some guidance in his life. In the series' final episode, the rabbi reappeared, mysteriously parachuting into the Alaskan woods to help a different character — a Catholic young woman — learn to make decisions in her life. "There's an old Yiddish saying," he told her. "When you don't know where you're going, every road will take you there.")

An episode of *Seinfeld* was fortunately unique in its negative portrayal of a rabbi among the vast body of programs to have portrayed rabbis on TV. The story line focused on one of Jerry's single friends, Elaine, who is having a secret emotional crisis upon learning that her nebbishy friend George is about to be married. In a state of upheaval with no one to turn to (desperately not wanting her friends to know of her jealousies and insecurities), she confides in a rabbi who lives in her building after a chance meeting with him. Their talk, held in his apartment, is bizarre: the rabbi seems not to be paying any real attention to her plight, offers no helpful guidance, and even suggests fixing her up with his nephew, although Elaine told him that she is not Jewish.

The supposed humor of the story involves the rabbi ending up thoughtlessly blabbing details of Elaine's personal crisis to Jerry, countless other neighbors including a yenta and a fellow she was interested in dating, and eventually the whole city through a recitation of her woes on his cable TV show — to Elaine's great embarrassment, of course, and her astonishment that a rabbi would do such a thing.

Of course, no rabbi would. As in all spheres, of course, there may be the rare person who would so totally breach ethical, religious, and professional tenets to do such a bizarre, harmful, unethical, and simply wrong thing. But to portray a rabbi so blithely doing so—when Judaism speaks so strongly against gossip and commands utmost care for the words we utter, stressing the power and importance of the spoken word—is absurd (despite Jerry's "disclaimer" on that episode that the rabbi is not representative of most Jews, who "can keep a juicy bit of gossip to themselves").

But this is only half the picture. The character himself was portrayed in such an unsavory way with regard to his physical appearance, mannerisms, and speech that it merely completed the picture of disgust with which this character seems to be held by the show's writers. His nebbishy manner, whiny monotone voice, odd dress and hair, and Coke-bottle glasses were reminiscent of some of the worst anti–Semitic stereotypes of Jews.

There is of course nothing inherently wrong with Jewish characters being portrayed in a humorous way. The nature of comedy is to poke fun at human foibles, to expose our human weakness in a way that brings us to laughter. Why should Jews be immune to that? Let Jewish characters be *human*, as human as other characters, with all the pluses and minuses that entails, portrayed as multidimensional beings, not as some cardboard goody-goody nor as some cartoonish fool.

The problem with this show was not so much the humor or even the story line surrounding it. Perhaps if the rabbi had been portrayed differently, the humor could have come through. But he was simply beyond the ken, so off the scale in terms of any reality or nod to sensibility that he was merely a bizarre caricature. His very appearance as almost some kind of weird space alien set him apart, as a rabbi, from other human people. One can only shudder imagining what kinds of notions this show promotes about Jews and their spiritual leaders. Thankfully, this depiction was a rarity. Overall, the importance of rabbis' functions as responsible citizens, religious authorities, sympathetic and helpful counselors, leaders of their congregations, and men and women who are in charge of the spiritual well-being of their people is made clear.

Indeed another rabbi who was so loyal to a congregant's confidentiality that he was berated for doing so appeared on the law drama *The Practice*. In a complex story over the course of a three-part arc, a man commits a murder in revenge for his daughter's murder. It seems that he had gone to his rabbi before committing the avenge killing; but the rabbi had not sought to stop him nor to report him to authorities, although the father hinted at the course he might take. When the rabbi defends his own actions and justifies the deed of his congregant, discussions ensue about justice, vigilantism, morality, and religion. What is refreshing in this show is that there is no monolithic Jewish point of view. A woman in the law firm (how refreshing, too, to see her portrayed as attractive, smart, and likable—but of ample weight) who is Jewish takes extreme issue with the rabbi's stance.

Cantors too have evolved over the years. In a 1953 production of the famed

Philco TV Playhouse anthology series titled "Holiday Song" about a cantor who loses his faith just before the High Holidays, Cantor Sternberger looks the part of a pious and religious man. He is tormented by the tension he feels between his doubts and his responsibilities to his congregation, and he searches deeply to find some answers. A 1965 episode of *Ben Casey* features another cantor, Nathan Birnbaum, in a very similar story.

On the other extreme is a 1996 episode of *The Nanny* in which the chic and fame-seeking cantor at Fran's synagogue is catapulted to theatrical fame much to the dismay of his congregation, which depends on him.

A story that encompassed both extremes, with a journey from one to the other, stemmed from the theatrical film *The Jazz Singer* and was produced anew for television in 1959. A more modern and quintessentially New York setting found a traditionally garbed cantor plaintively singing as he descends a staircase to the subway platform, where his melody is picked up by an African American saxophone player jamming on the platform. Appearing as one of several dramatic vignettes on an HBO production called *Subway Stories: Tales from the Underground*, the story — which began with a woman singing gospel music — was titled "Sax, Cantor, Riff" and is meant to evoke the mosaic of New York and the commonality of music in religious experience.

Women cantors, too, have sung their way into television in such series as *Archie Bunker's Place* and *Northern Exposure*.

Hasidim

Few shows have gone to any lengths to differentiate among Judaism's various ideologies and movements or provide any explanations about their distinctive approaches or beliefs. Although several programs have touched on the issue — and only in the vaguest of ways — one strain of Judaism has been most prominent and visible. While for the vast majority of TV's Jewish characters a particular denominational affiliation is not laid bare, the identity of television's Hasidic characters is visibly, immediately obvious.

The appeal of Hasidic Judaism to television fare undoubtedly lies in its exoticism — its distinctive manner of dress, speech, and custom — as well as its supposed position outside mainstream America. Such curiosity and mystery has led to a number of television excursions into Hasidic life.

A textured and multilayered picture of Hasidic Jews emerged on a 1981 episode of *Barney Miller*. Based on actual events, the story revolved around the Hasidic community's feeling that it was not being adequately protected by the police. A recent mugging of their cantor brings Mr. Ya'acov Berger to the precinct to complain and ask for protection: "Friday night, Avram Meyer is attacked by three hoodlums outside Gramercy Park. He was walking home from *shul*— a fine, peace-loving man. How we all love him — never mind he has a crack in his voice that would frighten a cow. A woman saw all this from a window — she broke her Sabbath and telephoned for help. Twenty-five minutes later the police were kind enough to show up." When nothing is done to remedy the situation, the Hasidim stage a demonstration described by a police officer as "a bunch of Hasidics gathering outside the precinct." When inspector Lugar decides that he wants to help alleviate the tension between the police and the people who "look like the Smith Brothers," Captain Barney Miller warns him, "These people have different ways. They're very sensitive." Lugar bungles the job, causing the demonstration to erupt into a riot. Captain Miller reflects on the havoc wreaked upon his precinct by the Hasidim, referring to them as "men of law and faith behaving like animals." Although Berger returns to the precinct following the riot both to apologize for and at the same time excuse the destructive actions of his people, the story ends on a realistic note of uneasiness.

One type of foray into Hasidic circles has been that of criminals posing as Hasidic Jews, a disguise assumed to cast any suspicion off them. In the 1981 *Cagney and Lacey* made-for-TV movie, for example, the detectives investigate a series of murders in New York's diamond district of Hasidic Jews who were Holocaust survivors. When the evidence points to an inside job, they reveal that a Nazi war criminal posing as a Hasidic concentration camp survivor is the perpetrator.

Juxtaposed with this have been depictions of police officers going undercover as Hasidic Jews to solve their cases. Sergeant Belker in *Hill Street Blues* did this, and a police officer on *Pacific Station* hid from an escaped convict in disguise as a Hasidic Jew.

On an episode of *NYPD Blue*, the detectives assume Hasidic identities to recover a stolen *Torah*. Similarly on *New York Undercover*, one episode told the story of a jewelry heist in New York's diamond district, sending the police undercover with a Hasidic family. In a twist on this not unusual plot, a hint of romance develops between one of the detectives and the family's daughter.

Another romantic possibility erupted on an episode of *The Days and Nights of Molly Dodd*, in which a Hasid comes to take piano lessons from Molly; they develop an attraction towards each other.

Underlying these potential love stories is the Hasidic Jews' tension between an allegiance and connection to their community and the allure of the outside world. A similar tension plagued a Hasidic boy with a gift for painting in the series *Bronx Zoo*. Ms. Callahan, a teacher in the school where Hasidic father and son are hired as exterminators, wrestles with her conscience when the artistic youngster asks her to teach him to paint, although, he says, his religion deems it a sin. They have several conversations about religion, art, and community, as both wrestle with the issues raised.

Lovejoy, a BBC-produced lighthearted mystery series about a sleuthing antique dealer (named Lovejoy) seemed to have a propensity for featuring

Hasidic characters. While its early efforts resulted in one-dimensional caricatures, a fascinating and very human picture of Hasidim emerged on a later
episode. When a suspicious cache of rare and antique Judaica surfaces in rural
England, Lovejoy, seeking a buyer, contacts the Solomon family in London. A
Hasidic father and son team, the Solomons display an easy camaraderie with
old friend Lovejoy. They are cultured, articulate, humane, worldly, and at the
same time Judaically knowledgeable and dedicated — an unusual portrayal for
TV, which most always depicts Hasidic Jews as weirdly exotic and removed
from society. Moreover, the elder Solomon very eloquently and movingly
expresses a love of his heritage that this Judaica collection represents and the
need for its preservation on that basis rather than any financial concerns.

Doctors and Lawyers

In an unexpected departure from the common current presupposition
that doctors and lawyers are "Jewish professions," television's early medical
and law shows — such as *Dr. Kildare, Ben Casey, Marcus Welby, M.D., The
Defenders*, and *Perry Mason* — featured non–Jews in these positions of prominence. Of course, those series included Jewish episodes, with one episode on
Dr. Kildare even revolving around a Jewish doctor and his family.

The beginning of TV's Jewish doctors and lawyers came along with a new
television era introduced and propelled by the *All in the Family*. Throughout
the series Archie Bunker would insist on having Jewish doctors and lawyers
handle his affairs because of his stated belief that they are smarter and shrewder.
An update of this bigoted view aired years later on an episode of *Chicago Hope*,
in which an unsavory patient fends off a black physician who tries to treat him,
stating that he wants to be tended to only by a Jewish doctor. Many other shows
have included passing references regarding the assumed skill of Jewish doctors,
some to show the bigotry of a character, as in *Chicago Hope*, others for purely
humorous purposes.

While specific episodes of series and TV movies would continue to feature Jewish doctors (as on *Medical Center, Golden Girls, Mrs. Delafield Wants
to Marry*, and *Fight for Life*), in more recent years many series began appearing that featured Jewish doctors as part of the regular cast of characters. Such
series included *Buck James* (Dr. Rebecca Meyers), *St. Elsewhere* (Drs. Daniel
Auschlander and Wayne Fiscus), *Nurses* (Dr. Hank Kaplan), *Chicago Hope*
(Drs. Aaron Shutt and Jeffrey Geiger), *Doctor, Doctor* (Dr. Grant Linowitz), and
Northern Exposure (Dr. Joel Fleischman).

This change, while significant, may not be as bold or sweeping as imagined. The newer shows that include these regularly featured Jewish doctors are
in fact part of television's trend of recent vintage towards ensemble dramas.
Whereas the very titles of older programs indicated the show's focus on a

Marcus Welby or a Ben Casey, today dramatic dictates and the democratization of medicine offer titles that highlight a team, rather than a particular physician. Thus the world will have to yet wait for a medical series on the prime-time schedule titled *Joel Fleischman, M.D.*

Television's Jewish lawyers, bearing the same historical precedent and contemporary course, have become a familiar and ongoing presence on the small screen in such made-for-TV movies as *The Caine Mutiny Court-Martial, Terrorist on Trial: The United States vs. Salim Ajami,* and *Skokie*; and such series as *L.A. Law* (Stuart Markowitz), *Civil Wars* (Eli Levinson), *Law and Order* (Adam Schiff), *Homecourt* (Sidney Solomon), *Courthouse* (Myron Winkelman), and *Reasonable Doubts* (Tess Kaufman). In a blending of fiction and reality, one episode of *Picket Fences* had the regularly featured Jewish lawyer Douglas Wambaugh getting legal advice on his upcoming Supreme Court appearance from real-life lawyer Alan Dershowitz (who appeared playing himself).

It was a television lawyer who became the first ongoing Jewish character in a regular series to always wear a *kippah*. On *The Trials of Rosie O'Neill*, public defender Ben Meyer was an observant Jew who often referred to and called upon his Jewish heritage in both his professional and personal lives.

Another Jewish lawyer who drew on an aspect of his background, in an amusing and unlikely turn, was the character of Felix Frankfurter, as portrayed on a miniseries *Separate but Equal*. Dramatizing the historic 1954 Supreme Court decision (*Brown vs. Board of Education*) declaring segregation illegal, the show pointed up the fact that Justice Frankfurter was both Jewish and a towering and humane intellect. When the Court's deliberations on the case stalled, Frankfurter — in prelude to his plans to break the deadlock — drew upon his knowledge of Yiddish to suggest the need for "a *kochleff'l*— a cooking spoon to stir things up."

The abundance of TV's Jewish doctors and lawyers is clearly a reflection of the disproportionate number of Jewish doctors and lawyers in the real world as well. Television programs themselves have offered various explanations for this phenomenon, one of the most humorous in an episode of *All in the Family* titled "Maude." In response to being accused of having made an anti–Semitic remark, Maude defends herself and her admiration for Jews, saying, "I happen to feel that Jews are brilliant — which is why I have a Jewish doctor, and a Jewish lawyer, and a Jewish accountant."

Cops, Cabbies, Politicians, and Others

Maude's husband, listening quietly to her lauding soliloquy, pipes in to temper her exaltation, reminding her, "You forgot to mention your brilliant Jewish plumber!"

Indeed television has depicted Jewish plumbers and just about every other occupational endeavor. Although doctors and lawyers are the stereotype of Jews — and there have been many on television — TV has not relegated Jews to these occupations. Rather, there has been a wide variety of Jewish engagement in all manner of professional, occupational, social, economic, and political spheres.

A profession not traditionally associated with Jews is that of police officer. Yet television, recognizing the reality that there are many Jews in law enforcement fields, has depicted dozens of Jewish police officers and detectives. Many of these have been series regulars, including Captain Barney Miller (*Barney Miller*), Lieutenant Bert Samuels, Detective Victor Isbecki, and Desk Sergeant Ronald Coleman (*Cagney and Lacey*), Detective Mick Belker and Lieutenant Henry Goldblume (*Hill Street Blues*), Captain Mickey Schwartz (*Under Suspicion*), and Detective Barney Ruditski (*The Lawless Years*).

With great shades of variety, the made-for-cable movie *Legacy of Lies* depicted a multi-generational Jewish family — some in the mob, others police, both honest and crooked. Part gangster tale, part thriller, *Legacy of Lies* clearly depicts Jewish bad guys during the Prohibition era, with gangsters named Adler and Resnick who even show up in *shul* on Friday nights. Focusing on the Jewish good guys, another clan of cops, the Feins, was the subject of two made-for-TV movies (*Family of Cops I* and *II*).

One of television's most popular Jewish characters was in the transportation field: Alex Rieger, taxi driver, on *Taxi*. Although his Jewishness was not a major theme, it was alluded to in a few episodes and was a part of his persona.

Jewish characters in the entertainment and communications industries have also been recurrent portrayals. As in the case of TV's doctors and lawyers, these fulfill a widespread expectation that a large percentage of Jews fill such roles in real life. Many of the TV characters portrayed in this way toss about Yiddishisms as if the language were a lingua franca in show business, signaling the character's ethnic as well as professional affiliation.

Such characters have been regulars on series, like comedy writer Buddy Sorrell on *The Dick Van Dyke Show* and talent agents Al Floss and Abe Werkfinder on *The Famous Teddy Z*; have made recurrent appearances on story arcs, like movie producer Ben Flicker on *L.A. Law*; and have been placed strategically in numerous shows for ambiance.

On the political front, few Jewish characters have held positions of formal political prominence. One Jewish woman (Laurie Bey) became mayor on *Picket Fences*; another was an illegitimate daughter who became a political liability to her senator father (and whose Jewishness was an embarrassment) when she resurfaced in Washington, D.C., on *The Powers That Be*. Where TV's Jewish characters *have* made their political mark is in the role as outsider — as agitator, as civil rights worker, as labor organizer, as 1960s radical. This frequently seen motif projects a sense of the Jew as one absented from conventional channels but working outside the system in a feisty effort to make it better. On *Homefront*, Al Kahn was a dedicated labor organizer; on *L.A. Law*, Barry Glassman was a 1960s radical, a fugitive from the law come in from the cold. He had taken part in an attempted prison escape of a Black Panther in which prison guards were killed; now, he said, he's been "living like a nice Jewish boy." Although short-lived, another law drama, *Eddie Dodd*, managed to include a similar theme. At times the notion of the Jew as political outsider is taken to an extreme, with bigoted characters often being shown to denounce Jews and communists in one breath, as in HBO's *Fellow Traveler* about the McCarthy era.

The Jewish role in the civil rights movement was pointed to in TV movies like *Murder in Mississippi*. On the miniseries *Separate but Equal*, Justice Frankfurter's Jewishness and his legal activism for integration were highlighted during the show about the Supreme Court's 1954 desegregation ruling. It was even noted, as the NAACP prepared for arguments before the Court and assessed each of the justices, that Frankfurter was the first on the Supreme Court to employ a black law clerk.

Progressive politics on the part of Jews was even expressed by as unlikely a character as Fran Fine, always dressed out to the nines, on *The Nanny*. After her refusal to cross a picket line ruins an evening and a potential career coup for her employer Maxwell Sheffield, she lectures him, saying unapologetically, "I'm sorry, but the Fines don't cross picket lines. It's against our religion."

Television's Jewish characters have varied not only with regard to profession and political stripe but recently even with sexual orientation as well, as this topic has attained a high visibility. A short-lived series *The Crew*, about an airline crew included a Jewish, homosexual flight attendant. On *Chicago Hope*, Dr. Robert Lawrence is homosexual; the surprise revelation, which he later relates to a colleague, is that he is Jewish and once attended rabbinical school. A more in-depth look at the subject surfaced on Showtime's cable movie *Twilight of the Golds*, about a Jewish family with an adult homosexual son. When his married sister learns she is pregnant and discovers that her fetus carries the genetic makeup for homosexuality, the entire family becomes involved and difficult emotions arise.

This diversity of characters points to a comfort level regarding the presence of Jews in every aspect of American society. In fact, so comfortable are other Americans shown to be with their fellow Jews, whom they now encounter in every sphere of life, that a number of Christian TV characters took upon themselves an enthusiastic exploration of Judaism or the possibility of converting to the religion. On *Blossom*, the lead character was Jewish for a week as part of a school assignment and took viewers with her through a journey of learning about Judaism. Another teenaged girl, on *Party of Five*, explored Judaism with an eye toward converting, as did school-aged Zachary Brock on *Picket Fences* and a young African American boy on *Diff'rent Strokes*. On *Seinfeld*, Jerry's dentist converted to Judaism, but Jerry is convinced that he only did so to be able to tell Jewish jokes and still be politically correct. (Conversions in the context of an interfaith relationship are discussed in Chapter 6, "Intermarriage.")

While non–Jews are generally shown to be at ease with Jews — working, playing, living with them side-by-side — several TV characters are portrayed as among those who still do not usually meet or get to know Jews in their daily lives. Such people, who of course exist in real life as well, serve to highlight yet again the importance and necessity of examining television's Jewish images for the notions they impart to viewers about Jewish people, religion, and life. As one TV character herself said — Maggie O'Connell's Midwest grandmother who was fascinated to meet Dr. Joel Fleischman — "I've never met a Jewish person before. The only Jewish people I've ever seen are on TV comedies: *Seinfeld*, and that little know-it-all on *Murphy Brown*, and those nice people on *Brooklyn Bridge*."

* * *

The sheer diversity of Jewish characters on television belies the notion that Jews are depicted only stereotypically on the small screen, and their oft-expressed attachment to Judaism flies in the face of charges that such characters are only minimally Jewish. One need only sample the vast array of personalities depicted over the last half century to understand and celebrate the trove of wide-ranging Jewish characters. While not every TV Jew has, of course, been depicted as possessing only positive traits, most have been portrayed as being as human as the next guy — with whatever faults and shortcomings that may entail.

While concern for stereotyping on television is an important one, the eradication of all negative images from television would equally distort reality. Real life has its share of Jewish doctors and mothers; their absence on television would offer a false view and impoverish the TV landscape. Naturally, focusing only on these kinds of characterizations should be avoided in favor of greater diversity and depth, which have been apparent to a significant extent on popular TV.

In fact, the growing diversity of Jewish characters and the capacity to portray some who are less than perfect bespeaks an expanding maturation of the medium. Yet popular television has always offered a generous picture of Jews in American life.

The phenomenon of Jewish characters peopling America's TV screens even during the medium's early days of ubiquitous Westerns demonstrated a belief that the nation, from its earliest days, was host to a diversity of ethnic groups and that Jews were actively engaged with America from its formative origins. Television's picture of the immigrant experience expanded this portrait as the nation swelled with new citizens and viewers saw Jewish characters grapple with the pains and pleasures of adapting to a new land.

That in recent years Jewish characters have been portrayed on TV in every conceivable role that America has to offer demonstrates just how complete that adaptation has been. The full integration of Jews into American life is reflected by the presence on TV of Jewish men and women who are doctors, lawyers, police officers, taxi drivers, clergy, criminals, musicians, architects, and on and on. No profession, no facet of life is off limits. The excitement of America's ethnic mosaic has placed Jewish characters in interactions with TV's blacks, Asians, American Indians, Muslims, Latinos. The range of experience, the spectrum of portrayals is nearly endless. Though not without problem, not without cost, television's Jewish characters — like their real-life counterparts — have been embraced by America and have embraced back eagerly.

3

Anti-Semitism

While many of the positive and distinctive aspects of Jewish life and America's open and welcoming spirit towards them have been depicted on popular television, so have the disruptive forces of religious bigotry.

The varied manifestations of anti–Semitism that popular television has portrayed have been almost unlimited. Depictions have ranged from the genteel bigotry of restricted country clubs to the crude thuggery of modern-day skinheads; from dramatized recountings of the Dreyfus affair in nineteenth-century France to beleaguered Jewish peddlers in the American Old West; from ancient church anti–Judaism to modern-day anti–Zionism and Holocaust revisionism. Hatred toward Jews has been shown to come from the high class, the low class, the polite, and the crude, even, in more than one case, from a Jew who had renounced Judaism.

In this regard, TV dramas have reflected the reality of the age-old phenomenon of anti–Semitism, a phenomenon that has existed with a "consistent continuity,"[1] although it has taken many different forms in different times and places. Drawing on contemporary issues, however, most shows have focused on modern-day manifestations of anti–Semitism that are current in the world today. Few deal with older anti–Judaism — the hatred of Jews on religious grounds, which prevailed for many centuries, usually at the instigation of the Roman Catholic Church. When this became outmoded and unacceptable as nineteenth-century reason and enlightenment superseded medieval superstitions and beliefs, anti–Judaism was replaced with more modern "scientific," "rational," and racial anti–Semitism.

The continued existence of modern anti–Semitism is reflected in the numerous programs that dramatize its many manifestations. As a reflector of reality, popular television has naturally taken on this issue; it is significant that as a shaper of social attitudes and behaviors, it invariably depicts anti–Semitism as an ugly, abhorrent trait that must be fought at every turn.

The fight against religious bigotry is fought in varying degrees and by various methods, by both Jewish and non–Jewish characters. Non-Jews often have a strong and prominent role in the battle against anti–Semitism. In fact,

103

whenever religious prejudice is expressed by certain non–Jews, they are over-shadowed — and ultimately overpowered — by a positively portrayed non–Jew who opposes such viewpoints. The depiction of non–Jews leading the fight against anti–Semitism in no way minimizes efforts by Jews to do so; indeed Jews are often shown also leading such efforts. But the participation of non–Jews demonstrates that the fight against anti–Semitism is not just a Jewish concern. For the vast majority of Americans who are not Jewish, watching their favorite TV character do battle with religious bigots can be an important influence. And often, non–Jewish characters can make inroads against anti–Semitism on their own turf in ways that Jews cannot.

"No Jews Allowed"

Indeed, it is on their terrain, in their relating to fellow Christians that non–Jews can have particular impact. One recurring TV portrayal where this is the case is the issue of restricted country clubs, a subject that has been portrayed as the central story line of several shows. This anti–Semitism of the upper crust was depicted as early as 1957 in a program called *The Trophy* that dealt with the story of a restricted college fraternity. After learning that their Jewish friend could not be admitted because of religious restrictions, a group of young men struggle to overturn the regulations.

The immensely popular comedy series *The Mary Tyler Moore Show* aired an episode on this theme in 1972. Mary befriends Joanne, an upper-class chic young woman who wines and dines her in the fanciest and hippest clubs and restaurants. While spending time with her new friend, who seems to demand exclusive attention, Mary neglects her Jewish friend, Rhoda Morgenstern. Realizing this, and in need of a fourth person for a doubles tennis game at Joanne's club, Mary suggests they ask Rhoda. Joanne becomes very uncomfortable and objects, saying that Rhoda is not the right type for her club. As it dawns on Mary that her friend is anti–Semitic, she confronts Joanne but receives only stammering denials. Motivated by loyalty, true friendship, and a hatred of bigotry, Mary defiantly declares that she too is Jewish,[2] thus ending her acquaintanceship with Joanne and restoring her close friendship with Rhoda.

Some fifteen years later, an episode of *The Golden Girls* closely paralleled the *Mary Tyler Moore Show* story. One of the golden girls, Dorothy, meets a suave novelist, is beguiled by her intellect and worldliness, and the two women become fast friends. But Dorothy's three women housemates dislike the new friend, Barbara, and complain that she's a snob. Dorothy is undeterred, but their feelings are confirmed when they are all prepared to spend an evening on the town together at Barbara's exclusive club. When Barbara learns that one of the men joining them as dates has the decidedly Jewish name of Murray Guttman, she quickly takes Dorothy aside and explains that the club is

restricted. As did Mary's friend, Barbara insists that these are not her prejudices, just the policies of the club. Dorothy is disgusted nonetheless, and saying, "You're not the kind of person I want to have for a friend," she throws her
out and tells her to "go to hell."

Jews being unwelcome at certain posh apartment buildings was the
premise of a 1972 episode of *Bridget Loves Bernie*, in which the couple moves
into a ritzy Manhattan high-rise. When the building management learns that
Bernie is Jewish, they try to evict them. Bernie and Bridget fight back, and
ultimately all management is fired for their bigoted actions.

The notion of a restricted club was used as the backdrop for a 1988 episode
of the family drama *Our House*. When avuncular Joe Kaplan is barred from a
local men's lodge, he assumes it is because he is Jewish, only later discovering
that is not the case. The reverse, where a Jew assumed a club was not restricted
but learns that it indeed is, appeared on the comedy *Doctor, Doctor* the following
year. Self-absorbed, social-climbing Jewish heart surgeon Grant Linowitz was
completely oblivious to this possibility until it was forcibly thrust in his face.
After successfully operating on a grateful Harlan "Hoey" Babcock — a quintessential Wasp who moves in all the right circles — the ambitious young doctor
senses an opportunity to gain membership to Babcock's exclusive Naragansett
Club. Grant's desire to enter Mr. Babcock's milieu merges seamlessly with his
desire for the patient's daughter, Catherine "Khaki" Babcock. Everything seems
to be progressing perfectly as Grant is invited to join the posh club and he
delightedly tells colleagues and friends that his relationship with Khaki is getting serious. When they reply with disgust that Babcock is a snob, that his club
is restricted (it had rejected the membership application of the black doctor in
their medical group), and that Grant is meant to be the token Jew, the surgeon
dismisses such notions, arguing, "Hoey Babcock is not a bigot — I'm dating his
daughter, for God's sake." But it is through his relationship with Khaki that
Grant is aroused from his blindness to Babcock's anti–Semitism. When a fellow doctor, the uproariously mischievous character of Michael Stratford, shows
up at the club to join the cocktail-sipping threesome of Grant and the Bab-
cocks, he loudly — and purposely — toasts "the future Dr. and Mrs. Grant
Linowitz." Hoey and Khaki burst into laughter at the ridiculousness of the
notion, laughter that turns to anger when Grant fails to see why the idea is so
absurd. Hoey elucidates: "The two of you married? Not while I'm alive... It's
not a question of good [enough for her]. It's a question of *right*." He goes on
to list undesirable traits of "you people," demonstrating the unacceptability of
marriage to a Jew for solely bigoted reasons. For Grant, who had no difficulty
with the idea of interdating and the prospect of intermarrying, this anti–Semitism is a rude awakening, and he resigns from the club and breaks off acquain-
tance with all its members.

That popular TV shows have been dealing with this issue for forty years
indicates that the struggle for Jews to gain acceptance in areas as seemingly

innocuous as a country club has not yet been resolved. Indeed, the ongoing relevance of this issue has been pointed up in headlines of just a few years ago—with presidential appointees forced, in the spotlight of media scrutiny, to resign from allegedly restricted clubs. Just as the response to this controversy was an individual one—resignations from clubs rather than policy changes—the TV dramas focus on the individual's speaking out on this question from a sense of moral uprightness rather than a group's altering its ways and practices.

For the most part, it is generally the Christian who takes the stand in this moral struggle. The Jewish characters are left out of the fray, with little focus on how such discrimination affects the Jewish victim's sense of self, identity, and quest for assimilation.

One exception to this, and a wry twist on the issue, appeared on an episode of *L.A. Law*, in which law firm head Leland MacKenzie invites prospective partner Eli Levinson to join his club. As Leland wines and dines him in the club's posh dining room, Eli perceives a very staid and Waspy atmosphere into which he feels he will not be welcomed. Leland persists, insisting that the club does indeed include Jewish members, and sets up an interview for Eli with two of its directors. Eli, unconvinced, now faces a dilemma: he wants to be a friend to Leland and accept his invitation, yet he feels monumentally out of place at the club and is certain that his obvious Jewishness will preclude his membership—and place Leland in a difficult situation. As a solution, he decides to go to the interview but pass himself off as a Wasp. His attempts to do so—he describes his fictitious sailing and squash exploits, portrays himself with gin and tonic in hand hailing from Darien, Connecticut, and even bestows upon himself the nickname Topper—create a scene that is comically delicious yet subtly uncomfortable. Later, when Leland informs him of the good news that he has been accepted for membership into the club, Eli expresses surprise, saying, "It was painfully obvious that I didn't fit in." In a gentle rebuke, Leland replies, "I think you may have an overly narrow view of what it means to fit in." Here notions about anti–Semitism are viewed from a different perspective. While there is, to be sure, still much persistent anti–Semitism that causes great consternation and discomfort to its targets and to all decent people, Leland's comment warns of the peril of seeing anti–Semites in every corner. The advice of this Christian friend to Eli to be who he is without undue fear is an important message.

That others may be more accepting than Eli imagines was an idea that propelled a remarkable episode of *Picket Fences*. One character, the eccentric, abrasive Jewish lawyer Douglas Wambaugh, had been subjected to widespread criticism both on screen and off. His tactics, mannerisms, and what some perceived as his coarse "shysterism" had many real-life viewers up in arms over their perceptions that Wambaugh was perpetuating and promoting a negative stereotype of Jews. To deal with this issue head on — and on screen — the program devoted an episode to a sort of trial of the Wambaugh character. Set in a *beit din* (court of Jewish law), the episode dealt with the issue of stereotypes and images, real and perceived, and their role in the fomenting of anti–Semitism.

Events unfold when Wambaugh gives a crude and tasteless eulogy during a memorial service at the synagogue and is later barred by the rabbi and the temple board from thereafter entering the house of worship. An outraged Wambaugh brings the case to a *beit din*, where each side presents its arguments. The synagogue's Rabbi Levin berates Wambaugh and his offensive actions and behavior as detrimental to Jews and the Jewish image and thus an encouragement to anti–Semitism. The counter argument is raised that Wambaugh is just a single character, not emblematic of a whole people, and that others will view him as such. To assume otherwise, to believe that people will be quick to take on anti–Semitic views as a result, is in itself a form of prejudice because it assumes the worst about others. As one of the rabbis on the *beit din's* three-man panel tells Rabbi Levin, "Where you are egregiously wrong is in attributing one man's conduct to an entire race of people." Levin protests, saying, "I'm not doing that. I'm saying the general public does that." "Then it is *you* who is bigoted," replies the *beit din's* rabbi. "Mr. Wambaugh is a man complete with his flaws. If you are offended by him, condemn his as a man, not as a Jew." Levin persists, countering, "But he's *perceived* as a Jew, and it hurts us."

Finally, the rabbi on the *beit din* rules. "You see that young woman there?" he asks, pointing out a former, non–Jewish employee of Wambaugh who had earlier in the proceedings risen to his defense, enumerating many of the lawyer's positive and generous traits that had gone unmentioned. "If she's an indication of how he's perceived, any religion should be glad to have him. It is the order of this *beit din* that Mr. Wambaugh be readmitted to your synagogue." The exoneration of Douglas Wambaugh — and thus of the TV image of the character as well — bespeaks a view that Jews, both on-screen and off, have less to fear from anti–Semitism than from their own fear of functioning as full and complex human beings, free to be as good, mediocre, or human as anyone else. The words of *L.A. Law's* Leland MacKenzie urging a release from being fettered by "an overly narrow view of what it means to fit in," resonated in *Picket Fences'* beit din.

Anti-Semitism from the In-Laws

While these episodes of *L.A. Law* and *Picket Fences* present an interesting angle and an important counterpoint, most TV images dealing with anti–Semitism portray it as an active, ugly, and ever present threat to be found lurking in virtually every avenue of American society, from boardrooms to barrooms, from sidewalks to salons. Even in the venue where Jews would seem to be most accepted — in the situation where they marry or date non–Jews — television has portrayed a plethora of scenarios in which anti–Semitism extends a threatening grip. Jews facing anti–Semitism within the context of an interdating or intermarriage situation (as in *Doctor, Doctor*) are a very common TV portrayal; often the Jewish characters have a forceful reaction. One noteworthy example was an episode of *L.A. Law* dealing with an impending intermarriage. At first, the upper-crust prejudice that is depicted takes a subtle form, even in the guise of compliments, as Jewish accountant and tax attorney Stuart Markowitz meets the mother of his bride-to-be, Ann Kelsey. Over dinner, Mrs. Kelsey admiringly expresses her perception that Jews possess great accounting abilities and that Jewish men "put their wives on pedestals." Stuart reacts with wry aplomb, but later, during a party given for the engaged couple at the home of the mother's friend, things take a turn for the worse. He overhears the friend conversing with an attentive Mrs. Kelsey, warning her of the awful things that await Ann in this marriage and exclaiming, "I can't believe she couldn't do better than some awful little money man." She lets Mrs. Kelsey in on these views of hers as well: "Jews are not like us. They look different; they think differently. Let them keep to their own kind." Visibly welling up with anger, Stuart approaches the friend and asks if any Jew had ever done anything to her to cause her to express such hostility to him and to Jews in general. When she bursts out a flustered no, Stuart pushes to the floor an immense chest full of valuable china and glasses, and as it shatters at her feet before a roomful of stunned and silenced guests he announces, "Now one has!"

Trying later to understand his reaction, uncharacteristic both in terms of its vehemence and its strong Jewish component in light of his admitted lack of Jewish affiliation, Stuart explains to Ann that he suddenly "felt the weight of five thousand years" and affirms his Jewish identity with conviction by exclaiming, "It's who I am!" Coming face to face with anti–Semitism in the most polite and ordinary of settings, Stuart felt suddenly part of a people vulnerable in any set of circumstances, in any milieu, no matter how assimilated they may be. Not until he felt personally maligned and belittled did he come to this realization and have the rage and ability to speak out.

Another Jewish character who faced unkind reactions about her Jewishness within an interfaith romantic relationship went even further in expressing her Jewish identity. On an episode of *The Waltons*, a Jewish girl begins dating one of the Walton sons, Jason. When the family learns at the dinner table that their guest is Jewish, there is stunned silence and a suddenly chilled and unwelcoming air. The young Jewish woman, named Toni, flees from their home in tears, leaving Jason to chastise them by asking, "How would you like to be the only Baptist at a table of Jews?"

Toni is unsettled by the event, particularly since, as she tells Jason, she knows little about her religion and has never practiced it. As a result, she is moved to study and explore Judaism, driven by what she describes as "a hunger I've never felt before."

Anti-Semitism arising in this context also elicits activism from non–Jewish characters. In the 1986 made-for-TV movie *Mrs. Delafield Wants to Marry*, genteel anti–Semitism rises when the proper widow Mrs. Margaret Delafield intends to marry the Jewish Dr. Marvin Elias. When her friends and family voice strong anti–Semitic objection, the elderly matron proclaims her disgust, saying, "God knows I don't want to do battle with prejudice at my time of life, but if I have to I will." Another older interfaith couple about to marry but facing familial anti–Semitism appeared in a humorous context on the short-lived sitcom *The Home Court*.

Although Mrs. Delafield and Dr. Elias's wedding plans did survive anti–Semitism, a different relationship did not. On a 1972 episode of *All in the Family*, which featured the visiting character of Maude, Edith Bunker's cousin who would later be the main character in a spin-off series, Maude's daughter is about to marry a Jewish man. Like Mrs. Kelsey on *L.A. Law*, Maude has only compliments for the Jewish people, saying that "the Jews are brilliant" and all have "that wonderful sensitivity." Carol, the prospective bride, scolds her mother for making what she explains to her are reverse anti–Semitic remarks. But provoked by a separate issue, the bride and groom begin arguing, and Carol is shocked to discover that in her anger, she hurls anti–Semitic remarks at her husband-to-be, David. The notion of bigoted sentiments, however positively they may be couched, being passed down from one generation to the next is here on display.

Suddenly the target of anti–Semitic remarks from his wife-to-be, David reacts to the crescendo of conflict by bursting out, "I knew it. I was waiting for this. My mother told me it might take a year, two years, maybe three. But sooner or later, if I married into this family, one of you would crack, and the anti–Semitic remarks would come pouring out." Suddenly, from a person wholly at ease with intermarrying, about to enter into a mixed marriage the following day, David is faced with the surfacing of another part of himself— formerly deeply buried and rejected — that harbors the notion that anti–Semitism will emerge in even the best of intermarriages. When Carol denounces his anticipation of anti–Semitism as "anti-gentile feeling," the picture is one of unbridgeable animus and mistrust.

Although the situation cools and Carol and David retract their insults, they are beyond the point of reconciliation — despite Maude's comically desperate efforts to reunite them. ("Everybody knows that Jewish boys make the best husbands," she pleads to Carol. "It's a known fact. Look it up!") But shaken by the animosity and differences revealed, and newly aware of unresolved attitudes and religious gulfs between them, the couple calls off the wedding.

Anti-Semitic in-laws — or potential in-laws — have been portrayed not only in upper-class and suburban homes but in working class and rural settings as well. In *Chicken Soup*, the Jewish Jackie Fisher comes under incessant attack from his Gentile girlfriend's brother, an Irish Catholic bar owner named Michael who is full of stereotypical and bigoted notions about Jews. Cast in the mold of an Archie Bunker, Michael is depicted not as malicious or threatening, but as a foolish, uneducated person who is almost likable in his irascibility. Jackie responds to this sort of anti–Semitism with humor, characteristically making jokes to get his point across and show the absurdity of Michael's attitudes.

On an episode of *Little House on the Prairie*, the Jewish set of in-laws are visiting the prairie town because their son and daughter-in-law are about to have a baby. The situation becomes very uncomfortable when they are greeted with great hostility and unceasing anti–Jewish clichés and stereotypes from their non–Jewish in-laws.

The Jew as Different

Another Jewish family that faced anti–Semitism on the American frontier appeared on a modern Western, *Dr. Quinn, Medicine Woman*. They are defended by the good doctor who fights the townspeople's prejudices and leads them to an acceptance of the new family.

In two earlier Western settings, the Jewish characters react to anti–Semitism by attempting to show their persecutors that although their customs and traditions are different, they are human beings just the same. A 1966 episode of *Rawhide* deals with an ancient anti–Semitic myth — that of the Jew as the Wanderer. The program tells the story of Michob, an itinerant Jewish peddler who joins up with a group of cattle drivers on his way to a town to clear a man unjustly accused of murder. When bad luck suddenly befalls the drivers, some of them become suspicious of Michob's different ways and customs and point out such strange phenomena such as rain falling around him but not on him. One of the men tells of the Christian legend that while on the way to crucifixion Jesus asked to sit in front of a shoemaker's shop to rest. When the shoemaker refused him, Jesus denounced him with the curse, "You shall travel forever." After the storyteller ominously announces that Michob is one name of the Wandering Jew, the other men begin circulating rumors that Michob is the Wandering Jew and should be forced to leave the group. The cattle drive leader advises his men to leave Michob alone, but it is to no avail. Michob is ambushed and beaten, but he finally fends off his attackers to the astonishment of the mob that had gathered to watch. Turning to them, he rises in indignation, and in an effort to dispel their primitive biases, he implores them, "Look at me — all of you! Look past superstition and fear and ancient tales of incantation and boiling pots and *see* me! I am a man — I bleed, I rage, I laugh, I cry, I see, I feel — and I even pray. But it isn't enough! I'm still a myth, a denizen of darkness, a harbinger of disaster and ruination. And why? Because I have committed the crime of being different!" Even in the face of hostility, Michob refuses to give up his distinctiveness, but he does ask them to see beyond it, saying, "I may be different, but I am a man. Just as you are men." This speech, coupled with the concern and compassion he shows for a dying cattle driver who had previously been antagonistic towards him, win Michob apologies, new friendships, and respect from the entire group.

His ultimate acceptance relays the positive message that those who are different should not be treated cruelly for that reason. But the show does have a disturbing aspect. One is left with a sense that the actual anti–Jewish legend is never really refuted; indeed as Michob goes on his way, there is a suspicion that he is a mystical, tormented being who has somehow fulfilled his appointed role. One could gather from this presentation that while the Wandering Jew should be treated fairly, the legend itself has merit. As opposed to most other shows where the anti–Semitism is roundly refuted, here the entire show seems to be a play on this legend.

In a similar but more benign vein, the plea of the Jew to remain different, to retain his or her own beliefs and principles in the face of anti–Semitism and yet to demonstrate equal humanity was expressed by a Jewish character in another Western, *Here Come the Brides*, in 1968. Here, it is a Jewish woman in an 1870s Oregon logging camp who is faced with the hatred of other young women there when it is disclosed that she is Jewish and wants to marry a Jewish man, which may — in a convoluted series of events — cause the ruination of the whole camp. When many of her former friends turn against her, the leader of the camp defends her right to be Jewish as he leads the fight against bigotry.

Like Michob, the young girl is undeterred in her Jewishness by surrounding hostility and seeks to reason with it. She tries to show her former friends that they have no cause to fear and hate her. When at last she finds a Jewish bridegroom, in preparation for her wedding she undergoes the Jewish ritual of *mikveh* in a natural lake nearby the camp. And she brings along a particularly hostile girlfriend, explaining to her, "People who hate usually don't know what they hate... Ever since you found out I was Jewish, I've become strange to you, something foreign, and that's just not true. This ceremony, it is Jewish, but the idea, well it's just what every bride would like to be."

While these Jewish characters are terribly upset at being ostracized for their different customs and ceremonies, they are not deterred from holding fast to their ways. But in their desire to fit in as a minority and be accepted by the non–Jewish majority, they try to stress their similarities with all people, emphasizing that which they have in common rather than that which separates them.

In a more modern setting, a sense of being an outsider propelled a Jewish character to explore his own Jewishness and distinctiveness. On an episode of *Picket Fences*, an unidentified body is found and thought to be an alien deposited by a UFO. When the body is finally identified as a very ordinary earthling, who was Jewish, connections are made between space aliens and Jews as outsiders in society. Stirred by this event, lawyer Douglas Wambaugh is moved to explore his own Jewishness.

Anti-Semitism in Context of General Bigotry

Television has often portrayed the idea of Jews being different within the broader framework of *all* ethnic minorities being different. Many programs have depicted anti–Semitism as a part of a more general bigotry, where no specific ethnic minority is the focus of the program, but rather a general picture is presented. In an episode of *Family Ties*, for example, Alex's parents are terribly distressed to learn that he has been going to a restricted club. They are disappointed with his lack of judgment in wanting to be part of a club that discriminates against, as his mother says, "Blacks, Jews, Hispanics, or any other group that didn't come over on the *Mayflower*."

In such programs, an association between racism and anti–Semitism is often made. In an episode of *L.A. Law*, for example, when young, black attorney Jonathan Rollins is incensed that his firm is retaining a client with holdings in South Africa, he berates the patriarchal senior partner, Leland McKenzie, for his agreement in this. In an effort to change McKenzie's mind, Rollins recounts moral stands the elder lawyer took on other issues in the past, reminding him, "You refused to join your own father's club because they wouldn't admit Jews."

Often, blacks and Jews are shown to share a kinship as victims of prejudice. In a 1970 *Hallmark Hall of Fame* presentation titled "A Storm in Summer," the relationship between an elderly Jewish man and a black youth from Harlem is transformed from initial hostility to friendship and understanding, as they get to know each other and together experience the realities of bigotry. They first meet when ten-year-old Herman Washington is thrust upon unwilling deli owner Abel Shaddick after Abel's irresponsible nephew reneged on his offer to care for the youth as part of a two-week social program. Young Herman expresses his negative feelings towards Jews, which stem from the fact that "the guy who owns our building is Jewish ... he's a pretty bad cat ... Nobody likes him." As Herman threatens to leave, Abel says to him "So go ... I don't need a three-foot-tall Ethiopian anti–Semite." Abel notifies Gloria, the non–Jewish social worker in charge of the case, that "between a seventy-two-year-old Jew and a ten-year-old black boy there's not what you'd call a mutuality of interest." Yet their relationship grows closer; Abel even takes to calling Herman by the endearing Yiddishism *boychik*.

Overcoming their own difficulties with each other, Herman and Abel

become common targets of bigotry. At one point, they are harassed by a group
of delinquent teens who tell Abel that he must be Moses and that Herman must
be "one of the children of the lost tribes of Israel." The two experience bigotry
once again when Gloria invites them to her high-class country club, where
they are surrounded by unfriendly and unsubtle whispering. Gloria, however,
is not intimidated and insists that they remain.

Jews and blacks as common targets for prejudice in the South was portrayed in the 1978 made-for-TV movie *Summer of My German Soldier*, which
takes place in rural Georgia during World War II. Patty Bergen, an adolescent
Jewish girl abused by her father and fairly friendless in the world, hides out a
young German POW escaped from a local prisoner camp, whom she tentatively
befriends. Her secret is discovered by Ruth, a black woman who works as the
Bergen's housekeeper and is who is ever protective of Patty. Their shared secret
bestows a special bond and subjects them both to harassment when suspicions
arise. Hints of racism and anti–Semitism towards them, which underlie much
of the program, finally erupt full-blown when their deed is discovered. In the
final scene, the two walk steadfastly down the town's main street hand in hand
as bigoted epithets are hurled from either side.

A more recent era in the South was depicted in the 1990 made-for-TV
movie *Murder in Mississippi*, in which Jews and blacks were also linked as victims of the worst kind of bigotry. The drama recounted the 1964 murders of
the three Civil Rights workers Mickey Schwerner and Andrew Goodman, who
were Jewish, and James Chaney, who was African American.

On a different scale, and in an Old West setting, a Jewish and a black student were portrayed as common targets of a bigoted teacher on a 1962 episode
of *Bonanza*. The community schoolteacher, Mr. Norton, systematically expels
from his class of youngsters all troublemakers, all of whom happen to be
minorities — Asian, black, Jewish. The story focuses on the expulsion of the Jewish boy, and it is his particular plight that draws family patriarch Ben Cartwright
into the fray. The expelled Jewish student is young Albert Michelson, a brilliant boy with a tremendous future. But Albert conducts physics experiments
in the streets and often causes some sort of mishap — a possible reason for his
expulsion. Discovering that Mr. Norton was motivated purely by prejudices,
however, Ben takes up the fight against the anti–Semitic teacher, who ultimately reforms his ways and asks for — and receives — forgiveness.

Anti-Semitism in History

The *Bonanza* episode combined a portrayal of anti–Semitism with the
early life of an actual American Jewish figure: as a voice-over by Lorne Greene
(Ben Cartwright) informs viewers, Albert Michelson was in fact the first American ever to win a Nobel Prize for scientific achievement, for his precise

measurement of the speed of light. Other programs also drew on actual events to depict issues of anti–Semitism. A 1953 episode of the anthology series *Suspense*, based on the radio classic, dramatized the anti–Semitic charges against the French Jewish army captain Alfred Dreyfus and his defense by the non–Jewish Emile Zola. This theme was reexplored decades later when HBO presented its version of the Dreyfus case in the 1991 movie *Prisoner of Honor*.

In another historical dramatization, anti–Semitism of nineteenth-century England and its Parliament was depicted in a 1963 presentation of the *Hallmark Hall of Fame* series titled "The Invincible Mr. Disraeli." This biographical account of the English prime minister — who was later elevated to nobleman, with the title first earl of Beaconsfield, Lord Benjamin Disraeli — depicts various anti–Semitic incidents that affected Disraeli and profoundly shaped his life. He recounts how he was born Jewish but was baptized at the age of thirteen because his father, who thought little of religion, allowed "a friend to convince him that my sister, my brother, and myself would get on better in this world if we belonged to the Church of England. Had it not been for these pressures, I would be a Jew in faith as well as in race." Despite his father's move, Disraeli faces anti–Semitism at every turn. He is characterized in cartoons as "Shylock's heir" and "the bumptious Jew-boy." He watches as colleague Lionel Rothschild wins election to Parliament seven times yet is never allowed to take his seat because, as a professing Jew, he refuses to take Parliament's traditional oath on a New Testament — the Christian Bible.

Disraeli protests this and successfully fights to allow Rothschild to take his parliamentary oath on an "Old Testament" — the Hebrew Bible. Years later, upon leaving Parliament to take on the life of a nobleman, Disraeli recalls in a flashback his speech on this issue — and his first ever in the House of Commons — when he declared, "I have been witness to an outrage. Perhaps it is ingenuous of me to feel such shock and surprise at the rejection of this most valuable man, the honorable [Lionel Rothschild] from the borough of London. Perhaps this outrage is no more than the following of precedent... We are approaching the season of Christmas, the sacred time which I assume this august body will celebrate by petitioning against the Jews." When someone cries out, "This is a Christian body!" Disraeli responds, "Whose body is it that we Christians celebrate? It is the birth of a Jew! Were the holy family on this Christmas Eve to seek shelter in this house, would you gentlemen extend to them the comforts of your manger?"

Although separated by eras and continents and broadcast twenty-five years apart, this program and the episode of *L.A. Law* share a similar theme. Both depict people detached from their Judaism — whether by assimilation or even conversion — who nonetheless face anti–Semitism. This anti–Semitism is blind to level of commitment or observance and finds even the most attenuated Jews. And they, rather than remaining in the obscurity they sought, visibly and vocally fight it.

Medieval England was the setting for yet another display of historical anti–Semitism in TV dramatizations of Sir Walter Scott's 1819 classic novel about chivalry, romance, and politics. As the Normans and Saxons battle in twelfth-century England, noble knight Ivanhoe is rescued by Isaac and his daughter Rebecca, who falls in love with him. The cruel anti–Semitism to which Isaac and Rebecca are subjected appeared in versions of *Ivanhoe* on a CBS TV movie in 1982 and a three-part miniseries on A&E in 1997.

Another portrayal of British anti–Semitism was depicted in — of all things — a TV dramatization of the bloody Jack the Ripper case that promised to reveal the real killer after years of doubt. Although the issue of anti–Semitism is not dealt with in a major way in this 1988 miniseries, it is an anti–Semitic scrawling (and its misspelling) of "Death to the Jues" that provides the pivotal clue for solving the notorious murders in this reading of the legendary case.

Anti-Semitism closer to home was a theme of another miniseries that same year, *The Murder of Mary Phagan*, which was based on the real-life Leo Frank case. The television drama about the Brooklyn-born Jew accused of murdering a young girl in 1913 Atlanta, Georgia, portrays the anti–Semitic element of the accusations. Leo Frank is Jewish *and* a Northerner — a volatile combination that causes him to be branded irrevocably as an outsider. Coupled with other damaging developments, it eventually leads to his lynching by an angry mob in 1915.

Synagogue Vandalism

One of the most historic and ongoing ways anti–Semites attack Jews is by attacking the symbols of Judaism — synagogues and *Torah* scrolls. For TV shows dealing with anti–Semitism, it is a dramatic way of demonstrating the violence and potentially destructive power of anti–Semitism. It has been a frequently depicted theme on popular TV, on such series as the 1960s law drama *The Defenders* and the 1970s police drama *Adam-12*.

Often it is the brutality of this act that galvanizes both Jewish and non–Jewish characters to rally to react. It even moved, eventually, a reluctant Archie Bunker to join a group to fight synagogue vandalism on an episode of *Archie Bunker's Place* titled "Trashing of the Temple." Archie's young Jewish niece, Stephanie, and his Jewish partner, Murray Klein, belong to Temple Beth Shalom. When anti–Semitic vandalism hits the community and surrounding areas, the rabbi asks Murray to join a group to protect their temple, and he unhesitatingly volunteers. Archie is also asked — implored — to join by Murray and the rabbi. They urge Archie to join forces with them because he is a prominent non–Jew in the community, and thus his solidarity would lend another dimension of strength to the fight against anti–Semitism. Archie, however, remains unconvinced and will not join.

Shortly afterward, during Friday night services — with Murray and Stephanie in attendance — the synagogue is firebombed. It is a frightening scene of shattered glass, smoke rising from extinguished fires, swastikas smeared on the doors, and a very scared Stephanie is shown. She then initiates a remarkable exchange, asking Murray why people do this. He answers, "We've been trying to find the answer to that for five thousand years — we haven't found the answer yet." When Stephanie pursues the issue and asks if it will ever stop, Murray replies, "Sure! They'll stop when we all go away — when we disappear from the face of the earth." Both vow that they will never allow this to happen.

Having heard about the bombing and concerned for Stephanie's safety, Archie arrives to take Stephanie home — for good. Over Murray and her strong protests, he insists on withdrawing her from the temple Hebrew school. Nothing will sway him until a regular customer at his saloon — a blind man — tells Archie, "There's a famous saying: They came for the Black people — I wasn't Black so I didn't speak up. Then they came for the Jews — I wasn't Jewish so I didn't speak up. Then they came for the Catholics — I wasn't Catholic so I didn't speak up. Then they came for me, and there was nobody left to speak up."[3] Finally moved to take responsibility for helping to fight anti–Semitism, not only for Stephanie but for himself as well, Archie goes to the synagogue and volunteers his time to help protect it.

Synagogue vandalism in a 1969 episode of *Ironside* also galvanizes the community to come together, eliciting the support not only of Christian laity but of leaders as well. A small storefront synagogue is invaded and defaced with swastikas, and the rabbi is injured upon surprising the vandals. Chief Ironside, an old friend of the rabbi, is determined to recover a stolen *Torah* scroll removed during the break-in and now being held for ransom. The reverend of a nearby church wants to help raise money for the ransom that is being sought for it. (That he is black adds another dimension to the intercultural depiction.) When the rabbi's wife demurs his offer, saying that she doesn't want him to make their problems his own, the reverend insists that "that's what it's all about."

This theme of a community coming together to rebuild a vandalized synagogue has informed several shows including most recently, *Promised Land* (a spin-off series from *Touched by an Angel*), about the Greene family, who travels from town to town helping others in distress. In one town, they come face to face with anti–Semitism when the synagogue is vandalized, the rabbi assaulted, and a Jewish classmate that one of the youngsters has befriended is the target of bigotry. The family spearheads the rebuilding of the house of worship but discovers to its dismay that anti–Semitism in the community runs deeper than a few errant youngsters. Their efforts to bring the town together are ultimately successful, as all join in an ecumenical service at the rebuilt synagogue.

Christian Clergy Fight Anti-Semitism

The picture of Christian clergy in the forefront of the fight against anti–Semitism, like the reverend in *Ironside*, is a recurrent one on popular television and one that is an important example of interfaith cooperation.

Another priest reacted even more strongly to an act of synagogue desecration on a 1989 episode of *Wiseguy*. This series chronicled the life and work of Vinnie Terranova, a rugged, down-home Brooklynite who is really a government undercover agent. Vinnie's brother is a priest who rushes to help clean up a synagogue that has been vandalized. He appears on the evening news that night, in his collar, denouncing this anti–Semitic act, saying, "The violation of this temple is a terrible thing ... the people who did this violate their own human spirit. They diminish all of us in this act. They are pathetically ignorant people." He seems to have been transformed by the whole experience, telling Vinnie that for the first time in eighteen years in the priesthood, since entering the seminary, "I felt to my soul what made me become a priest." It was through the act of fighting anti–Semitism that he had his own spiritual experience. As he says with reflective humor, "I guess it's ironic my revelation came in a synagogue."

One portrayal where the Christian clergy was even more determined in the fight against anti–Semitism than the aggrieved Jewish party was in *St. Elsewhere*. In a flashback episode that aired in 1986, a young Dr. Auschlander arrives at St. Eligius Hospital in Boston in 1945 and discovers that he is the only Jew on staff. Greeted with anti–Semitic comments from a troubled teenager who scrawls swastikas on the doctor's office walls, Auschlander decides to leave the hospital. It is the hospital's Irish Catholic priest who urges him to stay and fight it rather than flee. When the priest chides the doctor's apparent timidity, saying, "First incident — you're going to run?" Auschlander reveals that this is by no means the first incident. In fact, he says, "just a month ago, I was to be named to the Board of Medical Quality Assurance. 'Underqualified,' they said — too Semitic was the truth." He had faced anti–Semitism in the army too, from a soldier who had asked why he was defending America "as if it wasn't my country — and my family's been here for over a hundred years!" He seems merely tired of the constant battles against anti–Semitism that he repeatedly faces and that in the past he had resisted.

While this hospital priest's efforts to combat anti–Semitism were set in 1945 at the end of the war, several programs have depicted other Christian clergy who risked their lives while the war was going on to save Jews from the Nazis (see Chapter 4, "Holocaust"). These and other portrayals of Christian religious leaders fighting anti–Jewish bigotry have the potential to set a very positive example for their constituents. Such programs may reflect current efforts in the Christian community to redress age-old, Church-inspired persecution and hatred of Jews.

While commendable, these depictions sometimes include Christian clergy voicing statements that project a view of Judaism and anti–Semitism that is problematic. For example, in *Evil in Clear River*, a program about Holocaust revisionism, a minister speaks out against anti–Semitism by saying, "Jesus did not equate the Jews with evil. Now, maybe he condemned the Pharisees, but what he was condemning was greed and selfishness and hypocrisy — not people, never that." To suggest that the Pharisees as a whole — who included some of Judaism's greatest moral, religious, and ethical teachers and thinkers, not to mention the Apostle Paul, his father, and his teacher — represented greed, selfishness, and hypocrisy borders on a condemnation of Judaism and perpetuates one of the myths that formed the basis of early anti–Judaism and that continues to fuel anti–Semitism. The priest's motivation seems to be surely good, in that he is stating unequivocally — in terms that Christians will relate to — that Jews are not evil. And yet at the same time, his words imply that only Judaism should be condemned, not Jews; that Jews should not be hated just because of their religion. The best of intentions notwithstanding, care should be taken not to perpetuate this sort of ideology.

Youth-Oriented Shows

Young people confronting — or perpetrating — anti–Semitism has been the subject of many shows. These depictions are particularly important for the paradigms they present in terms of how young people, whether Jewish or not Jewish, deal with issues of religious bigotry and intolerance. These take on heightened significance when the shows are in fact teen or young people's shows, viewed by large young audiences all over the country, as in the case of the very popular *Beverly Hills 90210*.

This wildly popular series (teens as well as college students would gather together each week to hold viewing parties) presented two episodes about anti–Semitism. In both, the Jewish Andrea Zuckerman finds herself in the vortex of campus controversies regarding issues that could very well confront real-life college students. In one episode, loosely based on the real life Leonard Jeffries case, she leads the fight to bar a racist ideologue from speaking on campus. In another, she confronts perceived anti–Semitism in the sorority she wants to join, taking a strong and self-sacrificing stand against it.

Another Jewish college student who faced anti–Semitism was Jessica Cohen on *Class of '96*, a short-lived but critically praised show set at a fictional college. Although Jessica's Jewish identity went unmentioned initially in the series, it emerges when she confronts campus bigotry in the form of JAP jokes. With little connection to her Jewish heritage and identity, Jessica seems nonplused by the sudden surfacing and public circulation of JAP jokes at Havenhurst College, even when they are repeated by some of her friends. As meetings are convened, petitions circulated, and protests organized to respond to this calumny, she refuses to become involved, resisting the personal urgings of her friends, Jewish activist students, and the campus Hillel director, Rabbi Nancy Silverman. But as the issue continues to gain in notoriety, at one point becoming the topic of intense classroom discussion, it serves as a turning point for Jessica both in terms of her own increasing sensitivity to the problem and a new and genuine exploration and assertion of her Jewish identity. The story line includes a series of incidents, reactions, confrontations, responses, revelations, and discussions before the issue is ultimately resolved. Important questions about free speech, prejudice, quotas, college fraternities, and campus behavior are raised. In its head-on tackling of the issue of JAP jokes as a form of prejudice against Jewish women, this episode was laudable and unusual.

Young people involved in committing anti–Semitic acts and the efforts to change their lives were the topic of a *CBS Schoolbreak Special*, a one-hour drama show that aired periodically in the afterschool hours. Titled *The Writing on the Wall*, it dramatized the real-life tale of a New Jersey rabbi whose synagogue is set upon by three teenagers. Rather than recommending their imprisonment, Rabbi Eugene Markowitz presses for a plan that he has devised: to rehabilitate them by teaching them about Judaism, the Holocaust, tolerance, respect, and responsibility. The judge agrees to this approach, and viewers see the boys visiting a Holocaust museum, studying with the rabbi at the synagogue, and having their lives take a turn for the better.

A more pessimistic view involving young people as perpetrators of anti–Semitism, although on a very adult show, appeared on a powerful episode of *Law and Order* titled "Blood Libel." The outstanding series, each episode of which presents first the police work and then the legal aspects of a particular case, is known for offering complex plots, delving into real and complicated issues, and serving up no easy answers. This episode was a stellar example of such qualities. When a young woman who is a high school teacher is found murdered at the school, detectives discover that some students had been buying grades from a different teacher. It first appears that Sara Aronson was murdered by the teacher who was selling grades, a scheme that Aronson had apparently threatened to reveal if it was not stopped. But, things not always being what they seem on *Law and Order*, the detectives begin to discover anti–Semitic literature and threatening secret codes among the belongings of some of Aronson's students. The investigation takes a different turn, pointing to the students who were doing the grade buying.

When one of them is eventually charged with Aronson's murder, his lawyer — described as a "Klan lawyer" — rather than denying his client's anti–Semitism, seeks to utilize and exploit it to play upon the potential anti–Semitism in others, particularly the jury, as a defense tactic. The lawyer, Roy Payne, charges that a Jewish conspiracy is responsible for his "innocent" client being charged. After all, he argues, since the first suspect (the other teacher) was Jewish but was cleared, "my client is an innocent victim of a pernicious conspiracy to frame him and protect the real murderer. The Jews got together to protect him, and I'll prove it.... A Jewish detective led the investigation, a Jewish teacher was inexplicably dismissed as a prime suspect, another Jewish teacher lied to implicate my client, a Jewish forensic technician allowed evidence to be contaminated." Although the charges are outlandish and absurd, the judge allows Payne to raise them in court as an alternate theory.

When opposing counsel berates Payne for trying to "confuse and inflame the jury" and raising wild conspiracy theories, the lawyer counters, "It's the golden age of conspiracy theories. People love them. They help them to make sense of an irrational world." Indeed, it is just such a need that fuels the fires of anti–Semitism. Payne seems to know this when he goes on to confidently tell the prosecutors, "We've got reasonable doubt. You go outside with me right now. We'll ask twelve people what they think about Jews. And all I need is just one."

Payne turns the ensuing trial of his client into a trial of the Jews. He elicits derogatory but sympathetically received statements from his client about his fellow Jewish students: they made him feel like an outsider, they put him down because he was a Christian, they acted like they knew more than him, they went to Ivy League schools while he plodded through. Despite the fact that under astute cross-examination, the defendant loses his temper and nearly blurts out that he killed Sara Aronson, he is cleared of the crime. Payne's devious tactics playing on anti–Semitism are successful; the jury acquits his client eleven to one.

"One holdout," a dejected prosecutor muses during the postmortem. "I wonder which one." "Whoever it is, they blended right in," says another. A world-weary district attorney, who happens to be Jewish, asks, "What else is new?"

With those lines closing the program, the show certainly offers no simplistic answers to the question of anti–Semitism. Indeed it portrays it as so deeply imbedded within society and as such a known, anticipated quality that it can be astutely harnessed to serve one's unjust ends even within the legal system. Although, as perhaps a silver lining, only a single juror accepted the outrageous conspiracy theory, the persistent, palpable, and rooted quality of anti–Semitism emerges as a tenet of this presentation, in a dark but realistic outlook. In this view, it evokes Murray Klein's comment on *Archie Bunker's Place* about anti–Semites: "They'll stop when we all go away — when we disappear from the face of the earth."

With its portrayal of anti–Semitism as a given, television often presents it as the obvious motive when a Jew is murdered. The dramatic twist of surprise comes when the unfolding of the plot reveals that in fact other motives were at work. Such scenarios were played out on a different episode of *Law and Order* (when killings were at first attributed to Arab terrorists) and on the summer series *Bodies of Evidence* (where neo–Nazis were at first to blame).

Neo-Nazis

Although the swastika in Dr. Auschlander's office on *St. Elsewhere* had been painted by a confused young boy, neo–Nazis bearing swastikas and with more serious intentions have been the subject of many shows. Viewers are alerted to the neo–Nazi content of such shows as they are confronted with characters spouting Nazi ideology, parading swastikas, uniformed in brown shirts, expressing admiration for Hitler and calling for the completion of his Final Solution to the Jewish problem. Their leaders are shown to be sinister yet intelligent and clever enough to draw to their ranks disaffected Americans, convincing them that the Jews and other minorities are responsible for all their woes and all evil in this country and the world.

As early as 1963 an episode of the law drama *Sam Benedict* dealt with a white supremacist group. And the synagogue vandalism in the 1962 episode of *The Defenders* mentioned above was the handiwork of a neo–Nazi youth who painted the temple with swastikas, stating when caught, "I don't like the people inside ... I'm not ashamed of it." His own defense attorney, the very Waspy and respectable Lawrence Preston, is appalled by these views, asserting, "The Nazis started by putting a little paint on walls. They ended up committing the biggest crime in history."

In the 1970s, an odd twist on the neo–Nazi theme was depicted in an episode of *Lou Grant*, where journalists covering the story of such a hate group discover that its leader is a former Orthodox Jew now named Donald Stryker (changed from Sturner). One of the reporters, Billie, investigates the story further, trying to glean from interviews with those who knew him earlier in life what led to this bizarre transformation. She visits his family and synagogue and from a teacher learns that as a youngster he had been badly beaten up because of his religion. Donald's psychiatrist tells Billie that "a person is being attacked, but instead of defending himself he begins to identify with the attacker. He can't bear to be a victim any longer, so he simply changes sides." This extreme scenario of the Jew becoming the anti–Semite — of one taking on the cause and even assuming the identity of one's enemy — is shown to be an unhealthy and self-destructive reaction yet one that is plausible and manifested in varying degrees in reality.

This theme was revisited years later in an episode of *Murder One*, in which one Jewish college student, Jonathan Miller, targets another with hate mail, phone calls, and painted swastikas, which culminate in a vicious anti–Semitic attack that seriously injures the other student. In the trial that follows, the prosecuting attorney puts a psychologist on the stand to ask him, "How is it possible for a person to be Jewish and at the same time anti–Semitic?" The doctor attributes this to the fact that Miller's grandfather was a concentration camp survivor and that "very often, survivor guilt creates a generalized dissociative anxiety in the family, particularly among the offspring." The doctor traces this phenomenon in Miller's family, saying that his parents responded by spearheading a number of Jewish causes in the Jewish community and beyond. "This placed even more pressure on the defendant, who was already despondent over his perceived inadequacies. He lashed out — projecting his hatred onto anything Jewish." Although it turns out that the most extreme forms of Miller's behavior were actually due to a brain tumor discovered during the trial, the show makes a case for a psychological basis for instances of hatred of one's own ethnic group.

On the other end of the spectrum, as opposed to a Jewish character who reacts to anti–Semitism by lashing out against his own people or by joining a group dedicated to their destruction, a Jewish character on a 1973 episode of *All in the Family* responds by intensifying his devotion to protect his people, through whatever means, even taking up arms. In this episode, neo–Nazis who mistakenly believe that Archie's house is the home of the Jewish Mr. Bloom paint it with a swastika — a mark that is to target the home for subsequent violence. When Paul Benjamin, member of a militant Jewish defense organization, is alerted by the swastika on Archie's home and comes to protect him, the stage is set for a discussion among Paul and the Bunkers about the pros and cons of meeting violence with violence. The sitcom ends on a very serious and tragic note when the Bunkers hear the explosion of a car bomb planted by the neo–Nazis, which kills Paul.

In Paul's death there is an uncanny and ironic parallel with the *Lou Grant* story. In that episode, when Billie's newspaper refuses Donald's request not to print the story revealing his identity, he commits suicide. For both Donald and Paul, who display two diametrically opposed reactions to anti–Semitism, the scourge of anti–Semitism that pained them both ultimately kills them both. The dangers of anti–Semitism, no matter what approach one takes toward it, are shown to be very real and ever present.

In contrast to these two extremes, a more complex and layered reaction characterized a Jewish woman encountering neo–Nazis on *Reasonable Doubts*. Over the course of a three-episode arc about the murder of a Hasidic Jew by neo–Nazis, deaf attorney Tess Kaufman, who is prosecuting the case, exhibits a range of strong emotions. She is incensed by the hate murder and dismayed about a Jewish lawyer defending the Nazi; she finds herself in turmoil when conflicting feelings surface within her as a result of the case.

The story opens as three neo–Nazi boys attempt to vandalize a store and the owner, a Hasid who lives above the store, runs down to intervene. One of the boys pours gasoline over the man and sets him ablaze, burning him alive while his family looks on helplessly. Although the boy is arrested, he is charged as a juvenile, only later to be tried as an adult. Intensifying the drama is the fact that this criminal is defended by a Jewish lawyer, outraging both Tess and her non–Jewish investigator Dicky Cobb. (In a different setting and show, another non–Jewish character, John Hemingway on *The John Larroquette Show*, was similarly upset when he encounters a Jewish lawyer defending a neo–Nazi's right to charter a bus for a Nazi gathering). Tess is driven to win this case not only because it is so repugnant but because, as the show makes abundantly clear, of the added element of her Jewishness. She struggles to deal with this case on both a professional and an emotional level.

In trying to break the case, Dicky Cobb pursues and leans on one of the three assailants, pressuring him in powerful and moving ways to come clean. In the course of his investigations, he evokes memories of the Holocaust. Not only does the whole sordid affair disturb him, but he too is perturbed and taken aback by a Jewish lawyer defending the Nazi. Confronting the attorney, Dicky asks him, "Just out of curiosity, how does a Jew represent a Nazi and still live with himself?" He is told, "Being Jewish means having respect for the law. I have a moral duty to give the best possible defense to everyone I represent, even if that person is charged with killing a Jew. Does that answer your question?" Unflinchingly, Dicky says, "No."

Ultimately Tess emerges from this nightmare with a heightened sense of her Jewish identity, becoming more sensitive to anti–Semitism, and realizing that her being Jewish makes her relate differently to the Holocaust.

This issue of neo–Nazism has been the subject of increasing attention in recent shows, paralleling the actual upsurge in anti–Semitic and skinhead violence in recent years.[4] The *Wiseguy* episode that included the priest and synagogue vandalism was actually the first segment of a five-part arc[5] that portrayed the dangers of a neo–Nazi group and their deep hatred of Jews. Similar groups were depicted on such series as *Knightwatch*, *Grand Slam*, and the youth-oriented *21 Jump Street*, in which high school students confronted these questions.

The effects of neo–Nazism on an entire town was the subject of a 1997 TV movie based on actual events, titled *Not in This Town*. When white supremacists arrive in Billings, Montana, to spread their message of hate and recruit new members, one local housewife, Tammie Schnitzer, is horrified and begins a campaign to oust them and to rebuild the homes they have vandalized. When she takes her cause to the local press, she and her family (who are Jewish) are personally targeted. Despite her family's initial pleas to back down and opposition to her efforts from many town residents who are indifferent or fearful, Tammie presses on in her campaign against hate. Tensions come to a head during the December holidays when a rock is thrown through a window at the Schnitzers' home that has been adorned with a paper menorah — and just narrowly misses her son. At last the town is galvanized into unified action: in a dramatic showing of support for their Jewish neighbors and a demonstration of their disgust for the racist extremists, thousands of residents — although they are not Jewish — place menorahs and anti-hate messages in their windows. Even the local newspaper discards impartiality to publish a full-page menorah on its cover the next morning. One by one, townspeople post the newspaper menorah in their windows until the entire town is blanketed by a sea of menorahs and the supremacists are forced out.

This theme of a single courageous individual mobilizing a reluctant community and leading it to take the right moral course against an invasive evil is a common one within programs dealing with anti–Semitism. Interestingly, in the case of *Not in This Town* and the Chanukah episode of *Sisters*, this fight is spearheaded by women who have converted to Judaism. The point is forcefully made that it is often those who *choose* Judaism as their way of life who are the ones to most determinedly defend its honor.

The particular dangers of a reborn Nazism on German soil were explored in a made-for-cable HBO movie. *The Infiltrator* was based on the true story of an Israeli journalist's undercover infiltration of Germany's neo–Nazi movement, and it painted a frightening picture. Visions of a global Nazi resurgence and worldwide neo–Nazi conspiracies to reestablish the Third Reich propelled such TV movies as *Hitler's Daughter*, *Fatherland*, and *Apocalypse Watch*.

In an effort no doubt to underscore the danger of neo–Nazism — by showing the real consequences of this lethal anti–Semitic ideology as played out in the past — several shows have portrayed the confrontation between neo–Nazis and Holocaust survivors.

Undoubtedly the best known program on this topic was the 1981 made-for-TV movie *Skokie*, which dramatized the real-life controversy, of a few years earlier, surrounding the proposed march of the Chicago-based Nationalist Socialist Party of America in Skokie, Illinois. The TV drama portrays the intense emotional and ideological conflict that ensued between the many Holocaust survivors living in Skokie and the American Civil Liberties Union (ACLU), which defended the right of the Nazis to march there.

This conflict, between the imperatives for free speech and the dangers of providing platforms for Nazi ideology, allowed for a powerful drama and the presentation of various viewpoints. Personifying the pain and rage of Holocaust survivors was the character of Max Feldman, a survivor who declares, "Nothing will keep me from fighting them if they march in Skokie. On the grave of my mother, which was a lime pit in the death camp at Mauthausen — a pile, a heap of naked Jewish bodies — on that grave I swear it." Other Jews are depicted as advocating different approaches to this most extreme form of anti–Semitism. A Mr. Rosen, representing the Anti-Defamation League of B'nai B'rith (ADL), suggests that since the neo–Nazi marchers pose no real danger they should be ignored and thus denied the publicity they seek. Far differently, a Jewish Defense League spokesman threatens to "take care" of the marchers, since "it would be a desecration of the graves of six million Holocaust victims if we didn't meet those Nazis face to face and fight them."

The viewpoints of the ACLU, a civil liberties organization with a large Jewish membership and leadership, are expressed by two main characters based on real-life participants in the controversy: Herb Lewisohn, the lawyer pleading the case, and Aryeh Neier, a leader of the ACLU. Both are Jews, a fact that is fully expressed in the movie. Indeed, both are shown to draw their conclusions about the need for allowing the neo–Nazi march based on their own understandings of Jewish suffering. Lewisohn, forcefully arguing that prior restraint of free speech is a clear violation of the First Amendment and therefore unconstitutional, implores an audience of Holocaust survivors to realize that "it's always the despised and the unpopular who are the first victims of oppression — ask the Jews."

Neier takes a similar approach, explaining to the group that he was born in Berlin and that most of his family was killed in Auschwitz, and then asking them to see the necessity of "free speech for everybody — for Nazis … [because] defending your enemy is the only way to protect a free society against its enemies."

Max presents a different survivors' viewpoint when he rises indignantly to respond, "If the day should come when we are both forced by the Nazis to march into the gas chambers, on that day you should be at the head of the line so that you can holler smart slogans for freedom of speech — freedom of speech for the murderers who are pushing you into the oven."

The advocates for free speech are eventually victorious, when after extended legal battles and continued controversy the Nazis are granted permission to march, although they decide to do so in a neighboring town. While the free speech arguments were presented eloquently and fairly, never was the portrayal of the marchers themselves sympathetic. Throughout, they were depicted as hateful and despicable beings; in court their leader, Frank Collin, testified that he agreed "perfectly with everything Adolf Hitler said." Strong contempt for them from non–Jews was expressed in the words of Skokie's mayor, who attended a synagogue meeting to declare that he wanted to "make something absolutely clear to all our Jewish friends here this evening — and that is that your Christian neighbors here in the village of Skokie hold hoodlums like Frank Collin and his ilk in the utmost contempt." Clearly, the emotional sympathy lies with Max, who, standing outside a synagogue, has the program's final word as he laments the fact that "those bastards" won the right to freely express their Nazi ideology. And yet he perceives a bright side to the outcome of these events, recalling that although there was a time not so long ago when people said, "'There's nothing you can do,' this time there was. This time they couldn't wipe their feet on me; this time they couldn't spit on me; this time, they couldn't kill me."

Ten years before Max Feldman appeared on TV, another dramatized Holocaust survivor faced the threat of neo–Nazism on an episode of the crime drama *Adam-12*. Although this group of young hoodlums was not portrayed as explicitly espousing Nazi ideology, their use of Nazi symbolism to intimidate elderly shopkeepers clearly evokes neo–Nazi connections. In an effort to extort money from the store owners, they splatter the shops with swastikas. The besieged store owners are ready to give in and make the necessary payoffs — except for the Holocaust survivor among them who urges them not to do so, declaring, "Strange how soon we can forget. You make a deal with tyranny, it only gets worse."

Here again is the image of the Holocaust survivor who is propelled — and impelled — by a unique and terrible past history to be a leader in fighting all reminders and expressions of anti–Semitism.

More recent shows have continued to include Holocaust survivors as a reminder of the horrors to which anti–Semitism can lead. In a 1989 episode of *MacGyver*, a survivor of Auschwitz stumbles upon a neo–Nazi plan to take over the United States through a carefully detailed, step-by-step plan. Some fifty years after his enslavement in a concentration camp, his life is again threatened by those in Nazi uniforms when they learn he has inadvertently uncovered their scheme.

Holocaust survivors were similarly endangered by a neo–Nazi group in a 1988 *Miami Vice* episode, which portrayed a neo–Nazi organization bent on killing off elderly Holocaust survivors before they have the chance to testify against a captured Nazi war criminal. A survivor depicted in this episode made the link between the anti–Semitism of Nazi Germany half a century ago and expressions of it today when he stated, "The Holocaust did not end in 1945, my friends. It continues today in Russia, in the Middle East, and right here in Miami." Even so beatific a series as *Highway to Heaven* portrayed the violence to which an Auschwitz survivor and his grandson were subjected to by home-grown Nazis in 1987.

Still another neo–Nazi group appeared on a broadcast of the new *Mission Impossible*, a brief revival — lasting only a few episodes in the 1989-90 TV season — of the older, classic espionage series. Unlike every other TV depiction of neo–Nazis that includes some Jewish character or raises the Jewish "connection" in one degree or another, this episode did not even once mention the word "Jew." The Mission Impossible force learns of a German-based neo–Nazi group that dresses in full Nazi regalia, kidnaps young boys to indoctrinate them in the teachings of Hitler, sings Hitlerian songs, and generally revels in all things Nazi. Repeatedly and explicitly the group is shown to hate blacks, and in fact its ultimate punishment upon discovery at the show's end is to be forced to view filmed speeches of Martin Luther King, Jr., and Robert Kennedy on the topic of black-white racial harmony.

To present a rather involved picture of Nazi ideology, as this episode did for an hour, without a single mention of Jews is Holocaust revisionism at its height. While the "real" Nazis despised all of whom they termed "inferior races," the unparalleled focus of their hate and targets of their master plan for destruction was unquestionably the Jewish people. Ironically, although the ostensible subject of this episode was not Holocaust revisionism, it was revisionism in and of itself.

Holocaust Revisionism

The danger of just such anti–Semitic revisionist history about the Holocaust has been the topic of several popular TV shows. One show that devoted a very detailed episode to this question was the forensic medical series *Quincy, M.E.* In a 1982 episode, Holocaust survivor Chaim Zugorsky happens to hear a radio program on which the guest declares that facts about the Holocaust "have as much truth as Mother Goose." This guest, it turns out, is Cornelius Sumner, head of the Committee for Purity and Truth, an organization that denies the occurrence of the Holocaust. Obviously incensed, Chaim calls in to the show, brands Sumner a liar, and is sued for libel.

The remainder of the show lays out in careful detail a full refutation of Sumner's stance. Quincy, the medical examiner who became involved in the case when a Nazi-hunting friend of Chaim's was murdered, wants to help the accused survivor. He visits Chaim's Holocaust Remembrance Museum called "*Gedenk*" (Yiddish for "remember"), where the survivor describes the exhibits, such as "pillows and mattresses made from hair of Jewish inmates," and "lamp shades from skin." Quincy, reeling from the statistics Chaim quotes, says, "It's hard, almost impossible to comprehend such a massive loss of life." Quincy goes to Sumner's office to argue with him but to no avail. He leaves saying, "If someone's life is erased, it's called murder. What do they call it if someone's death is erased? That's a crime too, you know, and you're trying to erase six million of them."

At his libel trial, Chaim has an unlikely ally — an unrepentant Nazi war criminal who testifies for the defense because, as he says on the stand, "men like Sumner are worse than the Jews. They try to rewrite history, take away what we did. The Final Solution was the most courageous act in modern history. Nothing will change that." He turns to Sumner and says, "Anyone calling you a liar, even a Jew, he is speaking the truth." Viewers have learned this through the eyes of Quincy as he himself became aware of this history.

In the 1988 made-for-TV movie *Evil in Clear River*, another non–Jewish character comes to the realization of the truth, enormity, and horror of the Holocaust as a result of a confrontation with a Holocaust revisionist who seeks to deny it. Based on a true story,[6] *Evil in Clear River* depicts the heroic and self-sacrificing struggle of Kate McKinnon, a seemingly ordinary rural housewife, to oust the town's mayor and most popular schoolteacher, Pete Suvak. Through her son's homework assignments and his increasingly hostile statements about Jews, Kate discovers that Suvak is teaching his high school social studies students anti–Semitic propaganda and Holocaust revisionism. She herself knows little about history or the Holocaust, but she intuitively feels something is wrong and begins to read library books about the Holocaust — with pictures of children during the Holocaust that deeply move her. During a visit to a university, she learns that the books Suvak assigned his class to read as textbooks are a combination of classic anti–Semitic tracts used in Nazi Germany and mere crackpot literature.

Her efforts to untopple the beloved Suvak are met with universal opposition and hostility — she is virtually shunned in the small farming town. But she does have some measure of success: first he is ordered by the school board to stick to the assigned curriculum and texts, and then he is dismissed from teaching altogether. Ultimately, when a few allies emerge — including the local minister (whose comments were discussed earlier in this chapter) — Kate gains support and the townspeople vote him out of office. The final blow to Suvak is a court trial on charges of "willfully promoting hatred against an identifiable group — to wit, the Jewish people." Due primarily to testimony from Kate and her son — who had been a great admirer of Suvak and had fought his mother at every turn — Suvak was found guilty and forbidden to teach in Clear River.

This powerful program included no Jewish characters. It could not be said by anyone that Jews inflamed the issue in Clear River or even brought the matter to Kate's attention. Indeed, the absence of any Jewish characters in this particular program made Kate's actions all the more astounding and courageous.[7] The viewing audience is presented with someone who could almost be labeled a Righteous Gentile — the term used for non–Jews who risked their lives to save Jews during the Holocaust — for her heroic and lonely fight against anti–Semitism.

Later that year, the same story was dramatized in a somewhat different manner in the made-for-TV movie *Scandal in a Small Town*. Although the first piece was far more powerful — this one had a more hokey, melodramatic format — the program was commendable for its similar portrayal of a brave and righteous gentile battling anti–Semitism at great personal cost. Like *Evil in Clear River*, *Scandal in a Small Town* was significant for its absence of any Jewish characters.

Programs like these reflect the growing numbers of anti–Semites who declare that the Holocaust was a "hoax invented by the Jews,"[8] and that the gas chambers never existed. These pernicious doctrines are distributed through various publications and national organizations that are dedicated to disseminating this material.[9] While these revisionist theories are even being considered academically relevant in various historical institutions,[10] prime-time television has taken a role in heightening awareness of the falseness and harmful effects of these revisionist theories.

In fact, an entire made-for-cable movie dramatized the real-life case of a Holocaust survivor who took on such revisionists in a court of law. *Never Forget* told the story of southern Californian Mel Mermelstein, who lectured to various schools about the Holocaust. When a group called the Institute for Historical Review, which claims that the Holocaust was a "concoction of the Jewish imagination," challenges him to prove in a court of their own making that anyone was gassed at Auschwitz, Mermelstein — whose parents died in concentration camps — manages to maneuver them into an actual court of law. There, Mermelstein's Roman Catholic lawyer achieves a landmark result: the judge declares the Holocaust "an indisputable fact," in the first-ever judicial notice by a U.S. court that the Holocaust did take place.

Anti-Semitism in the Guise of Anti-Zionism

Although the Holocaust — the supreme example of anti–Semitism — was the ultimate horror visited upon the Jewish people, anti–Semitism did not end with the Holocaust. While certain forms of anti–Semitism have become less acceptable since the Holocaust, in the guise of anti–Zionism or anti–Israel attitudes it has taken on a certain measure of popularity in some circles. Indeed, scholars have noted, "An area of major concern today is that very complicated issue of anti–Semitism masquerading as anti–Zionism. ... Whether one deals with Israel as a people or Israel as a state, anti–Zionism is an anti–Jewish program."[11]

Several TV programs dealing with Arab terrorism and based on real events have depicted this connection. For example, the two made-for-television movies about the 1976 hijacking of an Air France plane by Arab and German terrorists to Entebbe airport in Uganda depicted, of course, the terrorists' hatred for Israel. But also portrayed was their demand that all Jewish passengers — from whatever country — be separated from the others. This idea of selection, with the implicit threat of who will live and who will die, is highly reminiscent of the Holocaust. In case any viewer missed the connection, it was voiced by a Jewish passenger who had survived Auschwitz and who described to a younger passenger the human sorting process upon arrival at the concentration camps: "Selection — to the right, to the left. You see, when we got off the trains, they were waiting for us with a list... To the right meant death — the gas chambers." The portrayal of this action — which actually occurred at Entebbe — and the dramatic underscoring of its linkage to the Holocaust demonstrated the integral relationship of anti–Israel hostilities and anti–Semitism.

A similar scenario was depicted in the 1988 made-for-TV movie *The Taking of Flight 847: The Uli Derickson Story*, which was based on the actual hijacking of TWA flight 847 in 1985. The chief Arab terrorist, wildly denouncing Israel and the United States and seeking to wreak havoc on the passengers, demands that head stewardess Uli Derickson read each passport to find Jewish names and then separate them from the other passengers. She is German; she tearfully objects to this dreadful action and refuses to be part of any selection. He forces her to read all the names aloud, however, and then proceeds to personally select the Jewish-sounding names and does indeed separate the Jewish passengers.

This link between anti–Semitism and anti–Zionism is also depicted in programs about life closer to home. Many shows that depict American neo–Nazis show to them be anti–Israel, voicing in standard phrases common to these groups such ideas as America being the "Zionist occupation government" (initials for this, *ZOG* was painted all over the vandalized synagogue in *Wiseguy*), or the Holocaust being a Zionist lie.

Similarly, two shows of the 1970s portraying Arab characters depicted no demarcation between their anti–Zionism and their anti–Semitism. On an episode of *Medical Center*, when a wealthy Arab potentate learns that his son has fallen in love with an American Jewish woman, he comes to the United States to break up what he deems an unsavory and disgraceful relationship solely because the woman is Jewish and he threatens to disown his son. Dr. Gannon, the series' main character, castigates the elder Arab and convinces him to accept his son's marriage and return home.

In *The Pirate*, a 1978 miniseries, an Arab named Baydr is in an open marriage with his American wife and says that she may sleep with anyone except a Jew. Baydr's expressed hatred for Jews was not directly opposed by anyone in the program, although the message ultimately transmitted was that mutual needs and interests eventually bring about cooperation and understanding. The final scenario of Jewish characters helping to save the lives of Baydr's family and the subsequent gratitude that he feels toward them is one that demonstrates the futility and harm of bigotry.

* * *

Just as in reality the existence of anti–Semitism has been a consistent continuity in its various guises, popular television has depicted this subject with a consistent continuity throughout the history of TV. Many varied expressions of it have been portrayed, with recurring issues (such as restricted clubs, synagogue vandalism, neo–Nazism) depicted decade after decade. This alarming repetitiveness bespeaks the persistence of anti–Semitism in the real world. For their part, these programs have convincingly relayed the warning message that anti–Semitism can occur in any setting and among any group of people.

It has been asserted that "it is not television's role to propose any particular solution to society's ills."[12] And yet, anti–Semitism is clearly presented in these television dramatic programs as an injustice that should be constantly fought. In virtually no program is the derogation of Jews and Judaism left unchallenged either by inference, word, or action. In fact, as we have shown in this chapter, often a well-known TV-series hero takes the lead in this effort.

This kind of portrayal projects the important message that fighting anti–Semitism is not solely a Jewish concern but the responsibility of all people. It was this very concept that underpinned the *Archie Bunker's Place* episode about synagogue vandalism. No one was more forceful against this terrible form of anti–Semitism than the rabbi or Murray Klein, who led the campaign. And yet, they urged Archie to join forces with them *because* he is a non–Jew, and thus his solidarity with this cause lends another dimension of strength to the fight against anti–Semitism.

The picture of Archie Bunker's joining a group to fight synagogue vandalism can be a potent symbol for the 97.5 percent of Americans who are not Jewish. Seeing a celebrated and beloved television hero like the ever-popular Mary Richards of the *Mary Tyler Moore Show* declaring herself a Jew in order to expose the bigotry of an anti–Semitic friend may strike responsive chords in viewers since TV heroes are the icons of our age, known by all and emulated by many. This is extremely significant in that, as one television scholar has stated, "if television reinforces attitudes and behavior, as social scientists claim, then to see a television character engage in a struggle and win it may well encourage viewers to persevere in their own battles against inequities."[13] Indeed, exposure of millions of viewers to such depictions may have a positive influence on the fight against anti–Semitism.

The fact that non–Jews are shown helping in the fight against anti–Semitism in no way paints the Jews as helpless or powerless. As shown here, there have been numerous programs that feature Jewish characters who vehemently oppose anti–Semites and are depicted as strong, independent characters. And just as the forms of anti–Semitism have not been monolithic, neither have been the responses of these Jewish TV characters. They have displayed a whole range of emotions, a wide gamut of reactions to being despised, and thus defy any notion of a stereotypical response to this issue.

For Stuart Markowitz of *L.A. Law*, an experience with anti–Semitism may have been a positive event. All at once — in a way that nothing else in his life had ever done before — anti–Semitism awakened Stuart to the fact of his identity. He realized that being Jewish is the very essence of who he is, and he reacted with a violent rage. For another Jew, depicted in the *Lou Grant* episode, the rage turned inward, and seeking to shed the burden of suffering and to identify with his persecutors he became a neo–Nazi. Violence directed outward toward the enemy was the answer for Paul, the Jewish defense organization member on *All in the Family*. *Skokie*'s varied responses to neo–Nazis ranged from legal remedies, to physical battles, to ignoring the whole matter. On *St. Elsewhere*, Dr. Auschlander was just plain tired of dealing with the issue altogether, having already fought some battles and now wishing to return to the safe ease of New York. In the Old West, on the *Rawhide* episode, the set-upon Michob tried logic, reasoning with his attackers to look beyond the differences that frightened them and see that he was a man just like they. Murray Klein of *Archie Bunker's Place*, sitting in a burned out synagogue, said there is no logic about it: "They'll stop..., when we disappear."

But popular TV programs reflect the reality that neither Jews nor their anti–Semitic adversaries will disappear. For the most part, these shows do not

depict die-hard anti–Semites, like neo–Nazis or country club bigots, unbe-
lievably changing their ways. But a whole parade of fairly ordinary folk — a
rural housewife, a Midwest mayor, a chief medical examiner, trial judges, attor-
neys, a chief of police, store owners, clergy, physicians — both Jewish and
non–Jewish, are shown in their fight against anti–Semitism to be endowed
with a great sense of justice and moral courage. Perhaps their counterparts
among the millions of viewers of these programs can be encouraged by the element of hope in this vision.

4

The Holocaust

The Holocaust, anti–Semitism at its most extreme and destructive, has been a persistent image on popular TV. Although it would seem an incongruous pairing — the "frivolity" of television and the most devastating catastrophe of Jewish life — popular television programs have approached the subject in a multitude and variety of ways. This apparently incongruous juxtaposition naturally raises serious questions about the appropriateness, effectiveness, and possibilities of TV portrayals of the Holocaust. Arguments that the constrained parameters of television entertainment cannot but trivialize the Holocaust state the obvious: one need only read some of the personal accounts written by survivors of the Nazi death camps to understand that the horrors and brutalities inflicted by the Nazis on their victims can never be accurately and fully portrayed.[1] Yet, this stance fails to acknowledge the equal reality that popular depictions of the Holocaust — particularly on television — are often the sole channels through which great numbers of people receive any information about the Holocaust. If it is the case that "how the Holocaust will be remembered depends increasingly on how it enters popular imagery,"[2] as one commentator wrote when reviewing a *book*, how much more applicable this is to television, which is the quintessential popular medium. Through popular TV programs that dramatize various aspects of the Holocaust, vast numbers of people who would otherwise have little or no exposure to information about the event acquire at least some familiarity with it.

Miniseries: Holocaust Overviews

Indeed, it was this effect that was most visibly noted following the airing of the 1978 program *Holocaust*, a four-part miniseries that chronicled the life and ultimate decimation of a German Jewish family as Nazism overran their country. Shortly after it aired, it was noted that "hardly a week goes by without hearing in the press and on the air, at mass rallies or kosher chicken dinners — about the Holocaust, as if the event had just been discovered."[3]

The great attention that this miniseries and its impact received, not only in America but in Europe as well — particularly in West Germany — was such that this show is often pointed to as the be-all and end-all of the Holocaust on TV. However, long before *Holocaust* was broadcast in 1978, at least a score of popular TV shows — starting in the early 1950s and airing throughout the 1960s and 1970s — dealt with many aspects of the Holocaust, from powerful depictions of concentration camps and ghettos to emotion-laden dilemmas faced by survivors in America.

Most of these shows, however, were not miniseries, a genre of TV show that developed and peaked in the mid to late 1970s, and that was able to have unusual impact because of the concentrated effect of many hours over a period of several consecutive nights. During the heyday of miniseries, this new and exciting TV genre was accompanied by much publicity fanfare, which added to its viewership and impact. Indeed, it was the 1977 miniseries *Roots*, the renowned and immensely popular production about a black family's odyssey from slavery to freedom and exploration of its African heritage, that inspired the view of miniseries as a respected and admired format with great potential for teaching people about history and affecting their consciousness. A year later, *Holocaust*— emerging during that heyday of the miniseries era, building on the huge audiences for the format generated by *Roots* and drawing directly on the genre's great popularity, hype, and sense of novelty — portrayed Holocaust issues on a massive scale for the first time, attracting tremendous audiences and international attention.

While it was far from the first time that the Holocaust had been portrayed on television, the miniseries *Holocaust*, in its sheer, unprecedented scale, attempted to present — through a tableau of representative characters — a composite picture of the Holocaust in its entirety. *Holocaust* traces the lives and differing fates of members of the German Jewish Weiss family and interweaves their tale with the rise of Nazi officer Eric Dorf up through the ranks of the Third Reich. In following the lives of these characters, the miniseries takes viewers from prewar Germany through the rise and fall of Nazism, exposing them along the way to Kristallnacht and the Nuremberg laws and taking them into the ghettos, the concentration camps, and the gas chambers of Auschwitz. The miniseries also incorporates such issues as Righteous Gentiles (non–Jews who risked their lives to save Jews during the Holocaust), Jewish Resistance, intermarriage when such marriages were forbidden by the Nuremberg laws, and prestate Israel as a symbol of hope during the Holocaust and as a haven for Jewish refugees after the war.

The Weiss family of *Holocaust* consists of Joseph Weiss, a Berlin physician, his wife, Berta, and their three children, Karl, Rudi, and Anna. That they are a highly assimilated family is indicated in the opening scenes, when Karl marries a Christian woman, Inga, in a civil ceremony and Joseph tells his more religiously observant brother Moses from Warsaw, "You musn't think too harshly of us — we still celebrate the High Holy Days." Despite the Weisses' assimilation, their rights are methodically stripped away through the discriminatory Nuremberg laws, and they are subjected to the violence of Kristallnacht. As the miniseries chronicles Nazism's escalating force and brutality, the family finds itself increasingly engulfed and ravaged by the Holocaust: Anna, who ventured out of her house and was raped, is sent to a sanitarium where she is gassed by a truck's carbon monoxide fumes; Joseph, Berta, and Moses are deported to the Warsaw ghetto. Amidst depictions of the Warsaw ghetto, the show presents a debate among members of the ghetto and its Jewish Council about how to confront the forces of Nazism. The council leader insists that compromise and obedience to the Nazis are the only means of survival, yet the opposing point of view urging resistance wins out and results in the Warsaw Ghetto Uprising.

This picture of Jewish resistance is also personified by Rudi Weiss, who earlier had escaped Berlin to join the Partisans fighting the Nazis. One thread of the miniseries follows his efforts with the fighters, and his love and marriage to Helena, an ardent young Zionist who is later killed during a Partisan action.

The role of some noble Christians during the Holocaust is played out as the story follows Inga, Karl Weiss's Gentile wife. In one scene, she attends church and hears a priest speak out on behalf of the innocent Jewish victims of the Nazis. Later, when that priest is harshly reminded by Nazi officer Dorf that Jews are "enemies of the Reich" and that most church leaders support Nazi policies, the priest responds: "In that case, I must draw a distinction between what Christianity teaches and how some people distort and betray that teaching." He is later deported to Dachau for his stance. Inga goes through much humiliation and suffering in efforts to help her Jewish husband.

The evolution of the Final Solution for the Jews[4] is chronicled through the character of Dorf and his Nazi cohorts, as they meet to discuss the need for innovating new methods of mass murder. They speak with pride of their plan to annihilate the Jewish people, concluding, "anti–Semitism is the cement that binds us together. Christians may disagree on a number of things, but as men of conscience, they can unite in their hatred of Jews," thus the world is silent in the face of what Germany does to the Jews "because deep down they admire what we're doing." Dorf boasts that Hitler will be remembered for one thing — "having wiped the Jews from the face of the earth."

This policy in action is shown as members of the Weiss family are deported to concentration camps. Joseph and Berta are transported to Auschwitz, where they die in the gas chambers. Their son Karl is sent to Buchenwald and then transferred to Theresienstadt, the Nazis' "showcase" camp that they present to Red Cross officials as a happy village. The reality is illustrated in paintings that Karl makes of the camp's real horrors; when the works are discovered, the Nazis break his hands and ship him to Auschwitz, where he dies just moments before the Allies liberate the camp.

Another concentration camp, Sobibor, is included in the miniseries, when Rudi — the Partisan fighter — is captured and sent there. Yet his struggle to resist the Nazis continues even there, as he joins with a group planning escape. It is he alone among the Jewish members of the Weiss family (along with Inga) who survives the war, and at its close he is recruited by the Jewish Agency to smuggle Jewish children to Israel.

The defeat of the Third Reich is represented in the capture of Dorf by the Allies. In keeping with the miniseries' depiction of Dorf as a good family man who had no compunctions about spending many a day's work murdering Jews, he remains unrepentant at the program's end as he declares to his interrogators that "what we did were moral and historical necessities ... we have committed no crimes ... we have merely followed the logical history of Europe," and he then commits suicide. This final image of Nazism, as personified by Dorf, avoids any attempt to whitewash or soften the evilness of Nazism.

In showing so many facets of the Holocaust, with a cast of characters representing a spectrum of its various aspects, *Holocaust* took on a daunting task. A great deal of the worldwide attention lavished on the production noted many of its successes — and failures — on this count. While its faults were more a matter of erroneous details — no insignificant matter since misinformation can clearly lead to misconceptions — its chief significance lay in transmitting a comprehensive picture, on a grand scale, of the overwhelming enormity of the Holocaust and presenting it undilutedly as a Jewish event to an audience unprecedented in its massiveness.

Another miniseries event began five years later, in 1983, with the airing of an even lengthier epic, *The Winds of War*, a sweeping drama of World War II with a particular focus on the Holocaust. (The event continued in 1988 and 1989, when the massive sequel, the thirty-hour *War and Remembrance* aired.)

The Winds of War interweaves World War II military history with the tale of two families: the non–Jewish naval family headed by Victor (Pug) Henry, and the Jastrows, Aaron — a world renowned scholar and writer — and his niece Natalie, who are Jewish. Their lives converge when Pug's son, Byron Henry, goes to work with Aaron Jastrow (an expatriate American) at the scholar's home in Sienna, Italy, and falls in love with Natalie, also there on a visit. She, however, is in love with foreign officer Leslie Slote.

As they enjoy Aaron's estate in Italy, the rise of Nazism is the topic of conversation. Aaron, who possesses profound Judaic knowledge but has been long estranged from his Jewish identity, calmly responds to Byron's curiosity about why he, as a Jew, is so tranquil about the rise of Hitler stating, "If Hitler wins out, the Jews will simply fall back to the second-class status they had for so long under the kings and the popes. We survived seventeen centuries with that. We have quite a store of wisdom and doctrine for coping."

But some of the harsher realities and hints of times to come arise when Pug is sent to Berlin as a naval attaché. When he and his wife Rhoda seek to rent an estate and are offered an outrageously low rental fee by the Jewish owner, the owner describes the "new ruling about Jews owning land," explaining that Germans can now seize any Jewish property unless it is being used by someone with diplomatic immunity.

The spread of Nazism is more graphically shown when Natalie, who is traveling to be with Leslie at his new diplomatic post in Warsaw, stops at a small village to visit a cousin of Aaron's named Berel. The *shtetl*'s celebration of a wedding that night is shattered in the morning when Poland is attacked by the Nazis and the village is bombed. As Natalie and Byron escape, Berel sends a message with them for Aaron: "Two simple Hebrew words: *lech l'cha*—'get out.'"

The rest of the show focuses largely on Aaron's stubborn refusal to heed these words, believing that the Jews of Italy will never suffer the rumored fate of those of Eastern Europe. He finally relents, when it is too late, and the program follows his and Natalie's efforts to escape out of Nazi-controlled Europe, a trek complicated by Natalie's pregnancy (she had fallen out of love with Leslie and in love with Byron Henry, whom she married).

In a concurrent story, naval attaché Pug Henry encounters many Nazis in his diplomatic capacity, is subjected to their virulent anti–Semitism, and argues them at every chance, in a forceful portrayal of official American repugnance for Nazi views.

The grim manifestation of such Nazi views is evident in Minsk, where Berel has photographed deportations and mass killings of Jews. Berel submits the photos to Leslie Slote, stationed at the American Embassy in Moscow, who is eager to help—but the embassy all but ignores the evidence. When Berel meets Pug, on assignment in Moscow, he asks him to inform the president about Nazi atrocities, which Pug, after much consideration, does. Still, at the conclusion of *The Winds of War*, the tide of Nazism rolls unabated.

The evolving rivalries and romances continued to unfold in the sequel that aired five years later, *War and Remembrance*. This thirty-hour miniseries aired in two sections: seven episodes comprising the first eighteen hours in November 1988 and the concluding twelve hours over a series of five nights in May 1989. *War and Remembrance*, while continuing to paint the war years on a large canvas that includes a detailed military and diplomatic history, delves in an even more detailed manner into the Holocaust. Indeed, the very first episode of *War and Remembrance* introduces Hitler's plans for the Final Solution, when a German priest smuggles the secret proceedings of the Wannsee Conference to Leslie Slote, then stationed in Switzerland. Clearly stunned and shaken by the Nazis' blueprint for the destruction of Europe's Jews, the non–Jewish Slote once again urges his superiors to show it to President Roosevelt, but to no avail. Patronizing his "compassion," they refuse to act without authentication, a feat made impossible when a speeding truck suspiciously mows down the priest on the streets of Bern. (Slote had earlier reported the massacres of Minsk

Jews to the *New York Times* but complains that the paper gave it "only ten lines on the back page.") The depiction of Slote and the German priest, who risked career and life to stop the impending genocide, is yet another acknowledgment of the many Righteous Gentiles who endangered themselves to save Jewish lives during the Holocaust.

Their brave efforts, however, are futile, and *War and Remembrance* goes on to depict the Jews' worsening plight. The Polish Jew Berel is imprisoned in Auschwitz and assigned to a construction crew that is building up the death camp. But it is not through his eyes — or those of any Jew — that *War and Remembrance* viewers initially witness the horrors of Auschwitz. Through an unusual dramatic approach, a complete "extermination action" is depicted — from the Nazis' point of view — as Auschwitz commandant Rudolf Hoess hosts visiting SS chief Heinrich Himmler and proudly showcases his camp's operations. In an intense forty-five-minute sequence — as Himmler nods approvingly — TV viewers witness the arrival of a trainload of well-dressed Dutch Jews, their deception by Nazi lies, their reduction to naked flesh herded into "showers," and finally the dumping of their corpses into large pits already filled beyond capacity. As the audience views the sequence through the eyes of the perpetrators — and thus fully sense their matter-of-fact demeanor and pride in their smooth-running operation (Hoess is rewarded on the spot with a promotion) — the events are rendered that much more repugnant and unsettling.

Depictions of concentration camp atrocities become even more stark in the concluding segments of *War and Remembrance*. As Aaron, Natalie, and her son, Louis, continue their perilous trek to escape Europe, they are introduced at every turn to the growing horrors of the Holocaust. Transported to Theresienstadt, they find Berel, who manages to spirit Louis away to safety through his contacts with the Resistance. Eventually Aaron and Natalie are shipped to Auschwitz, where Aaron meets his death in the gas chambers and crematoria, while Natalie somehow survives to the war's end. Frantic and relentless searchings lead Byron first to Natalie, who is deeply scarred and traumatized by the Holocaust and by her separation from her son, and ultimately to Louis, as they are all reunited.

Despite this seemingly redemptive ending, the series' overriding sense is of a world fraught with danger and destruction. Set in the broader context of World War II, the tragedy of the Holocaust is highlighted as the ultimate representation of evil and horror in the world. While the Holocaust is depicted as above and beyond all else, it is inexorably linked with the universality of tyranny and the dangers faced by all. The two prime targets of the Nazis in this program were American citizens, demonstrating that holders of American passports are unprotected. Such portrayals carry significant weight and are rendered more believable and cautionary to ordinary viewers as they watch world events endangering innocent Americans and others who happen to find themselves trapped by some evil and tyrannical regime. In this sense, while the Holocaust is portrayed clearly as a Jewish catastrophe, the terrible impact that it is shown to have on others as well offers a great potential to draw viewers into a deeper emotional connection with the events. Ultimately — such portrayals advise us — while Jews are most vulnerable to the anti–Semitic vehemence that surely figures prominently into the tyrant's quest for overwhelming power, few people — of whatever religion or nationality — are exempt from his or her unstoppable and amoral methods of attaining it.

The Ghettos

While these sprawling miniseries sought to present an all-encompassing picture of the Holocaust, most other programs, less massive in their length and scope, have focused on specific aspects of the tragedy.

Life in the Warsaw ghetto was the subject of a number of prime-time shows. In 1960, the dramatic anthology series *Playhouse 90* presented "In the Presence of Mine Enemies," a tale of the Warsaw ghetto written by Rod Serling in which debates about how to fight the Nazis — with books or bullets — and issues of guilt and forgiveness hold center stage. The teleplay focuses on the family of Rabbi Adam Heller, a bearded, elderly spiritual leader of the ghetto. The rabbi's faith in God and his patient wait for goodness to reappear on the earth is at odds with his son Paul's violent and passionate hatred of the Nazis. A member of the Resistance, Paul has become so hateful and distrustful of the world that he even despises a dear old family friend who is non–Jewish, Josef Chinik. Chinik, in a portrayal of yet another Righteous Gentile, wears an armband with a yellow star to identify with and be near his Jewish friends. He later confesses to and dies for the murder of a Nazi that was committed by Paul.

The vehement arguments between Paul and his father about the proper response to the Nazis are paralleled by those between a Nazi officer, Captain Richter, and his young subordinate, Sergeant Lott, regarding their treatment of the Jews. During a visit to the Jewish family, Captain Richter shows the inexperienced and sensitive sergeant how to beat a rabbi without feeling badly. But when the young sergeant later questions the morality of it all, Captain Richter explains — in terms similar to those expressed by Dorf in *Holocaust*—"There is a morality in hatred. It happens to be a clue to survival. Nations can feed on it. They can find their strength in it. ... But there must be an object of hatred. Suddenly, in front of us, out steps a Jew. He can be all things to all men: moneylender, communist, world banker, revolutionist, an unassimilated foreigner in our midst. And so we hate him. And in the process, we're unified. ... The Jew dies so that we can live. This is morality." He explains that he can order the extermination of Jews because of this and because "indignation and outrage are the most perishable items known to man. The memory of what we do to this ghetto will decay like a corpse."

With these speeches, the captain aims to gird Sergeant Lott for the task of bringing him Rabbi Heller's daughter; he then rapes her. When Paul hears that his father allowed Rachel to be taken away, he erupts with fury, calling his father "a caricature of a Jew. You bury yourself with chants and dirges and prayers while your people are being slaughtered. You may have exceptional faith, Papa, but damn it, you have no honor." With the end approaching, Paul makes his father look out the window at the corpses and the starving children lying in the streets.

Wracked with guilt over his actions, Sergeant Lott comes to beg for mercy and forgiveness from the Jewish family and asks Rachel to let him help her escape. He kneels before the rabbi with his head bowed in the rabbi's lap, crying out, "Oh, God, rabbi, forgive us, please forgive us." But when Paul returns to the apartment and sees Lott, he strikes him. It is the rabbi's turn for fury, and he calls his son a Nazi — the only one in the room "who hates like a Nazi ... who has a hunger to kill like a Nazi." He tells Paul that Sergeant Lott is asking for "the one luxury we have left to give — mercy. He asks for mercy much as we have asked for it since time began."

This early attempt to portray Nazis beyond the one-dimensional characterization more common to popular television featured an important image of a repentant Nazi trying to atone for his crimes and for those of his cohorts. But this potentially positive characterization is severely undermined by the odious comparison between Nazis and Jews, an abysmally offensive distortion of history. To parallel entreaties for mercy made by Jews, the innocent victims of horrific persecution and butchery for millennia, with one made by a soldier of the Nazis, the heinous perpetrators of the Final Solution, is a detrimental and indecent depiction, all the more obscene when emanating from the lips of a character who is a rabbi.

Yet the Nazi is indeed repentant, and the rabbi, in his desperation to ensure the survival of his daughter, accepts Lott's offer to help save her. The program closes with a most elegant, poignant, and sophisticated scene in which the viewer is not fed any easy answers but is made to feel the difficult and painful choices that confronted this Holocaust family. Against the background voiceover singing the poignant chant "Ani Ma'amin" ("I believe") and as Paul reaches for his gun, Rabbi Heller concludes, "Faith is a weapon too. And we have never lacked for faith — not in this ghetto, nor in the thousands of ghettos before this." Surrounded now by sounds of heavy fighting that has erupted in the ghetto, they leave together, bonded in love yet strikingly juxtaposed in method and philosophical vision. Paul, brandishing his rifle, tells his father, "I must go out and do this in my own way." Rabbi Heller clutches his Judaic books and states simply, "And I in mine."

Decades later, in a remake of this Rod Serling classic, the 1997 version of

"In the Presence of Mine Enemies" strayed widely from the original production. In the modern rendition, the final scene with the rabbi and his son is stripped of all its elegance and impact as the movie offers a different final scene[5] in which the father chooses not between mercy and cruelty and not between the survival of victim and perpetrator, but rather between his son and his daughter. And what a choice he makes — he kills his son to allow his daughter to escape with Sergeant Lott.

Rather than offering the audience open-ended questions without clear-cut answers, this "new and improved" edition of the movie seems to obviate our need and desire — and perhaps even question our ability — to ponder and reflect about two cogent and real yet opposing worldviews and approaches to life.

Controversy, argument, and the will to survive also emerge as themes in the 1982 made-for-TV movie *The Wall*. Set in the Warsaw ghetto, the program dramatizes Nazi atrocities — beatings, killings, and enforced starvation — as seen through the eyes of a small group of Jews hiding in the ghetto. The sense of devastation heightens when the group's leader, Dolek, escapes from the ghetto and embarks on a clandestine trip to Treblinka,[6] returning with the nightmarish report that rumors about mass exterminations of Jews are true. His news sets the stage for arguments within the Jewish council about the question of supporting armed resistance. Without the council's approval, a group of Jews forms the Jewish Fighting Organization, and it spearheads resistance efforts in the ghetto. But when Dolek learns of an escape plan to the woods to join the Partisans, he urges his followers to come along. Once more, a debate over methods of Resistance ensue. Some want to stay and fight in the ghetto because "it will appeal to the conscience of the world ... the thing to do is die defending Jews." Dolek counters, "Every time we raise a glass, we say *l'chayim* — 'to life.' There is nothing Jewish about committing suicide ... we are not destroyers but survivors ... the Germans want to wipe us off the face of the earth ... if we don't survive, there will be no future generations."

While Dolek and his group hide in preparation for their escape, the Warsaw Ghetto Uprising breaks out and the story of the Jews' fighting back against the Germans is dramatized. Finally, however, on May 16, 1943, the Warsaw ghetto is destroyed and the surviving fighters are herded away. Dolek's band emerges from hiding to a successful escape through the sewers, leaving the burning ghetto behind and heading for the forests to join the Partisans.

Hiding Out

Jews' hiding out in many different sites and settings throughout Europe in order to survive the Holocaust has been dramatized on various shows. Some years before the well-known story of Anne Frank's hiding in an Amsterdam attic reached popular TV another fact-based tale of a Jew who hid from the Nazis to survive the Holocaust was portrayed on a 1962 episode of the *Armstrong Circle Theatre* titled "The Man Who Refused to Die." When Polish Jew Abe Rothstein jumps a train headed for Treblinka in 1942, he manages to find his way back to his hometown. There he meets up with his sister, and together they live for nearly two years in a cave under the kitchen floor boards in the farmhouse of a Roman Catholic family.

Three made-for-television movies focused on the life of Anne Frank, her family, and some friends, who were hidden from the Nazis in an attic for two years. Two of these television productions (of 1967 and 1980) took their title — *The Diary of Anne Frank*— story line, and perspective from the famous diaries written by Anne while in hiding.

The diaries, as dramatized through these shows, open a lens on how these Jews survived for two excruciatingly long years and reveal the deepest thoughts and feelings of the sixteen-year-old Anne who endured the nightmare. The programs portray the incessant danger, the cramped attic's claustrophobic atmosphere, and the brutal paucity of food and supplies. Yet they also depict a joyful spirit reigning in the attic, much of it inspired by Anne's ebullient nature. Their efforts to maintain a normal and uplifting life in the face of their enforced hiding and the dangers that lurked around them are shown in such occasions as their celebrations of Chanukah. Despite external reasons to, they never stopped being Jews.

In television's 1988 rendition of this story, titled *The Attic: The Hiding of Anne Frank*, the emphasis is not on the Frank family but on the particular heroism of their protector, Miep Gies, and that of the Dutch people in general (although the show points out that she was from Austria).

In its opening scenes, with the German armies moving into the Netherlands, the made-for-television movie quickly sets the stage for the ensuing drama. Viewers learn that Miep, a Gentile woman, works for a small company owned by the kindly Otto Frank. With the imposition of Nazi rule, of course, comes increasingly harsh treatment of Holland's Jews, and when orders of deportation to camps eastward seems imminent, the Frank family decide to go into hiding and enlist Miep's aid. At a terrible risk to herself and her husband, she provides for the Franks with a boundless devotion, regularly bringing them food despite severe rationing and seeking to protect them in every possible way.

Although her individual bravery is amply shown, the program takes pains to portray it as part of a national courage on the part of the Dutch. In one scene, a sermonizing priest exhorts parishioners to wear yellow tulips to identify with their persecuted Jewish compatriots. In the montage sequence that follows the nation is shown breaking out into yellow tulips as each citizen defiantly dons one.

Righteous Gentiles

While Miep Gies's efforts on behalf of the Frank family are well known, many other Righteous Gentiles risked their lives during the Holocaust to save Jewish friends, neighbors, and even strangers. Their heroic efforts offer one of the few encouraging, hopeful, and uplifting aspects of the Holocaust. For this reason, doubtless, they appear in virtually every popular TV program that deals with the Holocaust, relieving the otherwise unbearable bleakness of the era and offering viewers the uplifting reminder that the bleakest of times was not devoid of people with extraordinary courage and exceptional goodness. Although they were few and far between, it would be an imbalanced view to convey only the evil without paying deference to a countering presence.

In addition to those who hid Anne Frank and Polish Jew Abe Rothstein, many other Righteous Gentiles — both actual and fictional — have been credited on popular TV. A 1959 episode of the *Playhouse 90* anthology series tells the sad story of Tanguy, a half–French, half–Spanish, non–Jewish child who, due to a variety of circumstances, finds himself alone in war-torn Europe. Although Tanguy is the focus of the show, great attention and respect is paid to Mr. Delivol, a Righteous Gentile who opened his house to many Jews seeking refuge from the Nazis and who risks his own life attempting to smuggle them out of Nazi-occupied France. After Tanguy is whisked to safety in Mr. Delivol's house, the Nazis discover the safehouse and send all its people to camps including Tanguy, who they assume is Jewish.

Age was not a determining factor in the makeup of a Righteous Gentile. On the made-for-cable movie *Hidden in Silence*, a teenaged Polish girl befriends a Jewish family in the prewar years. When the Nazis take over and ship the family to the ghetto, she strives to save them —first sneaking provisions into the ghetto, then hiding thirteen Jews in her attic until the end of the war.

A program that made quite an impact in Canada was a TV movie titled *Charlie Grant's War*. The 1980 production dramatizes the true story of a wealthy Canadian businessman working in Europe during the prewar years. Disgusted by the growing anti–Semitism around him, he protests the treatment of Jews to local authorities and has his mother back in Canada apprise government officials of the Jews' worsening plight in Europe. Both tracks are stonewalled: with the rise of Hitler, Grant finds himself persecuted for his support of Jews, eventually landing in a concentration camp. In Canada, his mother's efforts are met by deaf ears, a stance that the program denounces at its close when it declares that during the Holocaust, when six million Jews were murdered from 1933 to 1945, "The United States accepted more than 200,000 refugees. Britain took in 70,000; Argentina, 50,000; China, 25,000. Canada, despite countless pleas, accepted fewer than 5,000 Jewish refugees." In contrast to this, Charlie Grant's single-handed efforts succeeded in helping more than six hundred Jews escape the Nazis.

Many of the characters shown to help Jews during the Holocaust are Christian clergy. A very early example of this recurrent theme is the 1954 episode of the dramatic anthology series *Studio One*, which told the story of a bishop who takes extraordinary measures to protect the lives of Jews in 1944 Nazi-occupied Hungary. The episode, titled "Cardinal Minszenty," explains the dangers the Jews faced and shows the cleric — at much peril to himself — hiding Jews in his palace and ordering his monsignor to go to Budapest and there open up all religious institutions to them and issue them with false Christian papers. "Every cloister, every religious house, all parishes and churches, all religious institutions," he orders, "must throw open their doors to the Jews."

Two years later *Philco Television Playhouse* aired "Conspiracy of Hearts," the story of a group of Austrian nuns who smuggle Jewish children out of Nazi concentration camps and bring them to prestate Israel.[7]

These depictions continued in TV movies of the 1980s, including *Pope John Paul II* and *The Scarlet and the Black*. The latter told of the real-life exploits of Monsignor Hugh O'Flaherty, a Vatican official who spent his own time and energies, at great personal risk, working to hide thousands of escaped Allied POWs in German-occupied Rome. Although he was clearly dedicated to this specific cause, the movie suddenly introduces what seems to be merely a token scene of his meeting with a rabbi who asks for his help, thus rendering O'Flaherty one who saves Jews.

A PBS children's drama tackled the Righteous Gentile clergy issue in an episode of *Wonderworks* titled "Miracle at Moreaux," which portrayed a French nun who hides three Jewish children in a Catholic school, successfully protecting them from the Nazis of German-occupied France.

Not unexpectedly, television has also approached the topic of non–Jews protecting Jews during the Holocaust with a romantic twist, as seen in the 1985 made-for-cable movie *Forbidden*, in which a wealthy German countess falls in love with a Jewish professor whom she is hiding from the Nazis.

Perhaps the best known television production about a Righteous Gentile, owing to the public attention and concern that its real-life subject received at the time, is *Wallenberg: A Hero's Story*, a 1985 miniseries entirely devoted to this theme. The drama opens with a narration that pays tribute to all Righteous Gentiles. Against the backdrop of *Yad Vashem*, Israel's memorial to the Holocaust, a narrator explains, "Here on the outskirts of Jerusalem, there's a place known as the Mount of Remembrance. Each tree along its Avenue of the Righteous honors another Gentile, men and women who risked their own lives to save Jews during the Holocaust. The accompanying medal to each honoree — some living, others no longer — bears an inscription: 'Whoever saves a single soul, it is as if he had saved the whole world.'"[8]

The drama commences in Hungary on the night of April 30, 1944, as synagogues are burned and Jews rounded up, a scene starkly juxtaposed with that of the Wallenbergs, a renowned banking family, celebrating festivities at their estate in Sweden. Raoul Wallenberg's well-known opposition to the Nazis is expressed early on as he makes biting remarks about Hitler, even to their German guests. He is disgusted by his uncle's lending of money to the Germans, asking him, "Is Auschwitz a good investment?" and stating that he has trouble "trading truffles in countries where people are herded like cattle into freight cars."

These convictions lead Raoul to head a government mission to try to save the Jews of Budapest. Risking his life, he travels to Budapest and there issues Swedish passports and passes to as many Jews as possible, boards Jews in safehouses under the protection of the Swedish flag, and interferes directly with the roundups, transport, and forced labor of the Jews. He thus succeeds in saving many thousands of Jews but also arouses the ire of Adolf Eichmann[9] with whom he does constant battle over the lives of Jews and with whom he competes for their trust. In this effort to earn their confidence, Raoul often uses Yiddish phrases and celebrates Chanukah with a group of Jews in the basement of one of the safehouses he has established. His ongoing heroic efforts, including his enlisting the aid of other people of influence, results ultimately in the rescue of over 120,000 Hungarian Jews.

Having witnessed the horrors of Jewish roundups, abuses, and death marches, Raoul searches for an answer to such questions as, what does our Christian faith tell us about these Nazi scoundrels? who are they? what shaped them? but can only speculate that "perhaps we are witnessing the death of God himself." On January 17, 1945, Wallenberg drove from Budapest to meet some Russian officials in an effort to secure food and supplies for the surviving Jews under his protection. He was taken into "protective custody" at that time by the Russians, and his fate is not known for certainty to this day.[10]

In its depictions of Raoul Wallenberg and other Righteous Gentiles, popular television pays tribute to those who acted with uncommon morality at a time when abysmal immorality held the upper hand. Championing the actions of the individual, these portrayals promote the view that one person acting counter to powerful forces of politics and history and opposing the will even of the masses can make a great difference. Those who murdered Jews have been imprinted in popular television as the incarnation of evil; those who risked their own lives to save Jews are celebrated as heroes unafraid to stand up to evil with indignation and righteousness.

It is interesting to note that the important subject of Righteous Gentiles, which received considerable treatment on popular television beginning in its earliest years, was not dealt with in theatrical films in a major way until the blockbuster film created by Steven Spielberg, *Schindler's List*. The movie, about a real-life German and member of the Nazi party who saved the lives of thousands of Jews, garnered much critical acclaim and box office success during its theatrical run. But it was during its airing on television, in February 1997, when it earned its largest audience. As a press release from NBC trumpeted two days later, "The NBC research department estimates that 65 million people watched all or part of *Schindler's List*, more than doubling, in one night, the total number of people in the United States who have ever seen the movie in theaters (25 million)."[11]

The Camps

The vast majority of European Jews did not have the good fortune to find themselves in the benevolent hands of such Righteous Gentiles but instead were transported to Nazi concentration and extermination camps. Such camps, as the gruesome culmination of Nazi ideology and the horror most closely associated with its reign, have been the setting for numerous scenes in a myriad of dramas about the Holocaust. Here, under the shadow of the crematoria's smoking furnaces, questions of survival — and how one survives and at what cost — are most intense and have been the subject of much drama. How to portray such issues without trivialization, mawkishness, or a kind of macabre voyeurism has been attempted in a variety of approaches and with varying degrees of success.

Many programs or miniseries that deal with the large scope of the Holocaust have included concentration camp scenes. One widely seen depiction, unfortunately so softened for viewers that it was ludicrous and misrepresentative, appeared in the miniseries *Holocaust*. There, life in Auschwitz for husband and wife Berta and Joseph Weiss consists of clean and spacious barracks with family photos tacked to the bunk. When Joseph visits Berta in the women's barracks and the two make love in virtual privacy, they seem more like naughty teenagers away at camp than inmates at a center of extermination. A greater attempt at accuracy was made in the miniseries *War and Remembrance*. (The program's forty-five-minute sequence seen through the eyes of Nazi officers is discussed above.) Toward the end of the series, another relentless sequence follows Aaron Jastrow on a crowded, putrid train to Auschwitz that disgorges its passengers on a freezing night onto the snow-covered fields of the camp, where selections are quickly made. Aaron, pressed among the human waves of naked Jews pressed into the gas chambers, goes swiftly to his death.

While numerous programs about the Holocaust have included scenes of and references to concentration camps, some have been devoted entirely to life and death in the camps. The 1980 made-for-TV movie *Playing for Time* explores questions of survival and the responsibility of the artist in the face of surrounding horrors. It chronicles the wartime ordeal of the real-life Fania Fenelon, a half–Jewish French singer who is deported to Auschwitz.[12] In opening scenes that attempt to convey the trauma faced by new arrivals, Fania and the others are roughly stripped of personal belongings, their heads are shaved, and their arms are tattooed.

Recruited to sing and write arrangements for the camp orchestra, Fania is increasingly tormented by the thought that she is "pleasing the SS." Alma, the Jewish conductor of the orchestra and the niece of Gustav Mahler, demands that Fania concentrate only on the music, telling her, "There is life or death in this place — no room for anything else whatsoever ... in this place you will have to be an artist and only an artist ... create all the beauty you are capable of creating." These ongoing debates between Fania and Alma represent deeper issues about the struggle between survival and capitulation, and between self-preservation and cowardice, and they reveal some of the very difficult and painful choices forced upon concentration camp inmates.

Another apparent struggle faced by Fania was that of her identity in face of the Nazi oppression. At first she defiantly identifies herself as Jewish: addressed as Fenelon by a high camp official, she interrupts him to declare, "I must tell you my name is really not Fenelon. My mother's name was Fenelon; my father's name was Goldstein. I am Fania Goldstein." Later, informed that as a half–Jew she may cut off half her yellow star, she does so, only to sew it back on again that night. At the same time, however, she fiercely states that she is "sick of the Jews and the Gentiles, the Easterners and the Westerners, the Germans and the French... I'm a female, not a tribe, and I'm humiliated — that's all I know." Her initial identification as a Jew, it seems, is rather tenuous and short-lived, used only as a tool of defiance towards the Nazis, rather than as a genuine and deeply felt identification with the Jewish people. Her ultimate convictions and allegiances are clearly not Jewish, but rather universal — and French, as she triumphantly sings "The Marseillaise" when the Allies march in to liberate the camp.

The role of Christianity in the Holocaust, which has been praised in some shows by depicting Christian clergy saving Jews, is here — as in a number of other significant programs — severely questioned. Earlier, when signs of the Allies' approach first appear, a Polish member of the orchestra who had served in the Resistance tells Fania how guilty she feels for all the atrocities, pleading that she wants just "one Jewish female to understand. When I first came here I was sure that the Pope and the Christian leaders — when they found out — they would send planes to bomb the fires here and the tracks that bring them in every day. But the trains keep coming and the fires continue burning... Try to forgive me please."

As if in recognition of the wide and unbridgeable gulf between the few heroic individuals who resisted the Nazis and those peoples and governments who did nothing to save the Jews of Europe, Fania tells the resister not to feel guilty and that the problem is "the others who are destroying us and they only feel innocent ... you will survive and everyone around you will be innocent from one end of Europe to the other, and who will you ever be able to talk to again?"

Jews, however, did not always rely on outside help. Jewish resistance, and an approach to survival different from that in *Playing for Time*, was the subject of the 1987 made-for-TV movie *Escape from Sobibor*. Set entirely in the Sobibor death camp, the show dramatizes the daring real-life escape attempt of six hundred inmates, which was organized by Jewish prisoners in concert with a contingent of Russian POWs. The Russian soldiers were incarcerated in Sobibor — as opposed to a POW camp — because they are also Jewish. While the usual television romance blossoms in this program, as it does in so many others, the brutal inhumanity and cruelty of the Nazis is depicted with gruesome realism as whippings, beatings, point-blank shootings, hangings, and gassing of the innocent Jewish civilians caged in at Sobibor are shown as the course of a normal day. Although the escape is viewed as successful as three hundred Jews survive the breakout, the final moments of the program, in narration, reveal that the leader of this operation was murdered by anti–Semites in Poland less than two years later.

American Jews During the Holocaust

While the Holocaust occurred in Europe, as a Jewish tragedy it affected Jews the world over. Several programs depicted the notion that for American Jews the Holocaust was a time of strengthening identity and connection as a result of the suffering of their coreligionists.

Some who were caught in Europe even experienced this persecution firsthand. In a 1957 episode of the *Studio One* anthology series, Bernie Linton, a young American soldier who is Jewish, is among those captured and sent to a German prison camp. He has never felt particularly Jewish, and when the other Jewish POWs are to be placed in a separate camp, he denies his religion, until overcome by a sense of guilt and identification.

As described above in this chapter, the plight of American Jews Aaron and Natalie Jastrow trapped in Europe was a significant theme of the massive miniseries *Winds of War* and *War and Remembrance*.

Jewish characters within the incomparably safer milieu of America during the Holocaust era have also been depicted. The cataclysmic events in Europe are pictured as having a deep effect on them as well — in terms of a stirring of Jewish identity — but another phenomenon links them to these events: anti-Semitism. Invariably, these Jews are shown to be recipients of a homegrown strain of religious hatred, as they cope with reports of destruction of Jews in Europe in depictions that suggest a link between all forms of anti–Semitism.

This link was explicitly expressed by a young Jewish soldier in a 1972 episode of *The Waltons*, which chronicles his developing friendship with the Southern Baptist family. Ted Lapinsky first meets Jason Walton when the two are thrown together as barrackmates at a U.S. Army camp and Ted expresses his anger that his anti–Semitic sergeant refuses to recommend him for the position of drill instructor. After Ted receives news from overseas that his grandfather, a leader of the Warsaw Ghetto Uprising, died in Treblinka, his anger towards the sergeant mushrooms. Jason's efforts to soothe Ted by telling him that Sergeant Barnes does not have anything to do with his grandfather's death leave Ted unconvinced, and he replies, "Yes he does — he has everything to do with it."

When Jason invites Ted for a visit with his family on Walton's Mountain, a growing shadow of the Holocaust stretches over the peaceful rural setting. After Ted teaches the Walton family how to dance the *horah*,[13] he becomes sad recalling his grandfather's love for the dance. Trying to comfort him, the Waltons tell him of their own grandfather who recently died peacefully. But again, Ted is not to be comforted. He responds that peacefully is the way "all grandfathers should be allowed to go, but not my *zeydeh*.[14] My grandfather — he was murdered." Reading from the letter smuggled out of Europe that reported his grandfather's death — and his role in the crushed Warsaw Ghetto Uprising — Ted intones (translating from the Yiddish), "One of the leaders lived to be captured, taken to a place called Treblinka. For the first time now we learn of extermination camps. In Poland, in Germany where thousands have been taken, he was killed by poison gas."

The Waltons are shaken by such a report and have a difficult time believing it, especially after family patriarch John Walton contacts a senator friend of his who assures him that "there was no foundation to these rumors; it's propaganda." Despite Ted's pleas that they believe the news in the letter, John voices a skepticism that was in fact widespread in America at that time, insisting, "Maybe those kinds of mass killings happened way back when, but this is 1943! Human beings from one group doing that to another group? Not today — it's just unthinkable."

The folly of their disbelief is reproved by the contemporary perspective provided by the narrator who concludes each *Waltons* episode (the voice of a now-adult John-boy Walton), as he ruminates, "We were tragically mistaken. It was only near the end of the war that we learned that there had indeed been extermination camps — Belsen, Buchenwald, Dachau, Treblinka — where unspeakable and unthinkable horrors had been committed."

With this comment, the views of Ted Lapinsky the Jew are shown to be correct. Reviled by a bigoted sergeant and doubted even by the Waltons who warmly welcomed him but refused to heed him, Lapinsky pleaded on every front for justice and a sense of appropriate vigilance. In this depiction, the Jew is shown to possess a refined sensitivity to danger honed by a history of persecution — a sensitivity often derided in real life as "paranoid" but here vindicated and sadly proven, at great cost, to be warranted. An astute viewer could discern jarring parallels to continuing realities in the contemporary world.

Firsthand news about Holocaust atrocities comes not in a letter but via an escaped Jewish refugee in the 1980 made-for-TV movie *Long Days of Summer*. Here Joseph Kaplan escapes to America after his wife dies in a Nazi concentration camp; he finds refuge in the home of a Jewish family — the Coopers — in Bridgeport, Connecticut, and seeks to alert those around him of the horrors occurring in Nazi Europe. But in their effort to help Joseph publicize his eyewitness accounts of Nazi horrors, the Coopers themselves become targets of anti–Semitism. Ed Cooper, a prominent member of the community, arranges for Joseph to speak at a bar association dinner. At the dinner Joseph is largely ignored, and that night the Coopers' home is vandalized. Later, Ed is warned by colleagues in his law firm to desist from sponsoring Joseph and his campaign for help. Reminding him that Germany is one of the firm's largest clients, one of them tells him, "You're the first Jewish executive in the history of this company — that's a breakthrough, and I don't want to see you do anything to ruin it for you and your family." Joseph gives a talk at the local synagogue. The response is less subtle: blackhooded neo–Nazis burst in, defacing the sanctuary and beating those in attendance.

At the vortex of forces of anti–Semitism, facing them from overseas, from Ed's firm, and from their own community, the Coopers are compelled to confront their Jewish identity head on. Rather than denying this identity, they choose to affirm it, as encapsulated in a talk between Ed and his very young daughter. When she asks, "Do I have to be Jewish?" his reply, "Do you have to have brown eyes?" is met by her retort, "I was born with those." He replies, "And you were born a Jew. You know, being Jewish is a part of you ... like your hair, your eyes, your wonderful personality ... God only made one like you." For his part, Ed chooses to resign from his firm rather than bow to the anti–Semitic pressure being put upon him.

The program seems to toss aside its important central theme about Joseph broadcasting word of the Holocaust. A mini-crisis in which Joseph is threatened with extradition to Germany for high crimes against the state arises. This crisis is fancifully resolved when the Cooper children approach President Franklin Roosevelt, who is traveling by train through their town, to intervene on Joseph's behalf. Moreover, this glorified depiction of Roosevelt's intervening to save Jews during the Holocaust is hardly representative of his actions in this regard.[15]

This idealized motif continues in the program's final moments. The Cooper's teenaged son Daniel has been continuously baited and attacked by Freddy, the son of a neo–Nazi. Daniel finally beats him in a boxing match, and Freddy suddenly embraces Daniel in friendship. Without any given reasons or process of education, Freddy suddenly abandons all animosity towards Jews — in opposition to his father's vitriolic teachings — and has magically become civilized. The civilizing of Nazis and their ilk is generally a positive image for popular TV to depict; yet when presented without any context, reason, or credible struggle for repentance, it rings too hollow and contrived to be believable.

Despite its disappointing ending, *The Long Days of Summer* does address the sense of impact of the Holocaust on American Jews. Another program that did so, through quite different settings and circumstances, was *Summer of My German Soldier*, a 1978 made-for-TV movie set during World War II in a small Southern town bordering a compound holding German POWs. The program tells the sad tale of Jewish teenager Patty Bergen, a lonely girl so abused and unloved by her family that she pursues an extreme and forbidden relationship: she hides out an escaped Nazi soldier in her treehouse and develops a warm friendship with him. The obvious oddity of this secret friendship is punctuated throughout the movie. Even before the two met, when the train carrying the POWs first arrives in town, Patty waves to it but is reprimanded by a severe older woman: "They're only Nazis, and this town don't wave no nice hello to no Nazis. Especially you — Jewish people like you especially don't wave no nice hello." Later, even the German soldier, Anton, whom Patty is sheltering is shocked to learn that she is Jewish. He exclaims, "You are a Jew, little girl. I am a soldier of the Third Reich. We are enemies, you and I. We do not help each other, Jew." Patty, however, seems oblivious and in her confused innocence seems to have no sense of her actions — until she goes to synagogue. Once there (the family drives to a distant town once a month to attend services), she hears the rabbi speak out about "Nazi atrocities against our fellow Jews in Europe." This news stirs new feelings in her, and she returns home to tell Anton that the rabbi's speech gave her a "funny feeling in [her] stomach" and made her "feel like a Jewish person, and I've always thought of me as an American." Despite this awakened sense of identification, Patty assures Anton that she is his friend and promises not to betray him.

All of this is told against the backdrop of a Southern town seething with bigotry. The Bergens, although owners of a popular dry goods store in town, unquestionably exist on a clearly defined and tenuous plain of limited tolerance. In one scene, guffawing customers negotiating a sales transaction with Mr. Bergen caution him, "You're not going to *Jew* us down, are you?" In another, when FBI agents hunting for Anton enter the Bergens' store to question them, Mr. Bergen gives a speech that seems more a pronouncement of his loyalty to America than a comment on his Jewish identity in which he declares, "I am a Jew, my wife is a Jew, my daughters are Jews, and we don't help Nazis escape any more than we help a mad dog out of the pound ... Bergens are *patriots*."

When Anton is caught at last and discovered to have been hidden by Patty, the native bigotry is unleashed. As Patty and the Bergen's black housekeeper (who had secretly helped Patty shelter Anton) walk through the town, they are targets of religious and racial epithets.

While the Holocaust was surely an important subject of this program, the underlying purpose of its inclusion seemed to be its use as a platform to condemn all forms of bigotry. In all its forms, bigotry is to be shunned, whether it is directed against a "good" Nazi (Anton reported to Patty that his father had been killed for opposing Hitler), a Jew, or a black, and regardless of who the bigot is, even if portrayed, as in this movie, as "bad" Americans from the South. The lines of distinction between the good and bad characters in this production are blurred and ultimately so is its message. Possibly this is meant to underscore the deep confusion, despair, and loneliness felt by Patty herself, symbolic perhaps of the abandonment experienced by the Jews in Nazi Europe during the Holocaust.

These programs depicting American Jews during the Holocaust emphasize the historic, emotional, and unbreakable ties among diverse Jews the world over. Of greatest significance is the recognition of the strength of these ties during times of pain, struggle, and tragedy that — in one way or another — affect all Jews, even to this day.

Holocaust Aftermath

With the end of the war in 1945, the Holocaust was not about to be set aside and forgotten; rather, it was to be the basis of the post–Holocaust era, as this cataclysmic event would live on in the minds and hearts of the survivors, the victims' families, and all Jews, and forever affect — directly or indirectly — every aspect of their lives.

The fate of both Nazi war criminals and Holocaust survivors after the war — and the explosive situations when they meet (as they often do on TV dramas) — have been the subject of many prime-time shows. Television's picture of life after the Holocaust focuses on Nazis seeking to elude capture but ultimately being caught, and on survivors seeking to reconstruct their lives and to at times exact revenge. (The prominent role of Israel in these issues is addressed in Chapter 5.)

PURSUIT OF NAZI WAR CRIMINALS

For many Nazis, including high-ranking officials, the end of the war and the defeat of Nazi ideology led to suicide. This swift end to some in the Nazi upper echelon was depicted in *The Bunker* (1981), a made-for-TV movie that dramatized the collapse of the Third Reich and the final days of Hitler and his closest cohorts in the notorious Berlin bunker.

Some of those who did not commit suicide were captured and tried at Nuremberg; others eluded the Allied net, sought to hide, and became the subjects of organized hunts to track them down and bring them to justice.

These hunts, with their inherent suspense and ultimate sense of justice, were the subject of several TV shows. Programs devoted to the pursuit of Nazi war criminals allow for a retelling of the Holocaust within a contemporaneous setting. The real-life capture and trial of Adolf Eichmann in 1960 inspired the season-premiere episode of *Armstrong Circle Theatre* that year, titled "Engineer of Death: The Eichmann Story." Through narrative (the authoritative voice of prominent news journalist Douglas Edwards), reenactments, and actual footage, the show details Eichmann's rise to power, his hatred of Jews, his role in the Final Solution, and atrocities at Auschwitz. The program opens as Edwards describes Israel's capture of Eichmann, and quotes Ben Gurion's announcement to the Israeli Parliament that "the man responsible for the murder of six million of our people has been captured by Israeli volunteers and will shortly be placed on trial for his crimes." The three-act teleplay goes on to juxtapose the story of Eichmann's youth and his Nazi career with the Nuremberg trials, including testimony of Nazis and of survivors. Along the way, viewers are presented with a detailed history of the escalation of Nazism, from Hitler's speeches scapegoating Jews, imposition of the Nuremberg laws, the Wannsee Conference where the Final Solution for Europe's Jews was charted, and then the carrying out of that policy at extermination camps like Auschwitz, enabled by the development of technology of mass extermination via gas chambers and Zyklon B gas. Stark statistics are intercut with personal testimony of Auschwitz survivors, footage, and reenactments. The program puts an emphasis on the Jews as the particular victims of the Nazis and projects a strong statement about the importance of not forgetting what took place. Even the *TV Guide* description emphasizes the Jewish component, describing how the program traces "the rise to power of this mass-exterminator of over six million Jews ... his 'discovery of the final solution to the Jewish problem.'" In an era when repeats were far less a staple of TV fare than they are today, this program was rebroadcast in the spring of 1961 to coincide with the April trial of Eichmann in Jerusalem, in recognition of the historic significance of the event.

The event still held interest more than three decades later, when TNT produced a new television version of events surrounding the capture of Eichmann. The 1996 drama focused less on factual details and more on the moral-philosophical component of Eichmann's deeds.

Other made-for-TV movies focused on the pursuit of Nazis not by governments but by individuals. The 1974 miniseries *QB VII* tells the tale of Abe Cady, an American Jewish writer who publishes a book detailing the Nazi past of Dr. Adam Kelno, a prominent physician, now a British citizen. Kelno, a non–Jewish Pole, was a prisoner doctor at the Jadwiga concentration camp during the war. After the war, he married, had children, and built a respectable medical practice in London. Although the Polish government sought his extradition as a Nazi war criminal, witnesses who testified to the horrifying procedures Kelno performed cannot identify him and he is exonerated. Fearing that his tarnished image will destroy his London practice, Kelno donates his services to the people of Kuwait for many years and is knighted for his dedication to humanity.

Cady's assertion in his book that Kelno conducted horrible experiments on thousands of "Jewish guinea pigs," elicits a libel suit from Kelno, which goes to trial in London. At the trial, Kelno's sadistic sterilization experiments at Jadwiga are described in detail, as one victim recalls that Kelno "showed me my testicle on a plate and said, 'Here is your egg, Jew. Enjoy the other one because that goes next.'"

Although the trial concludes with a verdict in favor of the plaintiff, Sir Adam Kelno, the judgment awarded to him was "the sum of one half-penny for the damage to his reputation." The worth of this Nazi's reputation, no matter what steps he had taken after the war to hide and deny his past, was virtually nil and was exposed as such for the world to witness.

A German Protestant woman dedicated to bringing Nazis to justice was the subject of the TV movie *Nazi Hunter: The Beate Klarsfeld Story*. The life of the real-life Nazi hunter is chronicled in this 1986 production, from her marriage to a Jewish man whose father was killed in Auschwitz to her exposure of Klaus Barbie, "the butcher of Lyons," from his hiding place in Bolivia.

Another biographical drama of a Nazi hunter was HBO's notable made-for-cable movie about Simon Wiesenthal, one of the world's most renowned Nazi hunters and himself a Holocaust survivor. The movie, *Max and Helen*, powerfully recounts some of the horrors he underwent as a Holocaust victim at the Matthausen concentration camp and how his survival of these atrocities motivates his subsequent lifework to bring Nazi war criminals to justice.

The hunt for Nazis is complicated when they take on other identities to elude detection and evade capture. Often, this goes beyond merely taking on a facade of humanitarianism to mask past crimes, as did Adam Kelno in *QB VII*, and entails a more bizarre disguise. In TV's most common twist of identities, Nazis pose as Jews or even as Holocaust survivors, in a final affront to their victims. This theme of enemies of the Jews' taking on their cloak and character reappeared in several shows. In each case, the Nazi, staunchly unrepentant, is discovered and captured.

An early instance of this plotline was a 1968 episode of *The F.B.I.*, in which a Nazi disguises himself as a Jew, speaking Yiddish and taking refuge in a synagogue. A similar theme appeared on two detective shows in 1981—on an episode of *Magnum, P.I.*, where Nazis posed as Israeli Nazi-hunters, and in the pilot movie for *Cagney and Lacey*, where they assumed the identity of Hasidic Jews working in New York's diamond district. *Law and Order* broached this subject a decade later, in an episode where the wife of a Polish immigrant — presumed by all to be a Holocaust survivor — is murdered after discovering her husband's Nazi past.

This notion of contorted identities was the premise of entire TV movies. In *Twist of Fate* (1989), at the end of the war a notorious Nazi undergoes plastic surgery and poses as a Jew to evade capture, then is carried along by circumstances to join a group of Zionists smuggling Holocaust survivors into prestate Israel. There he rises to the upper echelons of the Israeli army. But the ineluctable unraveling of his secret begins when his Israeli-born son delves into Nazi archives in Europe while researching a film on the topic of Nazi war criminals and begins to uncover startling facts about his father. At the same time, the Odessa group — a gang of surviving Nazis dedicated to the resurgence of Nazism and operating out of South America — threatens to disclose his true identity unless he supplies them with large amounts of uranium to which he has access. Devotion to his adopted country prevents him from providing the uranium, which will make terrorist bombs; he devises a plan to foil his blackmailers and maintain his secret at the same time, sacrificing his life in the process.

On a made-for-TV movie from the series *The Commish*, a Nazi's decadeslong disguise as a Jewish garment industry magnate begins to unravel. A German woman who assumes a Jewish identity after the death of her Nazi husband and later marries into a Jewish family in America was the subject of *The Ring*, TV's version of a Danielle Steel novel.

As Nazi war criminals age and die out, one would think that popular television's attention to hunting them down would likewise fade. But the headline attention to continuing revelations of the Nazi past of prominent citizens like former United Nations head Kurt Waldheim and the trials of war criminals Klaus Barbie and others make this topic eminently salable and ripe for current prime-time fare. As western civilization's ultimate symbol of horror, evil, and atrocity, Nazis — and their modern-day followers — will continue to be hounded and brought to justice on popular TV. Moreover, while other of the world's bad guys may undergo political rehabilitation with changing alliances and global developments, the Nazi stands alone — fixed in time — as the undisputed villain, a target without controversy for television.

HOLOCAUST SURVIVORS

On many programs, Nazi war criminals are found not as the culmination of an orchestrated hunt for them but as a result of a chance encounter with a Holocaust survivor. For such survivors, attempts to put the horrors of the war behind them are disrupted by these chance meetings with former Nazi tormentors, which reopen old wounds, stir painful emotions, and arouse a need for action. Indeed, the bulk of programs about Holocaust survivors deal with such confrontations — usually on American soil — and the various events that ensue. Such scenarios involving the plight of a single Holocaust survivor or a close-knit group of them facing an old Nazi foe are one way in which TV attempts to deal with the enormous issues of the Holocaust in a personalized and highly dramatized way. Into such encounters are compressed issues of memory, revenge, justice, and how American values deal with such extreme evil as Nazis and Nazism.

In these cases, and indeed in virtually all depictions of Holocaust survivors, they are shown to be consumed with memories of past horrors and
relentlessly determined to pursue their tormentors and bring them to justice.
Yet in some cases their desire for justice, or revenge, results in a kind of replay
of the Holocaust, with the Nazis murdering the Jews who recognize them in
an attempt to keep their identity secret. This was the fate of Holocaust survivors on segments of *Night Gallery, Cagney and Lacey, Quincy, M.E., Magnum, P.I., Airwolf,* and *Miami Vice.* Despite the awareness of survivors, in some
cases, that such dangers awaited them, they remained undeterred. In the *Miami
Vice* episode, although other survivors had been apparently killed off by cohorts
of a Nazi war criminal against whom they were about to testify, an elderly survivor places other factors above his own personal safety. Responding to his
son's fears about the risk he is placing himself in by going ahead with testify-
ing, he states that he is undaunted and insists, "I don't care about myself. No
one can hurt an old man. No, I do this for the others. For the ones who didn't
survive. And to let the world know — it can never happen again." His ultimate
murder makes his courageous sentiments even more searing.

Through depictions of Nazis' calculating and ruthless murder of survivors,
these shows mean to project the threat of Nazism as deadly and ongoing, both
on a personal level and to society as a whole. Nazism is not dead, nor are Nazis;
their intent — and ability — to kill Jews remains intact long after their military
defeat. Some of the shows state this quite directly. In *Quincy, M.E.,* for example, Nazis and their followers express regret not only for the fact that some Jews
survived the Holocaust but also for attempts to relegate the Final Solution to
history books rather than revitalize it as "the most courageous act in modern
history." The notion of Holocaust survivors as past and present victims offers
a picture of the Jew as ever vulnerable, a sentiment expressly noted in the
Cagney and Lacey segment. When questioned by police, the widow of a Hasidic
Jew murdered by the Nazi whom he recognized states, "To some crazy *meshugenneh,* a Jew is an enemy," explaining that her late husband, who was like her
a survivor of concentration camps, was "a Jew in the diamond business. That's
why so many Jews are in this business: you can put a million dollars of dia-
monds in your pocket [and] leave anytime." (These shows, not allowing evil to
triumph, always conclude with the capture or death of the offending Nazi.)

Despite this vulnerability, many of TV's Holocaust survivors defy vic-
timization when confronting Nazis a second time in their lives. Those Holocaust survivors who track down their former tormentors and manage to remain
unscathed face the question of whether to bring the Nazi to justice through
the law or through the gun. Many a dramatic showdown places a Holocaust
survivor, with gun poised and pointed at a Nazi war criminal, visibly agonizing over whether or not to shoot. The Holocaust survivor must weigh emotion, revenge, and a sure, swift outcome against confidence in the American
legal system (usually extolled by the series' hero).

On a 1984 episode of the series *Hotel*, at the San Francisco establishment that is the setting for the normally light drama, an elderly man attending his grandson's *bar mitzvah* spots his former Nazi tormentor, now a respectable corporate executive named Alex Huff, attending a business meeting. The show charts the emotional upheaval of the survivor, Joe Freilich, as he experiences first shock and then great confusion and indecisiveness about how to react. He is inclined to kill the Nazi. Reflecting on his grandson's *bar mitzvah* he tells his wife, "In some cultures, the rite of passage involves killing a wild beast." But later, he goes with a concealed gun to Huff's suite and once there merely makes small talk, leaving without withdrawing the weapon or revealing his true aims. He laments afterward to his friend the hotel manager, "I don't have the courage of my instincts ... It's hard to kill; it's easy to die. Six million of us proved it." At last, dressed in concentration camp prisoner garb, he bursts into a stockholder's meeting that Huff is addressing and orders him at gunpoint to read a confession of his crimes — that he was a member of the SS, third in command at Treblinka, responsible for "the systematic disposal of unfortunates shipped there from all corners of the Reich," and engaged in his spare time in torture and needless experiments. Huff denies it all until Freilich places the gun at his head, telling him of the "six bullets in this gun — one for every million you and your kind killed" and demanding the truth so that "you can live with yourself." With Huff's confession finally uttered and stunned bystanders aghast, Freilich fires the gun — discharging six blanks in methodical repetition. "I told you I don't have the courage to kill," he tells the hotel manager as he walks off, who replies, "You have the courage not to." In a final scene that provides an endorsement of Freilich's decision not to kill him, Huff is seen being led away by U.S. Justice Department officials.

Another Jewish survivor who faced a Nazi with a gun but did not pull the trigger appeared on a 1989 episode of the action-adventure series *MacGyver*. A very proper art auction is disrupted when elderly Jew Sam Bolinsky, arm tattooed, bursts in announcing that the painting being sold is really his, that it was stolen from his family in Poland by the Nazis during the war. To substantiate his claim, he later explains about the special Nazi unit devoted to thieving art from Holocaust victims throughout Europe that garnered over twelve million works of art. With the help of series hero MacGyver, a modern-day Robin Hood, Sam tracks down the painting's current, "hidden" owner — it is none other than his former concentration camp captor, Frau Brandenburg. She has been plotting a resurrection of Nazism in America, but her efforts to entrap and murder Sam, who has discovered her, go astray. At the show's conclusion, she finds herself the target of a gun he points at her head, and the two, Nazi and Jew, tormentor and victim, spar on matters of revenge, justice, and morality. As if she were still a concentration camp commandant, Frau Brandenburg derides the Jew, snarling, "You will not kill me — you Jews are weak." But no longer subject to Nazi tyranny, he denies her insults, adding that "in fact your hate has made us stronger" and telling her that she deserves to die, that "the world would be a better place without you." Her reply, "The feeling is mutual — perhaps we are not so different, you and I," which suggests an equality in their motives, reviles and disturbs him. The camera pans to a close-up of his hand on the gun, and then to an extreme close-up of his finger on the trigger, as if anxiously awaiting his response. He concludes that they operate on separate planes of morality, and his arm falls as he utters, "No, we are very different," and pushes her out, presumably to her arrest and prosecution.

These programs unambiguously put forth the position that the proper action to be taken by survivors is to not stoop to the Nazis' level of killing but to allow a system of law to prevail and deal with this matter. Yet the moral course of action is by no means as clear-cut as these shows would have viewers believe. While the *MacGyver* conclusion asserts that Sam Bolinsky and Frau Brandenburg are indeed very different, that difference is not demonstrated by his decision not to kill her. Her purpose is to exterminate his people; his to prevent that from happening. A campaign of annihilation, and an attempt at self-preservation cannot be equated.

A recognition of this difference is found in a number of law dramas that depict Holocaust survivors who have in fact killed a Nazi but are defended by the Gentile lawyer-hero of the show. In episodes of *The Defenders* (1962), *Sam Benedict* (1963), and *The Mississippi* (1983), while criticism about taking the law into one's own hands is expressed, the survivor's killing of a Nazi is presented as understandable and worthy of defending and not as uncourageous or immoral. In *The Defenders*, Mayer Loeb kills a renowned medical scholar who was in fact the Nazi responsible for the deaths of his wife and son in a Polish concentration camp. The series' father-and-son legal team, Lawrence and Kenneth Preston, take on Loeb's defense, arguing it was justifiable revenge and that Loeb was temporarily insane at the time of the killing. In discussions between themselves, the two lawyers express rage at Nazis and what went on in concentration camps but disagree on whether Loeb's action was justified. The elder, distinguished Lawrence Preston insists that it was and that under similar circumstances, "I don't wonder [what I would have done]. I know. I would have followed the man who did it to the ends of the earth. And I wouldn't have used anything so humane as a .45-caliber revolver. I would have slaughtered him in the most brutal, barbaric manner my imagination could devise." The issue is further complicated as a sympathetic portrayal of the Nazi is painted by his grieving widow, who testifies that he was merely a victim of circumstances, following orders, and that had he not done so, someone of "less conscience would have ... and a worse tragedy might have occurred." This glorified picture, however, fails to sway the jurors against Mayer Loeb, as they return without a verdict, maintaining that "it happened in a different time and in a different place" and it is thus impossible to pass judgment. Given television's aversion to promoting lawlessness, particularly in its earlier years when no crime went unpunished, the jury's decision not to convict Loeb (the program certainly could have concluded otherwise — with his conviction and speeches about how American law must reign despite our obvious sympathy for your plight) is arguably a strong statement of understanding and support for a Holocaust survivor and an acknowledgment of the enormity and uniqueness of the Holocaust.

On another law drama the following year, *Sam Benedict*, a survivor of Dachau recognizes a well-known philanthropist as the person who informed on her family and was responsible for the deaths of her parents and husband. She tries to run him down and is defended by the series' eponymous lawyer.

Some twenty years later, a survivor of a German concentration camp stood trial for murder in a small Southern town on *The Mississippi*, a short-lived drama about a city lawyer seeking a quieter life as he plies his trade aboard a boat on the Mississippi River. He comes to the defense of the survivor who tracked the Nazi to his small-town hideout after hunting him for forty years.

On *Reasonable Doubts*, a Jewish lawyer finds herself in the reverse situation: she is prosecuting two young boys who kidnapped a former a Nazi, a task that brings on conflict within herself as a Jew and as a professional. A Jewish father and son, both lawyers, find themselves on opposite sides of the gavel when one prosecutes and the other defends a Jewish man accused of killing a German with Nazi leanings in a fifty-year-old murder case on *Picket Fences*.

A chance encounter between survivors and a Nazi and the ensuing issues of revenge, killing, and justice were the subject of a 1985 made-for-TV movie, *The Execution*. One evening during their weekly mah-jongg game, five women concentration camp survivors, one of whom is not Jewish, see a local TV feature about a restaurateur whom they recognize as their Nazi torturer in Birkenau decades earlier. As the women work to verify his identity and consider their course of action, they experience nightmarish flashbacks and anguished conversations, which expose viewers to various details and images of the Holocaust. When the women decide to kill the Nazi, the deed is assigned through secret lots to Marysa, the non–Jew. Because part of the plan is for them all to share complete responsibility for the act, they each confess following his death. The public rallies to their cause, supporting them with protests and demonstrations urging their immediate release. Even the police and the district attorney who is assigned to prosecute the women sympathize with their action, confessing that they "look like bozos harassing innocent women who struck a blow for humanity. There's no jury on earth that will convict them." Indeed, the women are released, as a result of public pressure and confusion over their multiple confessions. And yet, following this seeming vindication, in a plot twist that takes the bite out of their triumph, it is revealed that Marysa had only wounded the Nazi and that another non–Jewish victim of his had actually killed him. That both the presumed and the actual killer of the Nazi are non–Jews is odd and disturbing in the context of a program that itself emphasizes the Jewishness of the Holocaust. The program's general support for the women's action is further diminished at the program's end, as their sense of vindication seems to vanish when they state that "he is not dead ... he has scarred us forever, for what he did to us — and what we did to him." Although the movie portrays the women highly supportively, sympathetically understanding their pain and their consequent action, it raises in this final statement the objectionable premise equating perpetrator and victim. Here again, when television hints at any notion of support for vigilantism, it must be tempered.

The actions of a Holocaust survivor's seeking revenge traversed into further illegality and moral morass on an installment of the British import PBS *Mystery* series, "Original Sin." A series of inexplicable murders at a modern-day British publishing house is ultimately traced to an elderly Jew whose wife and young children had been deported from France during the war to their deaths at Auschwitz. The survivor committed the murders as part of a symmetrical revenge he devised: killing the son and daughter of the French collaborationist who fifty years earlier was responsible for betraying his family to the Nazis. For drama's sake, outlandish atrocity attributed to survivors goes further and further afield and raises conflicting morals within the show. The survivor is portrayed sympathetically ("Wait," he says plaintively to the police waiting to take him away. "I've been waiting fifty years to tell my story," he says as he mulls a photo of adorable, long-lost children), yet his murders of innocent people are reprehensible. The collaborationist is unmoved, impassive, unrepentant, smug and aloof, and repugnant — yet he claims he betrayed the Jewish family in order to get much-needed supplies from the Nazis so that the Resistance could continue. Moral ambiguity reigns on both sides.

A show where this was not the case was a 1985 episode of the medical series *Trapper John, M.D.* that depicts a survivor whose killing of a Nazi is not at all condemned, because she acted not before but after the wheels of American justice had a chance to turn — and to fail. Here the Nazi war criminal takes the form of a respected and renowned surgeon, Victor Kosciusko. The show revolves around the efforts of an Israeli agent, Sofia Koslo, to convince Kosciusko's colleagues — who hold him in highest esteem — that he is in fact Dr. Streibel, an infamous Nazi who distinguished himself as a young genius of medical cruelty during the Holocaust. Although the show starts off on a rather silly foot as the Israeli agent makes some comical and bumbling errors and no one takes her seriously, it turns more somber when she presents evidence that increasingly implicates the surgeon. With his colleagues' suspicions aroused, Kosciusko turns to a familiar ruse — he claims to be a Jew who suffered in the war and even shows a tattooed arm to prove it. Seeking to put an end to his deceptions and to finally convince his colleagues of his true identity, Sofia locates one of Kosciusko's victims and has the woman relate her harrowing memories to Trapper (nickname for chief of surgery Dr. John McIntyre). In a grippingly moving recounting, Madame Le Vasseur tells of her arrival with her five-year-old twin daughters at a concentration camp and her encounter with Dr. Streibel. In flashbacks that contain some actual concentration camp footage (a rare inclusion for series television), Streibel is seen ripping one of the twins away from her mother to conduct medical experiments in which he injects her with typhoid fever; and later taking the remaining, healthy twin and shooting her in front of her mother, so that he can perform autopsies on both children to compare the sick with the healthy. With this account and corroborating information Sofia receives from her headquarters in Israel she notifies the U.S. Justice Department and Streibel/Kosciusko's prosecution seems assured. Sofia and Trapper are therefore incensed and bewildered days later to see the former Nazi strolling unabashedly through the hospital. He boasts to them that he has effectively evaded legal justice by taking advantage of his American citizenship, "a gift [which] is difficult to strip away." With obvious glee, he explains that since proof against him is "difficult to find after forty years — so many of the so-called witnesses seem to have died, a pity," his appeals will be in the courts until he is "an elderly man." Taking leave of them on this triumphant note, Kosciusko enters the elevator alone but suddenly is made aware of — and the camera reveals — the presence of another person: Madame Le Vasseur. Greeting him with the words that he himself used to utter to "welcome" Jews to the concentration camp, "Welcome to the path to heaven," she points a gun at him, uttering "my babies" and shoots. The show's closing moments focus on his dying face, overcome with shock and pain.

By leaving viewers with this final image and omitting any expressions of censure about a survivor's killing a Nazi, the episode stands alone in depictions of this issue. Unlike other programs, the legal system is given first chance to render justice, but it brings about just the opposite when it ensures the Nazi's continual freedom. Left with no other recourse, the Holocaust survivor must become the agent of justice and does so without the show's reproach.

The sense of America's falling short in dealing with Nazi mass murderers — either by laxity of persecution or deliberate protection of them — is expressly alluded to in this program and several others. In *Trapper John, M.D.*, Sofia gives Dr. McIntyre some startling figures: "You should know that there are perhaps ten thousand Nazi war criminals living in the United States. Only eleven have been denaturalized." Nearly a quarter of a century earlier, a surprisingly candid comment on the U.S. role in harboring Nazis was voiced in *The Defenders*. A Nazi's widow declares that the U.S. Army had cleared her husband of any connection with the Nazi party or with war crimes, that he was invited to America by the U.S. government "in recognition of his ability and the invaluable assistance he could render this country," and that he was granted American citizenship by an act of Congress.

An entire TV movie was devoted to this theme, when famed TV detective Lieutenant Theo Kojak investigates a governmental conspiracy to protect Nazi war criminals living in America on *Kojak: The Belarus File*.

While these instances point to real lapses in the system, overwhelmingly programs dealing with survivor retribution project a strong view that justice must be done. The heroes of the shows uniformly express contempt for the Nazis, and the Nazis are inevitably punished in one severe way or another. The picture of Nazis living successful lives, free of guilt and of the past, while Holocaust survivors, their victims, are haunted and plagued by it is one of gross injustice that riles TV characters and, presumably, viewers. While disagreements are aired over how to right this wrong and achieve justice, there is never a question as to which side morality lies on.

In addition to physically confronting Nazis, TV's Holocaust survivors have taken upon themselves the mission of intellectually challenging Nazism in all its incarnations. They refuted and condemned Holocaust revisionists and deniers in *Never Forget* and a *Quincy, M.E.* episode and fiercely opposed the free and public expression of Nazi ideology in *Skokie*.

Featured in several programs are Holocaust survivors neither hunting nor confronting Nazis but simply trying to put their lives together after the war, to find lost loved ones, to deal with memories, and to keep memory alive, so that, in the refrain that underlies their actions and that they frequently voice, "it can never happen again." Several shows have explored these themes, with perhaps the most effective and searing doing so within the context of family, in plotlines where Holocaust survivors coming to America and encountering American relatives stir great tensions, memories, feelings, conflict and reconciliation.

One beautiful exposition of this was a *Brooklyn Bridge* episode that had as its subtext the question of the Holocaust's impact upon both survivors and a younger generation separated by decades and continents. It is 1950s Brooklyn and the Silver family is about to receive, with trepidation and excitement, an unusual visitor: a European cousin of Grandma Silver who lived through the war there. His appearance in the Brooklyn household opens up a world of turmoil and conflicting emotions for the whole family. Although thrilled to see him and happy to be of help, the grandmother of two young boys (one already a teenager) is determined to shield her American-born grandchildren from the unspeakable horrors her cousin has endured. The episode accurately captures 1950s attitudes that the children shouldn't know. Yet, in the tug between the grandmother's efforts to protect the children and the older boy's attempt to learn about his cousin's past and to forge a meaningful connection with him and with his own family's history, knowledge wins out. The show is a moving declaration of the importance of memory and of knowledge of history even at its worst.

The coming together of another Jewish family scarred by the Holocaust but reunited in New York some years later was the focus of *Hallmark Hall of Fame*'s "Miss Rose White," based on the off–Broadway play *A Shayna Maidel*. The show is about a family reunited after the war when a father and daughter already settled in New York are faced with the arrival of their daughter/sister fresh from Europe and concentration camps. It delves sensitively into issues of ethnic identity, assimilation and Americanization, and the often tattered state of family communication.

Another Holocaust survivor struggling to forge a new life in America was Gina Sloane, an Italian Jew who survived Auschwitz, on *Homefront*. She experiences painful flashbacks of the camps and her loss of family there, yet perseveres as a single mother in her new home in America, working at a job, raising her child, and falling in love.

While America presented its particular challenges to Holocaust survivors, for those remaining in Europe the end of the war did not mean the end of their plight, as displayed in the 1987 TV movie *Lena: My One Hundred Children*. A Polish Jewish woman, who had survived the Holocaust by posing as a Gentile, takes pity on the many Jewish orphans left starving and uncared for in postwar Kraków and devotes herself to their care. A character of great determination and forcefulness, Lena triumphs over bureaucracy and indifference to bring one hundred of the children to a home in the country. There she faces her greatest challenge: the pervasive anti–Semitism that threatens to bar the children from school and medical care and even endangers their lives. Deciding that Europe's obdurate anti–Semitism is too inhospitable to the children's recovery, Lena leads them on a perilous trek to new lives in Israel.

A reunion of survivors decades after the war coming together for the World Gathering of Holocaust Survivors was the topic of the 1982 made-for-TV movie *Remembrance of Love*. Dramatizing the actual gathering that took place in Israel the previous year, the program showed survivors airing issues of survival, heritage, strength, memory, and the complex relationships with their own children. Like the hunt-for–Nazis shows, TV dramatizations of such reunions provide an opportunity for a retelling of the Holocaust. While focusing on the story of a single survivor, his family, and — through flashbacks — his youth in Poland, the program covered various aspects of the Holocaust. Throughout the show, the overriding theme was one of remembrance. Speeches at the closing ceremonies, held at the Western Wall in Jerusalem, spoke of the tremendous losses of the Holocaust and concluded with the exhortation to "Remember it, dear friends and children — nothing dies that is remembered."

Another survivors' reunion, on a smaller scale, took place on a 1984 episode of *Finder of Lost Loves*, a short-lived series about an amateur sleuth who brings together star-crossed lovers. As a result of his efforts, two Holocaust survivors are reunited after decades of believing the other was dead.

The sense of dislocation and of a lost world faced by survivors expressed in their search for long-missing loved ones was even the subject of a sit-com.

On an episode of the 1980s series *Facts of Life,* one of the teenaged girls in the boarding school where the comedy is set is trapped on an elevator with an elderly Holocaust survivor. The buoyant young woman, fancily dressed for an event she was on her way to attend, is gradually drawn into the survivor's tale of his forty-year search for his brother — missing since the war — and is deeply moved by it. Viewers, and she, are left with the forlorn sense that he will never find him.

The idea of transmitting the Holocaust from older to younger generations takes on special meaning when it involves Holocaust survivors and their children. Children of survivors and the lingering effects upon them of their parents' ordeal were portrayed on *Remembrance of Love* and *Skokie*—where daughters of survivors emerge from a parentally imposed insulation from the Holocaust to a newfound exploration of the past and its impact on them and their relationship with their parents. Another daughter of Holocaust survivors undergoing this same process was the topic of an episode of the short-lived series about a New York City restaurant *Tattinger's.*

While these daughters are sheltered and overprotected by their survivor parents, for the son of a Holocaust survivor the roles are reversed, as he functions as protector of his elderly father on the *Miami Vice* episode. Fearing for his father's life (the survivor is about to testify against a Nazi), he urges him not to testify and to come live with him so that he will be safe.

While most of television's Holocaust survivors are shown in suspenseful conflict with Nazis for dramatic effect, the more realistic view of their living out ordinary lives made an appearance on the hit medical series *ER.* When Hannah Steiner, an elderly woman who is a Holocaust survivor becomes a patient in the emergency room, she and Dr. Mark Greene forge a bond of friendship and spirituality. Greene, a self-described "son of an agnostic Jew and a lapsed Catholic," and Steiner, who thought that "God and I had forsaken each other," surprise themselves by praying to God for the safe return of Steiner's granddaughter, who is missing in the carjacking that had landed the older woman in the hospital. Her own philosophy about retribution against the Nazis is expressed in conversations with Greene when she tells him, "After you have seen evil, you laugh, you work, you have children. You don't let it own you. That's your revenge: to live." Thankfully her granddaughter is safely recovered, and Steiner's whole family joyously celebrates Chanukah in the hospital with her, grateful for all the miracles.

NAZIS AND GERMANY
AFTER THE WAR

Just as survivors of the Holocaust are shown grappling with the terrible past, so also—though to a far lesser degree—are its perpetrators. Echoes of the Holocaust resound in several TV movies about modern-day terrorism against Jews, such as *21 Hours at Munich*, the Entebbe telefilms, and *The Taking of Flight 847: The Uli Derickson Story*, which all allude to German guilt about the mass murder of Jews.

The question of former Nazis' feeling guilt and the complex issue of "following orders" at times rounded out the picture of TV Nazis, in an effort, perhaps, to present them not merely as cardboard villains. The Nazi's widow in *The Defenders*, for example, claimed that he had been racked with guilt, spending countless sleepless nights recalling the cruelties he inflicted. At the same time, she maintained that for him it was a question of following orders and that if he hadn't done it someone else with less humanity would have, and with more tragic results.

A satirical treatment of a Nazi officer's feeling guilt was the basis of an offering from the BBC titled *Genghis Cohn*. Presumably it is guilt that causes a former SS officer to be haunted by the ghost of a Jewish comedian whom he murdered during the war — and who now causes him to take on Jewish characteristics.

The deep sense of guilt felt by a collaborator led to a form of artistic penitence in *Mistral's Daughter*, a miniseries aired in 1984. A French artist who had collaborated with the Nazis during the war, betraying the Jews of his town, discloses in a final dramatic scene set four decades later that his secret masterpiece, on which he has been toiling for years, is a series of portraits of the Jewish holidays.

Such attempts to flesh out characters who personify evil walk a delicate line between humanizing Nazis and exculpating them. A kind of revisionism can seep in that blurs definitions of guilt and innocence and erodes concepts of responsibility. During the time of the collapse of the Berlin Wall, for example, which brought a heady sense of a new Germany and an accompanying fascination with that nation, a new approach to Germans of World War II was discernible on popular TV. In a spate of shows they were portrayed not as perpetrators of an awful war but as equal victims of it.

Three such programs appeared over the course of just eight days in March 1990, only months after the fall of the Berlin Wall. In *Quantum Leap*, a series in which the hero zaps back and forth in time to redress historical quirks, a German girl in 1940s Georgia dies of apparent suicide. A subtheme of the program is the great suffering her family endured as a result of the American bombings of Germany.

The concept of Germans as victims not only in American bombing raids but in concentration camps was explored four nights later in a Perry Mason TV movie called *The Case of the Desperate Deception*. A tale of a hunt for a Nazi war criminal, the movie includes the observations by Perry and his assistant that most of the Maidenek survivors were Poles, French nationals, and Germans.

The Incident, airing within this same eight-day time frame, presents a sympathetic portrait of a young German soldier and projects the sense that he, too, although a soldier of the Third Reich, is a victim of Nazism. The year is 1944 and the setting a small Colorado town that borders a POW camp housing a contingent of German prisoners. When the camp doctor, an elderly townsperson, is found murdered there, one of the German soldiers, Wilhelm Geiger, is implicated and becomes the subject of revulsion and fury by the townsfolk. Yet, in a scenario that extols America's system of justice and sense of fairness, the soldier is staunchly defended in a court of law by a bedraggled but beloved town lawyer.

The lawyer's dedication to due process is underscored by his determination to defend the German soldier even though he learns that his own son-in-law has just been killed in battle overseas. The ensuing courtroom drama reveals that among the German POWs were deep ideological divisions between those who arrived in 1941 and persisted in their staunch devotion to Hitler and those recently arrived, younger soldiers, who sensed the imminent demise of the Third Reich and felt no support for the Führer. Geiger, one of the recent arrivals, describes a kind of secret police clandestinely established and operated by the veteran POWs to brutally enforce their political will; he explains that it was the leader of this rival group who murdered the doctor and is now framing him.

As he works to establish his innocence, Geiger emerges as a sympathetic — if emotionally aloof — victim of a kind of micro–Nazism that reigns at the camp. This benign portrayal is bestowed upon him even though he does not express guilt or remorse for serving the Nazi cause — as Sergeant Lott did in *Playhouse 90.*

Certainly, intelligent efforts to present political subtleties on popular television are desirable. But if these programs presage a trend in which, spurred by a popular enthusiasm to readily embrace a reunified Germany, history is forgotten and distinctions between perpetrators and victims are obfuscated, there is ample cause for concern.

Perhaps in response to this nascent shift in the political discourse, *L.A. Law* aired an episode — ostensibly about torture in Argentine prisons — that dealt with issues of the Holocaust and explored the question of who is a victim. In this episode, Jewish lawyer Stuart Markowitz prosecutes a former private in the Argentine army, Private Mendez, accused of torturing an American prisoner, Mr. Reynolds, years earlier — before the soldier emigrated to America and made good as owner of a chain of dry cleaning stores. In closing arguments, both Stuart and the defense attorney draw parallels to German atrocities. While Stuart explains that the Nuremberg trials established certain behaviors as unacceptable even in wartime, the defense attorney argues that the generals who gave orders — and not the privates who merely followed them — were tried at Nuremberg. When the jury decides in favor of the defendant, clearing him of any wrongdoing, the former torture victim takes matters into his own hands. Like many of TV's Holocaust survivors who seek retribution against their former tormentors, Reynolds holds a gun to Mendez's head, who pleads for his life maintaining that since he had no choice but to follow orders, he too was a victim. Reynolds scornfully rebukes this argument, insisting that Mr. Mendez "use precise language when characterizing our roles — you were not a victim."

While the episode gives fair and even sympathetic representation to Mendez's stance, in the final analysis it clearly distinguishes between the two characters' claims as victims. Private Mendez is deemed the perpetrator as one who has the power to refuse an order — the real victim, helpless and powerless, has no such luxury.

But it is Stuart and his personal musings that offer the final comments on this issue. His thoughts turn to the Holocaust and a great-uncle, "Heschie," who perished in the camps along with "all those Jews who were tortured. They disappeared into night and fog." In a comment that more reflects pre–German reunification sentiments, he tells his wife, "I was brought up to believe that every German was to blame." And yet despite recent political changes and his belief in nonviolence, he laments the fact that he can do nothing to avenge the extermination of six million of his people — the Jewish people — and declares that all you can do is "hold on to the hatred, that's what you do."

Stuart's stance seems to be a warning to temper our natural tendency to be carried off by sweeping events, no matter how exhilarating and filled with positive potential they may be. While his is a call for avoiding facile historical comparisons and historical amnesia, ironically another *L.A. Law* episode did just that.

In a story about a battered wife on trial for killing her husband, an expert witness testifies that abused women "think like victims of concentration camps. When human beings are subjected to daily terror, to constant punishment, options like escape cease to exist." While the plight of battered women is appalling and complex psychological factors shape their course of action or lack thereof, such a comparison is not appropriate. Could inmates of Auschwitz dial a hot line to get help? Imprisoned by barbed-wire, killer dogs, and machine guns and surrounded by starvation, disease, gas chambers, and death — which comprised an entire system of mass annihilation — these concentration camp victims truly had no options: there were no police, no court system, no shelters to turn to.

Overuse of the Holocaust as an analogy for various problems is a misuse and misunderstanding of the incomparable uniqueness of the Holocaust. Surely there are more accurate and appropriate ways to drive home the terrible plight of battered women and other appalling ills that beset our society and call out for our involvement and action. This strain of TV dialogue demonstrates the serious care that should be expended when the Holocaust is used as fodder for television programs.

TV's Post-Survivor Era

Such care is particularly important in the context of television's changing nature of Holocaust portrayals — and changing they are. In *L.A. Law*'s episode about Private Mendez, for example, the show's effort to grapple with an aspect of the Holocaust without having the Holocaust as its ostensible topic is representative of popular TV's evolving attempts to wrestle with this great catastrophe. As time moves forward, as political currents change, and as different issues and debates hold the world's attention, there is a corresponding change in approaches to addressing Holocaust issues.

One manifestation of this on the most basic level is the simple passage of time. The sheer march of days forces an alteration in the picture of Holocaust portrayals. In an attempt to deal with the Holocaust as time carries us further and further from the event, television has delved into the postwar lives of survivors — how they deal with memories, confront Nazis, rebuild their lives. But as survivors age and die out, their TV counterparts also have become more elderly, with many of them in recent years making a point of stating that there are few of them left. With their aging, TV has shifted to depictions of their adult children, even their grandchildren. Often the special emotional problems faced by such offspring as children of survivors drive a show's plotline. Their particular difficulties and challenges have been played out on such shows as *Law and Order*, *Murder One*, and *Tattinger's*.

This attempt to depict the impact of the Holocaust on people not yet born at the time (particularly relevant since most people viewing these shows were not) is not limited to portrayals of children of survivors. Stuart Markowitz on *L.A. Law*, for example, is not a child of survivors but an assimilated Jew, yet the Holocaust resonates powerfully with him.

This notion has even been depicted in a humorous manner. Bits of dialogue on shows such as *Murphy Brown* and *thirtysomething* have pointed to the deep-seated impact of Holocaust even upon the yuppie Jews depicted on TV in the late 1980s. When *Murphy Brown*'s young Miles Silverberg, producer of the fictional television news program *FYI*, experiences a string of bad luck, he ruefully comments, "This is God's way of punishing me for buying a German car." On *thirtysomething*, Michael Steadman, Americanized and intermarried, displayed a visceral identification with the Holocaust when visiting his wife's parents and feeling abysmally out of place as a Jew in their rarefied, Waspish milieu. Reluctant to attend a party of his in-laws' friends, Michael says, "I'll feel like I'm wearing a yellow armband with a Jewish star on it."

The continuing impact of the Holocaust, although we are now half a century removed from it, is as close as daily headlines. We read about newly revealed Swiss bank accounts holding millions of dollars from Holocaust victims, an Episcopalian U.S. secretary of state raised as a Catholic's discovering that her grandparents were Jewish and died in Auschwitz and Theresienstadt, and the medical community's debating the use of scientific data collected through Nazi torture in the concentration camps. All of these would seem to be the stuff of fiction, but are in fact real news events — that rapidly assumed their place as prominent story lines in entertainment TV shows.

The volatile issue of Swiss banks' hoarding funds and gold deposited by European Jews — or stolen from them by the Nazis — made an early appearance in a *Law and Order* episode in October 1996, even before the much greater extent of the matter was disclosed in further revelations. In this segment, the key to a coin dealer's murder lies in the anger of a woman whose father, a Holocaust survivor now deceased, spent decades trying to recover three rare gold coins that he had deposited in a Swiss bank before the war. His widow recounts the man's "forty-year obsession" to locate and claim them after surviving Auschwitz, where his whole family was killed. He wrote letters to the War Reparations Board, the United Nations, and presidents Truman, Eisenhower, and Kennedy — all to no avail. His daughter, who is under suspicion for murdering the coin dealer, is depicted as rife with psychological problems that the show states are characteristic of children of survivors. In explaining her father's obsessive hunt for the coins, she shouts in anger during a court-ordered therapy session that he lost everything during the Holocaust, "his family, his business, the house he grew up in, his dogs — he wanted to get *one* thing back."

Taking upon herself this task of her deceased father (along with a series of misdeeds by others) leads the daughter to murder, which she sorely regrets. But in the show's final scene, the district attorney and lawyers note an unseen culprit as they are reviewing the sentences each guilty party in the murder has received, and the question is raised: "And our Swiss banker friends? Who stole the money in the first place? What refugees are they taking deposits from now — as they yodel their way to the bank?"

Reclaiming not coins that vanished in the Holocaust but one's very identity was a theme that appeared on a 1997 episode of *Promised Land*. In a small town, a longtime resident watches as a synagogue across the street from her home is vandalized. When the woman refuses to provide any information to help catch the thugs and a young student finds materials about Nazism in her home, some suspect she is in sympathy with the anti–Semitic perpetrators. Reacting emotionally to these various events, she is compelled to reveal a fifty-year-old secret: she was born Jewish and fled Europe with her parents after her grandparents were taken away to Dachau. Yet she was raised as a Christian because, as she tells friends, upon arriving in America "although we were free, papa never forgot his fear. He told us that we were no longer Jewish. They wanted me to be safe. They didn't want me to live a life of religious persecution." This new twist in a dramatic portrayal of a survivor — one who as a child was raised Christian by parents scarred with fear by the Holocaust — clearly stems from the news stories about Secretary of State Madeleine Albright.

Another timely issue appeared on *Traders*, a Canadian-made drama series about stock traders. When a Jewish businessman and Holocaust survivor learns that a German corporation is profiting from a chemical formula used by the Nazis for their mass exterminations (including it now as a component of a top-selling garden product), he seeks to take over and disband the company. A few years earlier, a court case on *L.A. Law* explored related questions in an episode about a Jewish foundation's withdrawing its grant from a scientist after learning that she was utilizing research data obtained from Nazi medical experiments conducted at Dachau.

In treading on such territory, today's TV programs are doing more than merely mining the headlines for story ideas, they are seeking to fashion fresh approaches for sustaining a dialogue about the Holocaust. Even after fifty years, the subject lays claim on the nation's consciousness, and the need to teach about, remember, understand, and learn from the event remains. But the modes of doing so change over time. Television has already shown American viewers the facts about the Holocaust. On miniseries like *Holocaust*, *The Winds of War*, and *War and Remembrance*, dozens of TV hours brought viewers the horrors of concentration camps, the division and destruction of families, and the facts and figures. With those aspects already portrayed, TV stories have now moved to a new plane: ethical questions, moral ambiguities, theological searchings.

One case that charts this evolution is TV's depictions of the capture of Adolf Eichmann. In its first presentation in 1960 as the actual events were capturing world attention, the dramatization focused on Eichmann's capture and his role as architect of the Final Solution and included much actual footage to illustrate the terrible results of Eichmann's deeds. A different dramatization of the same story, some thirty-six years later, included no such footage. The central issue was the relationship between the Israeli captor (a Holocaust survivor who had lost relatives in the Holocaust) and the German high officer in private conversations between them. The Israeli agent was seeking to draw him out, to understand the workings of such a person, and to elicit an apology — which he never received.

This move from a recitation of Holocaust horrors to an investigation of existential questions is evident in several current, popular shows. On *Touched by an Angel*, a Holocaust survivor battles not Nazis or revisionists but the bitterness and loss of faith within himself. A postal worker who was just a child was he was interned in a concentration camp now sends angry replies to children who write letters to God.

Questions of moral ambiguity bubble under the surface in the many shows where Nazis take on the identity of Jewish survivors. (These notions of confused identities emerging from the morass of the Holocaust also presaged headline news stories: in the widely published listings of holders of Swiss bank accounts, nearly all Jews, were a number of Nazis who had thus hidden stolen wealth.) Moral certainties come unmoored when things aren't always what they seem, even as the line may be blurred between victim and perpetrator. *Weapons of Mass Destraction* was a cable-TV movie about warring media magnates unstoppable in their down-and-dirty tactics to overcome each other. But in a pivotal, climactic scene, one threatens to disclose that the father of the other — who had been held up as a hero of the Holocaust — was in fact a capo. Only then does the mutually destructive fighting cease. Under threat of this ultimate disclosure, the magnate surrenders and the two reach a compromise agreement.

Clearly, as we recede further and further from the Holocaust, creators of TV fare seeking to explore it will have to devise novel approaches with contemporary significance. One early and interesting attempt appeared in 1968, when an episode of *Star Trek* presented an extraterrestrial allegory of the Holocaust. Just recently, this same tack was taken when one of its successors, *Star Trek Voyager*, also presented an allegorical tale with parallels to the Holocaust.

How will entertainment TV approach issues of the Holocaust in the post-survivor era? As generations move on, as we press through history, our TV-mediated relationship to the Holocaust will necessarily be altered. If the current spate of shows is any indication, this issue will be a topic on popular television for a long time, creatively evolving with changing portrayals and plots as endless as the questions themselves we ask about the Holocaust.

5

Israel

Israel, although a tiny country, is regularly in the news in a very big way. Television news programs and documentaries often turn their focus to the Jewish state and the many Middle East conflicts that surround it. But another, very different picture of Israel — although rarely discussed or analyzed, yet perhaps of greater importance — emerges on the entertainment TV front.

In a bit of serendipitous timing, the rebirth of the state of Israel and the establishment of nationwide network TV in America took place in the same year, 1948. Since then, these two phenomena have been inextricably linked, as scores of TV dramas, comedies, and miniseries have turned to Israel and its stunning and turbulent history for subject matter. Many of these images have continued to be in the tradition of popular TV, which has generally portrayed Jewish themes in a positive light. On the whole, popular TV has conveyed the fact that Israel is the Jewish homeland with a strong emotional pull upon Diaspora Jews, that it lives in perpetual danger surrounded by foes, and that as a result of the constant and vital fight for its survival, it often takes extraordinary (sometimes rogue) measures in the fields of security and intelligence.

Israel and the Holocaust

Out of the ashes of the Holocaust came the modern state of Israel — at least according to popular television. Overwhelmingly, the TV dramas and made-for-television movies — and even some sitcoms — that involve Israel depict it within some historical context of the Holocaust. This connection between the attempted destruction of the Jewish people and the rebirth of their state is evinced through a variety of portrayals: prestate Israel as a haven for those escaping the Holocaust and later for those who survived it; Israel on a special moral mission to track down and capture Nazi war criminals; Israel as deserving recipient of world contrition after the horror of the Holocaust; and Israel, when the victim of Arab terrorism, dealing with echoes of the Holocaust.

Several programs present a picture of Israel bound up with the Holocaust even before the state was officially reborn in 1948. The plight of Jews fleeing Nazi Europe and seeking to reach Palestine[1] during the war, when few places on earth would accept them and when even their ancient homeland, then ruled by the British, was closed to them, is dramatized in many programs that depict the Holocaust.

An early depiction of this was the 1956 drama "Conspiracy of Hearts," which aired as part of the *Philco Television Playhouse*. In this show, a group of nuns try to spirit out Jewish children from an Austrian concentration camp to Palestine. The symbolism of Jewish children escaping Nazi Europe to find new lives in the Land of Israel evokes Israel's role as protector and preserver of the remnant of the Jewish people and site of its ongoing survival and future. It is a recurrent theme in TV dramas.

Another instance occurs in the 1989 miniseries *The Winds of War*, where the pregnant Natalie Jastrow, an American Jew trapped in Italy during the war, is repeatedly implored by friends to do everything possible to save her Jewish child in light of what is happening to the Jews of Europe. Pointedly, her only means of escape is via a Turkish ship smuggling Jews to Palestine, which has been arranged by an underground Zionist group whose leaders are portrayed as selfless, heroic, and determined. Although Natalie is ultimately unable to reach there, this vision of the Jewish homeland as a safe refuge for her threatened child is a prominent theme in this story.

It is this same vision — of regeneration of the Jewish people through children in the Land of Israel — that sustains a female inmate of Auschwitz on the made-for-TV movie *Playing for Time*. In the midst of great sorrow, she insists that all is not hopeless because she wants to live for the day "to see Palestine — to bring forth Jewish children in Palestine." The strength of this notion is undermined, however, by the casting of this character as a shrill, ugly, strident person whose "tribalism" is denounced by the hero Fania. The Zionist inmate seems to exist merely as a one-dimensional prop, a foil for Fania to espouse her own brand of universal redemption.[2]

The motif of bringing Jewish refugee children to Palestine continues in depictions of the period shortly after the war. In the miniseries *Holocaust*, Rudi Weiss, who by war's end is the sole survivor of the Weiss family, is recruited by the Jewish Agency for Palestine[3] to be a "shepherd," to smuggle some surviving children into Palestine. Earlier in the show, his mother Berta had taught the Hebrew words of the soon-to-be Israeli national anthem, "Hatikvah," to children in her music class within the Warsaw ghetto.

An entire made-for-TV movie was devoted to the theme of bringing Jewish children to Palestine. Based on a true story, *Lena: My 100 Children* depicts the story of a Polish Jewish woman who seeks to rehabilitate one hundred young and orphaned concentration camp survivors. But discovering that they cannot heal amidst the anti–Semitism she finds in Poland, she leads them on a treacherous journey to a new home in Palestine.

The plight of Holocaust survivors seeking to enter British-ruled Palestine was recounted in uncommon detail in a 1985 episode of the popular detective series *Magnum, P.I.* This description presents an unusual picture of a British soldier in Palestine with feelings of sympathy and justice for the arriving Jewish refugees. An elderly Holocaust survivor, Rabbi Solomon, recounts to the series' hero Thomas Magnum the origins of his friendship with Magnum's British associate, Higgins, explaining that immediately after the war, the rabbi and some friends sought to enter Palestine, "then ruled by the British, and for Jews it was impossible to emigrate — they wouldn't allow it. Naturally it didn't stop us." Under the cover of night, they took a lifeboat from the ship they were on to reach the shore, but "when we got there, there was a British patrol standing there. *Got in himmel!*[4] ... I was looking straight into that British soldier's face. I could see the struggle in his eyes. And all of a sudden he made a smart left turn as if he never saw us and walked away, leaving us free to scatter into the dark and to freedom."

Years later, Rabbi Solomon went on to explain, he spotted the soldier in London, embraced and thanked him and asked, "'How could a British soldier disobey a standing order?' And he answered very calmly, 'I was obeying a higher law that does not permit me to shoot unarmed refugees looking for a home.'"

A depiction of more typical circumstances — that of British soldiers indeed firing on Jewish refugees seeking to enter their homeland — appeared in the 1989 miniseries *Twist of Fate.* This convoluted tale of a Nazi who takes on the identity of a Jew to escape prosecution as World War II winds down follows him as he joins up with an underground group smuggling Jews to Palestine. They are Holocaust survivors, zealous to build Israel, and highly organized and efficient in their clandestine trek through Europe to Italy, where they have arranged for a ship to take them and two hundred other Jewish refugees to Palestine. The disguised former Nazi — clearly going along for the ride and not driven by the ideology that fires the others — finds himself falling in love with the beautiful and determined heroine. He tells her of the difficulties she will face in seeking to establish Israel and what a dream it seemed: "Why do you go on with this madness — fighting the rest of world for a lousy piece of desert? There won't be an Israel. The British won't allow you in; the Arabs don't want you." She replies, "We're not looking for anyone's approval. We want a homeland." But approaching the shores of that homeland, under cover of both dark and the Israeli music and dancing of a party that awaits to ferret them away once on shore, they face a barrage of British bullets. Some are killed or captured; many land safely through the hail of fire and go on to establish a *kibbutz* in the desert. The determination and hardships of these Zionists — mostly Holocaust survivors — are shown in many of the scenes that follow, as viewers see them on their *kibbutz*, cultivating the desert, warding off attacking Arabs, and celebrating in Israeli song and dance.

Israel's Hunt for Nazi War Criminals

Tragically, though, so many Jews who wanted to go home perished before they had any chance; and many who managed to arrive were shot on sight or turned back to the German ovens and gas chambers. The few Jews who successfully reached Palestine and the many who were already there, however, were witness to the rebirth of the State of Israel and there vowed never to forget the six million Jews who died at the hands of the Nazis during World War II. One way the State of Israel paid tribute to their memory was by taking on the mission of pursuing and capturing any surviving Nazis and bringing them to justice in the Jewish state. A grand success of this mission — the 1960 capture and the 1961 trial of Adolf Eichmann[5] — seized the world's attention and was one of the earliest international media spectacles, as the trial was broadcast live in Israel and transmitted all over the world.

The enormity of this event set off a spate of popular programs — peaking in the 1960s but continuing up until today — depicting Israel's hunt for Nazi war criminals. A number of these dramatizations dealt specifically with the Eichmann story and were ensured popular success by the free publicity and well-known public interest that the real-life story had garnered.

The first televised drama on this topic was "suggested by the Eichmann case," according to its press release,[6] and was broadcast in 1960 in an anthology series called *Moment of Fear*. The story revolved around a Nazi war criminal who after the war, in an effort to get away with his war crimes, disguises himself and escapes to the United States where he becomes a citizen. An Israeli group tracks him down and convinces his employee, who is a Jewish refugee from Europe, to assist in his capture.

Less than two months after this program aired, *Armstrong Circle Theatre* presented a live telecast called "Engineer of Death: The Eichmann Story," which depicted in docudrama form Eichmann's life, his war crimes, and his capture by the Israelis. The following year, the program was updated and rebroadcast to coincide with the October 1961 trial of Eichmann in Israel. In the program, retitled "Eichmann and Israel," host and narrator Douglas Edwards (a renowned news commentator of the day) proclaimed to the viewing audience, "Adolf Eichmann is now a prisoner of the people he had sworn to destroy ... [his] case is now before a court in Jerusalem." The program's very title, "Eichmann and Israel," and Edwards's words project a strong sense of irony and supreme justice that Eichmann is being tried in Israel and thus lend legitimacy and purpose to Israel's existence for its role as the nation who captures and brings Nazis to justice.

Almost twenty years later, the story of Eichmann's capture was still a subject for popular TV. A 1979 made-for-TV movie called *The House on Garibaldi Street* dramatized the real-life pursuit and capture of Adolf Eichmann by a team of Israeli agents. The opening scene depicts then prime minister of Israel

David Ben Gurion[7] approving the mission with the declaration that it is "our right and our duty." Later in Argentina, when Israeli agents interrogate the captured Eichmann, they hear his dry recitation of his role in the Final Solution,[8] and are tempted to kill him on the spot. They exercise restraint, keeping in mind their mission of ensuring Eichmann's ultimate destination — and destiny.

Television's most recent version of the Eichmann saga appeared in 1996 on a made-for-cable movie from TNT called *The Man Who Captured Eichmann*. Based on the book by the Israeli Mossad agent Peter Malkin, who actually apprehended Eichmann, the telefilm had as its dramatic center the one-on-one, behind-closed-doors discussions between Malkin and Eichmann during the Nazi's Argentine captivity. The Polish-born Malkin, who lost his sister and her three children in the Holocaust, calmly engaged Eichmann in conversation, seeking to draw him out in an effort to understand the workings of such a person.

The popularity of the Eichmann story, stemming from the American public's own hatred of Nazis coupled with its admiration for Israel's dealing with her enemies, spurred several other shows to devote episodes to the theme of Israel as Nazi hunter. A 1965 *Kraft Suspense Theatre* story called "The Safe House," a 1967 episode of *The Saint*, and Rod Serling's 1969 made-for-TV movie *Night Gallery* (which spawned the subsequent anthology series) all depicted stories of Israeli agents on the trail of former Nazis who were responsible for the deaths of thousands of Jews in concentration camps. *Night Gallery*, a macabre tale of supernatural retribution, includes a scene of the fearful, hunted Nazi telling a friend that he looks constantly over his shoulder for ghosts. The friend replies knowingly, in a phrase that encapsulates a recurring TV theme, "Israeli ghosts." The two then discuss the Nazi's relative place on an Israeli list that, they say, Eichmann once headed.

The overarching fear of Israeli capture and retribution was also portrayed in a 1976 episode of *Columbo* titled "Now You See Him." Here it leads to the murder of a Holocaust survivor who threatens to expose a former Nazi currently earning fame and fortune as a magician in America. When the survivor, in fact seeking hush money, reminds the ex–Nazi, "You do rather well, considering your circumstances — certainly better than spending the rest of your life in an Israeli prison," he is swiftly murdered by the Nazi.

Echoes of Israel's real-life capture of Eichmann continued throughout the 1980s. Mention of it was made on a 1980 episode of the action-adventure series *Hawaii Five-0*, which depicted yet another Israeli hunt for a Nazi war criminal. The following year, the detective show *Magnum, P.I.* aired an episode titled "Never Again, Never Again," which depicted the same theme with a peculiar twist. A member of the Israeli Nazi-hunting Masada[9] team, Dr. Kessler, conceals his identity by posing as a Nazi. He is pursuing an actual Nazi couple who — in yet another twist — are themselves posing as a Jewish couple to elude capture. To complete their disguise as Holocaust survivors named Saul and Helena Greenburg, the couple has even gone so far as to tattoo numbers on their arms. They enlist the help and protection of their unsuspecting friend, private investigator Thomas Magnum, by concocting an elaborate lie in which Saul is cast as a Masada agent targeted for death by certain Nazis.

The hoax is unraveled when Magnum finds agent Kessler's dead body, sees that he has numbers tattooed on his arm, and realizes that in fact he — rather than the Greenburgs — is the actual Holocaust survivor and the Israeli Masada agent. Emerging from this convoluted tale is the recurring picture of Israel's direct connection to the Holocaust, and the very human level of that connection is underscored when Magnum declares that Kessler stalked the Nazis because it was someone like "Saul [who] gassed his mother or his father."

This picture of Israeli agents who, although highly dedicated to their mission of bringing Nazi war criminals to justice, have particular, individual debts to repay the Nazis was depicted in a 1966 episode of the well-known series *The F.B.I.* Here Otto Mann, an Israeli agent, works with Inspector Erskin of the FBI to track down a former Nazi turned communist spy named Karl Schindler. Schindler had been personally responsible for putting to death Otto Mann's wife in a concentration camp.

Women not as victims of Nazis but as Israeli citizens responsible for hunting down Nazi war criminals were portrayed in several shows. One such woman, also driven in part by personal motivations, was the character of Sarah Lebow, depicted on a 1984 episode of the action-adventure series *Airwolf*. Sarah was the daughter of a renowned Nazi hunter, Israeli Harry Lebow, who had recently caught up with war criminal Helmut Kruger. But Kruger, upon being confronted by Harry Lebow and learning of Lebow's plans to bring him to Israel for trial, murders the Nazi hunter and escapes. It is Sarah, in seeking to avenge her father's death, who accomplishes the mission of bringing Kruger to justice.

The theme of Israeli women hunting Nazis appeared also on two medical series: *Quincy, M.E.* and *Trapper John, M.D.* In these depictions, the women are Mossad agents on missions to locate and capture infamous Nazi war criminals. Both women employ ruses — posing as someone else and initially deceiving the program's hero — to achieve their ultimate aim.

Despite the subterfuge, these Israeli agents — as all those in other shows — are painted in a highly favorable light. They are depicted as fervently dedicated to their missions, efficient, and ultimately successful. In fact, the regular hero of the program and the Israeli often work together to pursue the common goal of catching Nazis and display camaraderie and professional respect for one another. Invariably, the American character expresses admiration for the Israeli agents and sympathy for their cause while displaying contempt for the Nazis.

This American contempt for Nazis, coupled with the renowned sense of American justice, closely parallels Jewish sensibilities on this issue and is yet another instance of how the portrayal of a Jewish theme on television can strike a responsive and sympathetic chord in American viewers. It is the prevalence of these sentiments that doubtless account for the great number of shows on this subject. Indeed, it is not a difficult task for television programs to portray the Nazis as evil and their capture as a victory for all humanity. What is strikingly authentic and most relevant, however, is the central role accorded to Israel in these programs as the country with the moral fortitude and the greatest natural and justified right to bring these Nazis to justice.

Non-Jews in Israel

It is Israel's connection to the Holocaust that impels a non–Jewish woman to live there in the 1974 miniseries *QB VII*. She is a psychiatrist at Hadassah Hospital who witnessed the atrocities at Jadwiga concentration camp, about which she testifies in relevant court cases and currently devotes her practice to helping survivors to cope and to likewise testify. When asked why she chose to become an Israeli citizen, the doctor responds "I admire courage. I thought it was right to try to do something for these people to make up for what we — the so-called Christian world — have done to them."

For wholly different reasons, several other non–Jewish TV characters have been depicted visiting or living in Israel. There is no question of guilt but sheer admiration that brings a young Dutch woman to Israel in the miniseries *Evergreen*. Now working as a nursery teacher on a *kibbutz* in northern Israel, she reports to an American tourist that when she had an opportunity back in Holland for a two-week vacation, "I chose Israel. It's a new country — exciting place that deals in action, also a lot of young people." After touring the country, she found her way to a *kibbutz* and "I liked it so much I became a volunteer."

Israel's attractions as well as its vulnerabilities, are expressed by other non–Jews on an episode of the detective drama *77 Sunset Strip*. Private investigator Stuart Bailey, in need of certain information, journeys to Israel. Flying over Tel Aviv, he ponders out loud, "Tel Aviv. At this point in the map, Israel is barely twelve miles wide. If you lean too far out of your taxi cab window, you find yourself in Jordan."[10] Once on the ground, a tip leads Bailey to a Tel Aviv cafe owned by Patrick Cohan. Cohan explains that he is Irish — "the New York variety" — but his name is now officially Cohen, owing to, as he describes it, a "typographical error [which] kind of set the natives at ease at first … but I feel like I belong now." Upon learning that this is Bailey's first trip to Israel, Cohan enthusiastically recites some of the nation's virtues: "It's a great country. The whole place is about eight thousand square miles … that's one-quarter the size of the State of Maine. We got a lot of history here. Still a shovel in the ground turns up ancient relics." He goes on to explain why he so enjoys living there: "During the last war [World War II], you know how it was — the destruction by the hour. Well, here they build, new things going up all the time. Growth and progress and a hunger for knowledge. Right here in Tel Aviv they got a street — one street — that's got a hundred bookstores. Now we got a Philharmonic with a ten-month season, twenty-five daily newspapers in ten different languages. When I was a kid in the States, they used to tell us that the days of pioneering were over. But not here ... they're just getting started."

Another young American journeyed to Israel on an episode of *Run for Your Life*, a series based on the premise that a rich and successful lawyer, Paul Bryan, learns he has just two years left to live and thus determines to live life to the fullest by traveling the world over. Bryan goes to Israel and joins an archaeological dig, something that Israel is renowned for. The safety and task of the dig is threatened, however, when Arabs begin shooting at the civilian archaeologists.

Although Israel is the Jewish homeland, these depictions of non–Jews going to live there and taking delight in its attractions reflect the significance and allure the country holds for far beyond Jews alone. The sense of Israel being someplace "different, special," as a non–Jewish black character on the series *Frank's Place* described it, can perhaps best be described and transmitted by those characters who would seem to be most "objective" about it: a transplanted Irish New Yorker, a European psychiatrist, a black from New Orleans.

For that matter, Israel can best be described as someplace special by a Catholic priest, whose trip to Israel was the subject of humor on an episode of *Car 54, Where Are You?* When the local rabbi tries to recruit guests for Joey Pokrass's *bar mitzvah*, whose father is a hated landlord, he turns in desperation to the local priest, with whom he is on a friendly, first-name basis. Calling in favors, the rabbi reminds the priest, "When you needed people at that picnic to raise money for Father Flannagan's first trip to Rome, didn't I send over the girls of the Hadassah? They did all right, Charlie, didn't they, huh?" Charlie recalls enthusiastically, "They certainly did. Not only did they raise the $500 for Father Flannagan to go to Rome, they also raised an extra $140 so that he could take that side trip to Israel!" Underlying the humor are some interesting attitudes. In saying *Israel* rather than *the Holy Land*, the priest is acknowledging the country as the modern Jewish state. Further recognition of this lies in Charlie's association of Rome with Catholicism — the city is Father Flannagan's primary and most natural destination — and, through the humor of the Hadassah ladies' efforts, Israel as the place most connected to Jews.

American Jews and Israel

This juxtaposition of Rome, as the ideal vacation spot for Catholics, with Israel, as the natural place for Jews, was the premise of an entire episode of

Bridget Loves Bernie. Bernie's parents, the Steinbergs, buy a raffle from their Catholic in-laws, the Fitzgeralds — and win a trip to Rome that includes an audience with the pope. Desperately envious of such a trip, the Fitzgeralds buy two tickets to Israel, hoping to subtly entice the Steinbergs to trade trips. But each couple is too proud to admit that they really want to trade and instead extol the virtues of their intended travels: Mr. Steinberg praises the Roman ruins, the ancient Colosseum, the Vatican, friendly Italians, and his upcoming meeting with the pope. Mr. Fitzgerald speaks of Tel Aviv and Jerusalem and insists that "the Jews of Israel are friendlier than the Italians" and that "the *kibbutzes* [are] wonderful communities."[11] Eventually, the trade is made and each couple goes its delighted way.

Even a quarter of a century later, in a more difficult political climate, Israel remained a natural and favored place for TV's Jewish characters to visit. When nanny Fran Fine plans a winter vacation for the Sheffield family on *The Nanny,* she packs everyone off to a *kibbutz* in Israel, recalling fond memories of her own earlier trip there. The episode follows Fran and the family as they spend time on the *kibbutz* and take in the sights of Israel.

Other Jewish TV characters have gone to visit or even live in Israel. An episode of the 1960s medical series *Ben Casey* featured a Jewish character named Sholom Isaacs, who after laboring on the docks all his life and traveling widely, bids farewell to a friend and fellow worker. In response to the friend's query about where he is going "this time," Sholom replies, "I'm going home. My son, whom I know only as a child; my *sabra*[12] grandchildren unseen by me; Jerusalem, where I'll grow old under the shade of the cyprus trees and be at peace again. No more journeys."

While the interest of Jewish characters in the Jewish state is shown to be axiomatic, often within the same program non–Jews or children of mixed marriages are also shown going to Israel.

One such program that depicted a child of a mixed marriage deciding to move to Israel was set yet again within the context of the Holocaust. The 1982 made-for-TV movie *Remembrance of Love* depicted Israel as a gathering place for Holocaust survivors where they could obtain information about lost friends and relatives as well as a vibrant and attractive place for young people to visit and even to settle. The program dramatized the real-life World Gathering of Holocaust Survivors[13] and focused on the story of American Joe Rabin, Auschwitz survivor, now attending the event. He is accompanied by his daughter Marcy, a journalist covering the story. (Her mother, Joe's wife, was not Jewish and is no longer alive.) During the program, viewers learn about the central computer bank in Israel (one actually exists) that contains names and other personal data of all Holocaust survivors in an effort to facilitate the possible reunion of families. Joe Rabin, it turns out, hopes to use the computer to reestablish contact with Leah, a young girl with whom he was in love back in Poland during the war.

Paralleling the romance Joe rekindles with Leah after finding her, his daughter Marcy becomes involved with David, an Israeli security agent who proposes to her and asks her to stay in Israel. While declaring her love for him, she outlines the difficulties of staying in Israel: she will have to start her life anew, learn a new language (Hebrew), establish new professional contacts and — alluding to an issue that has become even more problematic and controversial since this show first aired — "by Orthodox standards I'm not even considered a Jew because my mother wasn't — so my children wouldn't be considered Jewish." David tells her that "if they happen to be my children too, they'll be Israeli." Eventually, despite the envisioned difficulties, Marcy takes the major step of giving up her American way of life and moving to Israel. In this depiction, Israel's connection with Holocaust survivors is extended into the next generation, to the children of survivors.

Another child of a mixed marriage who wants to make Israel his home after forming a romantic involvement there appears on the miniseries *Evergreen*. After falling in love with a young Dutch woman, Eric decides to move to Israel and make his life on the *kibbutz*. There he is killed when the Syrian army shells the *kibbutz*.

Israel plays a central role in the lives of three generations of Jews, the youngest of whom is again a child of a mixed marriage, on the miniseries *QB VII*. The tale chronicles the life of the Cady family, consisting of elderly Morris, an observant Jew; his middle-aged son, Abe, alienated from Judaism and intermarried; and Abe's son, Ben, who has learned something of his Jewish heritage from his grandfather. When Morris moves to Israel at the age of eighty-three, a whole series of events are set in motion that eventually bring the entire Cady family to Israel and to a new Jewish identity. Morris's sudden heart attack brings son Abe to Israel and, directly from the cemetery after his funeral, to *Yad Vashem*.[14] Abe explains that "it's the memorial to all the Jews who died in the concentration camps — my father always wanted me to go there." Moved by the experience, Abe finds his purpose in life: to stay in Israel and write a definitive work about the Holocaust. His son, Ben, in the meantime has moved to Israel, become an Israeli citizen, and joined the Israeli air force. At the close of the show, viewers learn that Ben has fallen in the service of his new country.

These various depictions of young people who are children of intermarriages going to live in Israel present an interesting angle on Israel's relationship to Jewish identity. Perhaps because they face a more complicated quest for Jewish identity, these characters ultimately express that identity in a most demonstrative form: by picking up and moving to Israel. It is Israel that reawakens a sense of Jewish identity that had skipped a generation. As Abe Cady of *QB VII* stated upon learning that his son had joined the Israeli air force, his family has charted a "full circle."

Despite this portrayal of Israel as a catalyst for Jewish identity, the TV picture of American Jews going to live in Israel is not very encouraging. Those who do so are somehow outside the mainstream in one way or another: children of mixed marriages; a sick, elderly man in *QB VII* who dies there; an old rabbi mentioned in an *All in the Family* episode. The young American men who arrive there eager and robust are killed soon after: Eric in *Evergreen*, Ben in *QB VII*, and even a character in a made-for-TV movie celebrating Israel's twenty-fifth anniversary who went to aid Israel in the Six-Day War. Nor do TV's Jewish characters, once in Israel, have much commitment to staying put: in an episode of *Chicken Soup*, Jackie Fisher's Jewish mother reminds him that an old girlfriend of his lives on a *kibbutz*, "but she's willing to relocate." The humorous premise of a 1977 pilot episode of the comedy series *Busting Loose* was built on the very idea of an American Jew *not* moving to Israel. When Lenny Markowitz moves from his parents' home into an apartment of his own in order to secure a sense of independence, he is reluctant to tell them for fear of hurting them. Instead, he says that he is going to Israel; after all, he rationalizes, "they always wanted me to go." One Jewish character who did successfully relocate to Israel, joining the army there, was a woman rabbi on the comedy *Platypus Man*.

In fact, while American Jews do not move to Israel in large numbers, some do so every year — comprising a significant presence in Israel — yet their story is virtually absent on popular TV. Indeed, TV's far more frequent depictions of non–Jews than Jews going to live in Israel is quite out of sync with reality. Perhaps this imbalance reflects a discomfort about depicting Jews going to Israel, a reluctance to give appearance to a sense of Jews abandoning America and somehow calling into question their role as good American citizens.

While remaining in America, however, most Jews feel a special kinship with Israel. This sense of Israel in the consciousness of American Jews surfaced in a moving episode of *Northern Exposure*. When Joel Fleischman, the Jewish doctor isolated in an Alaskan town, learns about another Fleischman, a former Soviet refusenik now living in Israel, he is almost compulsively drawn to the overarching sense of global Jewish family that this Fleischman, though unknown and unrelated, represents. With Israel cast as the welcoming refuge for this ex–Soviet Jew, the final scene has Joel making a late-night, long-distance call to Tel Aviv, stuttering through the language barrier, tentative yet joyous to make the connection, saying simply, "Yevgeny, how are things in Israel?" Feeling marginalized as the sole Jew in the faraway Alaskan town of Cicely, Joel finds a sense of home and belonging through this connection to Israel.

This sense of kinship was experienced by *Reasonable Doubts'* Tess Kaufman. When the Jewish attorney becomes involved — both professionally and personally — with Mossad agent Asher Roth over the course of several episodes of the series, it is clear that the two are connecting as well through a common link of history and heritage.

American Jews are intimately bound up with Israel on many levels and demonstrate support for the Jewish state in various other ways, many of which have been pictured on TV shows. Generally, such depictions or references revolve around three activities: visiting Israel[15] (as described above), planting trees there, and expressing political support for it.

It is a widespread and longstanding tradition among American Jews to plant trees in Israel, either with one's own hands while there on a visit or, more commonly, by contributing money in America for the planting of trees in Israel. This custom has found its way onto several popular TV shows, usually as a subject of humor. On an episode of the early 1960s comedy series *Car 54, Where Are You?* the Jewish, grandmotherly Mrs. Bronson confronts a band of New York City policemen sent to evict her from a condemned building that she has utterly no intention of leaving. She subdues them with honey cake and tea and organizes them into a game of bingo in which, as one officer enthusiastically explains to a late-arriving comrade, "the money goes to plant a tree in Israel."

Such references to planting trees in Israel appear not only alongside elderly characters in old programs but continue in the mouths of young people even on the "yuppie shows" of the 1980s. Programs like *Anything but Love, thirtysomething*, and *Baby Boom* (the short-lived series spun off the movie of the same title) have had their young stars either reminisce about tree planting in Israel or engage in some repartee on the subject.

On TV, you don't have to be Jewish to plant trees in Israel. The crusty character of Maude, when first introduced on an episode of *All in the Family*, seeks to demonstrate the absurdity of a charge that she is anti–Semitic by indignantly stating, "You can say that? Why just last month, I had a tree planted in Israel!"

American Jews' political concerns for Israel have also been depicted on popular TV, sometimes defining the very characters, as when Arab-Israeli relations are approached through the guise of relationships between American Jews and Arabs. One such instance was a 1975 episode of *Medical Center*, in which the son of an Arab potentate romantically pursues a Jewish woman whose feelings towards him are ambivalent. One of her problems, as she expressed to him, is that "if your people start a war with Israel, I'm going to be rooting for the wrong side." This statement reflects an awareness of past Arab aggressions against Israel and a presupposition of American Jewish support for Israel.

A similar view was expressed in an episode of *Cagney and Lacey* when the son of an Arab government official badly injures an elderly Jewish man in a hit-and-run accident and then refuses to accept responsibility, taking shelter in his nation's consulate. Highly upset over the situation, Detective Lacey states, "He's a criminal... He's trying to start the Arab-Israeli war all over again on Fifty-Second Street."

The waging of Arab-Israeli conflicts on American ground, and in this case between American citizens, was addressed in even greater detail on a 1980 episode of *Barney Miller*. An argument between an Arab American dry cleaner and a Jewish American liquor store owner over a disputed alleyway between their respective shops becomes a microcosm for the larger Middle East conflict, as the insults they hurl at each other take on the language of Arab-Israeli politics. In later summarizing their arguments to Captain Miller, an officer explains that "a six-minute war broke out." Yet the police, citing procedural constraints, can do nothing to solve the dispute. Ultimately, when the Jewish businessman is murdered by thugs, his erstwhile enemy states with regret that "he deserved better — from both of us." If one wished to read this story as the Jew representing Israel, the Arab representing the Arab world, and the police precinct representing America, then it becomes a metaphor for Israel as victim of Arab aggression and American indifference.

Political concerns for Israel have even been expressed by such Jewish characters as the very assimilated and intermarried Michael Steadman of *thirtysomething*. When asked to represent a political candidate, Michael inquires, "Where does she stand on Israel?" The cynical, realpolitik answer he receives from her campaign manager, "That depends on who she's talking to," does not seem to satisfy him.

Israeli-Arab Relations

Of course, television has not ignored the Arab-Israeli conflict as played out by the parties themselves. Several made-for-TV movies of the 1970s and 1980s dramatized the Middle East violence and acts of terrorism that burst upon American headlines.

One such event, the massacre of Israeli athletes by Palestinian Arab terrorists at the 1972 Munich Olympics, was depicted in the 1976 made-for-TV movie *21 Hours at Munich*. The program depicts the break-in and seizure by the Arab terrorist group Black September of the Olympic quarters housing Israeli athletes. They hold eleven athletes hostage, and threaten to kill "the Zionist prisoners" if their demand for the release of 236 Arab and other terrorist prisoners held by Israel is not met. The connection of Israel to the Holocaust is underscored once again when the Bavarian interior minister states, "six million ghosts have come back to haunt us." Later, in response to a plea for the release of the hostages on humanitarian grounds the terrorist leader says, "We did not come here to kill anyone — especially Jews in Germany. You know what the world would say." Nonetheless, after the German government ostensibly gives in to the terrorists' demand for safe transport out of Germany with their hostages — in fact a ruse to stage a counterterrorist attack that the Germans bungle — all the Israeli athletes are murdered by their Arab captors.

In the Munich tragedy, Israel — long the target of Arab terrorism and violence — did not have the opportunity to personally protect its citizens. (But its determination to hunt down those who murdered its athletes at Munich was the subject of HBO's TV movie *Sword of Gideon*.) More often, however, TV portrayals have focused on the image of Israel as a fierce and proficient fighter against terrorism. Two made-for-TV movies, which aired one month apart (December 1976 and January 1977), dramatized the story of Israel's famed commando mission to Entebbe, which rescued passengers of the Air France jet that had been hijacked by Arab and German terrorists.[16] While Israel's courageous and skillful response to terrorism was emphasized in these depictions, echoes of the Holocaust are also evident. For example, in a scene where the hijacked passengers are first brought to the Entebbe waiting area, the Jews and non–Jews are separated, reminiscent of the selection process awaiting Jews at concentration camps during the Holocaust. Yet the Jews at Entebbe — unlike Jews of the Holocaust who were helplessly alone in the world — have a source of potential rescue: Israel. This role of Israel as rescuer, not only of her own nationals but of the entire Jewish people and her commitment to fulfill that role is underscored in a scene depicting a cabinet meeting convened to discuss the terrorists' demands to release Arab prisoners. Defense Minister Shimon Peres states that Israel must decide "whether we're going to protect Jews against terrorists, or whether we're going to surrender."[17] The decision, as the world would soon know, was to reject the terrorists' demands and to stage a rescue operation, which emerged as a stunning success. The TV depiction of the operation concludes with the liberated hostages flying on planes back to Israel and expressing their joy at being rescued by singing traditional Israeli folk songs. The portrayal of Israel as rescuer of the Jewish people anywhere in the world, under the most dire of circumstances, is given added force by the inclusion of Holocaust imagery in this program, imagery that points to a time when Jews had no such protection.

A fictional terrorist attack was the climax of a 1978 miniseries *The Pirate*, a convoluted tale about Arabs and Jews entwined in a tangled twist of identities. When the program opens, it is 1925 and the Jewish Ben Ezra and his pregnant wife are trying to reach the Land of Israel so that their child will be born there. They are forced to cross the desert, visas having been denied them by the British. Harsh conditions and his wife's illness force Ben Ezra to seek shelter in the tent of an Arab, Samir Alfe, whose wife is also pregnant and who takes in the sojourners. But there is disaster when the women give birth: Samir's wife delivers a stillborn son and Ben Ezra's wife dies in childbirth — but the infant boy is saved when Samir, a physician, cuts open her womb. Grateful to Samir for saving the child's life and realizing that his son has no chance for survival alone with him in the desert, Ben Ezra goes on his way, leaving the child to Samir, who declares that "with me, he will be a Moslem, not a Jew." The boy, named Baydr, grows up to become a worldly financier and a powerful figure in the Arab world, unaware of his Jewishness.

Terrorism enters the picture when Baydr's daughter from a first marriage joins an Arab terrorist group — in part because of hatred for her own father. Headed by a terrorist named Yasfir, the group hijacks a plane carrying Baydr's current wife and their young son. When a tense hostage situation ensues, Baydr's assistant comes forward, offering to Baydr the services of the nation most likely to successfully handle the crisis: Israel. The assistant reveals that he actually works for the Israelis, because he despises Yasfir, who years earlier led a massacre in his parents' Jordanian village and falsely blamed Israel. The assistant is sure that he can enlist the Israelis' help "because Yasfir is the real enemy. You and I both hope that Arabs and Israelis can work and live together in peace. It's men like Yasfir who kill this possibility, and they're the enemy — they're the ones who have to be destroyed." The Israelis agree to unofficial involvement in the rescue operation and send one of their high-ranking officers to head the mission, none other than Ben Ezra, the biological father of Baydr. Baydr, still unaware of his origins, and his Moslem father Samir, aid Ben Ezra in the successful rescue operation. This picture of Israelis and Arabs cooperating to successfully rescue the hostages suggests that there is hope for peace, once it is recognized that the common enemy is terrorism.

The scenario of Israel's fighting terrorism to both protect Arabs who are victims of such terrorism and to further peace efforts reappeared in a 1986 made-for-TV movie called *Popeye Doyle*. When a "leading American advocate of an Arab-Israeli settlement" is set to meet with a Jordanian delegation for preliminary peace discussions, another high-ranking but renegade Jordanian diplomat arranges for a Cypriot terrorist to pose as an Israeli and to kill the American. Thus it will appear that an Israeli violently thwarted any chance for peace. The Israeli government, however, learns about the scheme, and anxious for the peace negotiations to go forward, sends a Mossad agent to New York to eliminate the terrorist before he can carry out his deadly task. While the Jordanian diplomat had later sought to cancel the arrangement for personal, not political reasons, the program clearly conveys the message that Israel actively pursues true opportunities for peace and does anything to protect such negotiations.

A similar theme was depicted nearly twenty years earlier, in a wholly different setting — the comic world of *Get Smart*. In an episode that aired four months before the Six-Day War in 1967, Israeli agents are called in to save the life of a prince from an Arab nation with whom they have good relations.

A far less benevolent image of Israel has been projected on some recent shows where Israel is portrayed not as the fighter of terrorism but as its unequivocal cause. While continuing to portray Arab terrorism as despicable and barbaric and labeling it as such by all decent characters in the program, such shows provide a forum for the Palestinian Arab characters to excoriate Israel as their harangues against the Jewish state go unchallenged. The presence of such depictions may in large measure reflect the current slant in news

and documentary presentations of the Middle East situation and efforts to
bring these points of view into the mainstream.

An instance of this was the 1989 made-for-TV movie that portrayed a
real-life terrorist attack. *The Hijacking of the Achille Lauro* chronicles the
takeover of the ill-fated Italian cruise ship by Arab terrorists and their murder
of American Leon Klinghoffer. While here too the victims of terrorism are
depicted with sympathy and terrorist methods are deplored, the political views
of the terrorists are given full vent without any other side. Thus, one of them,
addressing the bound and terrified hostages, states, "My family, see, live in
beautiful village, north Palestine — live in beautiful house, beautiful fields, olive
grove, almond trees, oranges. Then come Zionists, drive us out, take our land,
take house, make us live in camp, while stranger get rich from my stolen land.
We are not bad people; we fight for what is ours." Never is any challenge to
this railing invective expressed.

A somewhat more sophisticated condemnation of Israel was contained in
the 1988 made-for-TV movie *Terrorist on Trial: The United States vs. Salim
Ajami*. Ostensibly a paean to due process and the American justice system, this
fictional tale of an American Jewish lawyer who defends a Palestinian Arab
charged with slaughtering vacationing Americans in Europe in fact provides
an unchallenged platform for the terrorist's harangue against Israel and America. In this program, as in others of this type, America is linked with Israel as
bringing suffering to the Arabs.

Throughout the lengthy and dramatic courtroom scenes, it is only Salim
Ajami's methods that are challenged, but never the rightness of his cause. The
prosecutor naturally denounces the terrorism, but even in his denunciation
gives credence to its stated cause, in arguing that there are "two sides to every
story, [although] there are not two sides to terrorism. ... Yes, there are people
suffering that we don't pay attention to." Earlier on the stand, in a lengthy dia-
tribe, Ajami proclaimed that he fights for "the restoration of our homeland and
our rights. We fight to recover what is ours." "Just like the black majority in
South Africa," responds his defense lawyer, in an invidious comparison. Ajami
shouts from the stand, "This is our way of making America pay attention ...
the conclusion of those who have no home and no hope." In closing arguments, the prosecuting attorney accepts Ajami's claims, disputing only the
methods when he states, "The U.N. lists forty-five refugee groups with no
homeland. Why don't *they* kill people?" Omitted from the entire three-hour
show is any attempt to provide a modicum of historical context to challenge
what is here presented as axiomatic.[18]

Even the one element in this show ostensibly demonstrating support for
Israel is depicted as menacing and malevolent. Working late one night in his
darkened office, defense attorney Resnick is visited by a group of ominous-
looking men, self-described as the "chairman of a fund-raising organization
for Israel" and "major contributors." They threaten Resnick to get off the case

in such a foreboding and intimidating manner that both they and the concerns they express about a prominent Jewish attorney's defending an Arab terrorist are made to appear irredeemably sinister.

In their unchallenged presentation of the Arab point of view, these programs paint a picture of Americans as victims of terrorism, unsafe and vulnerable to murder anywhere in the world, as a direct result of Israeli actions — actions that are condemned as unjust and likened to those of South Africa under apartheid. This scenario was repeated somewhat less directly in the 1988 made-for-TV movie *The Taking of Flight 847: The Uli Derickson Story*. This program dramatized the real-life hijacking of a TWA jetliner to Beirut in 1985 and the murder of U.S. Navy diver Robert Dean Stethem, as Arab hijackers sought revenge for America's bombing of Lebanon and demanded release of Arab prisoners from Israel. They force German stewardess Uli Derickson to separate the passports of Jews and non–Jews, although she protests that she cannot because she is German. They force her to sing a German folk song about being "homeless" and "without a friend," which they say describes themselves. The American hostages are shown to be brutalized and beaten as word is awaited from Israel about meeting the hijackers' demands.

American involvement in Middle East politics has been depicted in less violent scenarios. Two miniseries that did not air on network TV were part of Operation Prime-Time, which was supposed to create quality programming for independent stations. These miniseries portrayed Americans not as victims of Middle East violence but as bringers of Middle East peace. Both *Golda* (1982) and *Sadat* (1983) depicted the high point of Israeli-Arab relations, when the United States brought Egypt and Israel together to sign the Camp David Accords. That America's connection to Israel is longstanding was reflected in the HBO TV movie *Truman*, which depicted the president's historic recognition of the newly formed State of Israel in 1948.

America's involvement in the Middle East was also referred to in *The Final Days*, a 1989 made-for-TV movie about the fall of the Nixon presidency, in which Nixon is shown to supply planes to Israel after it was attacked by the Arabs on Yom Kippur in 1973[19] just as he is in the thick of the Watergate crisis. When another government scandal, the "Iran-Contra affair," rocked the Reagan presidency, Israel's involvement in the covert "arms for hostages" deal became a matter of great speculation and controversy and was addressed in a 1989 miniseries *Guts and Glory: The Rise and Fall of Oliver North*. In this interpretation of events, senior U.S. officials clandestinely enlist Israel to ship American missiles to Iran in hopes of a hostage release. While implementing the operation, North is shown to be highly concerned about maintaining its secrecy to protect Israel, whom he characterizes as a great and loyal friend of America who would not "hesitate to cut a corner for us." However, when the operation is exposed, North and his colleagues are portrayed as lying about the origins of the operation, blaming Israel for devising and directing it.

The real-life scandal provided grist for fictionalized accounts of other such covert international arms deals. In the same season that *Guts and Glory* aired, a 1989 TV movie, *Shannon's Deal*, concocted an "arms for drugs" scenario that involved the United States, South America, and Israel.

Other headline stories relating to the Middle East are a regular source of dramatic themes for TV movies, among them *Secret Weapon*, about the Israeli arms technician who diverged details about the country's nuclear capabilities, and *The Path to Paradise: The Untold Story of the World Trade Center Bombing*. Another show involving Israel and an American character was *Desperate Rescue: The Cathy Mahone Story*, which dramatized the true story of a child kidnapped by her father to Jordan and rescued by her American mother via Israel. A kidnapping, this time to Israel, was also the premise of an episode of the series *Sweating Bullets*. (Not only did the story actually take place in Israel, primarily in Jerusalem, but it became the first and only regular American television series to film for an entire season in that country, when twenty-two episodes were shot on location in Eilat.)

Most recently, reflecting current peace-building efforts, an episode of the series *JAG* focused on an Israeli minister spearheading peace negotiations. Confined to an American hospital awaiting a heart transplant, he becomes the target of Hamas terrorists as they commandeer the hospital, demanding the release of an imprisoned comrade of theirs awaiting extradition to Israel. (With the PLO having gone in much of the world's view from terrorist organization to respected peace negotiation partner, it is no longer cast as the bad guy and source of terrorism on popular TV; that position has been ceded to Hamas, which has become television's new code word for Arab extremism and terrorism.) When the original donor heart is destroyed in a gun battle that ultimately brings the standoff to an end with the death of the hostage takers, a new heart suddenly becomes available. In a twist meant to symbolize a hoped-for reconciliation between former enemies who might live together in peace, the heart of one of the mortally wounded Arab terrorists is transplanted into the body of the Israeli minister.

The Mossad

Israel's intelligence service, the Mossad, has acquired over the years a legendary reputation for unparalleled proficiency. On popular TV this perception is reflected and no doubt perpetuated in highly admiring depictions of the intelligence establishment and its agents. As described earlier in this chapter, many programs have depicted Mossad agents successfully tracking down Nazi war criminals. They achieve success and earn esteem even when on different sorts of missions.

In a 1986 made-for-TV movie, *C.A.T. Squad*, about the killing of NATO scientists, Mossad agents become involved when an Israeli scientist falls victim. Their ultimatum to the Americans — take over the case within one week or hand it over to the Mossad agents to be solved (certainty that the Israelis will indeed solve it is implied) — spurs the Americans in their investigation. Later, during the investigation, the Americans' reliance on Israeli intelligence findings in leading them to certain suspects hints at the intelligence relationship between the two nations and the value of information America receives from Israel.

A similar race between American and Israeli agents was depicted on a 1989 episode of *Mancuso, FBI.* An apparent theft of weapons-grade plutonium points to the Israelis as the culprits. Those accusing Israel make reference to its presumed nuclear plant in Dimona, to the materials' mysterious origins and a concomitant theft of French nuclear material, and to instances of Israeli espionage in America, with the Pollards cited. Because the presumed Israeli theft jeopardizes an upcoming sale of American fighter planes to Israel, Mossad agents become involved to clear their country's name. The Mossad leader, named Ari and brimming with a combination of arrogant bravado and roguish charm, assures FBI agent Mancuso that Israel did not steal the plutonium, asserting, *"Yisrael* needs your planes, not your plutonium." Not only did they not steal it, Ari promises, but they will find it first — and he and Mancuso bet a dinner on it. In the midst of this guarded but evident camaraderie between the two agents, the vulnerability of Israel and its constant vigilance are expressed when Ari, complimented by Mancuso that he has "done his homework," responds, "Our survival depends on homework."

Eventually, Mancuso captures the real (American) culprit, and Ari is on the scene to extract from him a confession that will clear Israel's name at once, without awaiting legal machinations. When the thief refuses to talk, Ari — with great drama before a startled Mancuso — prepares a plutonium-laced drink and threatens to force-feed it to the villain; the confession quickly follows. Only then does Ari casually reveal that it's cocoa and slugs it down with a *"l'chayim"* in Mancuso's direction. They call their dinner bet a draw and bid each other farewell in Hebrew, Ari saying *"l'hitraot"* (Hebrew for "we'll meet again"), and Mancuso, *"shalom."*

This picture of the heroic Israeli desperately committed to the nation's survival and thus compelled to function on the outskirts of the law in a way that is at once applaudable and disturbing surfaced on a three-part arc of *Reasonable Doubts.* Viewers meet Asher Roth as a charming, simple Israeli-born bookseller with a love interest in leading character Tess Kaufman. But even as he happily courts a smitten Tess, a sense of danger surrounds him. "Yes, I have a gun," he tells a startled Tess when she happened upon a Baretta .22 in his apartment. "I'm an Israeli. I know how to shoot. I have to. Or would you rather I just lay down and die?"

As the plot thickens and Asher's connections to the Mossad and to an attempted kidnapping of a Nazi war criminal become clear, Tess finds herself in great conflict — as a lawyer and as a Jew. She is clearly committed to the American legal system and is unsettled by the covert methods employed by Asher. Yet she recognizes some validity in his arguments that the letter of the law must sometimes be swept aside to overcome a greater evil and that Israel is at times compelled to do so to fulfill its role as protector of Jews worldwide.

The image of clever, devoted agents employing calculating and questionable but ultimately swift and successful methods finds its expression in the portrayal of women Mossad agents as well. Indeed the depiction of female Mossad agents adds to the "Mossad mystique" and the casting of the intelligence unit in a romantic, invincible light. Their involvement in the hunting of Nazi war criminals was described earlier in this chapter. Another female Mossad agent was the main character in the 1989 miniseries *Brotherhood of the Rose*. She is based in America and is in charge of the Mossad's entire East Coast operation. Throughout this show, Mossad's prominent role in the international community is suggested by revelations that CIA personnel are trained by the Mossad in Israel and that American presidents are guarded by Israeli Uzis. Erica, the Israeli agent, eludes great dangers that face her throughout the two-part miniseries, earning the love of an American CIA agent, who, in the final scene, surprises her by showing up to join her on a flight to Israel.

Even comedy series have toyed with the Mossad image. In the *Get Smart* episode in which a Mossad-like Israeli agent is called in to protect an Arab prince, the chief of Control — the fictional American intelligence unit that is spoofed in the series — explains to his own agents that the Israeli espionage group is "one of the finest in the world." The reputation of Israeli intelligence and stereotypes of Jews are fused when the chief describes the name of the Israeli unit: "Your Espionage Network and Training Academy — it's referred to by its initials, *Y.E.N.T.A.* They know everything that's going on everywhere!"

Underlying popular TV's recurring allusions to Mossad's presumed ability to "know everything that's going on everywhere" is the sense that Israel's capacity to do so is a prerequisite for its very survival. Often, this is implied in depictions of Mossad as singularly clever, generally one step ahead of everybody else, and at times ruthless. Indeed, Israel is often portrayed as functioning — of necessity — outside the normal constraints of social and international relations (as when Ari forces a confession from the real plutonium thief, who has jeopardized Israel's lifeline to American military hardware, or when Israel penetrates foreign territory in the rescue of hostages at Entebbe). In an even starker explication of this notion of Israel unconditionally fighting for survival, a U.S. official in *Guts and Glory* explains that America, as a world power, "can't afford to damn the consequences" of its actions, in contrast to "Israel [which] is a tiny nation surrounded by enemies."

This prevalent picture of Israel in constant danger and struggling for survival finds expression also in TV references to the Israeli military, which, like the Mossad, has an enviable worldwide reputation. Its exploits were glorified in such productions as the Entebbe made-for-TV movies, and its reputation remained high in 1990 in no less than a *Magical World of Disney* presentation, which included a story line about Americans taken hostage by North Koreans. A teenaged daughter of one of the hostages, expressing anger and frustration at the American government's lack of action, exclaims that the hostages have been in there "30 days — the Israelis would have had them out 29 days ago!"

This image of infallibility on the part of Israeli security and intelligence was somewhat tarnished by the 1995 assassination of Prime Minister Yitzhak Rabin. Following that event, which was a stunning lapse in Israeli security, far fewer references to Israeli invincibility were presented on TV. One allusion to this new state of affairs found expression the following year on an episode of *Walker, Texas Ranger*, in which Interpol agents, local authorities, and Israeli security men argue over who can best protect a visiting Israeli ambassador targeted for assassination in Dallas. When the Israeli security officer stands his ground, insisting, "I'm just doing my job," the Interpol agent retorts, "If you had been doing your job, you wouldn't have lost a prime minister."

* * *

Despite a tragic assassination, a sense of admiration for the Jewish state informs nearly all the portrayals of Israel on American popular TV over the past fifty years. With the exception of a few recent programs, a broad array of prime-time series, made-for-TV movies, and miniseries have depicted Israel as a heroic, ingenious, miraculous nation but one whose survival hangs by a thread. Yet confidence in Israel's ability to survive and thrive, and praise for its doing so, permeate television's portrayal of Israel in a way that has seen little, if any, wavering or hesitation from the earliest years of network television until the present time. Almost invariably, these depictions include the expressing of much admiration by non–Jews for Israel's heroism, achievements, and pioneer spirit.

Through many of these programs, viewers have been exposed — either by sight or sound — to some of the beauty, history, locales, experiences, and accomplishments of Israel: the Chagall windows of Hadassah Hospital,[20] the Western Wall of the ancient Jewish Temple that was located on the Temple Mount,[21] *Yad Vashem*, life on a *kibbutz*, Israeli singing and dancing, the Israel Philharmonic, the streets of Tel Aviv, the hills of Jerusalem, scenery of the Galilee, the developed deserts of the Negev, and the archaeological riches of the ancient Jewish land. These attractions have been a magnet for several TV characters, both Jewish and non–Jewish, to visit and make their homes in Israel.

Against this backdrop of beauty and accomplishment, the pervasive vulnerability and danger of Israel has also been underlined. While details of the overwhelming dangers posed by the twenty-two Arab states surrounding are rarely enunciated, many shows do depict the constant threat of Arab terrorism faced by Israel and the killing of Israelis and Americans in Arab attacks. In light of all this, television has recognized Israel's need for security and the highest level of intelligence since, as was succinctly stated by an Israeli Mossad agent in *Mancuso*, the nation's "survival depends on it."

In a discomforting sort of symmetry, just as Israel is shown to exist on the precipice of destruction, it is depicted as having materialized out of destruction. The predominant theme portrayed in connection with Israel and one that permeates the greatest proportion of shows about Israel is the Holocaust. There is, of course, a strong historical connection between Israel and the Holocaust, and it is important for viewers to see the picture of Israel as sanctuary for Holocaust survivors and as a haven for them when the rest of the world closed its doors. And how extraordinary that TV even depicts from time to time a sense of Christian obligation to Israel in the wake of the Holocaust. Commendable and important as such depictions are, they have been shown almost to the exclusion of other vital aspects of Israel, primarily its historical and religious significance to the Jewish people. While indeed some attention has been paid to this, as described earlier, the focus on the Holocaust has been overwhelming and as such presents an apparent one-dimensional picture of Israel.

Television's portrayal of Israel within the context of the Holocaust is appropriate and relevant—but not if it is isolated from all that preceded the Holocaust. Israel's centrality to Jewish life, history, religion, and the Jewish people cannot be overstated. Programs touching on these aspects of Israel, as well as its invaluable contributions to world advancements in a wide variety of fields and its assistance to Arabs, Arab countries, and myriad developing nations, would help present a clearer and fuller picture of Israel.

6

Intermarriage

Perhaps no issue in the Jewish world is as emotionally charged and so fraught with implications for Jewish existence as that of intermarriage. Throughout its long history, the Jewish people, living often as a tiny minority scattered throughout the world, developed a unique awareness of the perils and possibilities of intermarriage. A wary and apprehensive eye has been continually cast upon it — and for good reason. The issue of intermarriage strikes at the heart of Jewish survival and the question of how Jews will remain an alive and distinct people in a world of "others."

As a result, TV's portrayals of intermarriage are among the most controversial of the medium's Jewish images, evoking great interest and often passionate reactions. This response reveals both the significance of the issue and its immediacy: with today's rate of intermarriage reaching as high as 52 percent,[1] the issue is one that not only faces the Jewish community as a whole but impacts in a very personal way on countless Jewish — and non–Jewish — families. Reflecting the breadth of interest and concern this issue commands, a whole array of activities has sprung up to address it. Recent years have witnessed a proliferation of scholarly inquiries, demographic surveys, organizational strategies, and grassroots seminars on the topic — along with a heightened attention to popular TV's influential say on the subject.

But television's portrayal of intermarriage — and all manner of interfaith romantic relationships — is anything but new and long predates the current outspokenness on the topic and the high visibility of such popular shows of the 1980s and 1990s as *thirtysomething* and *L.A. Law,* which featured intermarried couples. Even the controversial 1970s series *Bridget Loves Bernie,* the comedic premise of which was based on an intermarriage, was hardly the small screen's first approach to the issue. As early as 1948, the first year of network television, issues of interdating began to appear on popular TV programs. When the early anthology series *Philco TV Playhouse* aired "Street Scene" — a saga of immigrant life on New York's Lower East Side — viewers were introduced to the trials and tribulations of interfaith love when a young Jewish student courts a Gentile Irish neighbor.

The depictions of intermarriage and interdating that were to parade across the small screen in the following decades and the attitudes toward such relationships inherent in these portrayals would be as diverse as those expressed on the topic in the real world. Covering a broad spectrum of opinion, those attitudes range from approbation to objection, acceptance to rejection, and superficiality to seriousness.

Endorsement

Perhaps the least surprising of television's attitudes towards intermarriage, given the medium's reputation as a great homogenizer, is the notion that not only are interfaith romances problem free, but they offer a model of interfaith harmony and compromise at its zenith. Driving this outlook is the familiar idea of the melting-pot process, in which America's varied groups coalesce into a new, seamless, and better whole — in this case, through intermarriage. Quite a few programs have taken this tack, and such a scenario was played out quite explicitly in another early *Philco TV Playhouse* segment titled "And Crown Thy Good." Set in the mid-nineteenth century, the program chronicles the travails of immigrants in the Dakotas and tracks the love story between a non–Jewish Norwegian-born young man and the daughter of Jewish immigrants. The ubiquitous difficulties faced by the immigrant families are covered at length: acclimation to harsh conditions, coping with personal tragedy, and the older generation's difficulty in forging friendships with other new Americans. But any religious differences or controversy between the young lovers, Sven and Yanushka, is wholly avoided. Their union is presented as a harmonious and hopeful vision, the very essence of a new America to come.

The interfaith romance of another early American was seen by viewers of the Western series *Rawhide* in 1962. In the "Peddler" episode, intermarriage is presented not only as painless but as a welcome solution and kind of salvation for two oppressed minorities who feel like outcasts and come together through romance. When a beset-upon Jewish immigrant from Holland and an American Indian woman who has always been abused by white people meet and fall in love, marriage is the happy answer to their former troubles. Mendel the immigrant is portrayed as a proud and practicing Jew, yet he expresses no difficulty with the idea of intermarrying. Although he may have been compelled to intermarry due to the paucity of Jewish women in the Old West, the absence of any hint of reluctance to do so adds to the sense that their match is ideal. Any differences between them are projected as superficial, insignificant, and easily bridgeable, paling in comparison to those that divide them from the outside world. They are perfect mates, scorning a fate of second-class status to find solace with each other in their commonality.

Other of television's Jewish immigrants or children of immigrants are drawn to the path of intermarriage or interdating as a way into American society, as a swift and inviting agent of Americanization. The upward-scrambling Sammy Glick of "What Makes Sammy Run?" presented in 1949 on the *Philco Television Playhouse* and a decade later on *Sunday Showcase*, dates an apparently non–Jewish woman. So do Harold Sizeman, son of an immigrant garment boss in *Playhouse 90*'s 1956 version of "Sizeman and Son," and newly arrived immigrant Hyman Kaplan in "The Education of H*Y*M*A*N* K*A*P*L*A*N*," aired in 1958 on *Studio One*. The theme of Jewish immigrants' effortlessly marrying out of their religion continued in more recent programs, as in the 1984 miniseries *Ellis Island*, which chronicles the lives of four European newcomers finding their way in America. The Jewish one among them, Jake Rubin, a former victim of pogroms in Russia, marries a Gentile woman without a murmur raised about their different religious backgrounds. In these shows, the interfaith nature of the relationship is not explicitly addressed, and the assumption that these *are* interfaith relationships is based on the characters' mannerisms, speech, looks, and names. This presentation of intermarriage as so casual and natural a process reduces questions of religious differences and identity to an insignificant factor that merits no attention.

This matter-of-fact depiction of intermarriage as problem free and as a nonissue has infused many modern settings as well. One of the most notable was the mid–1970s comedy series *Rhoda*, a spin-off of *The Mary Tyler Moore Show*, on which the Jewish Rhoda Morgenstern had been a regular. Rhoda's much-heralded wedding to Joe Gerard—a civil ceremony presided over by a judge—was clearly the start of an intermarriage, yet the interfaith aspect of their relationship was never featured during the series' five-year run, nor did it figure in their breakup after two years of marriage.

Even characters who express a connection to their Jewish faith enter into an intermarriage without its being any issue at all. In a 1974 episode of *Medical Center*, a Jewish doctor falls in love with a female patient whose religion is not named but who is portrayed as seemingly not Jewish. Throughout the program, he explains Jewish concepts and quotes Jewish sources to her, apparently introducing her to the world of his religion. Later, their wedding ceremony takes place under a *chuppah*, complete with rabbi, wine drinking, and glass breaking, but throughout their courtship and marriage, no word about her religion is uttered.

In the late 1980s, the comedy series *Anything but Love* appeared, featuring as its centerpiece an interfaith friendship that comically teeters on the edge of a relationship. Coworkers Marty Gold (Jewish) and Hannah Miller (presumably non–Jewish, although her religion was not specified) have a deep affection for one another, but is it platonic or romantic? As they repeatedly try to sort this out, they explore with each other, with a kind of lighthearted angst, many issues of life and love. Yet questions of how their religious differences might figure into this equation are not raised. This absence is ironic, since one of the series' opening vignettes (each episode begins with Marty and Hannah in a humorous exchange at a luncheon counter) has Marty recounting the tale of a cousin in Russia who led a miserable life of oppression and cruel fate. When Hannah comments, "My, that is a tragedy," Marty replies, "No, the tragedy was that he intermarried." While the comment reveals, in a mocking sort of way, a significant Jewish attitude to intermarriage, it is not one that seems to be a part of Marty's own life. While at every turn he openly refers to his Jewishness, usually with sardonic humor, that Jewishness is never raised as a potentially complicating issue as his relationship with Hannah intensifies.

Marty Gold shared many characteristics with another one of TV's male Jewish characters, Miles Silverberg of *Murphy Brown*. Both are in the news field, comically neurotic, frequently referring humorously but affectionately to their Jewishness — and interdating. After several seasons on *Murphy Brown*, Miles develops an unlikely courtship with the statuesque and Southern-bred Corky Sherwood. In pairing these two, the show plays on the notion that opposites attract, as they have vastly different backgrounds, personalities, and demeanors — and are of different faiths. While these differences are grist for the humor mill (including when their families finally meet), questions of religious differences are not portrayed as of consequence to either of them.

In a similar vein, Jewish journalist Jake Stein of the comedy series *Love and War* was seriously involved with a succession of non–Jewish women. While a stream of references to his Jewish background served to highlight some divergences within the relationship, the interfaith component of his romantic liaisons was not a problematic issue.

Many couples of this sort — who display little or no consideration about the interfaith nature of their relationship — have populated the TV landscape, appearing on such shows as *Flying Blind*, *Something Wilder*, *Nurses*, and the TV movies *For the Very First Time* and Hallmark's *Mrs. Santa Claus*.

Another high-profile interdating couple, twentysomethings Leo Roth and Isabel Lukens, appeared on *Relativity*, a drama series from the creators of *thirtysomething*. Perhaps because the program lasted only a single season (1996-97), the Jewish Leo and the Christian Isabel did not address issues of religion in the minefield of problems through which their turbulent relationship sojourned during the show's brief run. With Isabel hailing from an ebullient, upper-middle-class family and Leo coming from a tattered, struggling, and working-class clan, their religious differences were merely part of a broader backdrop of contrasts that defined the couple and supplied the show's dramatic underpinnings. Their respective families, reluctantly at first, come to tolerate and even like each other, despite the wide socioeconomic divergence, onto which is layered the additional component of religious differences.

Some TV families provide a perhaps unexpected source of support for young people about to intermarry. On the youth-oriented series *The Heights*, romance bloomed for weeks between the Catholic Dizzy Mazzelli and his pregnant girlfriend, the Jewish Jodie Abramowitz. With their wedding approaching, Jodie asks her mother whether Dizzy's brother, a priest, "could marry us along with Rabbi Klein." An obliging Mrs. Abramowitz replies, "I got no problem with that. The Mazzelis are terrific people." In its absence of any thoughtful discussion on the issue and its reduction of the complex issue of intermarriage to a question of whether the parties are nice, this series represents television at its most simplistic and Pollyannaish.

A similarly superficial aphorism was expressed on the eve of another intermarriage, on *Beverly Hills 90210.* Notable for some other episodes in which it dealt intelligently with issues of anti–Semitism on campus, when Andrea Zuckerman (also Jewish and pregnant) is about to marry her Roman Catholic boyfriend, the youth-oriented series deals blithely with intermarriage. Learning of the wedding, her grandmother, a Holocaust survivor, comments, "Take life's blessings where you can find them."

Rejection

Given television's role as the quintessential mass medium appealing to a diverse audience, such upbeat portrayals of people coming together through intermarriage are not unexpected. But in contrast to the notion that romance between people of different faiths is the natural and accepted state, just the opposite has also been suggested and even expressly stated on several prime-time shows. These are rife with the message that dating and marriage between individuals of different faiths cannot and does not work and that only endogamous relationships are the proper, acceptable, and viable way of life. As a result, any interfaith romances must be deliberately halted by one of two possible means: conversion, by which process the relationship is no longer an interfaith one, or by a voluntary breaking off of the relationship. At times, it is the intrusion of anti–Semitism on the part of the Christian family that leads to the break up, suggesting through yet another scenario the impossibility of interfaith romances (see Chapter 3, "Anti-Semitism").

Non-Jewish characters who embark on conversion to Judaism often do so because they presuppose that Jewish-Jewish relationships are the only ones in which Jews will engage. On an episode of the family comedy *The Partridge Family,* teenager Danny Partridge takes a liking to Rene, a classmate whose father is a rabbi. In his pursuit of Rene, Danny pretends to be Jewish, and — undergoing a kind of pseudoconversion — he takes off from school for Jewish holidays and attends a *Purim* carnival with her. Only when his family is invited to Rene's home for a *Shabbat* dinner is his ruse revealed when he is asked to join in reciting Hebrew prayers. Trying to alleviate Danny's embarrassment, the rabbi kindly forgives his deceit ("Well, why not? Rene's a beautiful girl") with a nod toward interfaith harmony that might be construed as an acceptance of interdating. The more trenchant implication, however, is that Danny will no longer pursue Rene romantically, as the overriding notion that drives the episode is his belief that he could only date the Jewish Rene if he too were Jewish.

Another non–Jew was motivated by this assumption and embarked on a course of conversion on a 1978 episode of *Eight Is Enough*. Nancy Bradford meets and falls in love with medical intern Howard Stein. Assuming he is Jewish, she is hesitant to pursue their relationship because of religious differences and confides to her sisters, "We come from two different worlds — they're bound to conflict sooner or later." Although they dismiss her fears, Nancy is determined that the way to proceed with her relationship with Dr. Stein is to convert to Judaism, and she informs her parents that she is considering doing so "in order to form a more harmonious relationship." She goes to a synagogue, speaks to the rabbi, studies Jewish books, cooks Jewish food — all for the sake of romance with the presumedly Jewish Dr. Stein. At the program's close, Nancy discovers that he is in fact not Jewish, but she is unregretful of her efforts, which she deemed to be the only right course of action for pursuing a romantic involvement with a Jewish man.

A similar notion propelled a non–Jewish TV host who fell in love with a woman rabbi on the comedy series *Platypus Man*. So smitten is he that he even parachutes into Israel after learning that she has moved there and joined the army. On *Caroline in the City*, a Christian man attempts a perhaps more daring feat: he schedules a circumcision to impress the Jewish woman for whom he has fallen — and who will only date Jewish men.

The issue of conversion to Judaism arose in the 1980s hit series *Hill Street Blues* during several episodes that followed the budding romance between SWAT team commander Howard Hunter and Jewish nurse Linda Wolfowitz. Hunter — an inimitable mix of bigot, buffoon, loquacious right-wing patriot, and lunatic who is not without charm and intelligence — is wounded and lands in the hospital, where he meets and begins a swift and passionate affair with Nurse Wolfowitz. But when Howard asks her to marry him, she turns him down because, she explains, "my parents are very old-world, and I just could never marry anyone they disapprove of." Pressed by a disappointed Howard on the nature of their disapproval, Linda states coyly, "We're of different faiths…" Brightening, she adds, "Of course, there is a way — you could convert." It is a possibility Howard seriously considers, later inquiring of Jewish coworkers what it is like to be a Jew. Ultimately, Linda breaks off the relationship citing incompatibility, but the religion factor is raised once again when Howard questions her about her new boyfriend, asking, "Jewish?" Her offhand response, "It so happens — but that isn't why," might seem to contradict her previously expressed requirement for a Jewish mate. More likely, the deliberate casualness of her reply belies the fact that the requirement is still in place for her, only now it is more easily fulfilled. That questions of religious compatibility figured into her equation to break up with Howard is in fact his assumption, as evidenced by his first thought that her new boyfriend was Jewish.

Although Danny Partridge, Nancy Bradford, and Howard Hunter ultimately do not convert to Judaism, Lindley Gardner on *A Year in the Life* actually does, becoming the first major ongoing character in series television to do so. When viewers first meet the sprawling Gardner family of Seattle, Washington — around whom revolved the 1986 miniseries and subsequent series — Lindley is in the process of converting to Judaism and preparing for her wedding to Jewish patent attorney Jim Eisenberg. She cheerfully teaches her family the Yiddish phrases she is learning, and Jim is warmly welcomed by the Gardner clan. Yet in a subsequent episode, during the run of the short-lived series when her conversion was complete, a sensitive and searing portrait emerges of some of the challenges engendered by conversion.

Although the immediate point of contention focuses on the Jewish baby-naming ceremony for the Eisenbergs' infant daughter Ruthie, the program addresses questions of personal and religious commitment — exposing, confronting, and ultimately dealing with the issue of their future Jewish identity as a family. The first rumblings of trouble surface during an interview of the proud new parents by the representative of a gifted toddler program in which they wish to enroll Ruthie. When the starched young woman interviewer asks the parents if they are white, Jim — who has approached the whole session with a relaxed, satiric sense — replies, "Well, we're Jewish white." Quickly, a very serious Lindley adds, "*Jim* is — *I'm* not. I mean, I'm a converted Jew." Suddenly the mood changes, as Jim is visibly transformed by a silent but very apparent distress over Lindley's dissociation from Judaism. She apologizes the next day, explaining, "It's still kind of new to me," but the unresolved issue of the speed and comfort level with which she is entering what is for her a new world of Judaism continues to arise and plague the couple. When Jim asks her about attending the Jewish baby-naming ceremony they have planned for their daughter in synagogue, Lindley retreats once again, masking her reluctance by citing a general aversion to rituals. Jim responds with moderate prodding ("It's a Jewish tradition and one that's very important to me"), but his constrained patience turns to unbridled anger when Lindley does not show up at the ceremony, and he stands alone beside the rabbi with his daughter in his arms. In the explosion that ensues at home between the couple, Jim questions Lindley's commitment to the conversion she underwent, exclaiming, "You are backing out of something that you have put absolutely no effort into." By extension, he questions the sincerity of her obligations to him, their marriage, and their daughter. Trying to sort out her feelings during a calmer moment the following day, Lindley tells Jim an allegorical story of her childhood about a mountain climb she took with her father and how one particular stretch overwhelmed and petrified her. As a terrified child, she stood frozen, unable to move despite all cajoling and hand-holding. Not until she closed her eyes both to "where I'd been and where I was going" and focused on taking one step at a time did the child move on from that spot. As Lindley recalls, "It wasn't that I didn't want to climb the mountain — I did." The recounting seems to be for Lindley not so much an explanation to Jim as a statement of strategy with which to find her own strength and inspiration. In a concluding scene, viewers peer into a private moment as she takes Ruthie in her arms and reads to her the words of the baby-naming ceremony welcoming the infant into the Covenant of Israel. Unseen by the two, Jim watches quietly.

This moving portrayal of the Eisenbergs offers a picture of a young couple for whom Judaism is a central and pivotal part of their lives. As they seek to come to terms with their Jewish identity and observance, they face the particular challenge of achieving a common ground forged from their two different worlds — Jim, a born Jew confident in the practice and expression of his religion, and Lindley, who has just entered Judaism and is beginning to adjust to her new religion. The portrayal does not suggest that Lindley's conversion was unwise or unworkable, only that it will take thoughtful effort — rather than the instantaneous adjustment Jim initially requests — to ensure its fulfillment and success. It suggests a path that combines Jim's level of commitment and Lindley's vision of taking one small yet important step at a time. Emerging from two different places in Judaism, Jim and Lindley seek to find within it a path to take together.

This rare television portrayal of a marriage that includes a spouse converted to Judaism is a welcome contrast to the many intermarriages on TV where no such conversion takes place. Traditionally in Judaism, conversion to the religion for any reason other than a pure desire to become a Jew — such as for the sake of marriage — has been discouraged. But in light of the soaring rate of intermarriage and the growing acknowledgment that such marriages are today an unstoppable reality, the prospect of conversion by the non–Jewish spouse is one helpful approach to stemming the growing loss of Jews through intermarriage. The desirability of conversion in such marriages is supported by studies that indicate that couples in conversionary marriages and their children are far more likely to be Jewishly identified and involved than intermarried couples and their children.[2] With such conversions on the decline,[3] however, portrayals like the one in A Year in the Life take on added significance for their presentation of the possibility of this approach. To portray conversion to Judaism, along with its real difficulties and rewards, is a challenge that — if taken on by more TV shows — would enhance popular TV's diversity and reality on the intermarriage issue.

In fact, two programs following in the path of A Year in the Life depicted people seriously embarking upon conversion to Judaism, both within the 1992-93 TV season.

On Sisters, a moving series of episodes tracked the process by which

Frankie, intermarried to the non-observant Jewish Mitch Margolis, moved toward Judaism. She was first exposed to the beauty of Shabbat by her mother-in-law, who lamented her own son's aloofness from his heritage. Later, as Frankie and Mitch are expecting their first child, they attend a nephew's *bar mitzvah*, an occasion that touches Frankie deeply. She is moved both by the beauty of the ceremony and by the genuine warmth and affection extended to her by Mitch's family. Through much thought, tribulation, and contemplation, Frankie is ultimately certain that it is in the best interest of her new family — herself, her husband, and the son they are expecting — to practice together a single faith and that that faith should be Judaism. In short, she is creating a "traditional" Jewish family — the lack of which on TV has drawn much criticism.

The impetus for Frankie's initial thoughts of converting to Judaism, as well as the determining factors for her ultimate decision to do so, came from within herself, her own experiences and reactions to events, people, and circumstances — she was not coerced in any way. This is an important component of the program on many levels, but particularly when considering the reaction of Frankie's mother. Although she is extremely distressed with Frankie's decision, it is nothing about Judaism or Jews that seems to be the driving force in her reaction of horror and dismay. No anti–Semitism plays a part in her objections, as it almost always does in other TV depictions. Rather, Frankie's mother feels personally betrayed and abandoned, as she sees the years of raising her child in a very careful and particular way now seemingly thrown to the wayside, leaving her feeling a failure. This very real and understandable portrait of pain in no way clouds the depiction of a decision to convert to Judaism — in fact the opposite is true. By allowing for expressions of distress in a difficult situation, the depiction becomes more realistic.

Frankie's decision to raise a child in a single faith was echoed by a character that same season on a different series, *Homefront*, set just after World War II in a small Ohio town. Gina Sloan, an Italian Jew and survivor of Auschwitz, finds herself widowed, the mother of a young daughter, and welcomed into the upper-class Ohio home of the parents of her deceased American soldier husband. The attentions of Charlie, a kindly suitor, add a bright spot to her life, but her desire to raise her daughter in a Jewish environment supersedes her obvious affection for him. She breaks off the relationship with her Christian boyfriend Charlie, setting him off on an assiduous quest to learn more about Judaism and to embark on the process of conversion.

In presenting conversion as a solution to interfaith romances, television has shown it to be, as in reality, not one-directional. When conversions out of Judaism do occur, they are deeply painful to the Jewish community, as each one represents a significant loss of its precious few adherents. Popular television has infrequently touched on the issue of conversions out of Judaism in the name of love.

Not quite a conversion to Christianity but an abandonment of Judaism and an agreement to be married in a church was depicted in particularly egregious fashion in a 1964 episode of *Ben Casey*. The story follows the secret marriage — by a justice of the peace — of the Roman Catholic Marie Costo and the Jewish Harry Martin, who finds himself in Ben Casey's hospital after being pummeled by Marie's abusive father. Harry is a bitter and aggrieved young man who blames his own father, a rabbi, for all his troubles and rails against the Jewish heritage he now scorns. He foams with stereotypical and anti–Semitic comments, denouncing his father as "a jealous Jewish father punishing his children just to see how much they could take. Just like what *He* did to Job." In contrast, he finds solace from a kindly priest who is a fellow patient in the hospital and encounters in him an oasis of acceptance and kindly warmth. Harry's steps toward Christianity are also propelled by the anger of his Catholic father-in-law, who is most enraged that Harry is an atheist. As Marie tells her husband, "Of course papa wanted me to marry in my own faith. But what upsets him the most is the way you talk about not believing. If you were still a Jew, he could accept that." Brimming with complete disdain for his own religion, drawn to the gentle priest, and facing the wrath of Marie's father, Harry agrees to be remarried in the Catholic Church. Although Harry makes a point of saying that Marie's father "didn't convert me," the message of a loving Christianity's triumphing over Judaism, which is here the object of shallow and negative stereotypes and not given any voice of its own, is unmistakable.

A calmer portrayal of a Jewish character marrying in a church appeared on *Homefront* when the Jewish Al Kahn, a progressive urbanite, married the Catholic Ann Metcalf, a prim widow. Ann's fervent and meticulous devotion to her faith was in contrast to Al's remote attachment to his. Although he did not convert to Catholicism and later even commented that Christmas "is not my holiday," they were married by a priest after Kahn signed, at Ann's insistence, a prenuptial agreement to raise their children as Catholics.

A formal conversion to Christianity was an element of the 1979 miniseries *Studs Lonigan* which aired as part of the *NBC Novels for Television* and chronicled the lives of a group of friends growing up in Depression-era Chicago. One of Studs's friends — the Jewish Phil Rolfe — begins dating Studs's sister Loretta. While her anti–Semitic Irish Catholic family slowly warms up to Phil as the couple falls in love, Studs remains bigoted and vehemently opposed to their romance. When Phil finally tells his Orthodox parents, "I'm gonna marry this girl — if she'll marry me — even if I have to become a Catholic to do it," his father becomes enraged. Rather than offering moving, convincing, and cogent reasons for his objections to intermarriage and conversion from Judaism, the elder Mr. Rolfe inveighs a despicably foul and bigoted tirade against the Irish and severs all ties with Phil, who does indeed convert to Catholicism. Phil tells Studs "What a laugh! My parents — they're just like you." Unfortunately, while bigots exist — in varying numbers — among all peoples, portraying Jewish objections to intermarriage as based on prejudice demonstrates an ignorance of the issue from the Jewish perspective and negates valid Jewish concerns about the matter. Indeed, the conversion to Christianity shown here highlights in an extreme-case scenario the potential of intermarriage to diminish an already demographically fragile Jewish population.

When interfaith relationships are presented as taboo but conversion is not raised as an option, often the solution is the breakup of the relationship.

On a 1963 episode of *Bonanza*, young Adam Cartwright falls for the daughter of a Jewish peddler and helps defend her and her father from thieving outlaws. But as the grateful young woman develops a sense of greater respect and understanding for her own Jewish heritage, she realizes that her future is not with the non–Jewish Adam.

A humorous twist on the theme of breaking up over differing religions was played out on a 1985 episode of the popular comedy series *The Golden Girls*. Rose, one of the four "golden girls" sharing a house in Miami, begins dating Dr. Jonathan Newman, who happens to be a dwarf. She — and her initially startled housemates — are charmed by Jonathan's intelligence, gentleness, humor, and panache. But as the couple's relationship becomes more serious and Rose believes Jonathan is poised to ask her to marry him, she faces a dilemma: can she handle the public — and her own — reactions to being married to a dwarf? After a sleepless night of relentless soul-searching, revelatory dreams, and heart-to-heart talks with her housemates, Rose decides to gladly accept his anticipated proposal. At their lunch date the following day, she awaits his popping the question. Instead, he announces that because of differences between them they cannot see each other anymore. An understanding Rose reassures Jonathan, "I can honestly say it doesn't bother me you're small." Jonathan replies, "Small? No, I meant I can't see you anymore because you're not Jewish." For the audience, it is an intensely funny moment, with a consummate element of surprise as Jonathan injects a wholly unexpected factor into the scene by stating his previously undisclosed Jewishness and then rejecting Rose, when it was she who had been contemplating rejecting him. Beneath the humor, however, are Jonathan's very serious goals: his priority is not simply to marry, but to marry within his faith. Although marriage prospects would not seem to come easily his way — owing to his shortness in a world of normal-heighted people — he turns down, on religious principles, as desirable a catch as Rose. But she does not initially take kindly to his rejection. In a loud outburst, she decries the nerve he had for "dumping me because I'm not Jewish" after she had been "agonizing" over their relationship. Jonathan's stammering response offers her little explanation or solace: "Please understand; I come from a very religious family." Some humorous remarks from Jonathan and the passing of the shock combine to calm Rose, and the couple returns to a pleasant dinner. But Rose's sympathy-earning indignation in response to being summarily dumped and the hints of prejudice on Jonathan's part (Rose, after all, overcame *her* prejudices against his being short, but he rejected her because of religion) unmitigated by his paltry explanation that did not begin to hint at any real reason for Jews marrying within their faith, combined to paint Jonathan in a not altogether likable and sympathetic light. Some viewers may even interpret his actions as unfair and bigoted.

This implicit notion becomes an explicit accusation in a 1988 episode of the homespun family series *Our House*. When one of the show's principal characters, the Jewish Joe Kaplan, is denied membership in the local men's club, he believes it is due to anti–Semitism. His friend and neighbor Gus Witherspoon, a non–Jew and member of the club, confronts its leader head on with this charge only to learn of a very different reason for Joe's rejection. In a meeting of the three men, leader of the club Irving Clifford ominously asks Joe to recall a young man by the name Dennis, then reminds Joe of events that occurred ten years earlier. It seems that Dennis had dated Joe's niece, who was staying with her uncle while attending college, and the young couple was very much in love. "One night when he came to your house to see her, you met him instead. You told him that she couldn't see him anymore, because he wasn't Jewish — in my mind that's bigotry too." Crushed by the rejection, Dennis had dropped out of school and it took him years to restore his life. Dennis was the son of a now very bitter Clifford. Somewhat stunned by the unexpected unearthing of the past but remaining calm, Joe then has his say. He said, "In my opinion, the most precious thing in a person's life is his or her religious beliefs. Now my niece came from an Orthodox family. She was deeply in love with your son. She decided she couldn't marry him. She didn't have the heart to tell him — that's where I came in." Joe apologizes for in any way hurting Clifford's son but remains true to his convictions, adding, "I backed her up then, and I'd do it again."

Like Jonathan on *The Golden Girls*, Joe says little to explain the Jewish objection to interdating and places the "blame" on some amorphous "family." His generalized paean to religious beliefs may be an effort to earn him the respect and sympathy of viewers but it does little to explain to them the unique reasons for Jewish disapproval of interdating and intermarriage. While Joe's principles and beliefs are cast in a positive light, his explanation of the niece's rejection of Dennis is too vague to have any significance. The charges of bigotry leveled by Clifford seem to hang in the air and, as in Jonathan's case, take on added significance because the rejecting Jewish character turns out *not* to be the victim of bigotry. Although Joe is a well-liked if at times nudgy character, it seems that a parting comment from Gus to Clifford — "That's a pretty good man, you know, and one of the most honest I've met in my life" — is now needed to restore his stature.

While some Jewish characters have sought to excise themselves from potential intermarriage situations by "blaming" or recruiting family members, one young man took it upon himself to truncate an interfaith romance on a 1987 episode of *The Days and Nights of Molly Dodd*. When a young and lonely Hasidic widower, Martin Storm, seeks to rekindle some happiness in his life, he decides upon piano lessons — and is led to savvy New York City single Molly Dodd. She finds him as witty and personable as he finds her warm and charming, and their interest in each other grows. Molly does research on Hasidism and queries her Jewish girlfriend, who tells her, "There's something not quite kosher about the way this man is behaving. I mean, it's only piano lessons, but it's my impression that this guy is breaking the rules just by talking to you on the telephone, much less shaking your hand, much less going into your apartment." While in fact he refused to shake her hand the first time they met, a clear physical attraction develops between them. As they gaze at each other romantically and longingly one afternoon, Martin tells her, "I can't, even for you, no matter how much I want to." But they seem to succumb to the passion of the moment when he says, "Oh, what the hell." They kiss and walk toward the bedroom — until he suddenly stops and declares, "I'm sorry. This isn't right, I can't do it, it's not fair. I can't see you again."

The picture of a Hasidic Jew, bound by myriad strictures and steeped in an all-encompassing code of life, desisting from an interfaith involvement is hardly surprising. Indeed, the element of drama and unexpectedness in this plot lies in the black-coated Martin's attraction to Molly altogether and his inclination to act upon it. It is the reverse of the scenario on *The Golden Girls*, where modern psychiatrist Jonathan Newman is uneventfully involved in an interdating situation — until his suddenly revealed Jewishness and refusal to continue the interfaith relationship provides the surprising element. Taken together, these mirror images offer a picture of interfaith attachments as pervasive and unavoidable in any sphere, entangling both of two Jews who are worlds apart in dress, demeanor, outlook, attitude, and approach to the "outside world." Yet at the same time, both characters are driven by some allegiance — differing as it is in degree and expression — that impels them, against strong longings, to break off these interfaith attachments. In this vision, every Jew is both susceptible to interdating, and driven by some imperative to reject it.

Objection

The majority of programs featuring interfaith relationships, however, shun the extremes, presenting such unions as neither devoid of problems nor breaking up because of them. The relationships continue, as difficulties raised by religious differences or bigotries are overcome by the persevering couple. Such travails as anti–Semitism, family objections, and the couple's own religious stirrings disrupt but do not sever the impending or existing intermarriage.

In the most common of television's intermarriage or interdating scenarios, the couple itself has no problem with the interfaith aspect of their relationship, but they face the objections of relatives — usually parents — that are inevitably overcome. The relationship proceeds, embattled but prevailing.

One couple from vastly different backgrounds whose ultimate union and eventual wedding were presented as victories over the forces of bigotry appeared on a 1975 episode of *Medical Center*. When Pete Rashid, son of an Arab sheik, falls in love with a poor Jewish widow, he provides funds for the costly medical care of her seriously ill son. But the widow, Esther Kornblum, concerned about their differing religions and political views on the Middle East, is reluctant to become involved with Pete. Ultimately, she is swayed by his kindnesses — he also offers to donate one of his kidneys for the ailing boy — and reciprocates his love. The stage is set for the appearance of Pete's father, the emir of Qatar, who arrives incensed over his son's relationship to a Jewish woman. Threatening to cut off all funds to Pete — and to the sick boy — unless the relationship is broken off, the emir gets a lecture from series hero Dr. Gannon on the virtues of unbigoted compassion, and the romance is allowed to proceed. Both Esther and Pete clearly intend to maintain their respective religions, and the show's concluding words telescope its theme that two different religions can coexist harmoniously in a marriage. When Dr. Gannon asks about where the wedding will be held — in a mosque or a synagogue — so that he will know "whether to wear a burnoose or a yarmulke," Esther's son pipes up, "Try both."

At times, the pursuit of an interfaith romance is portrayed as a deliberate and conscious rebellion against parents and Jewish heritage, an act of defiance and disseverment that is part of the broad detachment from one's background and heritage. This theme infuses the well-known story of "The Jazz Singer," a television version of which aired in 1959 on the anthology series *Startime*. This same motif surfaces in the 1974 miniseries *QB VII*, where young journalist Ben Cady spurns his father's religious sensibilities when he meets and falls in love with a Gentile woman, marrying in a church. It is she who considers his aging father's feelings and offers to "go through a Jewish ceremony." Ben, however, distanced and alienated from his father, refuses to do so, replying that he does not "believe in the Jewish thing."

More often, however, children are depicted not as deliberately defiant but merely reacting to idealized imperatives of love or necessity of circumstance. They face parental objections always from the Jewish side and sometimes from the Gentile side. The voicing of these objections range from silly and superficial to sensitive and searing. In some programs, the uniquely Jewish concerns about intermarriage are raised in a fair manner; too frequently, however, there is little explanation of them, as parents moan about some unexplained, amorphous need to stay in the faith. As a result, such objections come across, at best, as neither intelligent nor intelligible, and at worst, as the basest kind of bigotry.

An early example of this was a 1961 episode of the law series *The Defenders* entitled "The Young Lovers." Two teenagers — he Jewish and she Greek Orthodox — marry in secret, knowing that neither set of parents will approve. When a child they also bear in secret dies of dubious causes, David, the young father, is charged with murder. Forced to reveal their secret marriage during the ensuing court case, the teenagers face their parents' full fury. They are reviled by their elders, who spew forth bigotries against each other and refuse to help to their children. Both sets of parents are painted as narrow-minded and cruelly intolerant, full of generalized distaste for marrying outside one's religion. To emphasize the suggested symmetry of their stances, series hero Lawrence Preston takes them aside to rebuke them, demanding, "Can't you hear how alike you are? Why, you're echoes of each other! The same superstitions, the same little rituals!" Despite this program's cursory equation of all religious objections to intermarriage and its censure of such objections, it is notable for being one of the few shows ever to give voice to non–Jewish concerns for intermarriage based not simply on anti–Semitism but on a desire to preserve religious identity, custom, and heritage. And yet, while this may be a shared view among various religious and ethnic groups regarding the undesirability of intermarriage, particular Jewish concerns, unique in their depth, complexity, and urgency, are virtually ignored in this show.

Antagonisms between families of an interfaith couple were approached in a comical and less vehement way on the very popular 1972 series *Bridget Loves Bernie*. The comedy show chronicled the intermarried life of Jewish Bernie Steinberg and Irish Catholic Bridget Fitzgerald, with many episodes focusing on the interfaith aspect of their relationship and the involvement of various relatives. As Bridget and Bernie prepare to marry in the pilot episode, for example, they are confronted by both sets of parents objecting to the impending union on "religious" grounds. Although neither family is very observant, intermarriage is anathema to both. Both families are portrayed as comical bigots, in different ways: the Fitzgeralds as genteel anti–Semites, the Steinbergs as coarse and narrow-minded. Out of this cacophony of conflict emerges the young couple as the picture of harmony, whose love defeats small-mindedness. Although they had eloped to avoid the problem of who would marry them, a priest or a rabbi, they return to find the issue still being fought. Mrs. Fitzgerald demands that Bridget and Bernie be married religiously, but her husband explains that the Steinbergs would not allow a Catholic wedding. Mrs. Steinberg also petitions for a religious wedding. With each family insisting the ceremony take place according to their ways, much fighting and anger ensue. Finally, a mixed ceremony is the solution, with a rabbi and a priest, Bridget's brother Father Mike, officiating.[4] Bernie wears a yarmulke at the ceremony, as does the presiding rabbi, who also dons a prayer shawl. The ceremony is ecumenical, with no specific Jewish wedding rituals present. Each clergyman utters words of brotherhood, harmony, and common ground.

This projected sense of concord dwarfing religious differences was show-cased in another episode on this series — dealing with the December holiday season, often a crisis point for intermarried couples and popularly known as the "December dilemma." Bridget and Bernie each recall very fond memories of how they used to celebrate their own holidays, Christmas and Chanukah, respectively.

Each of their families is preparing a celebration of the holiday and wants the couple with them. The newlyweds decide to go out of town and avoid favor-ing one family. But both Bridget and Bernie, unbeknownst to the other, go to the other's family to relay how upset their spouse is about having to go away and not be with them. Just before boarding the bus to depart, they decide they just cannot leave and return home only to find a surprise. Bridget had secretly arranged for both families to be at their apartment to celebrate Chanukah; the living room is decorated for Chanukah, Jewish music is playing, and the fam-ilies are dancing. But in an O. Henryesque turn, Bernie thanks Bridget and takes her into another room where a Christmas tree and celebration that he had sur-reptitiously arranged for her awaits. As the families delight in this resolution, Bernie's Uncle Moe says, beaming, "She gives him, he gives her — now that's a marriage!" This forced vision of an intermarried couple being able to harmo-niously blend their individual holidays impels an inevitable blurring and dis-tortion of those holidays, as epitomized by Bernie's summation that "Christmas, Chanukah ... is a time for brotherhood, a time when families come together and say things to each other that they've been too busy to say all year long — things like 'I love you,' 'I need you,' 'Stay close.'"

But *Bridget Loves Bernie* was to have a persistent life. Romance between a Jewish boy and a Irish Catholic girl would bloom on TV again when *Brooklyn Bridge* debuted some two decades later. The series, about a Jewish family in 1950s Brooklyn, focused on the romance between fourteen-year-old Alan Sil-ver and his girlfriend Katie Monahan. The series was often a warm and engag-ing comedy with a Jewish flavor, but it frequently faltered when those Jewish matters were brought to the forefront. One such instance was an episode in which the two families come together at the behest of the youngsters who, anticipating strong familial objections to their interdating, seek to make peace by having everyone meet and dine together at a Chinese restaurant.

The result is an anachronistic throwback to TV's days of the original *Brid-get Loves Bernie*, an outdated and preachy paean to social homogenization in which concerns about interfaith romance are summarily dismissed. Young Alan repeatedly gives grown-up speeches about how America means accepting all different cultures. In this way, a straw man is set up, by which his grandmother's deep anxiety about his interdating can be readily dismissed as un–American, old-fashioned, and outdated. Never are her concerns given any articulate voic-ing — they are presented as just some vague longings for the old country, which are unsubtly equated with the Monahans' longing for *their* old country.

In the Chinese restaurant, with the families uncomfortably settled in for dinner, the Monahans display a tradition that seems utterly startling but intensely lovely to the Silvers: the Irish family says grace before meals. It is as if Jews have no such concept in their lives (when in fact Jews are bidden to say a blessing for nearly every conceivable event). The one-upped Silvers finally do manage to mumble something of their own, when Grandfather Silver clumsily mutters the words of a prayer he barely knows. To top off the scene, cousins of the Silvers coincidentally show up at the restaurant. They are the loudest, coarsest stereotype of Jews one could imagine.

By the end of the evening, however, the awkwardness is overcome and the two families warm to each other and find they have much in common. The Monahans offer details of Irish history, describing British persecution of the Irish and explaining the development of headmasters (teachers), from whom they are descended. Grandmother Silver mentions only that "the Jewish schools were closed," without any explanation of why or under what circumstances. In this contrived analogy, everything is the same; everyone has the same history. In the final scene, those most adamantly opposed to the young love that is blooming — Alan's grandmother and Katie's father — seem to have found peace with each other and the notion of their children interdating, as they experience and appreciate a taste of each other's culture.

While the episode includes some high comic moments, it disappoints in its dismissal of Jewish concerns about interfaith romance in the context of Jewish survival and its premise that to appreciate another's culture one must abandon one's own.

This outlook reached a pinnacle on an episode of *CBS Schoolbreak Special.* Even the show's very title, "Same Difference," bespeaks a worldview that eschews distinctiveness and individuality. The show chronicles the springtime efforts of a Jewish girl and an Italian Catholic boy to overcome the opposition of their respective families — both of whom have strong ethnic identities and who object to the relationship. To do so, the teens try to blur their separate cultures by melding celebrations of their Easter and Passover holidays. At the show's close, they declare the two holidays to be so similar that they can in fact be called, as they laughingly coin a phrase, "Eastover."

Certainly, ecumenical harmony and peaceful relations between disparate cultures is a desired goal. But this program follows in a tradition of some TV shows that embark on a benighted effort to achieve harmony among groups by fostering the mantra that "we're all pretty much the same." Such shows promote a cult of sameness that posits that living in peace and having respect for one another *and* being different are mutually exclusive conditions, that only through a blurring of all differences, a homogenizing of particular backgrounds and cultures, a falsifying of the meaning of certain rituals, customs, and values can we live in peace.

Why the sense that harmony can come only when we negate our individuality and knowledge and appreciation of our own heritage — and that of others? The lessons of "Eastover" are hardly valuable ones for a young people's show — that only if we are the same can we get along, that distinctiveness tears us apart, that only when we are like everybody else will we be accepted and befriended. The premise of "Same Difference" is a simplistic and impoverished viewpoint that closes down real dialogue, maturity, and learning — and that will necessarily crumble when any differences do arise.

Another TV movie that concluded with a scene of merged religions was the 1986 telefilm *Mrs. Delafield Wants to Marry*. In a switch on the conventional setup where parents decry the interdating of their offspring, in this TV production it is the children who resent the interdating of their parents. When rich, Protestant widow Mrs. Margaret Delafield becomes gravely ill and is restored to health by middle-class Jewish doctor Marvin Elias, the stage is set for them to fall in love — and face the opprobrium of their respective children. Each set of offspring bitterly resent the other family, citing religious and class differences as reasons the marriage should not go forward. The objections of both are painted in derogatory and bigoted terms. Marvin's children insist that they have "the right to say no to a goy stepmother" and that Margaret "is in the enemy camp." Margaret's children brim with anti–Semitism, telling her they are ashamed of her and warning her against "this Jew." This formulaic symmetry equating all things culminates in Margaret's espousal of a universalist philosophy that she recites to her children to quell their opposition. Since both she and Marvin believe in God, she explains, "there are no religious differences because it's all one miracle. And if it's all one miracle, then it's all one religion, no matter how many forms it takes."

With familial antagonisms at bay, Marvin and Margaret proceed to make wedding arrangements, but their respective clergyman politely — and without explanation — decline to participate when they realize the interfaith nature of the marriage. Eventually, the couple weds in a church "that hardly cares who they marry." Performed by a justice of the peace, the wedding is a kind of humanistic ceremony with a sprinkling of Jewish traditions. They stand under a wedding canopy, and Marvin wears a yarmulke and breaks a glass at the end of the ceremony. The wedded couple then asks their families — who until now have sat on opposite sides of the hall in a final protest — to join hands in peace and love. The concluding picture, clothed in the guise of interfaith harmony, in fact caps the program's unrelenting message that distinctive religions are divisive and should be dissolved into one religion — or nonreligion.

Issues of intermarriage and familial objections have permeated several other made-for-TV movies. A 1975 television movie titled *Conspiracy of Terror* featured Jacob and Helen Horowitz, a husband-and-wife detective team who are intermarried. As they go about solving crimes, they must also deal with the wrath of Jacob's elderly father, Arthur, who strongly objects to his son's intermarriage. The father enlists his rabbi's help to talk to Jacob, but Rabbi

Sinvale can only tell Jacob, "I don't know where to begin." When Arthur suggests that the rabbi start by telling Jacob to take off his gun (that Jacob carries a gun everywhere, including to synagogue, evokes from his father the same degree of vehemence as does his intermarriage) the conversation with the rabbi becomes a lament on the violent state of the world that forces Jacob to do so. While no real issues about intermarriage are seriously discussed here, the capacity of the issue to disrupt relations between a parent and child is shown.

A more intense exploration of that issue appeared in another made-for-television movie the following year, *The Great Houdinis*, about the life of master magician Harry Houdini, born Eric Weiss. The TV production focuses less on his feats of magic and illusion than on his personal life, particularly his intermarriage to Bess and the ensuing strain in his relationship with his mother. Eric's ties to his mother Cecilia are portrayed as especially warm and close until his secret marriage to the Catholic Bess is revealed and Cecilia erupts with tears and tirades, telling Eric, "Your father is turning in his grave." When Bess is perplexed by this and asks Cecilia why this intermarriage is so troubling to her, she responds tearfully but gently, "Look at me! I'm five thousand years old, from the time of Abraham. You think that's nothing? Five thousand years — the same people! Who else can say it? Do I have to tell you what it cost us? With fire they tried to finish us, with swords, with guns, with hate. You think I want to see them do it with love?" Cecilia raises the option of conversion when Harry tries to comfort her, assuring her that everything will be all right. She agrees, saying "Absolutely! You'll get married again in a temple, by a rabbi — a rabbi like your father; and the girl will convert." But conversion is not to be a solution here, as Bess asserts she is a Catholic and intends to remain so, insisting that they first be married in a church. Cecilia's threats to Eric ("You do this to your dead father, to the day I die I'll never forgive you") are upheld. She continually shuns Bess, and relations with her son remain strained.

Unfortunately, Cecilia's histrionics and harsh treatment of her daughter-in-law distract from the moving and reasoned explanation that she offers Bess as to why she objects to the intermarriage. In fact, her stated desire to uphold the continuity of the Jewish people despite centuries of oppression is unusual for television, as it lends parental objections to intermarriage a new dimension of unequaled strength, consistency, and conviction. While popular television's predominant portrayal is of families coming around to accept and even embrace that which they view as a fait accompli, this depiction distinguishes itself on two counts. It offers a clear and convincing explanation of why intermarriage is so painful and problematic for Jews, and it depicts a character who remains steadfast in her unwillingness to go along with what she believes to be calamitous for Jewish survival. Moreover, her rejection of Bess cannot be construed as bigoted, since she clearly explains the historic and religious objections to intermarriage and its threat to Jewish survival.

The notion of Jewish survival endangered by intermarriage was raised by another parent in the series *Little House on the Prairie.* This popular family drama, set in the town of Walnut Grove in the 1870s American West, introduced a Jewish character named Percival Dalton. Originally from New York City, young Percival had changed his name from Isaac Cohen to better his chances for success as an accountant in the small town. Other changes would await him there as well. When Percival meets the non–Jewish Nellie Oleson, they fall in love and marry. Although Percival faces some anti–Semitism from his mother-in-law, his real troubles begin when his own parents arrive from New York for the birth of the young couple's first child. Percival's father strongly objects to the intermarriage, and the two engage in several discussions about Jewish identity.

To his disapproving father, Percival defends his earlier decisions to leave the family business and move out West (where, he allows, Jewish women are few and far between), change his name, and marry a non–Jew, telling his father that "these people are American, Papa, just like you." Rejecting the melting-pot concept when it comes to marriage, the elder Mr. Cohen replies, "Understand, my son, we Jews must survive. Since the beginning of time, other men have tried to destroy us." His words are punctuated with an ironic twist that lends them added strength when Percival impatiently responds, "Papa, people are educated now. That kind of craziness won't happen again — it's almost the twentieth century!" Mr. Cohen's strong personality and articulately stated objections have no apparent effect on his son and are ultimately eclipsed by his greater need to make peace with his intermarried son.

Another Jewish father with fervently expressed views about intermarriage was a main character of the 1985 miniseries *Evergreen.* Joseph Friedman, patriarch of the four generations chronicled in this immigrant family saga, is a proud and observant Jew who wants his son Maury to be so—and to also ascend to the pinnacles of American success. So there is great rejoicing in the Friedman home when Maury, who has been groomed for the Ivy League, is accepted to Yale. But, not sharing his father's religious convictions (the two had bickered when Maury was young about Sabbath observance and synagogue attendance), Maury returns from Yale announcing his imminent marriage to a young Christian woman; the Friedman family's glee turns to dismay. Joseph is crushed and evokes the Holocaust — then brewing in Europe — to dissuade his son from intermarrying. "Right now in Germany, our people are being persecuted for no reason, and this world does nothing — it doesn't care… We are a proud, strong people who enrich this world, and our religion is what unifies us, it's what keeps us together, and it's what keeps us strong." Maury sees only bigotry in his father's attitude and referring to the anti–Semitism he encountered from his fiancée's family, charges, "You're no different from her people — you're a bigot!" The judgment would seem to be belied by Joseph's deep friendship and longtime business partnership with the Irish Catholic Matthew Malone. Indeed, Joseph cites that friendship to Maury, saying, "Malone is a good Catholic who expects his children to marry Catholic, and I respect him for that and he respects me for my principles." But Joseph's obdurate opposition tries even Malone's initial support, who— along with Joseph's wife — thinks Joseph is overdoing it. This picture of Joseph as a proud but stiff-necked man with destructive prejudices is heightened when Maury is killed in a car accident — and Joseph blames himself for the tragedy by having turned his back on him. Through this portrayal of Joseph as unduly harsh and ridden with guilt, his deeply felt objections to intermarriage seem to be deliberately undermined and cast as strongly prejudiced.

Television's exploration of intermarriage through the drama of a father-son relationship continued in a 1975 episode of the series *Cagney and Lacey*. Head of the station house Lieutenant Bert Samuels is a likable, sometimes gruff on the outside bear of a man. When he gets a sudden, unexpected visit in his office from his long-estranged son, Samuels is shocked to learn the son had married a Vietnamese woman and is hurt and angered on various levels: that his son neither told him about nor invited him to the wedding and that his daughter-in-law is not Jewish. The lieutenant's pain and anger give way to reconciliation and a desire for family unity. By program's end, he attempts a reconciliatory gesture by bringing the couple a wedding gift: the Shabbat candlesticks that belonged to his son's grandmother. Handing them to his Vietnamese daughter-in-law, Samuels expresses the hope that the gift will bring light and love into their home. The rift between father and son, aggravated by intermarriage, is healed by a symbol of their Jewish heritage — the Shabbat candlesticks.

It was the daughter-granddaughter relationship that was explored through the interdating lens on the medical drama *Buck James*, when series regular Dr. Rebecca Meyers, a native New Yorker on staff at a Texas hospital, gets a visit from her grandparents. The visit provides an opportunity for the kind, elderly couple to have a quaint cultural exchange with Texas life — and for Rebecca's grandmother to question her about her love life. When she learns that Rebecca is dating a non–Jew and expresses worlds of displeasure with a single look, Rebecca protests, "He's a very fine man, Grandma." With wry Jewish humor that succinctly reveals her unmistakable views on the matter, Rebecca's grandmother replies, "So is the pope, but I wouldn't want you dating him either."

Undeterred, Rebecca pursues the relationship, yet it continues to be a topic of discussion and controversy between the two women throughout the visit. Each seems to come from a different world, with Rebecca espousing a worldview devoid of any ethnic or religious differences, thus rendering intermarriage of no consequence, while her grandmother's views emanate from a strong sense of Jewish identity that shapes her stance against intermarriage. The older woman, played with refreshing understatement and exuding a kind of persistent wisdom, asks Rebecca to "just think ten years down the line. You and this Mark are married, you have a family and a home, and Christmas comes around. He wants a tree and to take the children to mass. What do you do?" Rebecca fails to see any problem with this scenario, characterizing Christmas as merely a national holiday. Her grandmother goes on to insist, "You're a Jew in your heart, a Jew in your soul, and no matter what you do or who you marry, that will never change. It won't work." Although the two clearly have a close and loving relationship, they seem to be working at cross purposes, with Rebecca issuing pleas for her grandmother to treat her like an adult and to be more concerned about her happiness. The young doctor has little patience or understanding for what she sees as her grandmother's old-world ways, and she lectures her saying, "We don't live in a *shtetl* any longer. These are the 1980s in America, not Poland in the 40s. A person is a person, we go to the same schools, we live in the same neighborhoods. We're not that different." Her grandmother has the last word, sighing in disappointment and warning, "Aren't we?" The balancing of these two views seems to tilt in the grandmother's favor: Rebecca's judgment is called into question after she discovers that her "very fine man" is married, and as a result their romance breaks up.

Parental objections were a major component in the portrayal of one of television's more unusual interdating couples, featured in the popular but short-lived 1989 comedy series *Chicken Soup*. The program focused on the interfaith romance of fifty-two-year-old Jackie Fisher and his Irish Catholic neighbor, Maddie Peerce — along with the objections of their respective families. Maddie faces the displeasure of her working-class, anti–Semitic brother, while Jackie copes with his very motherly Jewish mother, Bea, who is temporarily living with him. In the pilot episode, Jackie first informs his mother that he and Maddie are "going to be a couple." His use of euphemisms when approaching his mother underscores his trepidation and hesitation, knowing the disapproval he will face. That a grown man well into middle age displays such evident anxiety over disclosing his interdating to his mother (although it is not sufficient for him to break off his relationship with Maddie) and that his mother goes on to forcefully express her views on it illustrates the strong family component in TV's interdating and intermarriage depictions. Whatever the ultimate outcome, the Jewish family exerts a powerful presence and influence in matters of interfaith relationships, bringing to bear fervid pressure against them. Pointedly, in almost every program where Jewish characters break off interfaith relationships or request their partner's conversion, they cite their family as the motivating factor, stating that they come from a "religious" or an "old-world" family.

Familial concerns often are showcased in a comedic manner and are the subject of countless humorous remarks and passing references and inferences on popular TV shows. An episode of *St. Elsewhere*, for example, opens with a torrid love scene between Jewish doctor Wayne Fiscus and a blond young woman. As they smear each other with whip cream with delighted abandon, a sudden knock at the apartment door freezes Wayne with fright. He sits up and gasps, "Mom?" Hiding his partner as best he can, Wayne greets his mother, visiting unexpectedly from out of town, and the two discuss plans of her next visit. As she leaves his apartment, she asks with a mother's intuition and feigned nonchalance, "Just one more question — the girl in the closet, is she Jewish?"

Even Archie Bunker seems to be aware of the Jewish concern about intermarriage, as he invokes the vision of a disapproving Jewish mother for his own ends in a humorous line from *Archie Bunker's Place*. When Archie thinks his niece Billie has been seeing too much of his Jewish accountant, Gary Rabinowitz, he threatens Billie with derailing the interfaith romance by calling up Gary's "little Jewish mother with the high blood pressure."

This comedy series addressed the question of intermarriage more seriously in other episodes. In the 1979-80 TV season, just weeks apart, two episodes focusing on the same character approached the issue from reverse perspectives. Together, they conjure up a sense of ironic justice being meted out by the generations.

In the first, Murray Klein is dating a non–Jew and is fully at ease with his interdating. Yet he is beset with apprehension upon learning that his elderly mother will be unexpectedly joining the couple for dinner at the Bunkers, anticipating and fearing the parental opposition he will face over his interfaith relationship. In the second episode, the focus is on Murray's role not as a child, but as a father — and as such he displays a wholly different attitude. Viewers learn that when his daughter Beverly married a non–Jew years earlier, he did not attend the wedding and in fact severed his relationship with her over the intermarriage. A sudden visit by Beverly to a still-rejecting Murray points up the extent and ongoing nature of his disapproval.

Both episodes are resolved through speeches about harmony and the insignificance of differences among people, and reconciliations abound. But the distinctive note is the apparently contradictory roles played by Murray — who is at once a fearful, interdating son seeking his mother's approval, and a disapproving father rejecting his intermarried daughter. His dual characterization telescopes the different attitudes toward intermarriage TV characters often assume based on their stage of life and the metamorphosis some undergo as they move from one stage to another.

Many adult children obliviously interdate and intermarry, defiantly shunning admonitions of previous generations about the dangers and problems of such relationships and denouncing such views as close-minded and old-fashioned. To them, parental objections are irrelevant, representing the voice of a past with which they want to break — until they themselves become parents. Suddenly, they become that past and their children the future through whom their heritage and identity will be transmitted. Suddenly, intermarriage — and religious identity — matters to them.

Personal Odyssey

The notion of personal odyssey found expression — in somewhat different form — in *Chicken Soup*. Here, Jackie's mother Bea is not herself involved in an interfaith relationship, but she is an assimilated, nonobservant Jew who finds herself suddenly focused on religious identity when faced with her son's interdating. The issue is raised during the exchange between Jackie and his mother when he first tells her about Maddie. Faced with his mother's strong protests over his interdating, Jackie responds, "I don't understand you — you're not even that religious." Bea's response is heartfelt but telling. "There is something inside me," she says, "that was passed down five thousand years ago, and I thought I gave it to you. But who knows? These days with the DNA and the RNA and the genes and the clones — sometimes it's hard to know what's happening." Her assumption is that knowledge of and devotion to Judaism will somehow magically be passed down genetically, despite the fact that Judaism is neither practiced nor taught at home. In the face of this kind of response, the adult child rightfully questions the parent's justification in objecting to intermarriage when the parent has lacked any strong Jewish identity or affiliation or observance all her life. This portrayal suggests that the role of family can be effective not when expressing objections to interdating at the time it occurs but in cultivating earlier a sense of Jewish identity that diminishes the possibility of its occurrence.

Seventeen years earlier, this important but rarely discussed aspect of intermarriage was exposed in the premiere episode of *Bridget Loves Bernie*. When Bernie Steinberg's assimilated parents — who apparently raised their son without any Jewish religious education, observance, or allegiance — are confronted with his impending intermarriage, they suddenly make a frantic grasp for a mantle of Jewishness. Bernie brings Bridget home for dinner on Friday night and encounters — evidently for the first time in that house — Sabbath candles, pronouncements that the family is Jewish, and the telling of jokes in Yiddish. So puzzled and angry is he with his parents' behavior that he cries out in disgust, "I don't believe this. I've lived with you people all my life. Now, why all of a sudden, is everyone being so Jewish?"

Such sentiments in nearly the same words were expressed again some twenty years later by an interdating young girl on the drama series *I'll Fly Away*, set in the 1950s South. As young Nathan Bedford falls in love with Diane Lowe, a Jewish classmate of his who has recently moved to his town from New Orleans, his best friend Paul Slocum vents bigoted and anti–Semitic feelings, nearly shattering their friendship. Yet Nathan is undeterred from pursuing his relationship with Diane, even when her parents vociferously object — although their objections are vague, leaving any Jewish concerns regarding intermarriage unarticulated. In a very telling and effective scene, Diane chastises her parents' seemingly unjustifiable objection to her dating Nathan, asking them why suddenly they are acting so Jewish when they never have done so before.

Behind these exchanges is the sense that the acquisition of religious identity is a lifetime enterprise of conscious involvement, and not a biological fiat, as envisioned by Jackie Fisher's mother. Such programs have the potential to arouse assimilated parents by pointedly raising questions about why their children should *not* want to intermarry and how — if there is no example to follow — Jewish identity is to be transmitted. Although these TV parents learn too late that their children will not likely grow up with any deep commitment to Judaism if it is virtually absent from the home, the depiction of them ultimately confronted by this notion can impart important messages for future generations of parents.

Indeed, a Jewish television parent for whom it is not too late finds himself grappling with these issues early on in the child-rearing process. His realization of the potential problem and his desire to act before it actually becomes one comprise one of the central and ongoing story lines of the popular drama series launched the late 1980s, *thirtysomething*. For the series' hero, assimilated Michael Steadman, being intermarried was never a problem. His wedding to the non–Jewish Hope, in fact, was one of those paeans to interfaith unions, with a rabbi and a priest presiding. But with the birth of his first child, Janey, Michael begins a soul-searching and often turbulent questioning about his own religious identity and his place in the link of Jewish generations. Like Murray Klein of *Archie Bunker's Place*, Michael finds his views on such issues changing as he assumes different roles in life.

His crisis is sparked by Janey's first Christmas-Chanukah season, as Hope makes grand preparations for Christmas, decorating the house and planning for a Christmas tree. The stark and sudden nature of the uneasiness that overtakes him is underscored in his comment to a friend: "It's just so weird. I love Christmas, I do. I used to. I used to love it with Hope, but now..." and his friend knowingly completes the sentence, "a tree's not just a tree." Michael suddenly views a Christmas tree in his home as something that cuts him off from both his past and his future: "I see it in my living room. I see my grandfather rising up from the grave and having another heart attack. Now there's Janey. What do I want to tell her about who I am? What if she totally loves this? I don't know where that leaves me." Now, in this new context of parenthood and engulfed by Hope's Christmas frenzy, Michael wonders and worries about transmitting something of *who he is* to his daughter. Suddenly, *who he is* is *Jewish*, and it is this aspect of his being that seeks expression on grounds that are new and unchartered to him. Ensuing tensions erupt in arguments between the couple: Michael expresses anger that Hope wants a Christmas tree when they had agreed in an earlier compromise not to have one. Hope, like TV characters Jackie Fisher and Bernie Steinberg, is perplexed and put off by such objections since Michael, as she acridly reminds him, hasn't "set foot in a temple" for as long as she has known him. Michael and Hope continue to bicker in a none-too-delicate renegotiation of all the rules for a harmonious intermarriage that they had laid down in calmer and simpler times.

Broadcast during *thirtysomething*'s first season, this episode was notable for showing with a reality and harshness uncommon for television some of the difficulties of intermarriage and the profound capacity of the holiday season and the birth of children to bring on rumblings of religious searchings in a previously untroubled intermarriage. But by program's end, all difficulties seem to dissipate, resolved in an O. Henryesque fashion akin to the *Bridget Loves Bernie* Christmas-Chanukah episode of some twenty years earlier. As Michael, in a turnabout, arrives home with a Christmas tree to surprise Hope, he finds her waiting to surprise him — as she lights a Chanukah menorah while holding Janey in her arms.

When Christmas and Chanukah rolled around the following year, viewers saw an intensification of Michael's religious explorations. The strain of the holiday season begins when Hope and Michael renegotiate how they will observe the holidays, agreeing in advance to have a Christmas tree and a Chanukah menorah. Tensions are compounded by the *yahrzeit* of Michael's father (the anniversary of his death, a time when the *kaddish* is traditionally recited) and later by Hope's involvement in a car accident, sending Michael into deep existential angst. He is openly plagued by doubts about having married a non–Jew, questioning whether it is the condition of intermarriage that is entrapping him in a discomforting sense of detachment. Reacting to the confluence of pressures, Michael has a bizarre dream that recurs in long segments throughout the episode. The main characters of *thirtysomething* are transformed into characters of the 1960s comedy series *The Dick Van Dyke Show*. It is a Gentile world of Christmas, where an all-knowing Santa Claus grants to everyone their fondest Christmas wishes and gifts — but not to Michael. His surreal journey into the world of Christian symbolism, where he finds no fulfillment, is intercut with his actual quest for his place in the world of Judaism. Stirred to thoughts of the synagogue by his cousin Melissa — who assures him that it is a quite different place from his Hebrew school days some twenty years earlier — Michael enters the synagogue and is astounded to discover that, beneath their different garb, the elderly rabbi and the Santa Claus of his dream are the same man. Their ensuing conversation is laden with allusions to Michael's sense of estrangement from Judaism. Trying to discern Michael's purpose in being there and seeking to be of help to him, the kindly rabbi repeatedly offers Michael an understanding ear. Yet Michael remains hesitant and remote, uncomfortably stating his purpose as merely wanting "to see how the place was doing." When the rabbi throws that question back to him, "So how *are* we doing?" Michael replies, "I don't know — I was just walking through. How do *I* know how *you're* doing?"[5] With this statement, Michael reveals that despite his religious searchings, he persists in positioning himself as an outsider to Judaism. Perceiving this, the rabbi dismisses him with a hard stare and the statement "We're doing fine." As Michael leaves, he is nowhere, an outsider to both of the worlds he has encountered. Even the news that Hope is not ill from her car accident but is in fact pregnant less cheers him than heightens his anxiety about his religious identity. In a conversation with Melissa, Michael again reflects on his intermarriage, which continues to trouble him despite his intensified love for Hope following the scare of her accident. He tells Melissa that after a great deal of thought and doubt, he has found that he does believe in God, but intermarriage vastly complicates this belief because he wonders "which God, who God, where God?" Compelled to make a choice, Michael takes a leap from the status of outsider to that of insider, choosing to continue his expression of religious identity from within Judaism. In the episode's final scene, he returns to the synagogue and enters the sanctuary where he hears an explanation of the *kaddish* as "solemn testimony to that unbroken faith which links the generations one to another." Michael joins in reciting the prayer, memorializing his father and linking himself to his people's history and destiny.

The evolution of Michael's character towards a closer Jewish identity entered a new realm in the premier episode of the 1990 season, which saw the birth of his son. While *thirtysomething*'s earlier approaches to intermarriage explored the question — and dilemma — of how two religions might reasonably coexist within a marriage (the Steadmans managed by having a *chanukiah* and a Christmas tree side by side), this episode seems to suggest that such religious intermingling is no longer tenable. The catalyst is the issue of a *brit milah* for the baby boy. The decision of whether to ritually circumcise the infant, in accordance with Jewish law and in keeping with a tradition that has a powerful pull on Jewish life, would call upon Michael to resolve within himself the question of whether he actively identifies as a Jew and to what degree he will partake in Jewish rituals as an outward sign of that identification. The episode focuses unremittingly on this issue, following Michael in his intense search as he veers between equivocation and determination in his quest for answers. Hope is wise enough to offer none. She has no objection to the *brit milah* and throws back the decision to Michael. After all, as she says to him, "You're the Jew in the house." Michael must also cope with his mother's intrusive new boyfriend, Ben, who lobbies hard for the *brit milah* and, without consulting Michael, hires a *mohel* for the as-yet-unplanned ceremony. Although Michael is highly resentful of Ben's crude efforts, the interloper is later shown to be sensitive and knowing, providing Michael with a sense of strength and direction that helps him ultimately decide to hold the *brit milah*. The ceremony takes place at the Steadmans', with friends and family joining in what is shown to be a moving and joyous occasion. In its public declaration of Jewish identity as expressed through this rite and in the notable absence of any "counterbalancing" Christian one (indeed, Hope did not even express interest in any), the

Steadman home seems to have made a quantum leap toward being a Jewish household.

The question of a child's religious identity in an intermarriage, which ignites a prolonged and anguished search by Michael Steadman on *thirty-something*, is a more clear-cut decision for other of TV's interfaith couples. In the comedy series *Cheers*, viewers see nothing of the decision-making process of intermarried doctors Lilith Sternin and Frasier Crane. But as the couple prepares to celebrate the *brit milah* of their newborn son, Frasier tells his drinking buddies, "I can't tell you how much it means to us. As you all know, I was raised without a religious tradition, and I'm determined my son shall not be similarly deprived. I'm so grateful to Lilith and her Jewish faith for providing Frederick a heritage of spirituality." That Frasier and Lilith are psychiatrists, presumably with superior knowledge about human nature and what is best for children, gives added importance to their decision to raise their child in a single faith.

Rachel and Tony Scali of *The Commish* seem to have resolved such issues early in their marriage — although questions still arise. The show's "holiday episode" includes a short but affecting scene in which the couple's ten-year-old son asks his mother (who is Jewish) if his father (who is Catholic) misses having a Christmas tree. Rachel tells her son David that they discussed this before they were married, that it was important for her that David be raised Jewish, and that his father agreed. The mother and son then discuss whether *David* pines for a Christmas tree, since he sees many of his friends with them. Assuring David that whatever feelings he may have about being left out are okay, she also reminds him of his own beautiful traditions and the fact that his parents wanted to raise him with as little confusion as possible. This small, quiet scene is unusual for its depiction of an intermarriage without the juxtaposition of Christmas tree and menorah but a reasoned and explicitly stated decision to raise the child as Jewish (although Rachel's reasons for that being important to her are not explored).

The determination to raise children of intermarriage in a single faith is a far cry from some of television's earlier depictions of the issue. One popular and of course ludicrously simplistic and fantastical solution is that of twins. On *Bridget Loves Bernie*, after the families feud over how the children will be raised, Bernie offers the solution: he and Bridget "decide" they will have twins so that one can be raised Catholic and one Jewish. This projected scenario came to pass in *Little House on the Prairie*, when the intermarried Percival and Nellie Dalton do have twins and decide to raise the boy as Jewish and the girl as Christian. This notion of raising each child in a different faith was advanced on the *Archie Bunker's Place* episode about Murray's intermarried daughter. When she tells her father the names of his grandchildren — Miguel and Rebecca — the implication through the use of one Hispanic and one Hebrew name is that both faiths are being represented.

More recent programs also give a nod toward religious pluralism within families. Stuart Markowitz and Ann Kelsey of *L.A. Law* are caught off-guard when asked by an adoption agency how they will raise their prospective adoptive child in light of their different religions. They reply offhandedly, "Oh, we thought we'd do a menorah and a Christmas tree, that sort of thing." Their casual response reveals the lack of thought they have put into the question, one which now seems to be insignificant to them but which may take on added importance as they raise their children.

When television depicts grown children of intermarriage, they are almost always shown to have a strong affinity for Judaism. Often this stems from the influence of a grandparent, in a kind of "skipping a generation" scenario. In the miniseries *Evergreen* and *QB VII*, religiously observant fathers lament their sons' intermarriages and then go on to see their grandsons develop an intense interest in Israel and move there. Daughters of mixed marriages also are shown to experience a kind of return to Judaism. In the 1985 miniseries *Mistral's Daughter*, a young woman whose Jewish mother was born in France sets about researching the two-millennia history of the Jews of Provence, with the help of a Jewish man whom she later marries. In *Remembrance of Love*, the child of an intermarried Holocaust survivor is also drawn to Israel, where she meets and marries an Israeli.

These portrayals of children of intermarriage initiating a kind of return to Judaism suggest that intermarriage may not be as devastating and final a blow to Jewish continuity as it is often considered. While such images may have little basis in reality,[6] their presentation bespeaks a kind of romantic, mythic notion that no matter how far removed one is from Judaism, the pull of one's heritage is an unstoppable, natural force that will ultimately express itself.

* * *

When popular television turns its attention to intermarriage, the sometimes silly or simplistic plots belie a much larger and more complex drama that moves simultaneously across the screen. In its depictions of intermarriage, television addresses the eternal battle — and the ever shifting balance — between the allure of a larger, pervasive culture and one's ties and loyalties to a small and specific religio-ethnic group. Through portrayals of personal love stories and feuding families, it focuses on the most intimate and emotional zone of that battle.

The complexity of the issue and its site at the vortex of so many conflicting strains results in a great ambivalence in popular TV's approaches to it. On the subject of intermarriage and interdating, television speaks in a variety of voices. It deals with other problems much more easily and unequivocally. Anti-Semitism is always shown to be bad — there are no two sides to the specter of ugly religious bigotry. And TV praises interfaith mingling — when it is platonic —

as a vision of social harmony and ecumenical cooperation. But while a family dinner with friends of different faiths is a popular and always positively portrayed scenario, the introduction of a romantic element almost always injects a wholly different tone — one of conflict and dissension. Objections are raised, insults are hurled, families fight, and characters are pained. To this conflict, there is no clear-cut resolution. Viewers are made aware of Jewish objections to intermarriage through the voices of disapproving parents and other relatives. But counter arguments are made and prevail — some of the time. All attitudes about intermarriage have come through on popular TV, both vehemence against and praise for it. The message is mixed on whether intermarriage is good or bad, inevitable or stoppable, workable or doomed.

The many sides to the issue portrayed on popular TV mirror the widely differing opinions about the subject in reality and the variety of passionate approaches to dealing with it. Indeed, the steady focus on the topic of intermarriage throughout the history of popular television reflects its position as a major issue in Jewish life. In a multitude of settings and scenarios, interfaith romances have blossomed on TV, revealing a widespread awareness — and self-consciousness — about the subject. Nearly always, it is presented as an issue that is problematic in one way or another and which must be dealt with. Each of these programs suggests a paradigm for doing so in some fashion, offering solutions befitting the particular vision it projects.

While the particular attitudes toward intermarriage vary from show to show, one common factor permeates virtually all of the many portrayals of the issue: intermarriage is depicted foursquare as a Jewish problem and as an issue of great concern to the Jewish community, as embodied by the characters of disapproving parents and other relatives. The objections they express, while only occasionally stated with full cogency and sympathy, manage almost invariably to nip at the edges of the serious Jewish difficulties with intermarriage, raising questions about Jewish survival and continuity. Whether they be bellowing fathers in *Little House on the Prairie* and *Evergreen* grabbing at phrases about those who "have tried to destroyed us," or mothers and grandmothers dispensing poignant pleas, these voices of opposition are generally cast with a degree of respect and sympathy, and their opinions are heard loud and clear. In television's dialectic of both endorsing and challenging intermarriage, these same voices often end up appearing antiquated and closed-minded, having been uttered and given equal time, it seems, merely to be countered and overcome by triumphant lovers. To deride the inclusion of these views as mere props, however, misses the point. For in the frequency of their utterance — they are ubiquitous in almost all shows about intermarriage — and the direction of their arguments, they project a background, a Jewish framework within which the drama of intermarriage conflict is played out. This can be seen in the stark difference between the portrayal of Jewish and Christian objections to intermarriage. Almost invariably, Christian families who object to their children marrying Jews are shown to be motivated by anti–Semitism, be it blatant or just beneath the surface. In marked contrast, Jewish objections are of the tenor expressed by Cecilia Weiss in *The Great Houdinis,* who spoke of Jewish self-preservation and the fear that love can accomplish what bullets could not.

Of course, there have been some dramatized efforts to paint Jewish objections to intermarriage as similarly bigoted to achieve a kind of facile but false symmetry. Such depictions fail to recognize the unique Jewish objection to intermarriage. As a tiny people who for millennia tenaciously sought to preserve and transmit a rich but imperiled culture, religion, and particular way of life, Jews have a heightened fear of demographic diminution and wariness of "marrying out." In depicting Jewish objections to intermarriage, popular TV could stand improvement in conveying this notion and expressing such objections in fuller and more complete terms.

Another area of concern is the predominance of TV's intermarried images. Popular television's focus on interdating and intermarriage reflects not only the controversy but the pervasiveness of such relationships in real life. With the high rate of intermarriage, TV's many interfaith couples mirror the social milieu from which they arise. No doubt, television's attention to such issues is amplified by the medium's mandate for controversy and conflict — emotions that interdating and intermarriage stories amply provide.

As a result, popular TV abounds with interfaith couples and thus projects the sense that such relationships are the norm. From a Jewish perspective, which views intermarriage as a threat to Jewish continuity, such a projection arouses concerns that the medium promotes and legitimates interfaith relationships. Stemming from an awareness of the influence of popular TV, these concerns duly question whether its images on this subject of vital importance for Jewish survival are damaging or helpful to Jewish life. In fact, they can be both.

That intermarriage appears on television is not negative in and of itself, given its widespread existence in reality. To thoroughly absent the issue from popular TV would be to pretend that it does not exist. But for television to depict romances involving Jews as almost always interfaith is inaccurate, imbalanced, and potentially harmful. The real problem lies not in the existence of such depictions, but in their preponderance — to the detriment of portrayals of Jewish-Jewish relationships. There are of course programs that depict Jews happily dating and marrying Jews, and Jewish couples and families have been matter-of-factly portrayed on several programs. (Indeed, on an episode of the short-lived series *Mariah,* a young Orthodox woman felt as if she were interdating — and betraying her father — when she fell in love with a Soviet Jewish émigré who espoused atheism.) While such shows are an important counterpoint to the abundance of interfaith relationships shown, they are underrepresented on TV, and their increase would be a welcome addition to diversity and realism on television.

Finally, in addition to more such shows, authentic depictions of some of the difficulties in intermarriage would go a long way toward discounting the idyllic view often presented. On this account, the program *thirtysomething* must receive high praise for its pathfinding efforts to dissect the workings of an intermarriage and lay bare some of the struggles within. With uncommon realism and superior craft, the program weaves a portrait with ever expanding scope and depth of an intermarried Jew launched on a path of questioning and religious searching. What is particularly noteworthy — and unusual — is that no external objections to intermarriage are voiced. Michael Steadman is not reacting to scolding parents, but to something much more influential deep within himself.

Such a show, despite the absence of expressed objections, can hardly be considered an endorsement of intermarriage. On the contrary, because it fails to offer simplistic solutions and depicts with a degree of authenticity the difficulties that arise, *thirtysomething* offers a sobering view of an otherwise often blithely portrayed issue. Here there are no simplistic solutions (as in some other shows where objections *are* raised), and the complexity of the issue is exposed. Indeed the indecisiveness and confusion that this complexity often engenders among real-life intermarrieds is reflected in *thirtysomething*'s irresolute handling of the issue as well. While viewers were left after the *brit milah* episode with the sense that the Steadmans were becoming a more Jewishly identified family, just a few months later a New Year's episode aired that showed a huge, decorated Christmas tree prominently displayed in their living room and had Hope offering ham to her guests. Michael and Hope, it seems, are bound for further exploration and negotiation in resolving the question of their family's religious identity.

Even a program where intermarriage is presented as aproblematic can offer a vision for some kind of Jewish identity within that marriage. When *L.A. Law*'s Stuart Markowitz is unsettled by the anti–Semitism of his mother-in-law-to-be, a sudden tidal wave of Jewish consciousness washes over him. Stuart admits to being "not a good Jew" and has not the slightest qualms about intermarrying — even following this incident. Yet such a character is compelled on some level to grapple with his Jewish identity and does so again in subsequent episodes, when, for example, he confronts echoes of the Holocaust or declares his affinity for Jewish-related cases.

The portrayal of such an assimilated character's considering questions of Jewish identity offers both a disturbing and a hopeful vision. That his intermarriage is presented as wholly untouched by religious controversy conveys the dubious message that mixed marriages raise no special difficulties and are a benign estate. And yet, the picture of one so thoroughly distanced from normal channels of Judaism but nevertheless openly grappling with issues of Jewish identity has the potential for positive impact on a segment of Jewish viewers.

Indeed, the particular appeal of popular shows like *L.A. Law* and *thirtysomething* lies in the reality of the issues; and many real-life Jews identify with these television Jews who are professional, successful, and often intermarried. They are reassured by people who are their coreligionists who are probably alike in lifestyle, demeanor, and tenuous Judaic affiliation that being Jewish is something to be proud of, to renew ties with, and to unabashedly explore.

The ambiguity of messages that imbues TV's intermarriage themes complicates the question of their impact but rightfully acknowledges the complexity of the issue and the diversity of those it concerns. Indeed, the different depictions seem to speak to different levels of commitment and awareness. The ideal Jewish picture, on both television and in reality, of Jewish-Jewish couples leading fully Jewish lives has found expression on the small screen. So has the inverse incarnation of this notion, in which Jewish characters are possessed of enough religious conviction to derail interfaith romances before they develop into marriages, as in *The Golden Girls* and *The Days and Nights of Molly Dodd*, for example. In other scenarios, where an intermarriage does take place, strong advocacy of endogamous marriages is often given voice. Articulate mothers and grandmothers, in such shows as *Buck James* and *The Great Houdinis*, for instance, argue forcefully and movingly against intermarriage.

But increasingly, such scenarios are ever more distanced from reality, as the rate of intermarriage in America's open society soars. While TV portrayals opposing intermarriage remain important — keeping resonant the Jewish ideal of endogamous marriage, other programs that reflect the reality of such relationships offer, perhaps, more realistic solutions and approaches. In the world of *thirtysomething*, an emergent Jewish identity materializes in raw fits and starts from an intermarried household. For those for whom such a scenario may come across as "too Jewish," a show like *L.A. Law* offers a thoroughly assimilated and intermarried Jewish character who still finds the need to grapple with his Jewish identity. Such programs carry an implicit advocacy for reaching out to intermarried Jews, by suggesting that such individuals bear an inerasable Jewish identity that is willing — and driven — to find some kind of expression. Finally, pointing to a new kind of ideal given the high rate of intermarriage, the conversion scenario that informs *A Year in the Life* offers a view of interfaith romance as not a negative force for Jewish diminution but a positive element in its growth. Given the unabating rise of intermarriage, such a perspective may be increasingly embraced, rendering its further exploration on popular TV timely and relevant.

Together, the many and varied popular television programs about intermarriage, underscore — and contribute to — the complexity and controversy of the subject. In their own way, they have become a dynamic part of the ongoing debate on this vital issue.

Epilogue: Finding Ourselves on TV

The half-century odyssey of Jewish themes and characters on popular television offers a dizzying palette of images drawn from every aspect of Jewish life. As this book abundantly illustrates, contrary to popular belief, Jewish matters have driven story lines, shaped characters, defined issues, and made appearances on countless TV shows throughout the decades.

Indeed, the presence of Jewish themes on television has been a constant throughout the history of television. From its earliest days until today, the great reflector of American life has amply recognized the active place of Jews within that life.

Yet despite the constancy of Jewish images, there *has* been a change in the manner in which these images are portrayed and the notions that they project. Over the years, television's Jewish themes and characters have evolved in ways that reflect changes in the wider world and developments in society at large.

For much of its early years, television did indeed take on the role often attributed to it of a great homogenizer — a common medium relaying images of unity and harmony to America's diverse population. Throughout its initial decades, TV programs brimmed with notions of assimilation and fitting in. Early instances of these appeared in the 1950s, with shows displaying the process of Americanization, some in an explicit way through the challenges of immigrant life, as in *The Education of H*Y*M*A*N* K*A*P*L*A*N**. This notion of blending into America was also espoused by many young TV characters who blithely looked to intermarriage as a means of achieving a desired homogenization over the "outmoded" objections of old-world parents, as on such early shows as *Bonanza* and *Wagon Train*, popular Westerns of the 1960s.

While characters could and did exhibit their own cultures and background, the overriding message was the beauty of everyone really being the same deep down despite outward appearances. Frequent parallels were drawn between different cultures and religions. A 1960s show of immense status did so on an episode that featured a priest and a learned Jewish man. On the classic series *Ben Casey*, the two men — both patients of Casey's and in hospital beds side by side — discuss with each other their respective religious texts and quote favorite sages. Their commonality and similarities are underscored, with only the details differing. That they are in this together is noted in a humorous way when one of them chuckles with conpiratorical glee, "Oh, we are going to drive the cook crazy on Friday."

In the 1970s, a show like the popular comedy series *The Partridge Family* included a story line that highlighted sameness in an even more explicit way. Young Danny Partridge, with a crush on a classmate who is a rabbi's daughter, tells her he is Jewish so that he can date her. Later, when Danny's family is invited to her home for Shabbat dinner, the rabbi asks Danny if he would recite *Hamotzi*, a Jewish blessing before eating bread said Friday nights over the challah as part of the traditional Shabbat meal. A flustered Danny must reveal his secret to the rabbi's family, which is forgiving and welcoming. When the rabbi proceeds to say *Hamotzi*, Danny erupts gleefully, announcing, "Hey, it's like grace!" His mom makes it even clearer: "See, people aren't as different as they think. We may have different beliefs, but we're all pretty much alike." The rabbi gives final approval to these sentiments, with a resounding "Amen to that."

These shows, although diverse in genre and theme, advanced a similar notion. In television's early years, when America's dominant and driving philosophy was that of the melting pot, many of the programs that included Jewish characters projected the idea that, at the core, Jews were no different from all those surrounding them. These characters were not ashamed of being Jewish. Indeed they unabashedly recited their Jewish prayers and proudly cited their Jewish texts — *But those are just like ours!* these shows told Christian America. While TV's early Jewish characters were proudly Jewish, and being part of a minority religion was depicted as certainly acceptable, the overriding sentiment was that of sameness and similarity — that we could all get along with each other *because* everything was basically the same.

This picture corresponded to conditions behind the small screen. For many of television's Jewish producers, writers, and network executives, who were seeking their own assimilation and acceptance into American culture, it was useful to create characters who could demonstrate that there was little difference between Jews and Gentiles and that the distinct Jewish religion, culture, heritage, and peoplehood was in essence nondistinct.

But all this would change with a cataclysmic shift that took place in the late 1970s. The perception and portrayal of Jews and others on television was to be forever altered by watershed events. In 1977, the phenomenally successful miniseries *Roots*, chronicling the history of an African American family from slavery through modern times, suddenly made ethnicity permissible and even desirable. Aired in the salad days of miniseries — the new genre was captivating TV audiences hungry for involving and ongoing stories — *Roots* attracted huge audiences and massive critical praise and attention. Coupled with the ethnic pride movements that had earlier ignited the 1960s, a new ethos took force: it became "in" to be demonstrably ethnic — both onscreen and off. Suddenly it became not only acceptable, but almost obligatory to wear one's heritage on one's sleeve. Melting pot was out; ethnicity was in.

One year later, the miniseries *Holocaust* aired. What *Roots* had done for black Americans and for others in a more generalized way across the board, *Holocaust* did for Jews in particular. Among its many other far-reaching effects, the miniseries — with its grand-scale portrayal of Jewish matters in such a highly visible forum and commanding such a large viewership — cemented the permission for Jews to be fully Jewish both on screen and off.

As a result of these various forces, almost on a dime the drive to assimilate screeched to a halt. This created a paradox: at the same time that ethnicity became a badge of honor, many Jews had achieved a consummate assimilation into American life. Hollywood's assimilationist Jews — having realized their goal of homogenization (Los Angeles holds the highest intermarriage rate in the country, at 70 percent), yet moved by the rise and swelling of ethnic pride — were faced with a stark and alarming reality: they no longer possessed a unique identity to distinguish them. Now that they and the characters they created had achieved acceptance and sameness (TV Jews, like most real-life Jews in America, now looked, talked, and celebrated like everyone else; lived in the suburbs; and married into Gentile families) television's Jews, both onscreen and off, were faced with a searing question: "Now that we are like everyone else, *who are we?*" We succeeded in being assimilated, but with little or nothing of our identifiable heritage remaining, what defines us? Who are we?

They would pose this urgent conundrum with growing seriousness and frequency. Increasingly, TV viewers were to see this soul-searching played out by popular TV characters who posed and probed this question as they grappled with their religious identity. Shows began to take on a new twist as characters said, in effect, I am proud of the new person I've become; I do want to fit in and be part of this much loved melting pot, but I can't lose a sense of who I am.

Many characters explored such questions within the context of an intermarriage. *thirtysomething's* Michael Steadman spent several episodes pondering the place of his Jewish identity in his marriage. Like many baby-boomers viewing the show — similarly alienated from their roots but now reclaiming them — Michael pondered fundamental issues regarding the place of religion and ethnic identity in the fabric of his personal life. How should his religiously mixed family celebrate "the holidays"? Should he enter a synagogue (after decades of distance) to pray on the anniversary of his father's death? Should he hold a *brit milah* (a Jewish ritual circumcision) for his baby son? These were no longer questions of general faith and open-ended spirituality; nor were fuzzy, feel-good answers possible. Now facing the real-life challenges of maintaining families and raising children on a day-to-day basis, TV's baby-boomers needed specifics, they needed the how-to for the nitty-gritty. Thus on one episode of *thirtysomething*, in which Michael has been sent into an emotional tailspin by a variety of factors, he tells a friend that he thinks he believes in God, "but which God, who God, where God?" He is later shown in synagogue reciting *kaddish* for his father.

Yet intermarriage was far from being popular television's only plotline for this burgeoning expression of religious identity. Many regularly featured characters were propelled to a renewed or heightened expression of Jewishness as a result of a variety of experiences. For many the trigger point was anti–Semitism, as for example Stuart Markowitz of *L.A. Law*. After being the target of upper-crust bigotry, he said he suddenly "felt the weight of 5,000 years" and asserted his Jewish identity by declaring, "It's who I am!"

For others it was a sense of isolation, as in the case of Dr. Joel Fleischman of *Northern Exposure*. Isolated in a small Alaskan town, Fleischman dealt frequently with his Jewish identity in a myriad of offbeat scenarios, in keeping with the program's famed quirkiness. He researched the Yiddish roots of native Alaskan languages, called Israel to reach distant family once trapped in the Soviet Union, discussed interdating with a rabbi in the belly of a fish, and sought out a *minyan* to say *kaddish* for a deceased uncle.

One episode of *Northern Exposure* sagely encapsulated the current search for roots and identity and precisely articulated the development of television's Jewish characters in this regard. It was Christmastime and Fleischman, the town's lone Jew, grapples with feelings of isolation and identity as everyone around him celebrates Christmas or the traditional Indian raven festival. Fleischman admires the beauty of the Christmas trees around him and finds allure in their aesthetic and evocative appeal. Yet he rejects them for himself, explaining that he is Jewish and that "a Christmas tree is a major Christian symbol. Traditionally Jews try to avoid Christian symbols." (This in itself was a rare-for-TV yet forthright statement that the ubiquitous, seemingly secularized Christmas tree is indeed a Christian symbol.) But he harbors second thoughts about this rejection: unmoored from all that is familiar and from any Jewish community, Fleischman ponders his relationship to the Christmas tree, considering whether to take one into his home.

Eventually he does so, and the towering plant looms hugely over his room. He doesn't know quite what to do with it and seeks the advice of non–Jewish friends. Although he tries to adjust to it, he is clearly uncomfortable.

By the show's end, Fleischman removes the tree from his home and deposits it on the front lawn of his Christian girlfriend. "I have something that I think belongs to you," he tells her. "I tried. I really did. I gave it my best shot. It just — didn't work. Scratch the plum pudding and there's a matzah ball underneath. I'm a Jew, that's all there is to it."

In those final, extraordinary sentences, the decades-long development of television's Jewish characters was stood on its head. Rather than promoting the notion, as Mrs. Partridge did on *The Partridge Family*, that despite outward differences "we're all pretty much alike," Fleischman asserted quite the opposite: We have all become the same on the outside. We Jews talk like you and look like you and do just what you do. Yet on the inside, somewhere deep down, there is an ineradicable Jewish core that will out. Even in isolation, detached from any other Jew, even romantically involved with a Christian woman, even drawn to the beauty of the Christmas tree — Fleischman finds that he possesses a powerful sense of Jewish identity that will not disappear, that cannot be erased. Even his best efforts, somewhat to his chagrin, cannot squelch it ("I tried. I really did").

For decades, many of TV's Jewish characters were portrayed as exotic — heavily accented, oddly dressed, immersed in a strange and foreign culture. While a few still are, today almost all of television's regularly featured Jewish characters are just like all the rest of us. And yet — or perhaps because of this — television's Jews seek to find within themselves that Jewish core, the "inner matzah ball" within even the most assimilated Jew. Whether it be a Philadelphia advertising executive, a Los Angeles attorney, a spaceship commander of the twenty-third century, or a child of Holocaust survivors, they each possess an indestructible Jewish essence that will have its day. This search for one's essential ethnic identity has become so popular that it was poked fun at in a wry episode of the comedy *Third Rock from the Sun*. The series has as its premise the efforts of four aliens sent by their distant planet to learn about life on earth by assuming the forms of a human family. Their comic attempts to be like earthlings provide grist for top-notch satire on the human condition. Although they have generally adapted well to living as humans, it comes as a rude awakening to them on one episode when they learn that every American has some *additional* ethnic tag. "To fit in you have to be something," announces one of the youngsters in the Solomon family upon returning home from school one day. "Well, we're something," his father replies. "We're human beings." "Everybody at school is something *extra*," the boy insists. "Like African American or Italian American or Asian American or Audiovisual Americans."

The family's search is now on to choose an ethnic identity, lacking a real one of their own. Hoping to pick "one of the really good ones" they study encyclopedias on the topic, badger people to tell of their own backgrounds, and seek to learn about the accomplishments and supposed traits of various ethnic groups. In exasperation, one suggests, "Well, we're carbon-based life forms. Just tell everyone we're Carbo Americans."

Finally, in a comic twist of events, the family decides that they are Jewish. Suddenly they start saying "*mazal tov*" and playing tunes from *Fiddler on the Roof*. In the last scene, when the daughter excitedly tells everyone about the perfect date she just had, her father gives her an affectionate yet suspicious look and asks, in his best Jewish-mother tone, "So— is he Jewish?"

Beyond the hilarious humor of the episode is a telling demonstration of the full circle that television has traveled in its approach to ethnic images. At one time, the medium conveyed the overriding message that it was important for everyone to fit in and be essentially like everyone else. Later, the quest to distinguish oneself and the importance of being different held sway. Now, television chronicles the paradox that *in order to fit in, one must be different.* To be an American is to be an ethnically identified American, to be, as Tommy Solomon said, "something extra." As the father of the Solomon family declared with great contentment and satisfaction upon achieving membership in a particular ethnic group, "Isn't it great to know who we are? I finally feel like I belong in this big melting pot they call earth." While the melting-pot philosophy, and its reflections on American television, once posited that one had to be the same to fit in, today — as the TV comedies tell us — to fit in, one must be different and dedicated to the quest for a unique identity.

This incisive fun poking at the sometimes frantic search for identity is unlikely to dampen the swelling phenomenon that seems every day to grow in fascinating new directions and manifestations. The headline news, for instance, about U.S. Secretary of State Madeline Albright's recently revealed Jewish past is yet another captivating chapter in the surprising twists and turns that Jewish identity sometimes takes. Her recent visits to Yad Vashem in Israel and to Theresienstadt in the Czech Republic, encountering connections to lost family and heritage, provide real-life credence to the notion — portrayed on so many TV shows — that Jewish identity is an unstoppable force, no matter what the vicissitudes and challenges. The phenomenon is worldwide, with recent reports about the Jews of Poland, nearly decimated by the Holocaust, experiencing a renaissance of Jewish life and culture, and news of a popular movement among many South Americans to assert that they are descendants of Marranos, or "hidden Jews," and to reclaim their identity. There, this trend to retrace family lineages and reclaim Jewish ancestry after centuries of dormancy is known as *la sangre llama,* "the blood is calling," a phrase that evokes the image of Joel Fleischman's matzah ball having its day. Everywhere, it seems, Jews are shedding their plum puddings in a resurgence of Jewish identity, pointing to the persistence of that identity — a notion addressed on numerous TV shows.

Fueled, as always, by real-life issues and trends, television will no doubt continue to focus on such matters. The ongoing search for meaning, the human quest for identity, have after all been at the core of television's flickering images in one form or another since its inception. That is why, in part, the small screen is the quintessential popular medium. Behind the dramas and the sitcoms, through the silly, the soporific, or the soaring, television fare has managed in its own way to grapple with the essential issues, large and small, that people face day to day. In the forefront of this sometimes difficult, sometimes exhilarating, always challenging journey will be — as they have been for half a century — television's Jewish themes and characters.

Notes

Preface

1. Sidney Head and Christopher Sterling, *Broadcasting in America*, 5th ed. (Boston: Houghton Mifflin Company, 1987), p. 84.

Introduction

1. A significant portion of this programming was explored, for the first time, in author Jonathan Pearl's unpublished doctoral dissertation, "Jewish Themes in Prime-Time Network Television Dramatic Programs, 1953–1986" (Ph.D. dissertation. New York University, 1988). Constrained by various academic and research delimitations, the dissertation identified 125 programs with Jewish themes and analyzed 72 of these. Any references in *The Chosen Image* to the lack of prior in-depth research in this field exclude this dissertation.

2. Philip A. Kalisch, Beatrice J. Kalisch, and Margaret Scobey, *Images of Nurses on Television* (New York: Springer, 1983), p. vii.

3. Harry F. Waters, "Life According to TV," *Newsweek*, 6 December 1982, pp. 140, 136.

4. John E. O'Connor, ed., *American History/American Television: Interpreting the Video Past* (New York: Frederick Ungar, 1983), p. xxvi.

5. Hannah Kliger, "Communication and Community: Ethnic Media Images and Jewish Group Identity" (Master's thesis, Annenberg School of Communications, University of Pennsylvania, 1977), p. 83.

6. W. Russell Neuman, "Television and American Culture: The Mass Medium and the Pluralist Audience," *Public Opinion Quarterly* 46 (winter 1982), p. 472.

7. Paul M. Hirsch, "The Role of Television and Popular Culture in Contemporary Society," in *Television: The Critical View*, ed. Horace Newcomb (New York: Oxford University Press, 1982), p. 290.

8. Lucy Maynard Salmon, *The Newspaper and the Historian* (New York: Oxford University Press, 1923), p. xlii.

9. Paul Smith, ed., *The Historian and Film* (Cambridge: Cambridge University Press, 1976), p. 1.

10. Through such books as Smith; Murray Lawrence, "The Feature Film as His-

torical Document," *Social Studies* (January/February 1977), pp. 10–14; Pierre Sorlin, *The Film in History* (Totowa, N.J.: Barnes and Noble Books, 1980); John E. O'Connor and Martin E. Jackson, *American History/American Film* (New York: Frederick Ungar, 1979).

11. For example, Randall M. Miller, ed., *The Kaleidoscopic Lens: How Hollywood Views Ethnic Groups* (Engelwood, N.J.: Jerome S. Ozer, 1980); Richard Oehling, "Hollywood and the Image of the Oriental," *Film and History* 9 (September 1978), pp. 59–67; Ina Bertrand, "'National Identity'/'National History'/'National Film': The Australian Experience," *Historical Journal of Film, Radio and Television* 4 (October 1984), pp. 179–188; Les and Barbara Keyser, *Hollywood and the Catholic Church* (Chicago: Loyola University Press, 1984).

12. Allen L. Woll, *The Latin Image in American Film*, revised edition (Los Angeles: UCLA Latin American Studies, vol. 50, 1980).

13. Gretchen M. Bataille and Charles L. P. Silet, eds., *The Pretend Indians: Images of Native Americans in the Movies* (Ames: Iowa State University Press, 1980), p. xix.

14. Other than those mentioned below, such books and articles include Thomas Cripps, "The Movie Jew as an Image of Assimilation, 1903–1927," *Journal of Popular Film* 4 (summer 1975) 53–58; Eric Goldman, *Visions, Images and Dreams: Yiddish Films, Past and Present* (Ann Arbor, Mich.: UMI Research Press, 1984); Nikki Stiller, "The Sephardic Image in Israeli Films," *Midstream* 21 (May 1975), pp. 59–62; David Weinberg, "The Socially Acceptable Immigrant Minority Group: The Image of the Jew in American Popular Films," *North Dakota Quarterly* (autumn 1972), pp. 60–68.

From Hester Street to Hollywood, edited by Sarah Blacher Cohen (Bloomington: Indiana University Press, 1983) presents a panoramic overview of Jews in the entertainment industry. This issue was also explored by Neal Gabler in *An Empire of Their Own: How the Jews Invented Hollywood* (New York: Crown, 1988).

15. Lester D. Friedman, *Hollywood's Image of the Jew* (New York: Frederick Ungar, 1982), p. ix.

16. Patricia Brett Erens, "The Image of the Jew in the American Cinema: A Study in Stereotyping" (Ph.D. dissertation, Northwestern University, 1981), p. 1.

17. Howard Suber, "Television's Interchangeable Ethnics: 'Funny, They Don't Look Jewish,'" *Television Quarterly* 12 (winter 1975), p. 50.

18. Kalisch, Kalisch, and Scobey, p. viii.

19. Stephen Farber, "John Corty, a Film Director Who Prefers TV," *New York Times*, 26 April 1986, p. 50. John Corty directed the made-for-TV movie *The Autobiography of Miss Jane Pittman*.

20. O'Connor, *American History/American Television*, p. xxxiv.

21. O'Connor, *American History/American Television*, p. xxxviii.

22. Frederic A. Moritz, "New TV Series Riles Chinese Americans," *Christian Science Monitor*, 2 February 1975, p. 2.

23. Tom Kagy Nahm, "Stop Stereotyping Me," *Newsweek*, 15 November 1979, p. 15.

24. Kay Gardella, "Polish People Have a Hero in Peppard Banacek Series," *Daily News*, 2 August 1972, p. 67.

25. Steven D. Stark, "Pop Culture Embraces Hispanic Images," *New York Times*, 11 November 1987, p. C-4.

26. S. Robert Lichter and Linda S. Lichter, "Italian-Americans in Television Entertainment," prepared for the Commission for Social Justice, May 1982, p. 60.

27. Andrew M. Greely, "TV's Italian Cops—Trapped in Old Stereotypes," *New York Times*, 27 July 1975, sec. 2, p. 1+.

28. Bonnie Downes Leonard, "Impaired View: Television Portrayal of Handicapped People" (Ed.D. dissertation, Boston University, 1978); Richard H. Davis, *T.V.'s Image of the Elderly: A Practical Guide for Change* (Lexington, Mass.: Lexington Books, 1985); and a documentary titled "Hollywood's Favorite Heavy: Businessmen on Prime Time TV," PBS, 25 March 1987.

29. Jack G. Shaheen, *The TV Arab* (Bowling Green, Ohio: Bowling Green State University Popular Press, 1984).

30. Shaheen, p. 4.

31. United States Commission on Civil Rights, "Window Dressing on the Set: Women and Minorities on Television" (95th Congress, 1st Session, 1977), p. 47.

32. See John F. Seggar, Jeffrey K. Hafon and Helena Hamonen-Gladden, "Television Portrayals of Minorities and Women in Drama and Comedy Drama, 1971–80," *Journal of Broadcasting* 25 (summer 1981), pp. 277–288.

33. John W. Donohue, "Images of Nuns," *America*, 23 November 1985, p. 349.

34. Sumiko Higashi, "Hold It! Women in Television Adventure Series," *Journal of Popular Film and Television* 8 (summer 1979), pp. 26–37.

35. Kalisch, Kalisch, and Scobey, p. vii.

36. J. Fred MacDonald, *Blacks and White TV: Afro-Americans in Television Since 1948* (Chicago: Nelson-Hall Publishers, 1983), p. xvi.

37. John J. O'Connor, "An Update on 'The Cosby Show,'" *New York Times*, 21 January 1988, p. C-26.

38. John J. O'Connor, "Cosby Leads the Way, but TV Still Stumbles in Depicting Blacks," *New York Times*, 30 March 1986, sec. 2, p. 1+.

39. Richard B. Koiner, "The Black Image on TV," *Television Quarterly* 17 (summer 1980), p. 43.

40. Zev Zahavy, "A History and Survey of Jewish Religious Broadcasting" (Ph.D. dissertation, Yeshiva University, 1959).

41. Zahavy, p. 66.

42. Gary A. Steiner, *The People Look at Television* (New York: Alfred A. Knopf, 1963), p. 229.

43. Judith E. Doneson, *The Holocaust in American Film* (Philadelphia: Jewish Publication Society, 1987), p. 143.

44. Doneson, p. 154.

45. Annette Insdorf, *Indelible Shadows: Film and the Holocaust* (New York: Vintage Books, Random House, 1983), pp. 6, 207.

46. Alvin H. Rosenfeld, "The Holocaust in American Popular Culture," *Midstream* 29 (June/July 1983), p. 53.

47. John Toland, "A Noted Historian Judges TV's Holocaust Films," *TV Guide*, 13 February 1982, p. 10.

48. For example: Martha Bayles, "Holocaust Hero on TV," *Wall Street Journal*, 8 April 1985, p. 14; Dan Isaac, "Entebbe Televised," *Midstream* 23 (June/July 1977), pp. 69–73; Isaiah Kuperstein, "Playing for Time: A Review," *Shoah* 2 (spring 1981), pp. 18–19; Robert J. Milch, "Why Bridget Loves Bernie," *Jewish Spectator* (December 1972), pp. 25–26; John J. O'Connor, "Hepburn, in 'Delafield,' Plays a Widow in Love," *New York Times*, 28 March 1986, p. C34; and Elliot Gertel's Media Watch column in *The Jewish Post and Opinion*.

49. One essay, although titled "Jews in American Film and Television," included but a brief passage about television, referring only to Archie Bunker's overall bigotry in the series *All in the Family*. Samuel Lewis Gaber, "Jews in American Film and Television," in *Ethnic Images in American Film and Television*, ed. Randall M. Miller (Philadelphia: The Balch Institute, 1978), pp. 43–47.

50. Most notably such series as *Rhoda*, *The Goldbergs*, and *Bridget Loves Bernie*, and more recently the widely discussed *thirtysomething*. While indeed significant, these well-known television series are far from representative of the large number of TV dramatic programs that have included Jewish themes.

51. Suber, p. 51.

52. Michael Elkin, "Jews on Television: The Image Changes," *The Jewish Standard*, 6 September 1985, p. 16.

53. Alan D. Abbey, "TV Today: Maybe the Cleavers Would Have a Jewish Neighbor," *Long Island Jewish World*, 6–12 October 1989, p. 8.

54. Jack Fischel, "Hollywood's Jews," review of *The Jew in American Cinema*, by Patricia Erens, in *Midstream* 31 (November 1985): 64.

55. *Ibid.*

56. Arthur Unger, "Minorities in the Media: TV is Offering a Fairer Image, but Mainly for Certain Groups," *Christian Science Monitor*, 10 May 1983, p. 12.

57. Paul H. Keckley, Jr., "A Qualitative Analytic Study of the Image of Organized Religion in Prime-Time Television Drama" (Ph.D. dissertation, Ohio State University, 1974), pp. 192–193.

58. Aviva Cantor, "TV's 'Holocaust': A Sellout to Assimilation," *Lilith* 5 (1978), p. 32.

59. Sergio Zavoli, "Italian Television, Italian History," *Historical Journal of Film, Radio and Television* 5 (March 1985), p. 57.

Chapter 1

1. The correct plural of the Hebrew phrase *bar mitzvah* is *b'nai mitzvah*, and the correct plural of the Hebrew phrase *bat mitzvah* is *b'not mitzvah*. However, for the sake of familiarity, ease of recognition and use for the general readership, the Americanized terms *bar mitzvahs* and *bat mitzvahs* will be used.

2. See George Gallup, Jr., and Jim Castelli, *The People's Religion: American Faith in the 90's* (New York: Macmillan, 1989), pp. 37, 39, 42, 45, 48.

3. Bryon L. Sherwin, "Bar Mitzvah," *Judaism* 22 (winter 1973), p. 53.

4. Edgar E. Siskin, "Bar Mitzvah American Style," *Journal of Reform Judaism* 28 (winter 1981), p. 89.

5. An anthology series that ran from 1955 to 1957, *Crossroads* dramatized the lives of real-life historical and contemporary clergy.

6. One *becomes* a *bar mitzvah* or a *bat mitzvah* at a specified age, attaining the status of the majority and thereby assuming adult religious responsibilities. *Bar mitzvah* is not something that is done to a person, and therefore one cannot correctly "get *bar mitzvahed*" or "get *bat mitzvahed*." Although these Americanized terms are widely used, they are both grammatically incorrect and distort the active meanings and implications of *bar* and *bat mitzvah*.

7. A young man is declared an orphan if he suffers the loss of one or both par-

ents; in such a case he attains the status of majority and becomes a *bar mitzvah* at the age of twelve instead of the customary thirteen.

8. The first recorded American *bat mitzvah* was celebrated in 1922 by Judith Kaplan, daughter of Rabbi Mordechai Kaplan, the founder of Judaism's Reconstructionist movement.

9. The term "Old Testament" is of Christian origin and represents but one of early Christendom's many attempts to render Judaism obsolete. By introducing the term Old Testament, Christianity was conveying its belief that the Hebrew Bible — which is the Jewish Covenant (Testament) — was old and had thus been supplanted by the New (Christian) Covenant (Testament). While this may accurately represent Christian thinking, it is obviously antithetical to Judaism. For Jews, of course, there is only one testament or covenant — the Hebrew (Jewish) Bible. The concept Old Testament is anti–Jewish in nature as it denies the eternity — and even the very existence and legitimacy — of Judaism and the Jewish people. Although the term has gained widespread use, it is a misnomer.

10. The presence at this Jewish wedding of an Irish ship captain explaining the rituals and helping the ceremony take place and the absence of a rabbi may seem odd and incongruous, but does not invalidate the Jewish wedding. In fact Jewish law states that after the couple is properly engaged, they become husband and wife upon the exchanging of vows before two competent witnesses. Thus, for a Jewish wedding to take place, the presence of a rabbi is not required, nor that of an Irish ship captain.

11. Jeremiah 33:10–11.

12. It is customary for Jews, in the midst of moments of joy, to bear in mind the existence of sadness. The destruction of the ancient Jewish temples in Jerusalem (the first in 586 B.C.E. by the Babylonians, the second in C.E. 70 by the Romans) brought to an abrupt halt Jewish sovereignty in the Land of Israel. Nearly nineteen centuries of exile, persecution, and unparalleled suffering followed, until the re-establishment of the Jewish state in the Land of Israel in 1948. The breaking of the glass at the wedding ceremony commemorates all the destruction and sadness that has befallen the Jewish people in its long history of existence and also reminds the wedding couple and those in attendance not to forget those in this world who cannot know the joy that they have on the day of their marriage.

13. Jewish practice does not permit faithful adherents of Judaism to mourn the death of an apostate. However, there exists a folk custom that if a child leaves his faith, his people, and his family through intermarriage, apostasy, or in an extreme case like this by joining the enemy, the child is as if dead to them and for that child they sit *shiva* and say the *kaddish*. See Solomon B. Freehof, *Current Reform Responsa* (Cincinnati: Hebrew Union College Press, 1969), pp. 181–3; Maurice Lamm, *The Jewish Way in Death and Mourning* (New York: Jonathan David, 1969), p. 83.

14. As Susan Weidman Schneider explains in her book, *Jewish and Female: Choices and Changes in Our Lives Today* (New York: Simon and Schuster, 1984), "New ceremonies for naming a daughter have proliferated in the ten years since Jewish women have made a concerted effort toward greater inclusion in Jewish ritual. Booklets describing these ceremonies are much in demand, and the Jewish Women's Resource Center in New York even has a large loose-leaf notebook filled with copies of ceremonies sent in by parents who know that whatever models people can find for such events will be welcome, since there are few formal guidelines.... Even the naming of the ceremony has been problematic to parents. Some popular favorites are *Brit B'not Yisrael* (the covenant of the daughters of Israel), *Brit Kedusha* (the covenant of sanctification), *Sim-*

chat Bat (rejoicing in a daughter) ... [or] *Brit Bat Tzion* (covenant of a daughter of Zion)." pp. 122, 123, 127.

When it was depicted on popular TV, the ceremony was called a *brit bat*, "covenant of the daughter," apparently some combination and or shortening of some of the choices listed above.

15. Although both holidays have distinct historical and religious significance, these aspects are neglected and forgotten, replaced by a focus on the secular, popular, and Americanized "Christmas-Chanukah season."

16. Monford Harris, "Christmas and Chanukah: Two Structurings of the World," *Jewish Frontier*, December 1976, p. 19.

17. Chanukah is considered one of the Jewish calendar's minor holidays (see note 25 below) and is still treated as such by Jews who are secure in their faith and are thus insulated from any attraction to Christmas.

18. See Chapter 4, "Holocaust," regarding these programs.

19. According to Jewish lore, it is the Hebrew prophet Elijah who will herald the coming of the Messiah and thus bring peace to the Jewish people, to Israel, and to the world at large. The hope and expectation for Elijah's arrival is expressed at the Passover *seder*—both in song and in custom, by setting aside a large goblet of wine for him.

20. As stated above, even in moments of triumph Jews empathize with those who suffer — even their enemies. On Passover, when Jews are celebrating their freedom from Egyptian bondage, they take a moment from this joyous occasion to remember the hardships that befell their Egyptian tormentors as a result of the ten plagues. Thus, each person at the *seder* removes a drop of wine from his or her cup as each plague is recited aloud, symbolically removing some of the sweetness that he or she is celebrating in memory of those who suffer. The infusion of a laugh track in such a solemn and meaningful ceremony bespeaks ignorance and poor taste.

21. Rabbi Aaron Pearl, "From the Rabbi," *Beth Rishon Monthly*, Wyckoff, N.J., January 1990, vol. 15, no. 6, p. 2.

22. The major festivals in the Jewish calendar, which are found in the *Torah* (The Pentateuch) include *Shabbat*, *Rosh Hashanah*, *Yom Kippur*, *Pesach* (Passover), *Shavuot*, and *Sukkot*. Among the minor holidays included in the Jewish calendar are Chanukah and *Purim*.

23. The Lubavitch is a Hasidic group very active in trying to reach unaffiliated Jews to draw them back to Judaism. One of their outreach methods is the "mitzvah mobile," a fleet of small motor homes that park at various locations and encourage Jewish men and women to practice certain rituals.

24. In pronouncing such words as *Sukkot*, *Shavuot*, and *Shabbat*, many Jews use the Ashkenazic pronunciation, substituting the final t with an s.

25. There are various differences between the observances of major and minor festivals on the Jewish calendar. For example, the Torah prohibits the performance of any work on the major holidays. In modern times, such prohibitions include attending school classes on that day. *Purim*, however, is a minor holiday not subject to this biblical prohibition that requires one to refrain from work. In other words, this is not a Jewish holiday on which Jews would take off from work or school. The depiction of a teacher asking which of her Jewish students will be taking off for *Purim* is incorrect and unrealistic. Public schools (and Jewish schools) would not grant their Jewish students a day off from school.

26. One of the Ten Commandments is devoted entirely to the holiness, impor-

tance, and sanctity of *Shabbat,* and furthermore it is the only Jewish holiday mentioned by name in the Ten Commandments; it is also celebrated every week of the year!

27. Hebrew for "the one who takes out." The blessing praises God as the one causes bread to come from the earth.

28. This is not to be confused with the popular *Cosby* show of the 1980s.

29. Shanghai of 1938 was "the only place in the world that offered asylum to the desperate, persecuted Jews" of Nazi-occupied Europe (Kranzler, p. 20). Thus Shanghai's open immigration policy requiring no visas for immigration saw the flight of some eighteen thousand Jews to its port of entry. Although this policy did not last and at the urging of Hitler 1943 witnessed the establishment of a "designated area" (ghetto) for the "stateless refugees" (those from Nazi-occupied Europe, thus exempting the previously existing Jewish community of Shanghai), Shanghai offered survival to thousands of Jewish refugees. After the war, most of these survivors resettled in Western countries, primarily Israel. See David Kranzler, *Japanese, Nazis, and Jews* (New York: Yeshiva University Press, 1976), pp. 19–25, 488–491, 580–82.

30. A reunion of some one thousand Jewish survivors from Shanghai took place in Oakland, California, during the weekend of August 3, 1980. "Shanghai Recalled as a Haven for Jews," *New York Times,* 4 August 1980, p. A8.

31. A rabbi cites the Sixth Commandment ("You shall not murder," Exodus 20:13, Deuteronomy 5:17) as the rationale for permitting the consumption of nonkosher meat for Jews who are in danger of losing their lives. While a number of rabbinic authorities stated that one whose life could be saved by eating nonkosher food but does not eat it is "guilty of a capital sin" (Rosenbaum), the basis of the rabbi's decision (in this program) to allow the eating of horse meat should have been based on a different biblical passage. It is central to even the strictest observance of Jewish law that "the saving of a life overrides the commandments of the entire Torah"(Babylonian Talmud, Yoma 82b), based on the biblical injunction "And you shall keep my statutes and judgements ... *and you shall live by them*" (Leviticus 18:5), that is, and not die by observing them. This legal concept, being the "watchword of Judaism" (Soloveitchik), serves as the rationale for permitting the consumption of such nonkosher meats as horse meat during such times of peril as the Holocaust. See Babylonian Talmud, Sanhedrin 74a; C. G. Montefiore and H. Loewe, *A Rabbinic Anthology* (Philadelphia: The Jewish Publication Society of America, 1963), p. 495; Azriel Eisenberg, *Witness to the Holocaust* (New York: Pilgrim Press, 1981), p. 280; Rabbi Joseph B. Soloveitchik, *Halakhic Man* (Philadelphia: Jewish Publication Society of America, 1983), p. 34; Irving J. Rosenbaum, *The Holocaust and Halakha* (New York: KTAV Publishing House, 1976), p. 136; *Encyclopedia Judaica,* 13:509.

32. Hillel, one of the most prominent, revered and beloved sages of the *Talmud,* was born in Babylonia during the first century before the common era and lived into the first century of the common era. He came to Jerusalem to intensify and deepen his knowledge and became before long the nasi (president) of the Sanhedrin (the supreme Jewish legislative body). Numerous maxims, stories, and texts attest to his knowledge, wisdom, and patience. See Nahum N. Glatzer, *Hillel the Elder: The Emergence of Classical Judaism* (New York: B'nai Brith Hillel Foundations, 1956), pp. 24–33.

33. *Pirke Avot* (Ethics of the Fathers) 2:5.

34. After a portion of the *Torah* is read during services in synagogue, an additional portion is reads from the "Prophets" section of the Hebrew Bible. This additional reading is called the *Haftarah.*

35. Although this was stated in *Hallmark Hall of Fame*'s "Have I Got a Christmas for You," *shalom* does not and cannot mean "merry Christmas." In the context of this "ecumenical" program, the attempt was made to draw parallels between Jewish and Christian concepts, here specifically between shalom as "peace" and the modern notion of Christmas as a time of peace and brotherhood. Like the unfounded parallels drawn between Christmas and Chanukah, these programs that desperately strive for ecumenism teeter dangerously on the precipice of dilution.

36. Although the term *mazal tov* is Hebrew, its pronunciation differs in Hebrew (with the accent on the second syllable of *mazal*) and Yiddish (with the accent on the first syllable). In almost all programs that have used this phrase, the pronunciation has occurred in its Yiddish form.

Chapter 2

1. The first Jews, twenty-four in number, arrived in New Amsterdam in 1654, refugees from the Portuguese Inquisition in Brazil, and from that time Jews have figured prominently in the formation, growth, and strengthening of the nation.

2. Rabbi Gershom Mendes Seixas (1745–1816) was descended from a Sephardic family who immigrated from Portugal to America in 1730. He served as the *hazan*-minister (*hazan* is Hebrew for cantor) of Congregation Shearith Israel in New York for many years and gained prominence and stature as the religious leader of New York's Jewish community. See David and Tamar De Sola Pool, *An Old Faith in the New World* (New York: Columbia University Press, 1952), pp. 167–73.

3. For example, Seixas quotes from the Book of Psalms (92:13): "The righteous shall flourish like the palm tree ... he shall grow like a cedar of Lebanon."

4. Rabbi Dr. Arnold Fischel was designated by the Board of Delegates of American Israelites to lobby Congress and speak with President Lincoln about changing an Act of Congress that stated that a military chaplain "must be a regular ordained minister of a Christian denomination" (Thirty-Seventh Congress, 1861, Session I, Chapter 9, Section 9). Due to Rabbi Fischel's efforts, Congress amended the previous act to read, "That no person shall be appointed a chaplain in the United States army who is not a regularly ordained minister of some religious denomination..." (Thirty-Seventh Congress, 1862, Session II, Chapter 200, Section 8). It should be noted that although Rabbi Fischel continued to visit soldiers in hospitals for a short while, he was never appointed as a military chaplain, despite a petition for such appointment. See George P. Sanger, ed., *The Statutes at Large, Treaties, and Proclamations, of the United States of America, December 5, 1859–March 3, 1863*, vol. XII (Boston: Little, Brown, 1863), pp. 270, 595; Morris U. Schappes, *A Documentary History of the Jews in the United States, 1654–1875* (New York: The Citadel Press, 1950), pp. 462–464, 698.

5. Undoubtedly, the government offer referred to in this program was the Homestead Act of 1862, which provided to the head of any household who was or intended to become a citizen of the United States a quarter section (160 acres) of land in the Dakota territories for residence and cultivation. Many Jews seized upon this opportunity. See Uri D. Herscher, *Jewish Agricultural Utopias in America, 1880–1910* (Detroit: Wayne State University Press, 1981), pp. 48–49.

6. A *greenhorn* refers to a new immigrant, one who is as yet un–Americanized, unfamiliar with the ways of the new country, and untutored in its niceties.

7. The harsh conditions of the land, the bitter winters, the struggle to survive, and the perseverance of those pioneers in the Dakota territories have been documented by a number of people who describe their personal experiences in North Dakota. Many aspects of the conditions they describe are quite similar to those portrayed in this program. See Kenneth Libo and Irving Howe, *We Lived There Too* (New York: St. Martin's/Marek, 1984), pp. 285–86; Bessie Schwartz, "My Own Story," in *The East European Jewish Experience in America*, Uri D. Herscher, ed. (Cincinnati: American Jewish Archives, 1983), pp. 156–57.

8. *Pirke Avot* 3:2.

9. Kishinev (located in the province of Bessarabia) was the capital of the Moldavian Soviet Socialist Republic. Responding to yet another scurrilous ritual murder charge hurled against the Jews, Russian mobs unleashed a vicious and devastating pogrom against the Jewish community of Kishinev in April 1903. News of the Kishinev Pogrom spread around the globe and sparked strong international reaction and widespread protests by Jewish communities. See Howard Morley Sachar, *The Course of Modern Jewish History*, (New York: Dell, 1958), pp. 247–48.

10. Genesis 27:22.

11. See Numbers 20:7–13.

12. See Babylonian Talmud, Sanhedrin 37b. Circumstantial evidence is not admissible in a murder case.

13. See Cecil Roth, *The Jewish Contribution to Civilisation* (London: The East and West Library, 1956).

14. See Kenneth Aaron Kanter, *The Jews on Tin Pan Alley* (New York: Ktav Publishing House, 1982), pp. x–xi.

15. Although use of the term "arc" for *The Lawless Years* may be somewhat anachronistic, as it first came into popular TV jargon with the series *Wiseguy*, debuting in 1987, it aptly describes the format used here: a self-contained, multiepisode story within an ongoing series. It is interesting to note that *The Lawless Years* employed this format almost three decades before *Wiseguy* drew acclaim for this innovative approach.

16. Although the Jewish population of North America was known and reported to be of a noncriminal and law-abiding nature, the early twentieth century saw this untarnished reputation dirtied by reports of the large criminal element among the foreign immigrants — including the Jews. The pre–World War I Jewish underworld consisted mostly of local toughs and gangs. Following their decline and markedly distinct from these were the postwar more sophisticated bootleggers and racketeers involved in the business of crime, who had little if any affiliation with Judaism, Jewish neighborhoods, or the organized Jewish community. See Jenna Weissman Joselit, *Our Gang* (Bloomington: Indiana University Press, 1983).

17. Randall M. Miller, ed., *Ethnic Images in American Film and Television*, (Philadelphia: The Balch Institute, 1978), p. xxv.

18. One could easily be misled, however, from a spate of recent articles in both the secular and Jewish press, from *Newsweek* to *The Forward*, which erroneously describe a dearth of Jewish women on the small screen. The dearth exists only in the minds of the writers of these articles who, owing either to faulty, superficial research or a wish to present a trendy (but in fact false) thesis are egregiously ignoring TV's Jewish women.

19. While the plot of this *Larry Sanders Show* episode (HBO) was Hank Kingsley's crush on the rabbi, its premise was that an explicit expression of Judaism is not welcome on TV. Kingsley's character is that of a sidekick to talk show host Larry Sanders;

when he starts taking on some outward forms of Judaism — like wearing a *kippah*, quoting from the *Talmud* on air, and changing his name to Hank Lepstein — the talk show is barraged by hate mail. Host Sanders, the show's producers, and network executives are all frantic and pressure Hank to stop being demonstrably Jewish. The message is that television audiences are unaccepting of Jewish expression and that television executives run as fast as possible from any explicit display of Judaism on TV. Obviously, based on the content on this book and the breadth and depth of shows with Jewish substance that it lays out, this is far from the case. Nevertheless, this erroneous view is widely accepted as conventional wisdom. Thus the show was praised as a landmark in a *The New York Times* op-ed by Frank Rich, who wrote regarding television, "Though Jews have had no shortage of clout in show business from day one, they rarely use it to portray American Jews or Judaism honestly on screen" (*The New York Times*, November 23, 1996, p.19) As we responded in our letter that was printed in *The New York Times* (November 30, 1996), numerous television programs since the dawn of TV have portrayed "myriad images of Jews and Judaism honestly and with relative depth...." This episode was neither unique nor accurate. Neither was Kingsley's attachment to Judaism very impressive: it was based solely on an impulsive crush on a woman rabbi. When she brushes him off by show's end (to her credit, she is interested in his forging a true commitment to Judaism, not his romantic advances) and he is worn down by the hate mail and threat of losing endorsement accounts, he quickly drops all his former trappings of Judaism as fast as a hot potato. Television has seen better Jews and truer landmark shows.

Chapter 3

1. Shmuel Ettinger, "Anti-Semitism in Our Time," *Jerusalem Quarterly* 23 (spring 1982): p. 95.

2. This act of a non–Jew identifying as a Jew for the purpose of fighting anti–Semitism is associated with the widely believed story that during the Holocaust, King Christian X of Denmark identified himself and his subjects as Jews by having them all wear the yellow badges that Jews were forced to wear.

3. This is a paraphrase of the famous statement made by Pastor Martin Niemoeller in the context of the Holocaust. The actual quote is, "In Germany, the Nazis first came for the Communists and I didn't speak up because I wasn't a Communist. Then they came for the Jews and I didn't speak up because I was not a Jew. Then they came for the trade unionists and I didn't speak up because I wasn't a trade unionist. Then they came for the Catholics and I was a Protestant so I didn't speak up. Then they came for me — by that time there was no one to speak up for anyone."

4. This dramatic upsurge has been documented in such reports and articles as "Hate Violence and White Supremacy: A Decade Review, 1980–1990" (Montgomery, Ala.: Klanwatch, a Project of the Southern Poverty Law Center, 1990); Jason DeParle, "1989 Surge in Anti-Semitic Acts Is Reported by B'nai B'rith," *New York Times*, 20 January 1990, p. 10; "Skinheads Target the Schools" (New York: Anti-Defamation League of B'nai B'rith, 1989).

5. The program *Wiseguy* presented episodes in what its producers termed arcs, groupings of four or five episodes tracing an ongoing theme.

6. Based on the actual controversy surrounding James Keegstra, high school

teacher in the village of Eckville in Alberta, Canada, who in 1975 began generating complaints from parents over his teaching of anti–Semitic material and Holocaust revisionism. Legal battles raged for the next thirteen years. During that time, he was removed from teaching, was forced to resign as mayor, and was charged and convicted of the Canadian criminal code prohibiting the incitement of hatred against a particular group—a charge that was overturned on appeal. Kate McKinnon is a dramatized, composite character.

    7. Although the real-life event included the involvement of Jewish groups, the TV depiction exists on its own and its messages and import are unrelated to whatever else might have happened outside the program.

    8. Lucy S. Dawidowicz, "Lies About the Holocaust," *Commentary* 70 (December 1980), p. 31.

    9. Examples include such books as Paul Rassinier, *Debunking the Genocide Myth* (Los Angeles: The Noontide Press, 1978) and Arthur R. Butz, *The Hoax of the Twentieth Century* (Los Angeles: Noontide Press, 1979) and such organizations as the Liberty Lobby and the Institute for Historical Review (in California).

    10. Dawidowicz, p. 31.

    11. Yehuda Bauer, "Anti-Semitism Today—A Fiction or a Fact?" *Midstream* 30 (October 1984), p. 28. Professor Yehuda Bauer heads the International Center for the Study of Anti-Semitism at the Hebrew University of Jerusalem. Other scholarly writings on this are Shmuel Ettinger, "Anti-Semitism in Our Time," *Jerusalem Quarterly* 23 (spring 1982) and Robert Wistrich, "The Anti-Zionist Masquerade," *Midstream* 29 (August/September 1983).

    12. Robert S. Alley, "Television Drama," in *Television: The Critical View*, Horace Newcomb, ed. (New York: Oxford University Press, 1982), p. 115.

    13. Robert Sklar, *Prime-Time America* (New York: Oxford University Press, 1980), p. 21.

Chapter 4

    1. One need only read some of the personal accounts written by the survivors of the Nazi death camps to understand that the horrors and brutalities inflicted by the Nazis upon their victims can never be accurately or fully portrayed. See for example Terrence Des Pres, *The Survivor* (New York: Oxford University Press, 1982); Primo Levy, *Survival in Auschwitz/The Reawakening* (New York: Summit Books, 1986); Sylvia Rothchild, ed., *Voices from the Holocaust* (New York: New American Library, 1981).

    2. Iwona Irwin-Zarecka, "The Vicissitudes of Decency," review of *Double Identity: A Memoir*, by Zofia S. Kubar, in *Midstream* 36 (April 1990), p. 48.

    3. Herbert G. Luft, "'Holocaust' Spawns History Lesson, Seminars, World-wide Apologia—35 Years Late," *Variety*, 3 Jan 1979, p. 10.

    4. Hitler's Final Solution aimed at mass extermination of Europe's entire Jewish population of 11 million men, women, and children. Plans for carrying out the Final Solution were "officially" agreed upon by a select number of Nazi officials at the Wannsee Conference on January 20, 1942. However, Hitler had conceived of the idea of destroying European Jewry long before this and had clearly communicated this idea to his closest confidants (e.g., Heinrich Himmler) between October 1940 and May 1941. In addition, the term Final Solution had been used before the conference by various Nazis

in the higher echelon, and Hitler's program for Greater Germany had already seen the implementation of the mass murder of Jews. The Final Solution was the Nazis' so-called solution to the Jewish problem. See Lucy S. Dawidowicz, *The War Against the Jews 1933–45* (New York: Holt, Rinehart and Winston, 1975), pp. 136–37, 154; Martin Gilbert, *The Holocaust* (New York: Holt, Rinehart and Winston, 1985), pp. 28–9, 76; Nora Levin, *The Holocaust* (New York: Thomas Y. Crowell, 1968), pp. 290–95, 298.

5. According to the show's press materials, Rod Serling's wife provided the new show's producers and writers with other revisions of the script written by Rod Serling. One of these versions supposedly included this scene.

6. Situated a short distance from Warsaw, Poland, the Treblinka extermination camp existed only for about one year. In that short period of time, between eight hundred thousand and one million Jews were murdered by the Nazis. As the experimental killing center, it was at Treblinka that the process of killing and destroying twenty-five thousand Jews per day — without a trace — was perfected.

The first victims of Treblinka's gas chambers were to be the inhabitants of the Warsaw ghetto. Indeed, as portrayed in this program, a number of people did try to warn the Jews of the ghetto of their fate.

After Himmler ordered the destruction of the camp and all traces of its task, mass corpse burnings began. As the Jewish workers realized their ultimate fate, they staged a heroic uprising, killing a number of guards and cutting the barbed-wire fences to freedom. Although few Jews escaped and even fewer survived the war, this was a phenomenal act of resistance. See Feig, pp. 293–311.

7. Interestingly, this story, written by Dale Pitt, was remade as a British theatrical film in 1960.

8. Babylonian Talmud, Sanhedrin 37a.

9. It was Eichmann who organized the mass deportations of at least two to three hundred thousand Hungarian Jews to the death camps — primarily Auschwitz — in 1944. See Gerald Reitlinger, *The Final Solution*, 2d rev. and aug. edition (London: Valientine, Mitchell, 1968), pp. 455–66.

10. There has been much contradictory evidence regarding Wallenberg's fate after falling into Russian hands. The Russians officially stated that he died of a heart attack in his prison cell in 1947. They informed the Swedes of this "fact" only after much prodding in 1957. However, various pieces of evidence — including direct sightings and contacts with him in the late 1950s and even as recently as the 1970s — while certainly inconclusive and incomplete, raise the possibility that Raoul Wallenberg was still alive somewhere in the Soviet Gulag. See John Bierman, *Righteous Gentile* (New York: Viking Press, 1981), pp. 153, 179–181, 185–189, 216.

11. NBC press release, February 25, 1997.

12. Named for the Polish town of Oswiecim near which it was situated, Auschwitz was the main killing center of the Jews of Europe during the Holocaust. When Auschwitz-I proved to be too much, a much larger extermination camp was built nearby — Auschwitz-II, called Birkenau. The large Auschwitz complex served as both a prison (maintaining a large inmate population working for the Nazi war effort) and an extermination camp. In its capacity as a killing center, it is estimated that one million Jews were murdered at Auschwitz by the Nazis during the Holocaust. Auschwitz has become the byword for the Nazis' unimaginable and indescribable cruelty and inhumanity — the symbol of all the horrors of the Holocaust. Konnilyn Feig, *Hitler's Death Camps: The Sanity of Madness* (New York and London: Holmes and Meier, 1979),

pp. 333–40; Martin Gilbert, *Auschwitz and the Allies* (New York: Holt, Rinehart and Winston, 1981), pp. 339–41; Raul Hilberg, *The Destruction of the European Jews*, rev. and definitive ed. (New York and London: Holmes and Meier, 1985), p. 894.

13. Israeli dance associated with the early twentieth century Jewish pioneer settlers (*halutzim*) of the Land of Israel. It is a group dance that is characterized by its exuberance and camaraderie, and its melodies in the Hasidic spirit. See Macy Nulman, *Concise Encyclopedia of Jewish Music* (New York: McGraw-Hill, 1975), p. 113.

14. Yiddish, literally "grandfather."

15. This depiction is rather inappropriate since, in fact, "Roosevelt rarely took a direct hand in the refugee-rescue problem"[Henry L. Feingold, *Zion in America* (Boston: Twayne, 1974), p. 286.] The implications of such depictions (which occurred in other programs as well; for example, in *The Winds of War*, President Roosevelt promises his help to Byron in securing Natalie's safety), which suggest that such action was not unusual, is contrary to evidence that has demonstrated that the State Department maintained a "stringent anti-refugee policy," often implemented more strictly for Jewish refugees (Feingold, p. 287) and that "Roosevelt rarely interceded with the State Department in favor of the refugee cause"(Feingold, p. 288).

Chapter 5

1. The name Palestine was applied by the Roman Empire to the Land of Israel soon after the Romans destroyed the Jewish State in C.E. 70, and exiled the Jewish people from their land. The Roman Empire's imposition of the name Palestine was an attempt to obliterate the historic, religious, unique, and integral ties of the Jewish people to their homeland. The term gained widespread use in non–Jewish circles from Byzantine times on and was used almost universally until the rebirth of the State of Israel in the historic Jewish homeland in 1948.

2. A major controversy erupted as a result of the casting of Vanessa Redgrave as Auschwitz inmate and heroine Fania Fenelon. Because of Vanessa Redgrave's public anti–Zionist remarks and support for the PLO, her casting in the role of a Jewish victim of the Holocaust was deemed particularly offensive and inappropriate by the Jewish community and the real Fania Fenelon.

3. World War II left homeless tens of thousands of Jewish refugees who thus found themselves in Displaced Person (DP) Camps. The Jewish Agency came to their aid and through its numerous on-site representatives, organized and aided massive "illegal" immigration of Jewish Holocaust survivors to Palestine. See Howard Morely Sachar, *A History of Israel*, (New York: Alfred A. Knopf, 1976), pp. 267–68.

4. This is Yiddish expression literally meaning "God in heaven," akin to the saying of "Oh, my God!" in a desperate situation.

5. During the early part of the war, Eichmann became the "expert on Jewish affairs," as part of the the the Security Service branch (known as the SD) of the SS, Hitler's elite private police-army. His early responsibilities included the expulsion of Jews from Germany and Austria into ghettos and concentration camps. Upon assuming command of the Gestapo's office of Jewish Affairs and Evacuation Affairs after 1939, Eichmann organized and managed the deportation of Europe's Jews to the death camps.

After the war, he eluded justice and escaped to Argentina, where he lived under the alias Ricardo Klement. Eichmann was captured there on May 11, 1960, and brought to Israel on May 14, 1960, to stand trial for his crimes. See Lucy S. Dawidowicz, *The War Against the Jews, 1933–1945* (New York: Holt, Rinehart and Winston, 1975), pp. 73–74, 102, 106, 115; Gideon Hausner, *Justice in Jerusalem* (New York: Harper and Row, 1966), pp. 35–40, 56; William L. Shirer, *The Rise and Fall of the Third Reich* (New York: Simon and Schuster, 1960), p. 271; Howard M. Sachar, *A History of Israel* (New York: Alfred A. Knopf, 1976), p. 552–58.

6. NBC press release, August 18, 1960.

7. David Ben Gurion, a major force in the founding of the modern State of Israel, was also the nation's first prime minister. He served again as prime minister of Israel during the period in which Eichmann was captured.

8. See note 4 of Chapter 4.

9. The use of the name Masada in this context is clearly a takeoff on the name of the Israel Secret Service, which is called the Mossad. The Hebrew word *masada* literally means "fortress" or "stronghold." When the Jewish rebellion against Rome began in C.E. 66, a group of Jews fled to the mountain-top fortress called Masada in the desert near the Dead Sea. After the Romans destroyed Jerusalem in C.E. 70, they had only the Jews on Masada to overpower. Unexpectedly, the Jews fought off the Roman army for three years. The Romans finally penetrated the walls of Masada in C.E. 73 only to find that a mass suicide had taken place. The 960 Jews — men, women, and children — were determined not to die at the hands of the Roman pagans but preferred to die in dignity by their own hands, in sanctification of their faith. Masada has come to represent Jewish courage, determination, steadfastness, and will to survive with dignity. In fact, it is on Masada that soldiers in the Israeli army take their oath of allegiance. See Yigael Yadin, *Masada* (New York: Random House, 1966), pp. 11–12, 201–202.

10. This episode was broadcast in 1963, before the 1967 Six-Day War in which Israel was under attack by five of its powerful Arab neighbors whose aim it was to destroy the nation and drive the Jews into the sea. During that war, Israel liberated some Jordanian-occupied territories — Judea and Samaria, the heart of ancient Israel — thus rendering the twelve-mile width of the country obsolete.

11. The Hebrew word *kibbutz* literally means "gathering, collecting, assembly." The *kibbutz* in Israel is a communal settlement whose members are collectively responsible for every aspect of their lives including education, child care, and working the land. The plural of *kibbutz* is *kibbutzim* (not *kibbutzes*).

12. *Sabra* is the Hebrew word to describe a native-born Israeli.

13. The World Gathering of Holocaust Survivors was held in Jerusalem from June 15 through 18, 1981.

14. This is a Hebrew phrase meaning "living monument," or "memorial," found in the Hebrew Bible (Isaiah 56:5). *Yad Vashem*, located in Jerusalem, Israel, is Israel's memorial to the six million Jewish victims of the Holocaust. It serves as an archive, museum, and learning center for the history, significance, and remembrance of the Holocaust. See *Encyclopaedia Judaica*, 16:697.

15. A wry and well-known TV observation on Jews visiting Israel came from Archie Bunker, who commented in an episode of *All in the Family* that the vacationing Doctor Shapiro "went to visit the land of his people — Miami."

16. The hijacking occurred on June 27, 1976.

17. This quote is from the *Victory at Entebbe* version of the event.

18. A more balanced picture could be achieved by also presenting, for example, a view that states the following: The "Palestinian" Arabs' claim of being a separate peo-

ple who have no home is without foundation. The Arabs are one people who emanated from Arabia and under the banner of Islam conquered and occupied an enormous amount of territory in and around the Middle East no earlier than the seventh to eighth centuries of the common era. They have had no national existence until only recently with the establishment of twenty-two modern sovereign independent Moslem states in the region, many of them on lands outside their Arabian homeland. One of the Arab-occupied states is a "Palestinian" state called Jordan, which comprises 77 percent of Mandate Palestine. The Jews are also one people — whether they be Sephardic, Ashkenazic, European, Arabian, Egyptian, Yemenite, Syrian, Iraqi (Babylonian), American, etc. — who emanated from the Land of Israel some four thousand years ago. As opposed to the Arabs, however, the Jews acknowledge with pride their unity as one people and have only *one* state — which is all they want — and that state is in its original site, in the Jewish national homeland, albeit only in a small portion of the land that the Jewish people have uninterruptedly inhabited, held national sovereignty in, prayed in, prayed for, dreamt of, wrote about, or returned to for four thousand years. If the Arabs' claim that they are not one people but are many peoples, each of which is entitled to one of the twenty-two states that they now occupy — plus one more in Israel — then the same logic must be applied to the Jews. Thus, every distinctive group of Jews is entitled to a state in the places where they have lived for centuries and in many cases even for millennia, often predating an Arab presence. A brief list indicating the rightful location of these independent Jewish states to be established upon withdrawal of the Arabs from occupied Jewish lands would include Egypt and Iraq, where Jews had large and well-established communities long before the arrival of the conquering Arabs; Syria and Yemen, where age-old Jewish communities have lived under the horrors of Arab persecution; and Jordan, which comprised part of the ancient Jewish kingdom and where today Jews are forbidden to live. The cry from 140 million Arabs in twenty-two states that they are threatened by Israel reveals simply that the Arabs need no more land — what they want is no more Israel.

19. In fact, although the Arabs attacked Israel on October 6, inflicting devastating losses, it was not until October 14 that any of the promised American arms shipments arrived in Israel.

20. Marc Chagall, the famous Jewish French artist, was commissioned to create stained glass windows for the synagogue located at the Hadassah Hospital in Jerusalem, Israel. He designed twelve windows, each representing one of the twelve tribes of Israel.

21. When many centuries later the Arabs first conquered and occupied Jerusalem, they chose this holiest of Jewish sites on which to build a mosque.

Chapter 6

1. Barry A. Kosmin, Sidney Goldstein, Joseph Waksberg, Nava Lerer, Ariella Keysar, and Jeffrey Scheckner, *Highlights of the CJF 1990 National Jewish Population Survey* (New York: Council of Jewish Federations, 1991).

2. Sylvia Barack Fishman, Ph.D., Mordechai Rimor, Ph.D., Gary Tobin, Ph.D., and Peter Medding, Ph.D., *Intermarriage and American Jews Today: New Findings and Policy Implications* (Waltham, Mass.: Cohen Center for Modern Jewish Studies, Brandeis University, 1990).

3. Kosmin, et al.

4. Contrary to what might be perceived from popular TV, the four ideological movements that comprise the Jewish religious community share a negative stance toward intermarriage and the question of whether or not a rabbi may officiate at or participate in conducting an intermarriage. What may separate the liberals from the traditionalists is the degree and form of their opposition.

Orthodox Judaism expresses its unequivocal opposition to intermarriage. Under no circumstances will an Orthodox rabbi perform an intermarriage or lend his official status as a clergyman to aid in the civil union of such a couple. While there are some Orthodox rabbis, past and present, who deal in a less strict manner with couples who are already intermarried, most strongly oppose accepting these couples into their communities (unless the non–Jewish partner converts in accordance with Orthodox procedures) and will not recognize the children of such couples as Jewish (unless the mother is Jewish or, if she is not, the child converts — again in accordance with Orthodox tradition). See David Ellenson, "The Development of Orthodox Attitudes to Conversion in the Modern Period," *Conservative Judaism* 36 (summer 1983), pp. 63, 71.

The Conservative movement is similarly "unalterably opposed to mixed marriage." See Jules Harlow, ed., *Proceedings of the Rabbinical Assembly, 1985* (New York: The Rabbinical Assembly, 1985), p. 198. Their Committee on Jewish Law and Standards has also ruled that a member of the Rabbinical Assembly, the Conservative movement's rabbinical association, is prohibited from officiating at a mixed marriage, co-officiating at such a marriage with a priest or minister, or presiding over a "civil" marriage between a Jew and non–Jew. See Rabbi Aaron Blumenthal, "Memorandum" (submitted to the Rabbinical Assembly's Committee on Jewish Law and Standards), 24 February 1972. This memorandum was carried unanimously by the committee. A Conservative rabbi who violates these guidelines can be charged with "unworthy conduct" and is subject to an investigation of the charges and potential suspension or expulsion from the Rabbinical Assembly. (Blumenthal; see also the Constitution of the Rabbinical Assembly, 1984 revisions, Article 7, Section 4.) However, recognizing the widespread practice of intermarriage, Conservative Judaism seeks to reach out to these couples for the purpose of "bringing them into the household of Israel." See Harlow, *Proceedings of the Rabbinical Assembly, 1976*, p. 322.

Reform Judaism is also opposed to intermarriage and has declared its opposition to any of its rabbis officiating at or participating in such a wedding. Intermarried couples, however, are welcomed into the Reform Jewish community and their synagogues; children of such unions are recognized and educated as Jews; support groups and outreach programs seek to ease the strain, educate the couple and promote conversion of the non–Jewish partner. See Walter Jacob, ed., *American Reform Responsa* (New York: Central Conference of American Rabbis, 1983), pp. 445, 464. It should be noted, however, that there are Reform rabbis who do officiate at mixed marriages; unlike Conservative rabbis, they are not subject to any punitive action.

The Reconstructionist movement, while unhappy about the widespread practice of intermarriage, recognizes its existence and instead of turning away mixed engaged couples and severing the lines of communication, recommends that their rabbis listen, help, encourage, and see the couples through the difficult time in the hope that this behavior will attract the couple to Judaism, thus increasing the ranks of Jewish adherents. While they prefer to reserve the Jewish wedding ceremony for Jews marrying Jews, they do not discourage their rabbis from attending "civil" ceremonies for couples that are contemplating maintaining a Jewish home. See "RRA Guidelines on Intermarriage," *Reconstructionist* 49 (November 1983), pp. 18–20.

Thus the depiction of a rabbi and a priest co-officiating at a mixed marriage is not erroneous, but it is certainly misleading. Indeed the occurrence of such a scenario in real life is quite possible. As demonstrated above, however, such a depiction without the benefit of any background information would likely lead to popular misconceptions.

5. The wording of Michael's statement, "How do *I* know how *you're* doing?" recalls a famous portion of the *Hagaddah* (read at the Passover *seder*) known as "The Four Sons" that addresses the notion of varying levels of knowledge, commitment, and attitude on the part of Jews towards their religion. In the narrative, a wise child, a wicked child, a simple child, and a child who does not yet know how to ask all seek — in their own way — an explanation of Passover, and instruction is given about how to answer them. Turning its attention to the wicked son's question, "What is this service to *you?*" the *Hagaddah* dissects his phraseology, commenting, "'To *you*,' and not to *him*; this indicates that he has cut himself off from the community and thus disavowed the core of his heritage and people." Michael's use of the word *you* when inquiring about Jewish concerns evokes a powerful similarity to the wicked son's self-imposed exclusion from his people and religion.

6. Barack Fishman, et al.

Index